Tradition, Modernization and Globalization

About the Editor

Prof. P.N. Pandey (*b.* 01.11.1947) (M.A.,L.L.B., Ph.D., Dip.Sc.Y.), is Professor of Sociology, former Dean of the Faculty of Social Sciences, and Former Director I.R.D.P., Banaras Hindu University. He is practising Sociology for the last 44 years and is popular as a vocal, radical and progressive man in the fraternity of Sociology, produced more than 42 Ph.Ds. on themes of diverse nature, published eighty papers in national and international journals, also presented nearly 120 research papers in national and international conferences, seminars and symposia in India and abroad. Sociological Theories, Rural-Urban systems, Social Change and Development are the areas of his special interest.

Education and Social Mobility (1988), Daya Publishing House, New Delhi, *Sport and Social System* (1999), Saraswati Prakashan, Varanasi, *Rural Development and Structural Change* (2000), Rawat Publication, Jaipur, are the books published by him. A recent volume on *Theoretical Perspective of Sociology* (in Hindi) has been released shortly by Concept Publishing Co. Pvt. Ltd., New Delhi. The present volume on *Tradition, Modernization and Globalization* is the outcome of a joint academic endeavour with Prof. S.K. Srivastava, he left for heavenly abode on 12 May 2012 in the mid journey of the publication.

Prof. Pandey has contributed from time to time in the columns of newspapers, especially in *Times of India, Aaj, Swatantra Bharat, Amar Ujala, Dainik Jagran,* etc.

He is a life member of Indian Sociological Society, UP Sociological Society, served as Secretary of Association from 1993-1996 and has been a member in the Board of Advisory of Sociological Bulletin, a Journal of Indian Sociological Society.

Tradition, Modernization and Globalization

A Commemorative Volume

Editor
Prem Narain Pandey
Professor of Sociology
Former Dean, Faculty of Social Sciences
Banaras Hindu University, Varanasi-5 (India)

CONCEPT PUBLISHING COMPANY PVT. LTD.
NEW DELHI-110059

ISBN-13: 978-93-5125-144-6 (HB)
ISBN-13: 978-93-5125-149-1 (PB)

First Published 2015

Published and Printed by

Concept Since 1974

Concept Publishing Company Pvt. Ltd.
A/15-16, Commercial Block, Mohan Garden
New Delhi-110059 (India)
T: 25351460, 25351794, *F*: 091-11-25357109
E: publishing@conceptpub.com, W: www.conceptpub.com
Editorial Office: H-13, Bali Nagar, New Delhi-110 015, India.

Cataloging in Publication Data--Courtesy: D.K. Agencies (P) Ltd. <docinfo@dkagencies.com>

Tradition, modernization and globalization : a commemorative volume / editor, Prem Narain Pandey. -- Enlarged edition.
pages cm
Includes bibliographical references and index.
ISBN 9789351251446 (HB)
ISBN 9789351251491 (PB)

1. Manners and customs. 2. Civilization, Modern. 3. Globalization. I. Srivastava, S. K. (Surendra Kumar), 1928-, honouree. II. Pandey, Prem Narain, 1947-, editor.

DDC 390 23

In Memoriam

Professor S.K. Srivastava (1928-2012)

Excerpts from one of his papers of historical importance based on his Ph.D. thesis titled, 'Culture Dynamics Among the Rana Tharus: The Past in the Present', in the book titled, '*Nepal: Tharu* and *Tarai Neighbours*' (edited by Harold O Skar) and published in Bibliotheca Himalayica Series III Vol. 16, 1999.

Edited by H.K. Kuloy

Publication supported by Norwegian Research Council and Print Federation, Printed in Nepal by Nepal Lithographing Co. Ltd., Kathmandu.

Culture Dynamics Among the Rana Tharus: The Past in the Present

Introduction

This conference has the unique distinction, of inviting scholars on the Tharus and other communities of Terai. Perhaps in the history of conferences this meeting has made a history itself. I, therefore, bring to you the greatest blessings and benedictions from Lord Shiva of Varanasi, India, and Lord Pashupati Nath of Kathmandu, Nepal and hope that both the Lords of common people of both countries will be satisfied with your deliberations and concern for those who are living under their benign care and protection.

I feel greatly honoured and delighted to be with you at this conference. I never imagined that my people, the Tharus, would receive worldwide attention from international scholars of great reputation. Nor did I anticipate that my work done in 1948-5.0 on the Tharus would be able to attract intellectuals at Norwegian institute in 1995 after a lapse of 45 years of after 33 years – 1958 being the year of my publication on the Tharus.

Many changes have taken place in the social organization of the Tharus of Naini Tal Tarai of Uttar Pradesh (now Uttarakhand) as a result of changes in the socio-cultural environment the Tharus have been living in for several centuries. These changes have been brought about by the contacts the Tharus have been developing with the neighbouring peoples of so-called 'higher cultures and civilization'. The psychological change that resulted from this culture contact and manifested itself in conscious attempts in the form of special reform movements, is one of the most vital aspects of change, since a group of the Tharus of the same society wanted to interfere with the existing pattern and change it into a new pattern by superimposing another 'superior' system on their indigenous one.

A Tribute with Memories

Professor Surendra Kumar Srivastava was born in 1928 in a village of district Sitapur in Uttar Pradesh. He was the seventh and the last surviving son to his parents. He completed his education upto intermediate from his home district and graduation from Lucknow. He joined Lucknow University in 1945 and did his M.A. and Ph.D. in 1947 and 1950 respectively under the patronage of Late Professor Radha Kamal Mukerjee. He was registered for his Ph.D. under the supervision of Late Professor Majumdar in 1948 in Anthropology on the Tharus of Sitarganj and Khatima the Two sub-divisions of district Nainital in U.P. (Now Uttrakhand). Professor Srivastava as a young research scholar devoted two years continuously in the remote rural and hilly regions of their habitat moving in the bullockcart from village to village. He surveyed 33 villages and lived in the hutments and worked as a participant observer of the community. In this way he completed this herculean task as per the desire of his mentor. As a young boy of 20 years he arrested the attention of the men and women of the community who provided him food, shelter, and other accessories and treated him as their kith and kin. The young girls of Tharu community when they knew that he was an unmarried boy were much more fascinated towards him and all the time helped him as peers and mates and very cordially treated him as family member.

I came to know about all his tough, rough and cordial treatment by male and female Tharus by his own conversation with me from time to time sitting and chating with him at his residence as a young professional practitioner of Sociology Department, B.H.U.

After completing his Ph.D. he was appointed lecturer in D.A.V. College, Dehradun but soon after 3 years he moved to the Institute of Social Sciences, Agra University, Agra. He got a good company of social scientists under the efficient patronage of Prof. R.N. Saxena as Director of the institute and Yogendra Singh, Prabhat Chandra, D.N. Dhanagare and several others as colleagues. Prof. Srivastava after a few years moved to Jodhpur University in Rajasthan as Reader and Founder, Head of the Department of Sociology.

Further in 1965, he was appointed Professor of Sociology in the Banaras Hindu University. The teaching of sociology was started during 1963-64 under the Department of Political Science for M.A. classes only under the headship of Professor K.B. Rao. Due to tense relation and dictatorial attitude of Professor Rao, it was difficult for Professor Srivastava to continue in the Political Science Department. He finally decided to have a separate department which was materialized in October 1966. Here again Professor Srivastava became the founder of an independent department. It was formally inaugurated by Professor Radha Kamal Mukherjee in the month of October 1966. Messages of congratulations were showered on him from far and wide. Smt. Vijayalaxmi Pandit from Delhi, Prof. K.M. Kapadia from Bombay University, Professor S.C. Dube from H.S. Gaur Sagar University (M.P.) conveyed their messages of blessings and congratulations. Professor Surendra Kumar Srivastava had a vision of an architect and devoted his whole efforts in setting the academic platform of the Sociology Department at the international level.

Before coming to B.H.U., Professor Srivastava had gone to the U.S.A. and joined the Harvard University with a project. He got there a very influential academic alliance with Professor P.A. Sorokin, Talcott Parsons, Edward Shills and several others and brought with him strong academic orientation in the Sociology Department of B.H.U. His oratory in English was par excellence and arrested our attention to learn something unique from him. Before he joined as Professor of Sociology in B.H.U., Smt. Surinder Jetley and Dr. G.S. Nepali had joined the Political Science Department as Lecturer and Reader respectively in Sociology.

He became very popular among his contemporaries and elicited the admiration and affection of the senior friends of fraternity like M.N. Srinivas, S.C. Dube, T.K. Unnithan, A.R. Desai, R.N. Saxena and several others. His charming personality, satiric expression and Harvardian way of Impression Management made him popular in the fraternity. His Sociology bears a perennial imprint of humanist concern. He has indeed, academic influences of R.K. Mukerjee, Talcott Parsons and Pitirim Sorokin. He has published a number of books. His study of Tharu, Tradition and Modernization and several monographs on Sociological literature are commendable contributions. Prof. Srivastava has produced nearly half a dozen Ph.Ds, published a number of research papers and has presented papers and participated in national and international conferences in India and abroad.

Prof. Srivastava has served as Head of the Department and Dean, Faculty of Social Sciences, Banaras Hindu University twice. His dramatic style of presentation during the seminars and conferences compelled the audience and his admirers to keep his figure fresh in the minds of his contemporaries and students.

I came in his contact some 47 years ago through an encounter of academic discourse on Shakespearean drama of Macbeth. While delivering some lecture in sociology to his students of M.A., he cited a statement, "Tomorrow, and tomorrow and tomorrow, Creep in thy petty peace"....I was then passing through the corridor of the lecture theatre and could not check my emotion of adolescence as a young chap of 19 years. I crept inside the theatre from backdoor and with due courtesy, I stood up and narrated the onward few lines of the drama where he had ended. Perhaps the onward lines were not clearly in his mind. I narred the onward stanza as follows:

To-morrow, and to-morrow, and to-morrow,
Creeps in this petty peace from day to day,
To the last syllable of recorded time;
And all our yesterdays have lighted fools
The way to dusty dealth.
Out, out, brief candle!
Life's but a walking shadow, a poor player
That struts and frets his hour upon the stage,
And then is heard no more: it is a tale
Told by an idiot, full of sound and fury,
Signifying nothing.

As a matter of fact, Macbeth receives the news of his wife's death with a profound reflection on vanity of life and inevitability of death. The news comes to him at a time of a terrible crisis and he goes on expressing this soliloquy saying that one-morrow follows another from day-to-day till the end of time till all our todays and tomorrows are turned into yesterdays and push us to our graves. Life is compared to a brief candle, which burns for a time and then is burnt out. Life is a shadow. It is hollow and empty. It is like some poor player upon the stage and makes fuss upon the stage for a short time. Then the actor is heard no more. The story is full of sound and fury, but it signifies nothing, these bloomy reflections were Macbeth's own. This is not Shakespeare's pessimistic view of life, but the judgement of Macbeth who had knowingly made moral war on his own soul.

It was all amazing experience thrilling the hearts of the students and the Honourable Professor by a stranger who was not formally student of the class. The Professor asked me to meet him in his chamber. By this way, I came in his contact and he motivated me to become provisionally a student of Master course in Sociology quite lately in the mid session in October 1967. He tested me many times. I was appointed Lecturer in 1969 after completing my M.A. At times, I had to work as his assistant for writing papers, putting his lectures in black and white. He was a man of profound sentiment but at the same time very tough and stiff disciplinarian. Sometimes, he was very unhappy on the issues of discipline among students in general. Malviya's vision and mission, Gandhian metaphysics of Truth and Non-violence and *Ramcharit Manas* of Tulsidas were the themes of his appreciation. He used to come to BHU usually after his retirement and inspired me for holding conferences and seminars on national and international issues. When I was Dean of the Faculty of Social Science (2006-09), he frequented his visit to the faculty and used to advise me to promote academic and professional interests of professors and students. Sometimes, he lamented for not doing much in black and white because of his engagement in the establishment of the department during his services. The Department of Sociology was cradled at his hand and we were the support persons at his command. By this way, he sacrificed his whole life in the making of the Department. Professor Srivastava was given LIFE TIME ACHIEVEMENT AWARD by the Indian Sociological Society in its annual conference organized by one of his students Professor Anand Kumar of Jawaharlal Nehru University in December 2011. He breathed his last on 12 May, 2012 at his residence in Varanasi.

P.N. Pandey

Acknowledgements

This new edition embodies the post-modern and global features of changes emerging all-over the world with specific reference to Indian society. This volume consists of the papers contributed by earlier sociologists along with the later generation of practitioners of the discipline. The book is divided into two parts. The first part consists of the papers contributed by veteran Sociologists during Seventies and the second part of the volume consists of some of the papers from the earlier sociologists who are still alive with their changed vision, modified interpretations about modernity and global development, while most of the other papers on the same theme incorporate the extended ideas and analysis of the features of modernity and post-modern development after the turn of twentieth century and especially, the new features which have emerged in the wake of global developments in the first quarter of twenty-first century.

The second part of the volume consists of the very illustrious pieces of work on the issues concerning modernity and global development. Prof. Yogendra Singh has tried to focus upon the issue of globalization with multiple modernity and those of rationalization and counter-rationalization. Prof. S.M. Dubey has made a very comprehensive approach to the conceptual shifts and ideological constraints in the prevailing issue of 'Tradition, Modernization and Globalization'. Prof. Yogesh Atal has very clearly pointed the persisting cultural diversities at the global level in the wake of globalization. These diversities, he has attempted to point out in the realm of culture and civilization.

Prof. D.N. Dhanagare in his presidential speech at the 27th All India Sociological Conference, held at IIT, Kanpur, December 18-20, 2002, perceives global development as a mechanism of separation and recombination of space and time as well as a crucial factor of dynamism of modernity.

Prof. T.K. Oommen in his paper, attempts to highlight the conceptual history and contemporary cultural trends in the process of globalization. Prof. Jai Kant Tiwary in his study of tradition and modernity has attempted to focus on the emerging repercussions on polity and social structure as well as the agrarian economy in the third world countries. Prof. Anand Kumar is very emphatic in discriminating the diverse pictures of modernity in the era of globalization with reference to the developed and developing world. Dr. Vishwanath Pandey has presented a micro case study in terms of actors and institutions with reference to Banaras Hindu University in the anti-colonial struggle. His paper presents a peculiar blend, of course, a symbiosis of tradition and modernity. Dr. Manjula Rathoure is again a promising writer who portrays a specific feature of continuity of globalization and local culture with reference to Varanasi in India.

In my own paper, Modernity, Post-modernity and Global Development, I have attempted to present a comprehensive scenario of the programme of Modernity, Post-modernity and Global Development and as such is indeed a very systematic and impressive record of the current processes of cultural changes and post-modern developments with its impact on developing countries in general and India in particular. The analysis of paper consists of the latest conceptual projections and their implications on developed and developing societies. It is really a step from sociological imagination to so-called sociological impressionism that focuses on the emerging changes in the structure of feeling and sensitivity in the cyber age of electronics and informatics.

Dr. Anupama Pandey in her paper Science, Technology and Changing Power Structure in Modern Societies has focused on the latest features times of culture and social changes emerging as a result of modern techno-electronic developments. Dr. D.K. Singh and Dr. S.B. Singh in the joint paper have attempted to indicate the impact of modernity and globalization on national identity. Dr. Mukesh

Kumar Srivastava has streamlined the features of modernity and the socio-economic empowerment through global development.

I am thankful to the contributors of this volume who have worked on different aspects of tradition, Modernization and global development in contemporary situations.

Professor S. Tripathi, former Head of the Department of Sociology, B.H.U.; Professor Jugendra Sahai former Head Dept. of M.G. Kashi Vidyapith, Varanasi; Professor I.S. Chauhan, former Vice Chancellor, Barkatullah University, Bhopal (M.P.); Professor S.M. Dubey former Vice Chancellor, Digbrugarh University, Assam deserve congratulations as they motivated me time and again to complete this volume.

I express my gratitude and thanks to the Professors and colleagues of the Department of Sociology who helped me with keen interest in the completion of this book.

My research scholars specially Dr. Mukesh Kumar Srivastava, Dr. Neeraj Kumar Rai and Dr. Vikash Kumar helped me at every step of the preparation of the script for final publication.

I also express my thanks to Mr. Ashok Kumar Mittal of Concept Publishing Company Pvt. Ltd., New Delhi, for accepting this manuscript and prompt publication.

My heartfelt sentiments go to the veteran sociologists who have contributed papers but left for heavenly abode. Their absence causes a vacuum which is difficult to be filled in near future.

P.N. Pandey

Contents

Contributors

Prof. A.N. Pandeya, Former Professor of Sociology, Department of Humanities & Social Sciences, Institute of Technology, New Delhi.

Prof. S. K. Srivastava, Professor of Sociology, Former Dean, Faculty of Social Sciences, Banaras Hindu University, Varanasi.

Professor V.P. Verma, Retd. Professor of Political Science, Patna University, Patna.

Prof. Sachchidananda, Professor of Sociology & Former Director, A.N. Sinha Institute of Social Science, Patna (Bihar).

Prof. Yogendra Singh, Professor Emeritus of Sociology, Former Chairman, CSS, SSS, JNU, New Delhi.

Dr. (Miss) Bina Roy, Former American Scholars Officer, The United States, Education Foundation in India, New Delhi.

Dr. (Mrs.) Leela Dube, Department of Sociology & Social Anthropology, Sagar University, Sagar (M.P.).

Prof. S.Shukla, Former Co-ordinator, Asian Institute of Educational Planning and Administration, Government of India,New Delhi.

Prof. S.C. Dube, Former Professor and Head, Department of Sociology & Social Anthropology, Saugar University, Sagar (M.P.).

Prof. Y.B. Damle, Former Professor Department of Sociology, University of Poona. Poona (Maharashtra).

Prof. S. Tripathi, Former Professor and Head, Department of Sociology, Banaras Hindu University, Varanasi.

Prof. H.C. Srivastava, Former Professor of Sociology Department of Sociology, Banaras Hindu University, Varanasi.

Dr. Yogesh Atal, Retired UNESCO's Principal Director of Social Sciences.

Prof. S.M. Dubey, Professor of Sociology, Former Vice-Chancellor, Dibrugarh University, Assam.

Dr. R.N. Saksena, Former Vice-Chancellor, M.G. Kashi Vidyapeeth, Varanasi.

Prof. M.N. Srinivas, Former Professor and Head, Department of Sociology, Delhi School of Economics, Delhi University, Delhi.

Prof. D.N. Dhanagare, Professor of Sociology, former Vice-Chancellor, Shivajee University, Kolhapur.

Prof. T. K. Oommen, Professor of Sociology, Former Chairman, CSS, SSS, JNU, New Delhi.

Prof. P.N. Pandey, Professor of Sociology, Former Dean, Faculty of Social Sciences, Banaras Hindu University, Varanasi.

Prof. Anand Kumar, Professor of Sociology, Former Chairman, CSS, SSS, JNU, New Delhi.

Prof. Jai Kant Tiwary, Professor of Sociology, Department of Sociology, Banaras Hindu University, Varanasi.

Dr. Manjula Rathaur, President, Centre for Applied Sociology, New Delhi.

Dr. Vishwanath Pandey, Former Public Relations Officer, Banaras Hindu University, Varanasi.

Dr. D.K. Singh, Asstt. Professor, Department of Sociology, Banaras Hindu University, Varanasi.

Dr. S.B. Singh, Asstt. Professor, Department of Political Science, DAV Degree College, Varanasi.

Dr. Anupama Pandey, UGC Post Doctoral Fellow, Department of Sociology, Banaras Hindu University, Varanasi.

Dr. Mukesh K. Srivastava, Department of Sociology, Banaras Hindu University, Varanasi.

Introduction

P.N. PANDEY

The present volume is an enlarged edition on **'Tradition, Modernization and Globalization'**. The previous edition consisted of some theme papers presented by the second generation of sociologists during the initial stage of the process and programme of modernization in the developed and developing countries but the enlarged edition in its present form embodies some of the very brilliant analyses done by the previous contributors and other sociologists of illustrious calibre belonging to the third generation of the practitioners of the discipline.

The second part of this volume deals with the papers on 'Tradition and Modernization' in the wake of global development which has been accelerated by sophisticated and latest scientific investigations and technological innovations. The use of informatics and the implementation of informatics and cybernetics have not only redesigned the overall process of modernization or even the continuity of traditions but have brought about unprecedented changes in the structure of feelings and sensitivity of human beings.

The papers in the first part incorporate the features of economy, polity and social structure as it prevailed during seventies in the twentieth century, a period when the whole programme of modernization was on the mid way to destination.

The second part which consists of the papers analyzing the features of modernity and post-modern developments at a stage when they have reached saturation point where the very boundaries of approved standards and norms of society are getting in the liquid process of change as pronounced by Zygmunt

Bauman. I would like to say that the present stage is a period of liquid modern society, a post-matured stage of development or in the words of Anthony Giddens, the late, advanced or radical modernity with its own juggernaut in the first quarter of the twenty-first century. The tremendous changes brought about by systems of information technology where truth is no more a yardstick of knowledge but performativity, the capacity to deliver output at the lowest cost replaces the truth as yardstick of knowledge. The excessive bureaucratization, computerization and commodification of knowledge, the internal colonization of the individual's life world (Habermas' remark) are the outcomes of radical or late modernity. All these have brought about serious changes in the structure and economy of the society at the global level. The increasing 'technetronic' structure of society poses hyper reality as if it were more real than the reality itself.

We are quite confident that this volume on 'Tradition, Modernization and Globalization' will stimulate the social scientists and the professional readers more intellectual interests in conducting researches and investigations in regard to the impact of information technology on social structure and human behaviour because the changes brought about by the so-called post-modern developments have reduced the differences between elite and mass culture and the local parochial identities of popular culture are being subsumed in the externally exposed mass culture as a culture of bazaar. The whole society is being converted into market-place and the major culture components are emerging as commodities of sale and exchange as having been cut off from the linkages of real life like dogs of the police squad whose specific organs are mutilated and they are glorified as sharp species of Dobermans, pamelion and so on. So is the case of modern man being cut off from the linkages of real life world having been subjected to the atrophy of individual culture and hypertrophy of objective culture and is being placed in the market as a client, a customer, an agent, a buyer or a seller or an employer or employee.

Professor A.N. Pandeya in his paper on 'Modernization of Complex Society—Some Theoretical and Methodological Issues'—raises important questions of conceptualization of modernization in the context of a national self-study. He critically examines different models of modernization and attempts to suggest the general approach to theory construction in this area.

Professor Pandeya's distinction between heterogeneous society and plural society as two ideal types on a continuum of socio-cultural integration stands as a good model of conceptualization for a complex society as ours. His paper has, therefore, thrown a new challenging perspective for the students of Modernization in India. Prof. S.K. Srivastava, in his paper on 'Tradition and Modernization', has emphasized on conceptualization of the theme explaining that modernity is a state of mind. He interprets the change and continuity in the process of Tradition and Modernization with regard to value system, social system and personality system.

Prof. V.P. Verma, as a political scientist, presented a conceptual framework for the study of Tradition and Modernization and citing references from Asian and African societies with reference to their administrative structures in terms of communism, totalitarianism and democracy.

Professor Sachchidanand gives an idea of the social change involved in the process of modernization, tradition and modernity are no necessarily opposed to each other. Modernity does not necessarily weaken tradition. Sometimes, old traditions and structures exist without conflict with new ones and there is no clash of opposites between modernizing processes and traditional forms. Sometimes, each derives some support from the other.

Traditionalism and modernism function like ideologies. In developing countries desire to be modern and at the same time, desire to preserve tradition are present. From this standpoint, Indian Nationalism is deeply committed to both tradition and modernity. The neo-Gandhians perceive the process of modernization within 'indigenous culture' to maintain both *growth* and *national identity*.

Professor Yogendra Singh's paper has shown a new perspective by emphasizing historicity of modernization both at the conceptual and empirical level. His analysis of Indian scheme is full of insight and has vigorous potentialities for future research. Professor Singh in his paper on 'Historicity of Modernization' distinguishes historicity from historicism! He discusses the process of modernization in the context of historicity at three levels of the social system, viz., (1) system of stratification, (2) value systems, and (3) political system. As an attempt at a realistic formulation of modernization Singh pleads for the distinct analysis of this process in terms of (*a*) role structures and changes in them, (*b*) a system of values representing a scientific world view, and (*c*) a parallel set of categorical values which may be unique to the particular society.

Professor Singh's distinction between instrumental values and categorical values may also mean that some categorical values would not be more consistent with modernization than others. The entire society may not modernize. It is likely that some sectors of the society modernize faster than others and, consequently, they may detach themselves from others. One may pay attention to the relative spread of modernization in the different sectors. And there are risks, at times, in generalizing for the society as a whole.

Dr. Bina Roy's paper deals with another important dimension of perception and modernization. She raises some important issues. Dr. Roy's paper deals with perception of modernization by applying the theory of perception to the process of modernization in the Indian context. For the purpose of her paper she chases to indicate a few problems related to perceptions of modernization with special reference to three areas, viz., (1) fundamental rights, (2) social legislation, and (3) the educated minority. She points out that perception of modernization in the area of fundamental rights was made difficult because there does not exist any stimulus in the field of action of the average citizen. In the field of social legislation we have enacted many laws, many of which are ideal on paper. But once the legislation is passed, not much is done for implementation so that legislation becomes a mockery.

An important dimension of the problem in modernization of developing societies, which has not been duly emphasized by scholars has been dealt with by Mrs. Leela Dube and Professor S.C. Dube in their brief but thematically extremely useful paper on Barriers and Modernization. If the modernizing elite is itself confused, what will happen to the entire process of modernization of developing nations? The authors have, therefore, laid emphasis on ideological, motivational, institutional and organizational barriers, which obstruct the progress of modernization in developing societies.

Professor Shukla in his paper throws light on two way relationship between modernization and education. Conceptually, he makes a distinction among three facets of education, viz., as an institution, a fiction and a process. The role of education in social change and economic development may be analyzed at different levels. He also throws light on how education influences class structure and politics in India. In this connection his main emphasis is on the problems of policy formulation to set strategies of modernization in different framework of modernization that a society adopts for its change.

Professor S.C. Dube in his paper highlights both the functional and dysfunctional roles that education plays in modernization of Indian society. He presents the major assumption basic to the concept of modernization. These according to him were tapping of the inanimate sources of power, development of associational capabilities and development of the complex organizational skills. To realize these objectives he formulates a set of requisite strategies and in their light specifies the contexts wherein education has a directly functional or dysfunctional bearing. These processes, according to him, also imply some dilemmas for a very modernizing society such as those of national needs *versus* social justice, quality *versus* quantity, strategic and selective planning *versus* operation of market laws of demand and supply, etc. These forces which create structural constraints should be controlled to smoothen the process of modernization.

Professor Y.B. Damle in his paper has pointed out that sociologically modernization has to be analyzed and understood at three different levels, viz., social system, cultural system and personality system. He emphasizes the characteristics and implications of modernization at these different levels and examines whether or not these different characteristics are present in Indian situation. In context to modernization the role of education is to create autonomy and identity.

Prof. S. Tripathi has highlighted on the role of elites in the process of modernization with regard to values and ideology and emphasized that in the process of modernization and awareness of the situation is important for the participant while focusing on the role of elites in modernization of India, he highlights three distinct order of cultural reality, viz., the traditional or conservative Indians, the westernized Indians and the Indians in transition. He perceives that Indian nationalism is well-concocted with traditional values as well as the modern values.

Dr. Yogesh Atal has pointed out the three approaches in the current social science literature indicating the relationship between political participation and modernization:

1. Political participation as one of the attributes of modernization.
2. There are some social scientists who separate political participation from modernization and believe that modernization serves as a precipitating agent for political participation.
3. Political participation is viewed as a precipitating factor for modernization.

Professor S.M. Dubey presented a paper on modernization among the Tribes of North-Eastern India. The relation between tradition and modernity may be decided on the basis of the experience and conclusions from 'field situations'. As a process of change, he regards 'modernization' as a 'broad category' which includes 'westernization', 'sanskritization' and development. Keeping in view the levels of development, the agents and indicators of modernization among North-Eastern tribes, three models of modernization namely, westernization, sanskritization and development have been presented by him.

Professor R.N. Saksena has drawn our attention to certain basic issues of modernization in relation to development. He has also emphasized both economic and social dimensions of Tradition and Modernization. Though he laments for lack of mobility in Indian society, he concedes that the processes of mobility have started with the growth of industrialization in the country leading to modernization. Both horizontal and vertical types of mobility are taking place in our social stratification. Modernization in India, therefore, has also led to open a comparatively closed society.

Prof. M.N. Srinivas' valedictory address of the seminar on Tradition and Modernization (1974) has been placed as a paper in the present volume, because the significance of his address has in it the precise and crisp summary of the first part.

This new edition embodies the post-modern and global features of changes emerging all-over the world with specific reference to Indian society. This volume consists of the papers contributed by earlier sociologists along with the later generation of practitioners of the discipline. The book is divided into two parts. The first part consists of the papers contributed by veteran Sociologists during Seventies and the second part of the volume consists of some of the papers from the earlier sociologists who are still alive with their changed vision and modified interpretations about modernity and global development, while most of the other papers on the same theme incorporate the extended ideas and analysis of the features of modernity and post-modern development after the turn of twentieth century and especially, the new features which have emerged in the wake of global developments in the first quarter of twenty-first century.

The second part of the volume consists of some of the very illustrious pieces of work on the issues concerning modernity and global development. Prof. Yogendra Singh has tried to focus upon the issue of globalization with multiple modernity's and those of rationalization and counter rationalization. Prof. S.M. Dubey has made a very comprehensive approach to the conceptual shifts and ideological constraints in the prevailing issue of 'Tradition, Modernization and Globalization'. Prof. Yogesh Atal has very clearly pin pointed the persisting cultural diversities at the global level in the wake of globalization. These diversities, he has attempted, to point out in the realm of culture and civilization.

Prof. D.N. Dhanagare in his presidential address at the 27th All India Sociological Conference, held at IIT, Kanpur, December 18-20, 2002, perceives global development as a mechanism of separation and recombination of space and time as well as a crucial factor of dynamism of modernity.

Prof. T.K. Oommen in his paper, attempts to highlight the conceptual history and contemporary cultural trends in the process of globalization.

Prof. P.N. Pandey in his paper on 'Modernity, Post-modernity and Global Development', has attempted to present a comprehensive scenario of the programme of Modernity, Post-modernity and Global Development and as such is, indeed a very systematic and impressive record of the current processes of cultural changes and post-modern developments with their impacts on developing countries in general and India in particular. His analysis consists of the latest conceptual projections and their implications on developed and developing societies. It is really a step forward from sociological imagination to so-called sociological impressionism that focuses on the emerging changes in the structure of feelings and sensitivity in the cyber age of electronics and informatics.

Prof. Anand Kumar is very emphatic in discriminating the

diverse pictures of modernity in the era of globalization with reference to the developed and developing world. Prof. Jai Kant Tiwary in his study of tradition and modernity has attempted to focus on the emerging repercussions on polity and social structure as well as the agrarian economy in the third world countries.

Dr. Vishwanath Pandey has presented a micro case study in terms of actor and institution with reference to Banaras Hindu University in the anti-colonial struggle. His paper presents a peculiar blend, of course, a symbiosis of tradition and modernity. Dr. Manjula Rathore is again a promising writer who portrays a specific feature of continuity of globalization and local culture with reference to Varanasi in India.

Dr. D.K. Singh and Dr. S.B. Singh in their joint paper, Globalization and National Identity highlight that in the developing societies of Asia and Africa, the national identities are still retained and continued strongly in the wave of global development and modern technology.

Dr. Anupama Pandey in her paper has attempted to highlight the role of science and technology in changing power structure in modern societies at the global level. She has shown how in modern societies the power of decision matching is shifting from in - and there who have means of production to those who have technical knowhow and those who participate in making the decisions.

Dr. Mukesh Srivastava in his paper, Modernity and Empowerment through Global Development, has attempted to explain the nexus between Modernity and Empowerment.

This volume indicates a sequential nexus of tradition, modernization and globalization. Modernization has not done away with the traditions. Almost in all global societies one may perceive practices a continuity of traditional sanctions and rituals with new scientific outlook, perceptions and new contents and modern accessories giving a positive support to traditional continuity. Mention may he made of the traditions of seasonal festivals being celebrated in modern costumes and coverage in different countries both developed and developing, for example, the religious and cultural pilgrimages in India, light festivals in European countries specially, 55 days light festivals in Amsterdom the capital of Netherlands also similar traditions being celebrated in the U.S., Canada, Italy, Germany, France as well as in the developing countries of Asia, Africa and Latin America. Such continuity of celebrations in Brazil, China, India, Hongkong, Thailand and other Asian countries within their own indigenous models of modernity certainly denote a bonhomie of tradition and modernity. Traditions sociologically supplement modernity and modernity invigorates traditions. Only the superstitions are being removed by scientific and rational temper of modernity. The pilgrimage to Bodh Gaya, Vaishno Devi, and hilly shrines of Badrinath, Kedarnath, Amarnath, Hemkund and Mansarovar have been more popular. The religious festival and observance and celebrations of *Karba Chauth, Dipawali, Dala Chhathi* and *Holi* in India have undoubtedly emerged from local and little traditions to great traditions as well as global traditions.

Most of the countries in the developed as well as developing world have preferred to emerge with their own models of modernity with indigenous ethos of culture and social structure. Modernization and development are themselves the outcome of culture growth and because of cultural variations there cannot be a universal model for the entire world. No doubt, some common denominations of modernity with rational application of science and technology may be seen everywhere.

Globalization as a multidimensional concept and worldwide trade mechanism is a new approach but its roots lie in the last seven decades of post-World War II period. The decades of I960, 1970, 1980 and 1990 started with the agenda of growth, modernization, social transformation, development and sustainable development respectively and finally at the turn of the twentieth century led to globalization with emphasis on liberalization and privatization (Pandey: 1997). The active motivators for globalization are (1) search for market, (2) multinational investments, and (3) new tools of technology and electronics with computer network. The most paradoxical aspects of globalization are disparity, inequality, injustice, insecurity, apprehensions of maintaining sovereignty of the newly democratic nations. The western countries specially the U.S.A., France, Germany, Italy, the U.K. have moved toward post-industrial economy from manufacturing to service economy and they are in urgent need of market place for their profuse technologized production. It demands huge market for consumption. It is the developing countries of Asia, Africa and Latin America which appear as huge consumer market place.

The sad impressions of modernization, development and sustainable development have created more disparities and discrepancies, though the slogans of globalization are more attractive. The developing nations have disenchantment with the Western programmes of development and globalization. The ever increasing disparities and discrepancies and the gap between the rich and the poor, the economically affluent and the deprived, the powerful and the powerless shows that the very ideology of development based on egalitarianism and equity has proved elusive and dilemmatic to the societies of Asia and Africa. Most of the countries of these continents are realizing that foreign aids are instrumental in perpetuating long term dependency in the developing nations and as such is a strategy to place them in the grip of their trade and technology with contractual fundings. In such situations the developing countries must evolve their own indigenous models and parameters to their social and economic development. The policies and programmes initiated by international agencies, for example, International Monetary Fund, World Bank, United States Agency for International Development, Inter American Development Bank accord and approve the international and national character of Western capitalistic countries in the garb of new techno-capitalism and aim at maintaining their supremacy over these countries. These international bodies motivate for creating free market, trade and technology and to rely on them with a sense of attachment and commitment.

The most sensitizing recent discourse about cultural change centres on the issue whether culture has taken a new turn, entered a new phase at the outset of the twenty-first century. The cultural analysis done by the Neo-Marxists and Neo-Weberian scholars are essentially modern in character. If society prefers to be dominated by a single set of ideas, then Gramsci of Frankfurt school can investigate how these ideas are manufactured, if society is divided by men into small and fixed number of classes, then Bourdieu, Abercrombie, Hill and Turner can investigate whether culture exhibits similar internal differentiation. Habermas (1987) observes that this move of modernity to post-modernity is somewhat disethicized and has decoupled the relation between the life-world and the system and is creating inner colonization in the individuals. Malcolm Waters (1992) observed the process of advanced modernity as a chaotic mass mediated individual preference based phenomenon. It has superimposed mass culture over popular culture. Janeson (1984) provides the hardest Marxist version. He accepts that cultural change is in train but interprets it as the 'cultural logic of late capitalism'. His proposition of three-fold perception of capitalism embraces Mandel's perception, i.e. (1) Market capitalism as envisaged by Marx, (2) imperial or monopoly capitalism as envisaged by Lenin, and (3) Multinational consumer capitalism as envisaged by Mandel himself.

As regards the global change, the media of mass communication revolutionizes culture and the ever-growing knowledge of science, technology and electronics give wider coverage to global space. The society is being transformed into a 'technotronic culture' with computer networking. The culture specifics are attempted to be subsumed into multiethnicity and multiculturalism as smaller clenches with secondary importance. A post-human future is emerging with biotechnological revolution (Fukuyama : 2004) the unprecedented changes brought about by cybernetics and informatics and overall techno-electronic developments are going to transform the planet earth into a wonderland of Utopia. But the developing countries in general and India in particular have a long historicity of grand narratives, metatheories, legends and myths. Globalization cannot assimilate all of them. In my assessment, India and other developing countries of Asia and Africa will ever manifest a peculiar blend of their historical identity even in the global modernizing attempts.

PART ONE
Historical Perspective of Tradition and Modernization

1

Modernization of a Complex Society

Theoretical and Methodological Issues

A.N. PANDEYA

[I]
INTRODUCTION

If modernization is to be regarded as a new term for an old process—the process of social change whereby less developed societies acquire characteristics common to more developed societies (Lerner, 1968), it is important to recall that effort to develop an adequate conceptualisation of the process extended to nearly a century. In fact, Karl Marx was probably the first to note the process as activated by inter-societal communication, when in the preface to Das Kapital he observed: "The country that is more developed industrially only shows, to the less developed, the image of its own future". This 'showing', one may argue, includes not only the 'images' transmitted to the elites and masses of the less developed countries through the normal channels of international communication and dissemination, but also the relatively sophisticated conceptualisations developed by the social scientists and theorists of the developed nations, transmit to their counterparts of the less developed nations. An interesting, though little noticed feature of this process in the recent past is the effort at 'self-study' to which the social scientists and scholars of the modernised societies have been progressively driven, while engaged in conceptualising the process of modernization.[1] The consequent reconsideration has not only entailed a substantial modification in the evaluation of the historical paths of these nations from the past to the present, but has also occasioned a considerable reorganisation of their societal theories and policies, including new ways of estimating policy paths from the present to the future. This is not to minimise the importance of the significant advances made by them in the theoretical task of conceptualising the complex process of modernization itself; for, despite conceptual and terminological differences of more or less importance, there appears today a large area of agreement in these circles regarding the salient characteristics (operational values) of modernity.[2] The question rather is whether in the case of the social scientists of the less developed countries, particularly India, one could discern firstly, a similar indication of a national 'self-study', as an offshoot or by-product of their efforts to conceptualise the phenomenon of modernization; and secondly, whether their theorisation is based on a critical appraisal of the available models of the process, both in respect of their analytical characteristics, as well as relevance and applicability to the Indian context.

This chapter seeks to suggest a negative finding on both these scores, as its initial premise (Section II). Thereafter, it seeks to appraise some of the more significant models of modernization as a prolegomena to an adequate conceptualisation of the process, both in terms of analytical soundness, as well as relevance to the Indian setting (Section III). Finally, it attempts to suggest the general approach to theory-construction in this area, which is likely to be fruitful both for empirical research as well as policy formulation (Section IV).

[II]
CURRENT CONCEPTUALISATIONS OF THE MODERNIZATION PROCESS IN INDIA

Current conceptualisations of the process of modernization in India fall into two broad categories of (*a*) historically oriented analysis, and (*b*) analytically oriented formulations. Mishra (1961), Ahmad (1968) and Broomfield (1968) and Srinivas (1966) broadly illustrate category (A). Despite important differences in approach, method and rigour, they share certain common features, the most notable of which are a scepticism of overly rigorous analytic frame, greater reliance on *ad hoc* imagination and judgment in discerning general trends and attempting *sui generics* interpretation, and a desire to keep to the main factual terrain as defined by their focus of study. The methodological and ideational parentage are mixed; and it is rather difficult to trace them to any particular source, even when individual theorists and scholars may be seen to have exerted some visible influence over them. To this extent, therefore, these studies may be firstly regarded as original and/or creative efforts of varying quality, towards a scientific understanding, interpretation or explanation of the complex on-going processes of social change, as seen in the historical perspective.

From our point of view, however, their significance is rather limited; largely because of their thin theoretical fall-out, in terms of which one could hope to undertake an empirical exploration of the contemporary situation or attempt a prediction of emerging trends.

One would, under the circumstances, turn with hopes to the second category, which is overtly analytic in its approach as well as intentions. About the most notable example of such a conceptualisation is Dube (1967, 1965); and a careful scrutiny of his frame is instructive for more than one reason, even if one is driven in the end to a somewhat negative finding.

Modernity, for Professor Dube, "denotes the common 'behavioural systems' historically associated with the urban, industrial, literate and participant societies of Western Europe and North America as well as those of the USSR and Japan. Modernization is the process through which their standards of performance and achievement can be accomplished by the less developed societies." (1967, p. 35). 'Modernization involves the emergence of a new behavioural system with certain distinctive characteristics. Such a system implies considerable value-change. Unless the traditional values undergo a radical modification, an innovative ethos, an entrepreneurial and industrial ethic cannot be created. Value-change is necessary also for institutional rearrangement considered essential for modernization' (*ibid.*, 37). 'Modernity thus is not just superficial acquisition of some isolated traits and elements characteristic of the more advanced countries. Their selection in a logical order and sequence, and integrations into the cultural pattern in a widely ramifying manner is essential' (*ibid.*, p. 35).

How is, then, one to conceive this 'logical order and sequence', along with their integration into the cultural pattern in a widely ramifying manner. Here one is appropriately warned about the multiplicity of models of modernization (*ibid.*, p. 36), since 'they are often perceptive and offer some meaningful insights, but from the sociological angle they lack coherence and miss certain important aspects of the human context' (*ibid.*, p. 37). In offering his own model, Dube draws from the works of Lerner (1962, 63), Almond and Coleman (1960), McClelland (1961), Ithiel de Soa Pool (1963) and Wilbert Moore (1963), and proceeds to telescope their hypotheses, while listing the characteristic attributes of modernity, as follows:

(*i*) Empathy,
(*ii*) Mobility,
(*iii*) High Participation,
(*iv*) Interest Articulation,
(*v*) Interest Aggregation,
(*vi*) Institutionalised political competition,
(*vii*) Achievement Orientation,
(*viii*) Rational—ends means calculation,
(*ix*) New attitudes to wealth, work, savings and risk-taking,
(*x*) Faith in the desirability and possibility of change,
(*xi*) Social, economic, and political discipline, and
(*xii*) Capacity to put off immediate and short-term satisfactions for higher satisfactions in the longer run.

The anatomy of this model is transparent as to its parentage. The first-three attributes are components of the Lerner model; the next three are adoptions from the Almond-Coleman model; the seventh attribute comes from McClelland; while the last five of the list are items relating to attitudes, values and motivations—articulated in the growing literature on the social and cultural implications of modernization, more specially Ithiel de Sola Pool (1963), Wilbert Moore (1963) and Dube (1965). To be sure, the author does recognize the importance of the sequence or specific form of linkage as between the items listed; witness, his comment: "Several interacting transformations are thus called for: personality must open up, values and motivations must change, and institutional arrangements must be reworked. An integrated combination of these attributes leads to modernization" (*ibid.*, p. 40). The critical question as to the specific mode of 'integrated combination', however, is left unasked and unanswered.

Is the model applicable and/or relevant to the Indian context? The issue is never faced frontally, though one could argue with considerable force that the author envisages an affirmative answer. The extended analysis of the 'Indian Context' (*ibid.*, pp. 40-45) seems to imply this; as also scattered comments like: 'The requirements of modernization are hard and almost inflexible. They will not yield, beyond a point, to particular societies; societies must yield to them. The dialogue on their adaptive demands on Indian society has so far yielded only polite nothings. Fashionable debates on the subject diplomatically avoid facing the real issue. It is necessary that they be faced with candour and conviction.' Indeed. Yet, it is difficult to avoid the feeling that even at the level of serious analysis, 'the subject diplomatically avoids facing the real issue'.

What, then, are the more important 'real issues'? To begin with, the strategy of telescoping hypotheses from logically desparate, even conflicting habitat—in terms of which this hybrid model has been developed deserves a—carefully articulated rationale. Given a complex referent like the process of modernization, a good case for this strategy can be made, for instance, in terms of the need for an interdisciplinary approach, within the overall frame of an adequate analytic model of the requisite range of coverage derived from sophisticated abstraction. Furthermore, it is necessary to ensure that the basal construct of the interdisciplinary model represent a logically permissible synthesis of the frames of reference of the individual disciplines, in so far as they do not belong to wholly different conceptual species, with different relevances, which demand to be used in wholly difficult ways. There is no indication that these elementary precautions have been observed in the present case. On the contrary, what has been presented, betrays a 'shreds and patches' quality all through (to borrow a phrase from Smelser, 1963). The distinctive frames of reference adopted by the source-theorists—(*i*) Lerner, (*ii*) Almond Coleman, (*iii*) McClelland, (*iv*) Ithiel de Solo Pool, and (*v*) Wilbert Moore, it should be noted, do not belong to the same logical family, nor do they reveal any form of family resemblance; consequently, they just fail to cohere together to yield an integrated model. Nor does the model yield any set of testable hypotheses to guide empirical research, as a result, it is impossible to detect evenly purely heuristic virtues or uses. Nor is its relevance to the specific case of the Indian setting terribly obvious, since no effort has been made to link it to the distinctive features of the social and cultural system of obtaining in the country currently. About the most disturbing assumption underlying the model is the unexamined proposition that modernity can be definitively defined only in terms of a specific cluster of traits discernible in the modernised nations of today. This puts the modernising nations in the Leatsian situation of the Greecian Urn, which depicts a never-ending chase between the pursuer and the pursued. It implies a picture of future for the modernised societies, which is, in its essential features, indistinguishable from their present face a position that is palpably false, if one recalls the current efforts at projecting future 'images', currently underway in these countries, centering around the 'technotronic' revolution.

[III]
SOME RELEVANT MODELS OF MODERNIZATION

Are we, then, in a cul-de-sac? Are we suggesting a total 'self-sufficiency' in model-building, in which insights and cues generated by social scientists of the modernised societies have no meaningful contributions to make? Are we, for that matter, arguing for a *swadeshi* conceptualisation? The foregoing is only a prolegomena to our argument in favour of a careful search for a relevant model that would be adequate for our situation. And one need not start from the scratch, for the labour of the scientific community has provided a minimum foundation for further construction in this difficult terrain. It would be, for instance, rewarding to pay some attention to two significant models of modernization, proposed by Eisenstadt (1966) and Levy (1966), as a prolegomena to better theory-construction in the area.

One of the chief merits of these efforts is the explicit recognition given to the great structural variety of the modern as well as the modernising societies. An attempt is, therefore, made to delineate the different patterns of modernization as they have developed in both the cases; these models, consequently, presuppose a minimal knowledge about the historical as well contemporary settings of the nations involved. The three models, to be sure, differ in their analytic rigour, areas of emphasis, as well as empirical infrastructure. It is, nevertheless, possible to treat them as three elements of a cluster, which, taken together, carries within it rich possibilities for further fruitful exploration and refinement.

The intellectual context of the Eisenstadt model, is, to a great extent, the same from which Dube derives the component hypotheses of his telescoped model. Harold Isaac, Myron Wiener, Robert Wood, Talcott Parsons, Robert N. Bellah and Edward Shils are the additional influences that have shaped the orientations articulated by Eisenstadt. The last of these has provided the crucial concepts of the 'consensual mass society' and 'centre and periphery' (Shils, 1961, 1960, 1958). An attempt has been made to present a sociological approach to the problems of Modernization, particularly for political modernization: the focal point of the approach is the proposition that the major problem facing such societies is the necessity to develop an institutional structure which is capable of continuously 'absorbing' the various social changes which are inherent in the processes of modernization. The most central characteristic of modern societies, from this point of view, is their basic mass-consensual orientation (*ibid.*, p. 15) rooted in the growing impingement of broader strata on the centre, in their demands to participate in the sacred symbols of society and their formulation, and in the displacement of the traditional symbols by new ones that stress these participatory and social dimensions. The culmination of all these developments can be seen in the crystallisation of the nation and the nation-state as the most important socio-political unit of the modern societies, and of the possibility of a civil order as the major type of socio-political order within it (*ibid.*, p. 16).

The structural diversity discernible in the processes of modernization Eisenstadt ascribes to the crucial variable of different starting points (*ibid.*, pp. 46.ff.). The pioneer of this approach was, of course, Gerschenkorn, whose six propositions are worth recalling:

(*i*) The more backward a country's economy, the more likely was its industrialisation to start discontinuously as a sudden great spurt proceeding at a relatively high rate of growth of manufacturing output.

(*ii*) The more backward a country's economy, the more pronounced was the stress in its industrialisation on the bigness of both plant and enterprise.

(*iii*) The more backward a country's economy, the greater was the stress upon producers', goods as against consumers' goods.

(*iv*) The more backward a country's economy, the greater was the part played by special institutional factors designed to increase supply of capital to the nascent industries and, in addition, to provide them with less decentralised and better informed entrepreneurial guidance; the more backward the country, the more pronounced was the coerciveness and comprehensiveness of those factors.

(*v*) The more backward a country's economy, the heavier the pressure upon the levels of consumption of the population.

(*vi*) The more backward a country, the less likely was its agriculture to play any active role by offering to the growing industries the advantages of an expanding industrial market based in turn on the rising productivity of agricultural labour.

It is to Eisenstadt's credit that he seeks to apply these propositions not only to the economic sphere, but to all major institutional spheres. The two additional variables of the nature of the initial impetus that gives the initial push to modernization, and the policies of the more active elites of a society the "modernizing elites, in combination with the first variable help to explain the structural variety of Modernization. Eisenstadt then proceeds to a comparative analysis of situations of breakdown and of sub-stained growth". To the basic question: what are the conditions of sustained growth as against conditions of breakdown or stagnation?—the answer given amounts to the negative proposition: "these conditions are not simply related to any of the socio-demographic or structural indices of modernization" (*ibid.*, p. 145). These are minimal conditions but beyond these minimal conditions the picture is certainly much more complex. The widely held proposition that the less traditional a society is, the more it is capable of sustained growth has been disproved. The structural indices of modernization indicate only the extent to which traditional, self-contained societies become weakened or disintegrated—the extent to which traditional society is passing; but they do not in themselves indicate the extent to which a new, viable modern society capable of such continuous growth may develop.[3] Similarly, the inter-relationship between economic and political development turns out to be rather complicated and paradoxical. As against the rather naive assumption that the two are always concomitant and reinforce each other, more recent evidence shows that they might sometimes run counter to each other. The final upshot of his analysis is paradoxical and brief: "Both—breakdowns and the possibility of sustained growth—are inherent in the process of modernity. They indicate the pitfalls, problems, and challenges of modernity—and the fact that modernity constitutes perhaps the greatest challenge that mankind has posed for itself in the course of its history".

Thus forewarned we are ready to consider the Levy model, which carries the search for variations in the processes of modernization several steps ahead, conducted with analytical rigour, which is model for such inquiries.[4] Levy (1964) is basically interested in formulating hypotheses relating to modernization. The first scientific requirement of such statements is that they be *conceivably falsifiable*—that they are neither non-empirical mystical propositions nor tautological propositions. Furthermore, they should be fruitful is that either proof or disproof of them will teach us much more than we already know (*ibid.*, p. 7). Thus, what has been attempted is the presentation of a sensitised tool. The theoretical propositions on which it rests are not nearby well enough worked out, or logically interrelated to claim more. It is no serious criticism of Levy to assert that hypotheses about facts have been flatly asserted without any accompanying attempt at empirical demonstration, since he is aware that we are not close to having adequate empirical materials for the definitive verification of many, if any, of the hypotheses presented (*ibid.*, p. 808). At the very least, his hypotheses may serve as challenges to the data which may some day be collected. If such basic research on societies in general can be done, the implications for making isolated bits of knowledge cumulative in their impact will be enormous. In any case, this is to be preferred to having details descriptions of more or less isolated aspects and organisations with the interconnections among them left largely on an *ad hoc* basis (*ibid.*, pp. 808-9). In scientific work, it is more important to be fruitful for further work than to be right (*ibid.*, p. 7).

What are, then, the Levy hypotheses about modernization? To begin with is the definition of the *concept* of modernization, as distinguished from a full or realistic *description* of the thing to which the concept refers (p. 10). His definition is arbitrary in two senses. First, these are an infinite number of other possibilities for defining this concept in such a way as to have exactly the same referent. Second, for different purposes, one might wish to define the concept as having a totally different referent. Levy then proceeds to define modernization in terms of uses of inanimate sources of power and the use of tools to multiply the effect of effort (*ibid.*, p. 11).

This is undoubtedly a rather startling beginning, for in the subsequent phases of his analysis of the structural features of the relatively modernised society (pp. 38-84) and the relatively non-modernised societies, this definition does not play any role whatsoever. The distinction has been an attempt in terms of *aspects* like (*i*) specialisation of units, (*ii*) salf-sufficiency of the units, (*iii*) increasingly universalistic ethic, (*iv*) combination of centralisation and decentralisation, (*v*) relationship aspects (pp. 133-174), (*vi*) centralised media of exchange and markets, and *organisational contexts* like (*a*) bureaucracy, and (*b*) family systems. Of these, perhaps item (*v*) of aspects deserves attention, since they are intended to provide a conceptual frame for analysis of relationships in any society. His hypothesis is best illustrated by Table 1.1:

Table 1.1

	Aspects	*Rational (X)*	*Traditional (Y)*
1.	Cognitive aspects	Rational	Traditional
2.	Membership aspects	Universalistic	Particularistic
3.	Substantive Definition aspects	Functionally specific	Functionally diffuse
4.	Affective aspects	Avoidant	Intimate
5.	Goal orientation aspects	Individualistic	Responsible
6.	Stratification aspects	Hierarchical	Non-hierarchical

Likewise, the aspects of any society are (*i*) role differentiation, (*ii*) solidarity, (*iii*) economic allocation, (*iv*) political allocation, (v) integration and expression (pp. 175-184). The last of this list constitute a catch-all category (p. 341), and is about the weakest link in Levy's chain. The organisational context of society, on the other hand, is distinguished as (*i*) kinship and family organisations, (*ii*) governments and associated units, (*iii*) predominantly economically oriented organisation, (*iv*) armed force organisations, and (v) other organisational contexts like churches, schools, recreational organisation, etc. (*ibid.*, pp. 375-650).

Against this backdrop, Levy attempts an analysis of the problem of modernization. The structures of modernization are always subversive of the *status quo* of relatively non-modernised societies for several reasons (*ibid.*, p. 748). Accordingly, he lists three most strategic problems of transition as these of (*i*) control, (*ii*) capital formation, and (*iii*) the elements of ambivalence created by the process of modernization itself (*ibid.*, p. 765). The last of these is probably the most important. Some people who start out in favour of the process inevitably end up as its most bitter opponents, while others who may not have thought much about it one way or the other come to be opponents. (*ibid.*, p. 772). The enthusiasm for things modern may also carry with it its own excesses. Sooner or later, thus, occur *fundamentalist reactions*, which may be defined as one in which the actors concerned regard the solution to present problems as they conceive them to lie in a return to the good old days from which they feel departure never should have been made (*ibid.*, p. 773). So the conclusion: "The problems of modernization for the numbers of relatively non-modernised societies are exceedingly serious ones about which we have little reason to be optimistic. We do not know nearly as much as we need to know to solve these problems to the satisfaction of anyone" (*ibid.*, p. 793).

Levy's analysis hinges implicitly rather than explicitly, on a distinction which should be introduced now. This relates to the distinction between *ideal* and *actual* structures. The main propositions derived from this distinction are:

(*i*) The members of all societies distinguish between ideal and actual structure.

(*ii*) The ideal and actual structures never coincide completely for any society or any sub-system of a society.

(*iii*) Some of the sources of stress and strain characteristic of the members of any society inhere in the fact that the ideal and actual structures do not coincide.

(*iv*) Some of the possibilities of integration in terms of any society inhere in the fact that the ideal and the actual structures do not coincide perfectly.

(*v*) Discrepancies between the ideal and actual structures in general are never adequately explicable in terms of hypothesis.

(*vi*) A part of the discrepancy is always explicable in terms of inadequate knowledge of the members of the society about the structures of their society and about the experiences which they are likely to have. It is questionable whether the members as a whole are capable of the amount of knowledge which would be necessary whereby such discrepancies to be eliminated completely.

(*vii*) Were there to be a society for whose members these discrepancies did not exist, that society would be impossibly brittle in the face of any changes in the setting of the society with any implication for the activities carried on in terms of the society (*ibid.*, p. 747).

[IV]
SUGGESTIONS FOR A NEW APPROACH

The foregoing analysis of the models developed by Eisenstadt and Levy carry some implicit suggestions as to further lines of theoretical developments. For one thing, an attempt may be made to work out the implications of Levy's distinction of ideal and actual structures for a better understanding of the process of modernity in the transitional countries. Is it possible, for instance, to assimilate the 'modern' image within the ideal structure for a society, whose actual structure is non-modern? Recent analysis in the field of *sociology* of knowledge, it may be recalled here, have focused attention on the social construction of reality, including social reality (Berger, Luckman, 1967). The problem of identity and self-image is as relevant for nations as for individual actors. If so, it would be fruitful to explore the question of Modernization in terms of a revised self-image on the part of a nation. Another and equally relevant way of putting the question would be in terms of Levian distinction between the ideal structure and the actual structure, as per the seven-fold propositions.

Similarly, it would be probably fruitful if an effort were to be made to link the two models to the analysed features of the social and cultural system of contemporary India. This would entail a systematic development of the neglected dimension of the Levy model, particularly the aspect of integration and expression, which has been handled in a crude and cursory manner. This should be possible in terms of an analytic frame appropriate for the understanding of a 'complex' society. The basic concepts of this frame can be indicated here, tentatively and briefly.

The foundational concept, to be sure, would be that of 'culture', in contra-distinction to society. Admittedly, there is considerable terminological as well as analytic confusion around this concept. Nadel (1951—for instance, states: "Actually, neither 'social' nor 'cultural' anthropology defines our subject matter satisfactorily as I hope to show, it is essentially two-dimensional, being always both 'cultural' and 'social'—Society, as I see it, means the totality of social facts projected on to the dimension of relationships and groupings; culture, the same totality in the dimension of action" *ibid.*, pp. 79-80). Likewise, the Tylorian concept of culture is not terribly helpful for theory of cultural modernization, since the concept was applied to a class of phenomena that is defined residually. Nevertheless, there does appear to be general agreement on the following propositions: (*i*) culture is historically derived; (*ii*) culture is essentially ideational; (*iii*) culture comprises cognitive orientations and values; and (iv) culture is patterned (Krocber and Parsons, 1958). Or, as Despres (1968) would put it: "Culture is a historically derived system of ideas and values delineated by and expressed through the institutional structures of society".

The question remains: Is it possible to delineate a conceptual framework more or less consistent with this paradigmatic view of culture and capable of defining particular problems of theoretical importance concerned with the modernization of complex societies? It may be useful, in this context, to recall some of the recent discussions concerning the idea of 'cultural pluralism' and its heuristic value for the study of developing nations (see M.G. Smith 1968, 1965, 1960, 1955). A fundamental issue is whether or not the plural model, when compared to the structural-functional model of the unitary society offers any specific advantage for analysing the problem of unity and diversity in society, particularly in relationship of the process of cultural change. Smith for one has recently (*ibid.*) suggested a model which is based on the

Malinowskian position that social institutions are the concrete isolates of organised behaviour; that each institution comprises a mutually supportive set of values, rules, activities and social relations; that institutions having to do with the same phase of life form ch est of sub-systems, which, in turn, combine to form the total institutional system. It follows from the foregoing that the core of a culture is its institutional system.

Based on these conceptualisations is Smith's distinction of three types of societies—(*i*) homogeneous societies in which all the groups of a political unit share the same total institutional system; (*ii*) heterogeneous societies in which the groups within a political unit share the same system of basic institutions but participate in different systems of alternative and exclusive institutions (most modern societies would be examples); and (*iii*) plural societies, in which groups living within a political unit have very different systems of compulsory or basic institutions (the best examples are to be found among the newly emerging nations). Dispres (1968), however, suggests that definition of a plural society must take into account two related sets of facts—(*i*) the extent to which specified groups are culturally differentiated in terms of the specific institutional activities; and (*ii*) the level at which institutional activities serve to maintain cultural differentiation as the basis for socio-cultural integration. When institutional activities serve to integrate culturally differentiated groups primarily at local levels, such groups might be referred to as 'minimal' or local cultural sections. On the other hand, when institutional activities serve to integrate culturally differentiated groups at the societal level, such groups might be identified as 'maximal' or national cultural sections. Short of a society being homogeneous, the existence of 'minimal' or local cultural sections expresses the smallest amount of cultural variation a society can have. A society that contains local cultural sections is socially and culturally heterogeneous. Short of a society being bifurcated, the existence of 'maximal' or national cultural sections is the greatest amount of cultural variation a society can have. In these terms, then, the heterogeneous society and the plural society are two ideal types on a continuum of socio-cultural integration. This conceptualisation permits the construction of analytic models which specify the criteria to be used to determine empirically the degree to which a society is pluralistic.

It is the concluding suggestion of this article that the above conceptualisation offers possibilities for both analytic constructions as well as empirical research on problems relating to modernization of a complex society such as ours.

Notes

1. Thus, W. Arthur Lewis (1955) building upon prior work on the conditions of economic progress by Colin Clark (1940), David C. McClelland (1961), building upon prior work in the psychology of 'achievement-aspiration ratios' since William James, Sevmor M. Lipset (1963), building upon prior work in sociology on the process of social change since Karl Marx and Max Weber, who has rewritten the history of the United States as 'the first new nation'.
2. Of the numerous summaries, we may cite the following, as an illustration: (1) a degree of self-sustaining growth in the economy—or at least growth sufficient to increase both production and consumption regularly; (2) a measure of public participation in the polity—or at least democratic representation in defining and choosing policy alternatives; (3) a diffusion of secular-rational norms in the culture—understood approximately in Weberian-Parsonian terms; (4) an increment of mobility in society—understood as a personal freedom of physical, social, and psychic movement; and (5) a corresponding transformation in the model personality that equips individuals to function effectively in a social order that operates according to the foregoing characteristics—the personality transformation involving as a minimum an increment of self-things seeking, termed 'striving' by Cantril (1966) and 'need-achievement' by McClelland (1961), and an increment of self-others seeking, termed 'other-direction' by Riesman (1950) and 'empathy' by Lerner (1958a), (Lerner, 1968).
3. During a seminar led by Daniel Lerner in the Department of Humanities and Social Sciences, I.I.T., Delhi on January 8, 1969, a participant posed his dilemma thus: Sir, I have found in my empirical researches a high score on all the structural indices of modernised, as implied in your model, yet I do not believe that these villages are really modernised. Professor Lerner apparently failed to grasp the basic problem posed, and processed to observe: "Oh I am delighted that Indian villages have changed so much!".
4. Another example of such an effort, though far less rigorous analytically, is Myrdal (1968). For elaboration of its analytical deficiencies, refer to the presentation on the theme by the present

writer to the Asian Seminar on Sociology of Development, December 1968, Delhi.

References

Ahmad, Aziz, *Islamic Modernism in India and Pakistan:* 1857-1964, 1968.

Anthropological Studies of Complex Societies in Current Anthropology, Vol. 2: 201-10, 1961.

Banton, Michael (ed.), *The Social Anthropology of Complex Societies*, 1966.

Beals, Alan R. and Siegel, B.I., *Divisiveness and Social Conflict*, 1967.

Berger, P.L. and Luckmann, T., *The Social Construction of Reality*, 1967.

Braibanti, R. (ed.), *Tradition, Values and Socio-Economic Development*, 1961.

Brode, John, *The Process of Modernization: An Annotated Bibliography of Socio-Economic Development*, 1967.

Broomfield, J.H., *Elite Conflict in a Plural Society: Twentieth Century Bengal*, 1968.

Cantril, H., *The Pattern of Human Concerns*, 1966.

Clark, Colin, *The Conditions of Economic Press*, 1940.

Coleman, J.S., *'Modernization: Political Aspects'* in *Int. Encly. of Social Sciences* Vol. 10, *Education and Political Development* (ed.), 1965.

Damle, V.P., *Socialization for an Unknown Future* (unpublished paper), 1966.

Despres, Leo A., *Anthropological Theory, Cultural Pluralism and the Study* of *Complex Societies in Current Anthropology*, Vol. 19, No. 1, 1968.

Deutsch, K.W., 'Social Mobilization and Political Development' *Am. Poli. Sc. Review.* 55, September, 1961.

_______, *Nationalism and Social Communication*: An Inquiry into the Foundations of Nationality, 1953, 1966.

Dube, S.C., *Modernization and its Adoptive Demands of Indian Society* in *Papers* in *Sociology of Education in India*, (ed.): Gore, Desai, 1967.

_______, *Human Problems of Economic Development* in *Economic Development and Culture Change*, 1965.

Eisentadt, S.N., *Modernization: Protest and Change*, 1966.

Feldman, Shel (ed.), *Cognitive Consistency*, 1966.

Fishbin, M., *A Consideration of Reliefs, Attitudes and their Relationship in Current Studies in Social Psychology*, (ed.): Stenier and Fishbin, 1965.

_______, *The Relationship between Reliefs, Attitudes and Behaviour* in Feldman, (ed): Cognitive Consistency, 1966.

Freeman, L.C. and Winch, R.F., Social Complexity: An Empirical Test of a Typology of Societies, in *Amr. J. of Socio*, 62: 461-66, 1957.

Guertz, C. (ed.), *Old Societies and New States*, 1963.

Gluckeman, May (ed.), *Closed Systems and Open Minds*, 1964.

Hagen, E.E., *On The Theory of Social Change*, 1962.

Halparn, Joel M. and Brode, J., *Peasant Society: Economic Changes and*

Revolutionary Transformation in Biennial Review of Anthropology, 1967.
Hoselitz, R.F., *Economic Development and Change in Social Values and Thought Patterns* in *Explorations in Social Change*, (ed.): Zolloschan and Hirescp, 1964.
_______, *Sociological Aspects of Economic Growth*, 1960.
Inkeles, A., *Industrial Man: The Relation of Status to Experience, Perception and Value*, 66, 1, *Am. J. of Socio.*
Kahn, Thomas, S., *The Structure of Scientific Revolutions*, 1962.
Kriesherg, Louis, *The Relationship between Socio-Economic Rank and Behaviour in Social Problems*, Vol. 10, No. 4, pp. 334-353, 1963.
Krocber, A.L. and Parsons T., *The Concepts of Culture and Social System in Am. Socio Rev., 23: 582-83*, 1958.
Lerner, Daniel, 'Modernization' in *International Encyclopedia of Social Sciences*, Vol. 10, 1968.
_______, *'Toward a Communication Theory of Modernization*, in *Communications and Political Development*, ed. Lucian W. Pye, 1963.
_______, *The Passing of Traditional Society*, 1958 and *Attitude Research in Modernising Areas*, POQ, 22, No. 3, 1958 (b).
Levy, Marion J., *Modernization and the Structure of Society*, 1966.
Lewis, Arthur, *The Theory of Economic Growth*, 1955.
Lipset, Sevmour M., *The First New Nation: The United States in Historical and Comparative Perspective*, 1963.
McClelland, David G., *The Achieving Society*, 1961.
McCuire, W.I., *The Current Status of Cognitive Consistency Theory in Feldman* (ed.): *Cognitive Consistency*, 1966.
McKenzie, H.I., *The Plural Society Debate; Some Comments on a Recent Contribution in Social and Economic Studies*, 15 (1): 53-60, 1966.
Milikan, Max F. (ed)., *The Emerging Nations: Their Growth and United States Policy*, 1961.
Misra, B.B., *The Indian Middle Classes: Their Growth in Modern Times.*
Moddie, A.D., *The Brahmanical Culture and Modernity.*
Murphy, Robert F., *Cultural Change in Biennial Review of Anthropology*, 1967.
Myrdal, Gunnar, *Asian Drama*: an Inquiry into the Poverty of Nations, 1968.
_______, *Rich Lands and Poor: The Road to World Prosperity* (First published as Development and Under-development, 1956.
Nadel, S.F., *The Theory of Social Structure*, 1957.
_______, *The Foundations of Social Anthropology*, 1951.
Parsons, Talcott, *Sociological Theory and Modern Society*, 1967.
_______, *Societies: Evolutionary and Comparative Perspectives*, 1966 (ed.), *Theories of Society*, 1965.
_______, *Social Structure and Personality*, 1964.
_______, *'Some Considerations on the Theory of Social Change'* in *Rural Sociology*, Vol. 26, No. 3, 1961.

Parsons, Talcott, *Structure and Process in Modern Societies*, 1960.
______, *Economy and Society*, 1957.
______, *The Social System*, 1951.
______, *The Structure of Social Action*, 1937.
Pepitone, A., *Some Conceptual and Empirical Problems of Consistency Models* in Feldman (ed.): *Cognitive Consistency*, 1966.
Pye, Lucian, *Aspects of Political Development: An Analytic Study*, 1966.
Radcliffe-Brown, *A Natural Science of Society*, 1957.
Riesman, D., *The Lonely Crowd: A Study of the Changing American Character*, 1950.
Schramm, W. (ed.), *Communication and Change in the Developing Countries*, 1966 .
______, *Mass Media and National Development: The Role of Information in the Developing Countries*, 1964.
Shannon L. W. (ed.), *Underdeveloped Areas: A Book Readings and Research*, 1957.
Shils, Edward, *The Intellectual Between Tradition and Modernity: The Indian Situation*, 1961.
Smelser, Niel I., 'Toward a Theory of Modernization' in *Social Change Sources, Patterns and Consequences*, (ed.): Etzioni, A., and Etzioni, Eva, 1964.
Smith, M.G.; *Pluralism in Africa*, 1968.
______, *The Plural, Society in the British West Indies*, 1965.
______, 'Social and Cultural Pluralism', in *Annals of N.Y. Academy of Science*, 83, 1960.
______, *A Framework for Caribbean Studies*, 1955.
Srinivas, M. N., *Social Change in Modern India*, 1966.
Steward, J.H., *Levels of Socio-Cultural Integration in South-Western Jr. of Anthro*. 7: 374-90, 1951.
______, *Theory of Culture Change*, 1955.
Voget, Fred W., 'Man and Culture', *Am. Anthropologist*—62: 943-65, 1960.
Weber, Max (Ir.), *The Sociology of Religion*, 1962.
______, *The Theory of Social and Economic Organization*, 1956.
______, *The Protestant Ethic and the Spirit of Capitalism*, 1930.
Zajono, R.B., *Balance, Congruity and Dissonance*, P.O.Q. 1960, Vol. 24, 2, 1960.

2

Tradition and Modernization

Concept and Process

S.K. SRIVASTAVA

Conceptual Frame

The present article is an attempt to focus on certain issues, problems regarding the concept and process of modernization in general. Modernization as a process began in Western countries of Europe in the later nineteenth century. It started with the advent of industrialisation and commercialisation bringing about the following fundamental changes in the Western societies:

(*a*) Ever-increasing new technology;
(*b*) Ever-increasing use of inanimate power and technology in competitive market situation;
(*c*) Ever-increasing rate of trade and voyage;
(*d*) A scientific world view against traditional world view; and
(*e*) Fall of traditional-feudal structure and rise of democratic and totalitarian systems.

The process of modernization brought in its fold many new ideas and concepts which were utilised for collective action for change. The concepts like equality, freedom, justice, democracy, *laissez-faire* economy, etc., determined the content of cultural ethos. The course of modernization proceeded with the decline of medieval conditions of life and thought. It helped the evolution of these forces and institutions which either overthrew the old structure or renovated it gradually.

All over the world, human societies are undergoing transformation in various degrees for the past five hundred years. The general process of Modernization is conceived of in developing phases from traditional (non-modernised) to modernising societies. The phenomenon of modernization has assumed significance only in the twentieth century world. The present century has witnessed the collapse of great political ideologies and rise of accommodated political systems. There has emerged an autonomous hope in mankind to increase the social product with fair shares for all. The degree, nature and rate of development through modernization process are the essence of the national form of polity and policy.

The attributes of modernization are conceived in different ways by different scholars and of contemporary society. We are presenting in Table 2.1 some of the attributes mentioned by certain known critics and scholars.

Table 2.1: Attributes by certain Critics and Scholars

Critics	*Discipline*	*Attributes of modernization*
Cyrial Black	Economics	Growth of knowledge/increasing capacity to understand the secrets of nature and to apply the new knowledge to human affairs
		Self reliance/achievement orientation
David McClelland and Alex Inkles	Psychology and Sociology	(*a*) Certain attribute-readiness to accept new ideas, interest in present and future, concern for planning and efficiency (*b*) Characteristics of modern man-internal (attitude and values); external (change in external condition)
		Development of skill and a spirit of creativity;
		Adaptation of institutions to the rapidly changing functions
Anderson & Shils	Sociology	Non-economic process/choice concerning normative, structural, behavioural aspects Intellectual commitment
C.E. Black	Pol. Science	Use of inanimate source of power and tools
Apter	History	
W.C. Smith	Sociology	
Levy		

The contents of the Table 2.1 reveal certain orientations basic about modernization from different vantage points and different discipline-approaches. But they have not made a clear distinction between modernization, modernity, traditionalisation and traditionality.

Primarily, modernity is a state of mind. It creates and grasps such elements in human consciousness which enable the individual to adjust from his inner being to the rapidly changing conditions of modern complex societies. It implies a scientific and rational world view and inculcates universalistic-secular values.

Modernization is not an ideology, but it can be the cornerstone of any political ideology or policy. It is ideology free in the sense that it indicates the *common need* of the modern times for an overall growth of individual and society. Because of the speed and acceleration of change, modernization as a mode of adjustment becomes a felt necessity of our time. It is a break-up from traditional mode of life which is no more adjustable to the changing conditions. It is an escape from ideological commitment. The goals of higher standard of life, freedom, security, social justice are some of the universally accepted goals of modernism. These goals and culture of a modernizing society need not be ideology-bound, but a political system, driving the task of modernization, has to inculcate them.

We can conceive modernization as a process operation at the following levels:

(*a*) *Value System:* At this level these social values and the entire complex of symbol system are included which define the goal, direction and means to modernization. The value system would define the degree and range of modernization a social system would like to accept. Accordingly, there can be 'little modernization' or 'multidimensional modernization'.

(*b*) *Social System*: At this level status role of the individual and collectivities are taken into consideration. Modernization creates differentiation in society in vertical form. Differentiation of social structure involves specification and separation of social activities. Difference-making process in modernization is problematic but also extremely important.

(*c*) *Personality System*: Modernization emphasizes the emergence of *social* personality distinct from competitive individuality.

On the basis of the above observation, we can distinguish modernization and modernity. Modernization is a form of development in which value system, social system, and personality system are interwoven in such a way that universalistic-secularistic positive values make differentiation in status-role system and create a social personality. Modernity from the point of view of individual is a state of personality trait-scientific world view. Modernity, from the point of view of a given society as a whole, is a judgment on its level of development in material and ideational aspects.

Modernization as value-concept is not synonymous with westernisation or industrialisation. Though both the processes have generated the process of modernization. An industrialised society, in spite of its advanced technological development, may not be modern in the true spirit of the term. Such societies reveal a gap between their technological advancement and actual style of modern life. Their system fails to give forth creative social personality to the individual.

Ideas of 'modernity' grow more slowly than the external conditions, that is why we find the great dilemma of our age in the so-called highly developed societies. Such societies are technologically, organisationally and economically very much advanced, but in their value system they lack the ideal content of modern, norms, and the mode of behaviour.

Concept of Tradition, Traditionality and Traditionalisation

"*Tradition* means habits, customs, attitudes, ways of life which get embodied in institutions and then tend to get frozen because of the stability, and autonomous existence of these institutions" (V.K.R.V. Rao). Traditionality implies rigidity. Jacob Katz says, "*Tradition* sets a pattern, a hierarchy of concepts, accepted norms, and moves, which guide the individual in thought and action and regards *traditionalism* as validation of current behaviour by reference to immemorial prescriptive norms." A traditional society denotes a type of society which regards its existence as based upon a common body of knowledge and values, handed down from the past.

There are variations in adaptive mechanism among traditional systems in response to the process of modernization. Not all traditional societies are resistant to modernization. There are societies which traditionalise innovation and thus adapt the process of modernization. Generally, they resist innovations in the fundamentals of their systems but would adapt instrumental acts which do not change their social institutions and values fundamentally. Traditionalisation is a two-way process—convex and concave. In the convex process, it stabilises the new elements and in the concave process, it upthrusts the past traditions to the present.

Both types of traditionalisation go together in any society and neither of them is hostile to modernization. It depends on the flexibility, adaptability and element of rationality which enable the tradition ready to contain modernization. The essential functional role of traditionalism is to provide significance (meaningfulness) to human existence in terms of established symbol system. One of the major drawbacks of modernism is that it cannot provide new symbolic system to make life meaningful in the face of worldly contingencies. Probably, a sort of existential despair is a prize of being modern. If in modern symbols life can be made more meaningful and significant than in traditional symbols, then human energies can be released for rapid growth. Increasing rate of personality disorganisation neurosis and anxieties are the indicators of the lack of meaningfulness of so-called advanced societies.

Traditional social structure generally lacks differentiation suitable to the process of modernization. Elite and achievement oriented non-elite are the agents of modernization. In the post- colonial period in the developing societies the traditional elite is relegated and the role of modernization has been taken up by the Government. Their process of development encount all the possible structural resistance. The forces of vested interests develop ideologies in terms of traditional symbols which delay progress.

Characteristics of Societies on Continuum

We are conceiving societies in a phase of development (distinct from evolution) from traditional to modernization on continuous. On the continuous several ideal types of societies are constructed on the level of analysis—social system, value system and personality system. An examination of these hypothetical constructs may reveal the distinctive characteristics of these models. Some of them are shown in Table 2.2.

The above typology also provides a criterion for judgement for the degree of development. In each construct there will be marked difference in its social structures, value systems and the system of personality. The purpose of the typology is to bring out the marked difference and conceive the process of change from tradition to modernization as a process of development influencing these three levels.

Some Important Indicators of Modernization

To measure development by only economic criteria, such as, GNF, National Income, per capita income, etc., would not satisfy the requirements of the multidimensional problem of modernization. Such criteria would have to be supplemented by the principle of equitable distribution and the avoidance of regional disparities which tend to become the sources of social and economic discontents and ultimately leading to upheavals, thereby holding up the process of development and modernization.

The achievement of this aim becomes possible only through efficient technology based on scientific principles. The organizing principles of the economic system, therefore, are to be the scientific control over the traditional economic resources of land, labour and capital. For the efficient management of these resources the growth of an entrepreneurial class is regarded as essential. In the context of developing nation the role of the state in promoting production and providing for equitable distribution is crucial. Some important indicators of modernization are mentioned below:

1. *Social:* The traditional attitude toward women and children will have to be replaced by an emerging rational consideration for assessing the contribution which men, women and children can make to development and modernization.

The traditional restrictions on occupational and social mobility will have to go and a high premium should be placed on individual achievement.[1]

Table 2.2: Characteristics of Relatively Unmodernised-Modernised Societies

Level of Analysis	*Societal Attributes*	*Types of Societies*		
		Traditional	*Developing*	*Modernised*
1. Social System	(*i*) Population	High birth rate High mortality	High birth rate Lowering mortality	Adapted birth rate (Income): Low mortality
	(*ii*) Economic	(*a*) Traditional self-sufficient	(*a*) Economic activities within traditional	(*a*) Planned, competitive, cooperative in large interest
		(*b*) Maintenance of *status quo* in social structure	(*b*) Particularistic economic goals for family, community, groups, etc.	(*b*) Economic society and higher individual consumption
		(*c*) Savings for conspicuous consumption	(*c*) Savings for limited groups life	(*c*) Savings for higher income and development
		(*d*) Agrarian Character	(*d*) Manufacturing	(*d*) Industry and human services
	(*iii*) Organisation for social action	Family, caste-group	Family, class caste and regional solidarity	Organised public services
	(*iv*) Compliance system and form of Government	(*a*) By tradition	(*a*) By tradition and charismatic leaders	(*a*) By national authority and expert management
		(*b*) Defence of feudal state	(*b*) Liberal democratic or authoritarian or military state	(*b*) Welfare and security
	(*v*) Tempo of change	Slow change	Slow development	Controlled rapid change
	(*vi*) Innovation	Adaptation to changes from outside	Conscious innovation by elite or authority	By scientists

(Contd.)

Table 2.2 (*Contd.*)

Level of Analysis	*Societal Attributes*	*Types of Societies*		
		Traditional	*Developing*	*Modernised*
2. Value religiosity	(*i*) Religious	Magic, myth, sects and great religious systems	Magic, myth, sects and great religious systems	Individualistic System
	(*ii*) Integration	By common fate and traditional bonds	Common authority and traditional bonds	Harmoneous opposition between interest individual groups
3. Personality System	(*i*) Dominant social value & style of life	Fecundity	Order and Hierarchy	Social personality (distinct from individual personality)
	(*ii*) Type of tension	Power struggle between local groups	Power struggle between local and functional groups	Conflicts and concensus and organised harmony

Source: These hypothetical constructs are conceived on certain vital elements of social organisation like population, economy, ideal and faith, system of authority, form of religion and adaptability to innovation. The trend is from unplanned to planned development; from local to wider human society; from magic to science and from no individuality to social personality. In between the polarities of tradition and mdernisation comes the category of developing society. We do not regard developing as transitional rather our emphasis is to conceive the growth from tradition to modernization (moving target) a process of continuous development.

2. *Educational*: Modernization of the educational system is needed for the emancipation of the individual and the efficiency of a modern economic system. In order to play a significant role of the contents, methods and institutions of education would have to be subordinated in the scientific principle of revisability and flexibility in the light of new experiences. All dogmatic adherence to tradition in these matters will have to be abandoned, and emphasis has to be shifted from cognitive to non-cognitive content, which is one of the major characteristics of modernization.

3. *Value*: Differentiation of roles is also considered to be an important feature of modernised society. Its consequent outcomes are proliferation of professions and the development of complex organisations.

4. *Political*

(*a*) Individual liberty and self-expression are the attributes of one type of modern political system—the type which at the present moment happens to be adopted by India.

(*b*) The primary criteria of modernization of the political system lie in the efficiency of its administrative and judicial sub-systems.

(*c*) The growth of legitimate bureaucratic methods is an effective indicator of administrative structure within which decisions are to be taken on impersonal rather than on personal basis.

(*d*) The growth of international understanding and dependence accompanied by a decentralisation of authority at home is an indicator of Modernization.

(*e*) Modernising the political systems, politicisation and modernization of traditional structures and organisation thereby making them more functional, may be a more correct approach than exterminating the traditional structures and organisations.

Of course, these are some of the commonly accepted indicators of modernization but it is difficult to lay down definite criteria of each of the indicators showing the level of modernization. For instance, when we take up standard of living as an indicator of modernization, then, in what degrees of high standard may be regarded as modern? The same problem is relevant to other indicators also. In this connection a comparative model may give a quantifiable criterion of modernization. We can take a highly modernised society at the present point of time and compare its standard of living with the society which is undergoing the process of modernization. Level of modernization will always be a "moving target", therefore, the actual criterion of modernization will vary from time to time. But a hierarchy or normative values, determining criterion of a better human existence, is an established fact. A level of development in accordance with the value expectations can be called 'modernised'.

Instruments and Agents of Modernization

The process of modernization needs the conscious participation of the agents of modernization. In developing countries the state is the most important agency of modernization. But sociologically speaking, a state represents elite and interest groups. The agents of modernization can be classified into two broad categories of elites and non-elites. Under the category of elites—who share the social responsibility of guiding society—we include the political, religious, organisational and managerial elites. The modernising societies are the creation of all these elites in harmony but often in conflict. The rate of modernization will be higher where the intensity of harmony is greater. Under the category of non-elites, we include the achievement oriented non-elites who are the careers of the process of modernization. They are conscious about the goals and direction of the society. Such non-elites are the builders of history and their role, as the agents of modernization, is not less significant than as the role of elites. The process of modernization, generated by the elites, fails or grows slow where the non-elites do not cooperate in carrying the modernising process.

The process of modernization is expedited through certain instruments. Instruments are the social techniques of manipulating positively the process of modernization. In Table 2.3 some of the basic instruments of modernization have been mentioned as they operate at the levels of social systems, value systems and the personality system.

In a given modernising society, all these instruments may not be effectively in operation. It depends on the nature of society and the agent of modernization who would employ the specific instruments to drive the society towards modernization. Some societies emphasize the economic instruments more than the others. In authoritarian system of modernization, instrument of economic development is heavily charged followed by a system of indoctrination. In liberal democracies, the emphasis is on economic growth without any attempt to enhance the value and personality system. These agents using the instruments drive the society toward modernization. The process is shown in Fig. 2.1.

Table 2.3: Instruments of Modernization

Levels	*Instruments*
1. Social System	(*i*) Form of Government and bureaucracy (*ii*) Fair distribution of income (*iii*) Foreign aid and co-operation, (*iv*) Concern of the UNO—through its world organisations for health, food, education and culture, etc.
2. Value System	(*i*) System of political ideology (*ii*) Education and communication (*iii*) Constitution and law (*iv*) Technology (as it effects human life)
3. Personality System	Minimum of violence and creative skills for adjustment

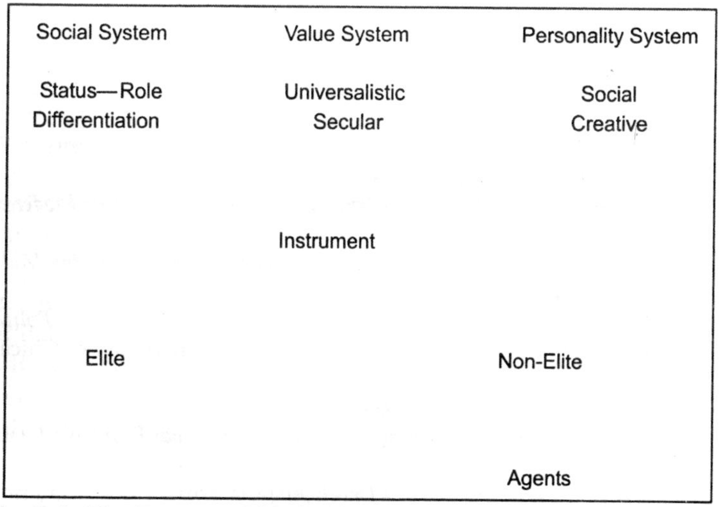

Fig. 2.1: The Process of Modernization

Integration

Rapid development is the essential attribute of modernization. It may disintegrate the age long traditional society and create problems of adjustment at the three levels of our scheme. It is difficult to conceive of moving equilibrium in the rapidly moving target of modernization. Some degree of disintegration is inevitable. Some have observed that the stability and harmony, characteristics of the past, can never be regained. A modernising society may become *temporary society* and the process of modernization may reduce the individual to a relatively isolated existence. The transfer of political power from traditional to modernising leaders may also lead to instability and violence. A modernised society is aptly termed as integrated society. Its task is to integrate within a single society of peoples of widely different race, religion, community and interest groups. The way in which a society reacts to the crisis of integration depends on the cultural tradition resources and the nature of leadership. Societies move towards integration gradually over many decades and even centuries.

References

Bernard Lewis, *The Emergence of Modern Turkey,* 1961.

C.E. Block, *The Dynamics of Modernization,* Harper.

Charles A. Micaus, Clement Hoore, and L. Carl Brown, Lunisia, *The Politics of Modernization,* 1964.

Clifford Geertz, (ed.), *Old Societies and New States: The Quest for Modernity in Asia and Africa,* 1963.

Daniel Lerner, *The Passing of Traditional Society: Modernizing the Middle East,* 1958.

Dankwart A. Rustow, *A World of Nations: The Dynamics of Modern Politics.*

David E. Apter, *The Politics of Modernization,* The University of Chicago Press, 1966.

Edward Shils, *Political Development in the New States.*

Everett E. Hagen, *On the Theory of Social Change: How Economic Growth Begins,* 1962.

Fred W. Riggs, *Administration in Developing Countries.*

Gabriel A. Almond and James S. Colomen (eds.), *The Politics of Developing Areas,* 1960.

Gabriel A. Almond and Sidney Verba, *The Civil Culture* (1963).

I.R. Sinai, *The Challenge of Modernization,* Chatto and Windus, London, 1964.

J.J. Spengler and R. Braibanti, (eds.), *Tradition, Values and Socio-Economic Development,* 1961.

John K. Fairbank, Edwin O. Reischauer, and Albert M. Craig (eds.), in the second Volume of their History of East Asian Civilization entitled *East Alia: The Modern Transformation,* 1965.

Jose Ortega Y. Gasset, *The Modern Theme* (Harper Torch Book).

M.S. Gore, I.P. Desai and Suma Chitnis (eds.), Papers in *The Sociology of Education in India,* National Council of Educational Research and Training, New Delhi, 1967.

Manning Nash, *The Golden Road to Modernity: Village Life in Contemporary Burma,* 1965.

Marion J. Levy, *Modernization and the Structure of Societies* (in two vols.) Princeton, New Jersey Princeton University Press, 1966.

Marius B. Janson, (ed.) *Changing Japanese Attitudes Toward Modernization,* 1965.

Myron Weiner, *Modernization: The Dynamics of Growth*—Study Circle Reprints Higginbothams (P) Limited, 1967.

Robert L. Tignor, *Modernization and British Colonial Rule in Egypt,* 1882–1914 (1966).

W.W. Rustow, *Stages of Economic Growth,* 1960.

William B. Hamilton, ed., *The Transfer of Institutions,* 1964.

3

Conceptual Framework for the Study of Tradition and Modernization

V.P. VERMA

The conceptual dichotomy of tradition and modernization reminds us of somewhat similar distinctions in the social sciences. Henry Maine referred to the dichotomy of societies dominated by status and societies where contract was the determining criterion. The German sociologist Ferdinand Tonnies familiarised the distinction between *Gameinschaft* and *Gesellschaft*. The former is characterised by primacy of intimate communion while in the latter rational and formal considerations are uppermost. The confrontation of modern explorers and investigators with the pre-literate tribal people and folk cultures in the different areas of the world have further strengthened the nation of a marked distinction between the patterns of action orientation in the industrialised nations of the world and other people who operate with underdeveloped technology and are not able to take advantage of the accumulation of knowledge. In the study of the emerging nations of Asia and Africa, several social scientists have put forward the trichotomy of traditional, transitional and modern societies.[1] The word transitional indicates that the goal-orientation of the various activities in the older civilizations of the world is towards the attainment of the technological efficiency and social, economic and political growth and levels of achievement-gratifications that characterise the scientifically developed countries. At a generalised level it is possible to state that this conceptual formulation indicates an awareness of the divergence in the levels of production and acquisition in the different sectors of national existence, among the different sectors of the peoples of the world. The intellectual activities in some of the universities as well as the research programmes sponsored by the UNESCO have served to focus attention on instigating and promoting innovations in the less developed countries so that they are also able to realise their creative potentialities in the not too distinct future.

The word tradition is an inclusive concept. It connotes the entitative character of certain dominant religious, theological, metaphysical and ethical values and beliefs. It also stands for the crystallisation of deference and reverence for certain symbols. Tradition also includes folk-ways, mores and semi-institutionalised patterns of action in a society. At a more extended level tradition may be identified with the totality of the historical heritage of a nation or a community. It is very true that the interpretation that will be put upon the soul of a culture, the mission of the people, the unique ways of identification of a group or the distinctive, particularistic elements of aggregate interpersonal existence, will differ because it is not possible to objectivise the meaning of the historical structure. But it is also possible that there may be some consensus on the generalized notions that a people have about their history and culture. It is also possible that there may be elements of exaggeration as well as understatements in the interpretations of the cognitive and evaluative components of the historical heritage but for purposes of clarification it may be stated that tradition is a generic term and is to a large extent identical with historical continuity in the fields of social, cultural and interpersonal existence. There have been philosophers and scholars who have emphasized the dynamic vitality that is imparted to a country or a people by its historical heritage. Hegel with his conception of the *Volksgeist,* Burke with his passion for history and prescription, Savingny with the preference for the historical roots of legal norms and other philosophical exponents of romanticism, conservatism and traditionalism have emphasized the value of tradition. These arguments may have appeal for the Eastern revivalists.

It will be improper to say that societies are either wholly traditional or wholly modern because in most of the so-called modern or industrially advanced countries there are deep roots of tradition. Some sociologists have gone to the extent of tracing the traditional roots even of modern economic systems.

The trichotomy of ancient, medieval and modern as applied in most of the schools of historical scholarship is basically an intellectual conception of the eighteenth century. With the advancement of science, this trichotomisation received credence and Spengler was one of the few scholars who had the boldness to challenge this trichotomy.

It cannot be denied, however, that since the Renaissance there has been a process of modernization in the Western world. It has had different phases. The growth of oceanic commerce, manufacturing, industrial and finance capitalism, steel, electric and atomic technology and power are some of its external characteristics. At the ideological level, modernization has been marked by the growth of the scientific scrutiny and rational probe in place of ecclesiastical theology and credal denominationalism. At the political level, modernization has symbolised the growth of the notion of individual rights, liberty, equality, participant citizenship, pluralistic associational structure and interest-groups, dynamics of political parties and social justice in place of patriarchal authority, power, regimentation and control. Furthermore, modernization has meant a future-oriented valuational adherence in place of a nostalgic longing for a primitive paradise *(Krita Yuga* and *Treta* and *Ramarajya)* or a golden past or an idealised state of nature.

In the Asian and African world, modernization has more or less become identical with the process of Westernisation. The historian Hans Kohn in several of his books has investigated the process of Westernisation in the Asian world. This process is now spreading in the emerging new nations of Africa, Asia, Japan, India, Turkey and China and have been the foremost in the adoption of Westernisation techniques and skills at different levels.

The entire Asian and African world today is in a great ferment and there is a quest for modernization but the growth of Chinese communism makes it essential to understand that modernization is now no longer identical with Westernisation as conceived by the older generation of historians and cultural sociologists. Communism in its basic roots is certainly a Western phenomenon. The ideological bases of communism were prepared by a German

Jew who was a product of Western educational system and who had his roots in the humanistic and liberal traditions of the French Enlightenment as modified by Hegelian dialectic. But Communism in action today stands for the repudiation of some of the dominant values or Westernisation. Communism with its totalitarianism, has scant respect for individual rights. It advocates centralised control. Its indoctrination and regimentation of the channels of communication make it essential to distinguish between the processes of modernization and Westernisation. It remains true, nevertheless that in the dimension of modernization the technological element is the determining indicator because the mobilisation of the non-human factors of power is common in both the political systems of democracy and totalitarianism. But there are marked differences of political and economic notions. Most of the political parties, leaders and intellectuals in the Asian world are agreed upon technological growth. But there are marked ideological differences among them. Some would accept the values of liberal democracy and socialism while others would adhere to the beliefs and techniques of totalitarianism. Another school which is more revivalist in its orientation would derive intellectual sustenance from past classics. This shows that it is possible to accept technological modernization without accepting the ideological bases, values and motivation which are associated with the West-European-American culture. This highlights the point that there is still meaning in the older dichotomy of a civilization based upon facts, techniques, skills and methods of controlling external nature as differentiated from the imbibing of cultural values, socialisation of emotions and articulation of interests. It is essential that in our studies of Asian societies in transition this distinction between modernization and Westernisation is emphasized.

Note

1. *Cf.* the Princeton University Volumes on Political Development.

4
Tradition, Modernity and Modernization in India

SACHCHIDANANDA

[I]

In recent times, tradition and modernity have loomed large in the conceptual baggage of sociologists. The process is an old one and earlier it was subsumed under the terms social change or development, whereby less developed societies tend to acquire characteristics associated with the more developed societies. Studies have revealed that an endless variety of meanings have been put on the term 'modernization'. Each meaning depends upon the professional training and discipline of the social scientist concerned. The different meanings lack logical consistency. Drawing upon the works of Lerner (1962, 1963), Almond and Coleman (1950), McClelland (1961), Ithiel de Soa Pool (1963), Wilbert Moore (1963), and Dube (1967: 46), they present a twelve point model of modernization. As the frames of reference of the source theorists do not belong to the same logical family, the model projected is not an integrated one. Horowitz (1966: 306) thinks that modernization lacks the merit of being a concept and every attempt to define modernization in terms of an operational set of variables results in the introduction of new ideas which have relatively little to do with the original concept.

Many modern writers have stressed the totality of the process of modernization in different spheres of life. The thoroughgoing changes involved in the transition to sustained economic growth tended to take a form specific and peculiar to them. They come to resemble one another not merely in their economic functioning but in their value systems, social stratification, family organisation, their religious beliefs and patterns of government. The conception of such a change is implicit in the dichotomous typological terms. It seems inevitably to invoke, such as *gemeinschaft* vs. *gesselschaft*, traditional *vs*. modern, folk *vs*. urban, universalistic specific *vs*. particularistic-diffuse, and so on. Sometimes, a characterisation of the traditional system is given as 'a series of agrarian villages in a setting of relatively unchanging technique limited economic opportunity and age-old conventional understanding, attachment to authority, respect for the pastness of things, dependence upon routine and an exaggerated respect for precedent' (Manning Nash, 1965: 3). The opposite of these conditions is held to be modern.

Implicit in such writings is the belief that tradition and modernity are bipolar opposites. Empirical evidence has shown that no society is completely modern or completely traditional. Social processes are not so simple as to be accommodated in this dichotomy. It is through tradition that the process of modernization is thrown into bold relief. Tradition and modernization represent a continuous process. Neither of them at the same time can be regarded as a static phenomena. Tradition cannot be completely identified with the past or modernity with the present. An element of modernity today can be enshrined as a tradition tomorrow. Thus, tradition and modernity are different moments of a continuous social process.

Toynbee tends to treat modernization as a unilinear evolutionary process whose development would bring all societies to a level of cultural homogeneity obliterating their original cultural identities (Toynbee, A.J., 1963: 543; Vol. VIII). In this school of thought modernization is identified with westernisation. Toynbee gives examples of the conflict between native traditions and modernity in China, Japan and India. Gandhi's insistence upon the spinning wheel was interpreted as an alternative to modernization. In all the three societies, it is shown how modernization and westernisation triumphed over tradition. Toynbee's analysis suffers from an erroneous identification between modernization and westernisation.

Parsons (1964) holds that modernization is reached by passing through certain structural evolutionary stages in the universal growth of societies through differentiation. He speaks of seven evolutionary universals which prepare the ground for modernization. Bureaucratic organisation, money and market complex, generalised universal norms and democratic associations provide the institutionalised basis of modernization. Although Parsons draws heavily upon the western experience of modernization, he does see the possibility of other modernising structural adaptations. The difference in modernization may thus be only in terms of scale rather than in quality and there may be no basic opposition between tradition and modernity.

The process of modernization is not necessarily empirical to tradition. Eisenstadt (1964) has shown that the structural changes which generate modernization begin first at the level of a few crucial sectors of society. The consequences of these changes may either accelerate modernization or lead to a regression to traditional forms. In certain circumstances, it may lead to a strengthening of traditional structures (Horowitz: 1966). At the level of values, it was held that modernization was opposed to the religious world view which was traditional. Bellah (1964) found that modernization did not bring in its wake a conflict between religious and scientific values. Both continued to co-exist in a changed form.

More recent analyses of social and economic change in the developing societies of Asia and Africa have pointed out the futility of the confrontation between the traditional and modern cultures. A great deal of economic development which goes in the name of modernization can be achieved within a context of general, social and cultural conservatism in which traditional values and social structures are adapted to more efficient economic practices. Studies in India, Indonesia, Japan and Ethiopia have revealed numerous cases and ways in which cultural traditions rather than posing recalcitrant obstacles to modernity have directly promoted various forms of modernization. Studies in Hongkong and Singapore suggest that economic modernization does not necessarily revolutionise the social system and a modern economic system may be compatible with a wider range of non-economic cultural patterns and social structure than has often been thought (Geertz, G., 1953: 144). It has also been shown that there can be different sorts of traditionalism and also different sorts of modernity. It all depends upon the differential interrelationship between economic and non-economic processes in a given social situation.

That traditional and modern forms are not always in conflict is evident from the fact that in Japan feudalism and industrial development combined to promote economic growth. Loyalty to such traditional institutions as the Emperor and the family, a collectivistic orientation and a high degree of vertical immobility have supported social and economic changes in the Japanese context while they were factors which produced resistance in the individualistic culture of the West. The loyalty of labour to a specific employer promoted economic growth in Japan while it was an impediment in the West. Traditional structures can supply skills and traditional values capable of being utilised in the pursuit of new goals and processes. Geertz (1963A) has shown how in an Indonesian town, the traditional mobility was the source of economic innovation and business expansion. Their wide social contacts and the force of authority, both of which were traditional in nature, helped them build up a strong business class.

[II]

In the light of the theoretical discussion made above regarding tradition and modernity, let us take a close look at the reality of the situation in India and explore the extent to which there is a confrontation between them and whether they are dichotomous and exclusive. Such an analysis reveals that the two concepts do not necessarily involve displacement, conflict and exclusiveness, nor does modernity necessarily weaken tradition. Both of these are sources of ideologies and movements in the polar opposites are converted into aspiration. The traditional forms may supply support for as well as against change.

In the context of developing societies, the concepts of economic modernization have sought to be generalised by social scientists at large. Some writers have viewed political modernization as the necessary framework within which nationhood can be achieved and operated. It has been realised that Weber's conception of traditional *versus* rational economic behaviour does not hold good in many concrete situations. The crucial question is that how pre-existing values and structures can provide a basis for identification with and commitment to larger social frameworks than those of segmental groups and primitive parochial loyalties. Traditional symbols and leadership forms can be vital parts of the value bases supporting modernising frameworks.

The word tradition is derived from *tradere* which means to transmit. Thus, tradition is transmitted value and behaviour patterns of a community. Traditions are quoted, recalled, esteemed, their age long succession becomes an assurance of value which has already accrued in the process of its instrumental functioning as a constituent of social cohesion or social solidarity. Traditions are not static. Old traditions die and new traditions are continually being built up. Leaving aside external influences, there are endogenous factors of change in tradition. In Indian social thought three principles of change are recognised. They are *ṣruti, smriti* and *anubhava.* The last one *anubhava* or personal experience is a revolutionary principle. In course of time the personal experience of money became the collective experience of the community and was then enshrined as a tradition. During the medieval period, a number of sacred cults or *panths* led by saints appeared on the scene and modified the existing tradition. Their teachings left a rich deposit on the sands of time and tradition.

Even such an isolated and antiquated culture as the Amhara culture in Ethiopia which Toynbee termed as a 'fossil in fastness' is not changeless. Levine (1968) has shown that change is constantly underway in Amhara. He has identified four sources of change, viz., the scope for authoritarian innovation, spontaneous rationalisation diffusion and the shifting status of cultural complexes. Empirical evidence has revealed that there is room for flexibility even in the most traditional of cultures and that modernization can be both congruent with tradition as well as discontinuous.

In the Indian context, it would be wrong to think that society has always existed in its present form. What we regard as traditional in Indian culture may itself be the result of a long period of development. India has been subject to a number of invasions from the West right from the Persian invasions in the sixth century B.C. to that of Ahmad Shah Abdali in 1761. It has gone through long periods of foreign rule each varying in its complexion and cultural legacies. A number of socio-religious movements have affected the life of people and changed their value systems. All these influences have left their mark on the family life, religious beliefs and practices and social structure in India over many centuries. Added to all this was the impact of Islamic and British cultures. The institution of caste which is basic to the Hindu social system, has been deeply affected. There has been constant change in its structure and norms through the ages.

Similarly, Indian villages have been regarded as a sink of ignorance and stagnation. It may, however, be noted that Indian villages were flourishing little republics with an efficient *panchayat* system and a more or less self-sufficient economy. Various kinds of village industries relieved the pressure on land. It is only towards the end of the first-half of the nineteenth century that Indian villages began to present a dismal look. The land tenure system which was held to be the cause of the lack of economic development was not very old. In eastern India it was established through the Permanent Settlement of Lord Cornwallis in 1791. Thus, it is clear that even before the encounter with the West, tradition was undergoing change.

The functional approach to the study of society has given birth to the view that all traditional cultures are sustained by a consistent corpus of norms and values. In India, recent studies have revealed a great deal of diversity in this field. Rules and values presented by tradition sanction a number of alternatives from which one may be chosen by the person concerned. Redfield has pointed out the existence of two parallel traditions current in India, the great tradition and little tradition. He conceives of these two traditions, characteristic of a primary civilization as currents of thought and action represented by the literate, the reflective elite, the school and the temple on the one hand by the unschooled, unsophisticated and diverse, local, regional and caste groups on the other. The process of interaction between the two traditions is continuous. Elements of little tradition are constantly taken into and absorbed by the great tradition. Elements of the great tradition are accepted by the carriers of little traditions being altered to fit particular contexts. We may think of a more detailed categorisation of tradition besides the great and little traditions such as regional traditions, caste traditions, local traditions and the emergent national traditions. It cannot, therefore, be maintained that all traditions embody a consistent body of rules and values.

Even within the literate forms of tradition with an all-India spread, traces of inconsistency are apparent. Diverse orientations to the image of a good life can find legitimisation in philosophical and religious books. The *Varnashrama* system conceives of good life as one in which men pursue different periods of life. A number of alternative forms of behaviour are in this way sanctioned by tradition. In popular religion and in scriptures we can find a moral basis for the accumulation of wealth, pursuit of happiness and mundane pleasures.

Homogeneity of social structure is held to be a distinctive feature of traditional societies. Indian society is a conglomeration of different ethnic, religious and caste groups. Different styles of life within and without the caste system are recognised as valid. It is generally held that Hindu traditions inhibit economic growth. The doctrine of *Karma* is said to be a drag on individual initiative and spirit of economic enterprise. Caste system is said to arrest mobility. It is, however, forgotten that within the framework of the caste system certain castes have performed occupations tabooed to other castes, but necessary for the running of the overall economic system. The Marwari, the Chettiar and the Bania have developed long standing traditions of business which though low in public esteem are perfectly legitimate for them. Outside the fold of Hinduism, the Parsees and Jains are the carriers of economic innovation and promoters of large scale industrial production. The old is not necessarily replaced by the new. The cultural roots of the past gave the rising middle classes an assurance of their own worth something which would reduce their frustration and humiliation. The acceptance of an innovation, a new religion or a new mode of decision making does not mean a replacement of older forms. The new forms merely increase the number of alternatives. The conversion of people to Christianity in Kerala did not mean the disappearance of caste. In Bengal Brahman converts to Christianity take care to marry their daughters outside their clan. Thus, Christianity and caste have existed without any opposition. Even Islam which believes in the basic equality of all its adherents tolerates the existence of endogamous caste groups in its fold in India.

Similarly, magic and medicine have co-existed. Even in highly modernised families when medicine fails, recourse is taken to magic and religion. They are used alternatively by some people to meet different situations at different times. The great tradition of the urban world has not displaced the little tradition of the village. Interaction between the two has led to a fusion and interpenetration. The modernising processes and the traditional forms do not necessarily clash. At the bottom Mahatma Gandhi accepted most of the modernization ideals, though he succeeded in associating them emotionally with traditional views.

The different components or dimensions of an institution do not respond in the same way to new influences. Indian institutions as caste and family were regarded as barriers to economic growth. Such a view falls down on deeper analysis. The inter-institutional relations are extremely complex and vary from one context to another. It seems that the baneful effects of caste on economic development have been exaggerated. The position of any caste has never been absolutely fixed. Within the compass of a *varna* caste groups have been known to slide up and down. Through persistent effort of its members some caste groups have improved their social position. The development of caste associations and emergence of caste as a political factor sometimes promote economic growth rather than retard it. In the same way, it has been shown that joint families are compatible with large industrial organisations. Milton Singer's work in Madras conclusively shows that "the traditional joint family system and many practices associated with it offer some distinct advantages for organizing an industrial enterprise." (1968:445). It provides nucleus of capital which can be used for technical and specialized education of its members, for starting new ventures and for operating and expanding the existing industrial units. It provides a well structured pattern of authority succession and inheritance based on family relationships. This structure fulfils many of the demands of industrial organisations for direction, management, diversification and continuity. The varied talents of the members of the family can be utilized for a number of industrial operations, viz., fiscal, administrative, engineering, etc. The big Indian industrial houses, the Tatas, Birlas, Dalmias, etc., are supported by traditional family units.

The growth of education, the development of a new administrative machine and modern industry during the British rule led to the emergence of an urban middle class consisting of professional classes, entrepreneurs, members of the bureaucracy, technologists, etc. They were relatively unknown in the traditional social structure. But they were easily fixed up in the social hierarchy as the emergent middle classes were all drawn upon higher castes and, by and large, class was subsumed by caste. As Singh has noted, "In role structures, it attributed to modernization, but in terms of stratification it further strengthened the power of the established traditional groups" (Singh Y; 1668: 12). Thus in one way modernised strengthened tradition.

As part of the modernization process politicisation of the people is proceeding at a fast pace. In this political process ample use is being made of such traditional institutions as village, caste and religion. It is through these that the individual and the family are drawn into the vortex of modern political organisation. Propaganda for political parties or candidates at the *Panchayat*, State or national level elections is carried on the basis of kinship and caste. Studies by Srinivas and others have brought into focus the prominent role of caste in the Indian elections. Morris Jones (1963) speaks of two contrasting political idioms or styles in contemporary India—the modern idiom of national politics with its plans and policies and the traditional idiom of social status, customary respect and communal ties. Indian political life becomes explicit and self conscious not only through western modern idiom. Thus, the two styles coexist without any contradiction.

In India, there is a growing demand for the spread of education. Education confers on the lower caste groups a respectability which is otherwise difficult to achieve. Higher education of a bridegroom enables his family to demand a higher dowry. Thus, education does not only provide new job opportunities for people but also gives them substantial status rise. Education which is a modernising agent satisfies the quest for status in traditional terms.

Similarly, modern law and courts sometimes serve to buttress traditional values. At the touch of the official law, a caste's prerogatives become the constitutionally protected rights of a religious denomination, a lower caste's ambitions become its constitutional right to equality. Property can be made to devolve on traditional lines and land reforms can be frustrated by transactions in good legal form. Traditional interests and expectations are thus translated into suitable legal garb, into nationally intelligible terms (Galantar, Marc: 1968: 34). If we regard tradition not as a stationary point, a way of remaining unchanged but as a method of introducing and legitimising change, we can say that the modern legal system has displaced the traditional methods within the legal system itself while it has supplemented them outside it.

It is a common experience that in villages courts were and are used as an arena in the competition for social status, political and economic dominance. Cases are instituted to harass one's opponents and rivals, as a punishment, as a form of land speculation and profit making and to satisfy insulted pride and to maintain local political dominance over one's followers (Cohn, B., 1965: 105). Feasts are held and drums beaten when a man wins a case against his rival.

In modern India, two social processes are working for mobility. The higher educated social strata of the Indian society are westernising their lifestyles, slowly giving up traditional ways of thought, speech and action. The lower castes on the other hand seek mobility through Sanskritisation. After getting some education and a petty job, a lower caste man does not allow his woman folk to do menial work, asks them to observe *purdah*, begins keeping ritual fasts and in general tries to adopt norms of Sanskritic Hinduism. Thus, some sectors of the population are moving towards modernity and some towards tradition.

After the achievement of independence, India was committed to democracy and socialism. Even these ideals of modernization were harnessed to a more traditional orientation. Means of communication expanded at a fast rate. Steps were taken for the eradication of illiteracy and there was a great deal of expansion of education. New job opportunities led to a growth in horizontal mobility. All this intensified the spread and influence of the great tradition over wide areas and across various levels. Through social education, dramas and other shows, rituals, worship and practices common to the great tradition were disseminated far and wide. As caste assumed importance as political pressure groups, a number of caste organisations have been formed. The spread of literacy has led to the publication of caste journals. Thus in village India, the winds of change are more often the carriers of tradition.

Tradition is not something far removed from oneself. It is created and shaped to present needs and aspirations in a given historical situation. People refer to aspects of the past as tradition in an effort to find legitimation for their present action. Thus, tradition is metamorphosed into an ideology. Similarly, to be modern appears in many developing nations as a goal, an aspiration towards which society is expected to approximate. Thus, the desire to be modern and the desire to preserve tradition are evident in many developing nations. These desires function as ideologies. They are not always in conflict. They do not stand face to face but shoulder to shoulder. The quest for modernity depends upon and finds support in the ideological tide of traditionalism. In this process, tradition itself may be changed, modified or stretched. That traditions change is engrained in Hindu social thought.

During the struggle for independence, the past was glorified. Indian culture and ancient traditions, norms and values were extolled to the sky. They provided the ideals or goals in the search for national identity—Indian civilization had to be saved from being swept off its feet by the high tide of western influences. The scriptures and holy texts of Hinduism were given a new interpretation to suit the challenges of the time. It was emphasized that the *Gita* lays emphasis on equal dignity and sacredness of all labour that falls to one's lot. It lays down in a unique manner the socialist doctrine in terms of religion. Swami Vivekanand's practical Vedanta, Tilak's interpretation of the *Gita* and Gandhiji's concept of *Rama Rajya, Varnashrama,* etc., were India's answers to the modernising challenges of the West. There was in fact a rediscovery of Indian traditions, so that they could provide support to our intellectuals in putting up a face against the West with honour. Tradition played a significant role in the nationalistic movements not only in India but also among other new nations of Asia and Africa. There was a reaction against the Dutch among the Indonesians, among the Japanese against the Europeans and among the Indians against the British. Despite a general commitment to modernization, Indian leaders fostered Indian national identity by adoption of customs and styles which were largely traditional.

Shils has referred to the existence of a high degree of tradition orientation in the life of the Indian intellectual. "Almost always the Indian intellectual speaks a regional language as his mother tongue, is steeped in classic Sanskrit literature and is deeply tied to an extended family. Parental arrangement is still the dominant mode of marital selection and he is often married to a highly traditional wife." (1961: 60-67) Narayan gives another illustration. "An Indian scientist acts rationally in a laboratory while practising meaningless rituals at home, combining in his own person varying degrees of ridiculousness, traits derived from western and his own culture without any sense of discomfort due to the contradictions." (Narayan, D., 1967: 130). Milton Singer on the basis of his study of Hindu industrialists in Madras believes that the separation of work and residence which follows industrialisation also symbolizes separate spheres of conduct and norms. The home becomes the sphere of religion and traditional values, the office and factory becomes the sphere of business and modern values. Old norms connected with family, caste and religion are thus kept intact. In the other sphere intercaste contact is frequent, food and drink which is tabooed at home may be taken. On going home, the industrialist changes into traditional dress and begins to play roles prescribed by tradition. This adaptive process has been made possible by the twin methods of compartmentalisation and vicarious ritualisation (1968:428-39).

Indian nationalism is deeply committed to both tradition and modernity. Even Pandit Nehru who more than any other leader of the post-Independence era was wedded to modernization and westernisation characterised India as 'both old and new. It has its roots deep in the past but it has also the dynamic urges of today.' (Nehru, J.L.: 1949). Tradition is a complement to the modernising process involved in the aspiration toward a unified nation. The awareness of history and the search for national identity do not in themselves endanger or even compromise allegiance to modernization ideals. The blend of tradition and modernity is seen in Gandhiji's work. He tried to graft new patterns of thought and action into the various stems of traditional culture. He attempted a merger of the three levels of the Indian social system, viz., social stratification, culture and policy into a pattern so that the breakdown of the Indian tradition could be averted. He aimed at reducing the gulf between social classes and power and also between power and the cultural system. This was done through a scheme of political and economic decentralisation and by laying stress on egalitarian norms which had their basis in tradition. He utilised the traditional authority and influence of the holy man for social action aimed at the reconstruction of Indian life. He aired most modern and revolutionary ideas in a language couched in ethical terms. When he organised non-violent civil disobedience against the British, it was from the *Bhakti* ethic that flowed the higher courage of the *Satyagrahi*. To him, politics was applied religion. The elevation of traditional values brought a new mass of national self-respect.

Among the Neo-Gandhians, there is a search for such political institutions as will cope with our problems within indigenous cultural forms. When *Panchayati Raj* was introduced, it was said that it was just a revival of the old system of *Panchayats* in the villages which had disappeared during the last hundred years of British rule. An effort was made to create a consensus for which a legitimising support was found in ancient tradition.

The process of political modernization contains the seeds of the new ideologies of tradition. Growth of literacy has promoted a common cultural identity but it has also encouraged regional languages and cultures. It has strengthened regionalism and parochialism and imperilled national unity. Thus, a move in the direction of modernization may foster a traditional element. It is thus difficult to disentangle tradition from modernity in the Indian situation. The common practice of viewing tradition and modernity as opposites tends to overlook the mixtures and blends which we find in the field situation. Thus, while tradition and modernity may be heuristically useful concepts, they are incapable of exclusive distinction in the field. They are related not dichotomously but dialectically. They are the two ends of a continuum rather than polarised. They show two sides of a coin. The Rudolphs have sketched the traditionalism of modernity in the Indian polity (1967). They have shown that modern societies possess characteristics often attributed to traditional ones, not as remnants in a process of decomposition but as strands integral to the social fabric.

India faces both directions. It stands half way between the past and the future. Dr Zakir Hussain echoed this sentiment sometime back as follows: "To survive we need a revolution in our thought and outlook. From the altar of the past we should take the living fire and not the dead ashes. Let us remember the past, be alive in the present and create the future with courage in our hearts and faith in ourselves." Indian genius can operate at the same time in the traditional world and in the modern world characterised by universalism, rationality and secularism. In the socio-economic institutions of present-day India, many of the traditional values, beliefs and skills are united with features of modernised economic systems. Thus in India, there is no confrontation between tradition and modernity. They are not only co-existing as parallel strands of thought but also continually interacting with each other. On closer analysis we find that traditional structures always adapt themselves to new situations. In this process new identities are created which cannot be regarded as merely revivalistic. On the Indian scene the systemic change in the caste system and the puritanical reinterpretation of Hinduism with its anti-ritual and anti-clerical slant are instances of such transformation. Cultures like individuals are, more often than not, ambivalent. All systems have their own internal contradictions which are not dysfunctional. It is through these that the thrust forward comes.

References

Almond and Coleman, *The Politics of Developing Areas,* Princeton, 1960.

Bellah, R.N., 'The Religious Revolution', *American Sociological Review,* Vol. 29, No. 3, 1964.

Cohn, B., 'Anthropological Notes on Disputes and Law in India', *American Anthropologist,* 1965, Vol. 67, No. 6, Part II.

Dube, S.C., 'Modernization and its Adaptive Demands on Indian Society, Papers in *Sociology of Education in India* (ed) M.S. Gore, I.P. Desai and Suma Chitnis, NCERT., New Delhi, 1967.

Eisenatadt, S.N., 'Social Change, Differentiation and Evolution,' *American Sociological Review,* Vol. 29, No. 3, 1964.

Galantar, Marc, 'Displacement of Traditional Law in Modern India Tradition and Modernity,' Conflict and Congruence, *The Journal of Social Issues,* October, 1968, Vol. 24, No. 4.

Geertz. C., 'Social Change and Economic Modernization in two Indonesian Towns', (ed) Hagen: On the Theory of Social Change, Homewood, III. Dorsey Press, 1963, *Peddlars and Princes.* University of Chicago Press, Chicago, 1963 .

Gusfield, Political Community and Group Interest in Modern India, *Pacific Affairs,* XXXVI, Summer, 1965.

______, Tradition and Modernity: Misplaced Polarities in the Study of Social Change, *American Journal of Sociology;* Jan., 1967.

Horowitz, I.L., *Three Worlds of Development,* Oxford University Press, New York, 1966.

Hoselitz and Moore, *'Industrialization and Society,* UNESCO, 1963.

Lerner, D., *The Passing of Traditional Society,* The Free Press, New York, 1958.

Levine, D.N., 'The Flexibility of Traditional Culture', *Journal of Social Issues,* October, 1968.
Marriott, M., 'Little Communities in an Indigenous Civilization' (ed) M. Marriott Village India, Chicago University Press, Chicago, 1955.
______, *'Changing Levels of Cultural Transmission in India'*, (ed) L.P. Vidyarthi—Aspects of Religion in Indian Society, Kedarnath Ramnath, Meerut, 1961.
McClelland, D.C., *The Achieving Society,* Princeton, 1961.
Misra, V., *Hinduism and Economic Growth,* Oxford University Press, London, 1952.
Moddie, A.D., *Brahmanical Culture and Modernity,* Asia Publishing House, Bombay, 1968.
Mooris-Jones, W.H., 'India's Political Idiom', C.H. Phillips (ed) *Politics and Society in India,* Alien and Unwin, London, 1963.
Moore, Wilbert, *Social Change,* Princeton, 1963.
Narayan, D., 'Indian National Character in the 20th Century', *The Annals of American Academy of Political and Social Science,* March 1967.
Nash, M., *The Golden Road to Modernity,* John Wiley & Sons, New York, 1965.
Nehru, Jawaharlal, *'Speech at the United Nations'*, Oct. 1949.
Parsonk, T., 'Evolutionary Universals in Society', *American Sociological Review,* Vol. 29, No. 3, June 1964.
Pool, Ithiel De Soa, *The Role of Communication in the Process of Modernization and Technological Change,* Industrialization and Society (ed) by Hoselitz and Moore, UNESCO, 1963.
Rudolph, Lloyd I. and Susanne Hoeber, *The Modernity of Tradition Political Development in India,* University of Chicago Press, Chicago, 1967.
Shils, E., *The Intellectual between Tradition and Modernity,* Mouton & Co., The Hague, 1961.
Singer, M., 'India's Cultural Values and Economic Development' in *Economic Development and Cultural Change,* Oct. 1958, *The Indian Joint Family in Modern Industry, Structure and Change in Indian Society.* (ed) Milton Singer and B. Cohn. Aldine Publishing House, Chicago, 1968.
Singh, Y., 'Historicity of Modernization', Proceedings of Seminar on Tradition and Modernity in India, New Delhi, 1969.
Srinivas, M.N., *Caste in Modern India,* Asia Publishing House, Bombay, 1962.
Toynbee, A.J., *A Study of History,* Vol. VIII, Oxford University Press, London, 1963.

5

Historicity of Modernization

YOGENDRA SINGH

The response of intellectuals to the ideas of modernization is widely heterogeneous. It is often ambivalent, and even between those who are committed proponents of evolutionary universalistic viewpoint of modernization, there are moments of credibility gap, so far as the prospects of poorer nations and communities is concerned. In this light, historicity of modernization assumes added significance, and should draw the attention of social scientists.

The term historicity should be distinguished from historicism which has a definite philosophical or even a methodological connotation. Historicism is treated as an approach to the social sciences which assumes that historical prediction is their principle aim, and which assumes that this aim is attainable by discovering the 'rythms' or the 'patterns', the 'laws' or 'trends' that underlie the evolution of history (Karl Poper: 1961: 3). Historicism also implies a viewpoint on social growth which is deterministic and prophetic and, therefore, open to doubt as a science (Karl Poper: 1962: 1-10). Historicity, on the other hand, is a *process* and not a philosophical or methodological standpoint. Historicity of modernization refers to the typical existential and structural factors which underlie the process of modernization in the various contemporary societies. Here we ask such questions as: (1) How far is modernization as a process evolutionary universal in nature? Are the forms of modernization likely to develop particularistic patterns in specific historical existential background of different societies?; (2) What is the role of 'initial stages' (M.J. Levy, 1955: 498), or of the established traditions in growth possibilities and acceleration of modernization? What are the similarities and dissimilarities in the historical experience of modernization in the socio-culturally homogeneous and heterogeneous societies?; and (3) What pattern or direction of a generalising nature could possibly be anticipated in the modernization of the new nations, particularly India?

Modernization as a Concept

A fuller treatment of modernization as a concept is necessary for an analysis of the above problems. Modernization has found varied conceptual formulations depending upon the professional training and inclination of individual social scientist. Also there is an obvious lack of logical consistency or even uniformity of connotations in this concept. No wonder that Horowitz thinks that modernization lags the merits of being a concept, and "every attempt to define modernization in terms of an operational set of variables results in the introduction of new ideas which have relatively little to do with the original concept" (Horowitz: 1966: 306, also Andrain: 1965).

Modernization consists of a composite set of processes each intwined with a variety of contextual meanings in which elements of history, cultural structure and existential factors each assume boundary maintaining functions. If, however, we wish to classify some important formulations of the concept we could group them into four types—(1) *The Psychological* (Danial Lerner: 1958, E.C. Banfield: 1958 and David McClelland: 1961, etc.), (2) *The Normative* (G.A. Almond and S. Verba: 1965, Lucian Pye and S. Verba: 1965, E. Shils: 1961, R.N. Bellah: 1964, G.Geertz: 1963, etc.), (3) *The Structural* (T. Parsons: 1964, K.W. Deutsch: 1961, D. Apter: 1965, R. Bendix: 1964, S.N. Eisenstadt: 1966, F.W. Riggs: 1964, M. Weiner: 1962 etc.) and (4) *The Technological* (M.J. Levy: 1966, E.E. Hagen: 1962, W.W. Rostow: 1960, etc.). The psychological formulations of modernization link this process with a set of motivational attributes or orientations of individuals which are said to be mobile, activistic and innovational in nature. Daniel Lerner calls it 'psychic mobility', an adaptive characteristic in man to respond to his environment with a sense of empathy, rationality and unconstricted participant style. The same phenomenon others characterise as achievement orientation (McClelland, 1961) or commitment to a consensual ethos (Banfield, 1958). Modernization as a normative construct differs from psychological, specially in the extent to which primacy here lies on a set of norms or values which form a pattern and enjoy relative autonomy over individual motivations or consciousness. Whereas psychic constructs are relatively free from the historicity of cultural traditions, the normative ones are inalienably a part of it, especially of the culture of modernization in the West. The representative normative formulations of modernization consist of such values as rationalism, universalism, individualism, humanism, pragmatism and a commitment to a liberal tradition, civic culture and secular values.

Despite the fact that a prominent section of social scientists formulates the concept of modernization either in psychological or normative terms the prominence is, however, held by its structural formulation. This formulation of modernization is in fact not entirely exclusive and includes elements both of normative and psychological dimensions. Nevertheless, the emphasis is mainly on structural ingredients such as bureaucracy, money and market complex, attachment to universalistic norms in social roles and democratic associations. These according to Talcott Parsons are the structural prerequisites of a modern society. Deutsch uses an inclusive phrase 'social mobilisation' to connote some important structural adaptations in society which form parts of the process of modernization (Deutsch: 1961). A rational administration, democratic power system, more integrative and consensual bases of economic and cultural organisations are some of the attributes of Modernization in its treatment by Apter, Riggs, Eisenstadt, Weiner and Bendix. Then there is a purely technological concept of modernization where it is described in terms of economic resources, or use of inanimate power. In such formulations modernization is associated with material inputs, and developmental infrastructures, which bring about qualitative and progressive mobilisation in the total resources of society. The structural, normative and psychic processes are either supposed to go along with them or follow them. None of the above formulations are, however, exclusive. The formulation of modernity is often also biased by attempts to see it as opposed to tradition. There is an implicit attraction in defining modernization through such a dichotomy. It follows from a simplistic view of social processes and completely neglects 'historicity' in modernization. Once science was similarly counterposed with religion, which has failed to draw conviction, and is far from the reality. Tradition is the very substance through which processes of modernization articulate themselves.

There are reliable data to support that processes of modernization may not always endanger the existence of 'tradition'. The structural changes relevant to modernization begin first at the level of a few crucial sectors of society and once these start, the consequences may either be high acceleration of modernization or regression to traditional forms (Eisenstadt: 1964). It may even mean a further reinforcement of traditional structures (Horowitz: 1966). The divergent patterns depend upon the historicity of circumstances.

The same is true at the level of values. Modernization is assumed to be in contradiction with religious world view. What in fact emerges following modernization is not increased conflict between religious and scientific values, but a coexistential continuity of both through a process of their respective self-transformation (R.N. Bellah: 1964).

Most of the above four formulations imply a contradiction between tradition and modernity. This aspect of these formulations needs a review. Is it possible to define modernization in a manner which may not be committed to this bipolar viewpoint? To our mind such an alternative is there if we could formulate modernization at two levels—first, as a system of new role structures, meaning thereby network of roles and contingent modern skills, and second, as a dual system of values—first, which is basic to a scientific world view, and lies in a scientific evaluational approach to normative problems of human life, is open ended, continuously revisable and relativistic; the second, the system of values which refers to the categorical values which are free from the instrumental definition of science, as they are rooted in the wider existential reality of man (Bellah: 1964).

The distinctive systems of role structures and values of modernity as defined by a scientific world view do not, however, rule out the meaningful role of 'tradition', which essentially is to serve as a reservoir for drawing categorical or moral values. The philosophy of science which articulates the scientific world view can possibly only serve as a basis for instrumental set of values; it fails to offer either confirmation (support) or disconfirmation (sanction) to categorical or moral values. If, however, an attempt is made to derive categorical values from the structure of science or a scientific world view these of necessity would be arbitrary and *ad hoc* in nature (C. G. Hempel: 1965) devoid of any scientific validity. Alongside scientific values, therefore, there would always be a parallel need for a source from where man could derive categorical values expressing the highest levels of his symbolisations. This source might develop as a *modern* religion (Bellah: 1964: 371-374) through a self-transcendence of the established tradition itself, which of necessity shall form a part of any cultural process of modernization.

Thus, a realistic formulation of modernization should describe this process in terms of (*a*) role structures emerging from the continual impingement of science and technology and continual differentiation of social structure on the social system; (*b*) a system of values representing a scientific worldview; and (*c*) a parallel system of values categorical in nature and representing both a self-transcendence of pre-existing traditions as well as the traditions of modern science. Such a formulation may be free from the fallacies of unilinear universalism, of insular dichotomies and of cultural ethnocentrism that most formulations of modernization imply.

Universalism *versus* Historicity in Modernization

An important question about modernization is that of the direction towards which this process takes societies. In this connection there are various formulations. One important view is to treat modernization as a unilinear evolutionary process whose growth would bring all societies to a level of cultural homogeneity washing away their original cultural identities (A.J. Toynbee, 1963: 543: Vol. VIII). Following this logic, some writers also treat modernization as equivalent to Westernisation. Modernization is thought of as a process of confrontation between the Western and the non-Western societies now with the help of technological and scientific symbolism rather than of Christianity as in the past.

In such formulations a universal stage of conflict between the native traditions and modernity is also postulated. Toynbee mentions in this connection traditional China's resistance to the

West, Xenophobia during the Tokugava regime in Japan and the recent effort of Gandhi in India to offer alternative solution for modernization. In all these societies, however, these efforts, according to him, finally failed under the impact of Westernisation.

The quintessence of Toynbee's treatment of modernization is based on the assumption that Westernisation is equivalent to modernization. Obviously, his concept suffers from the fallacy of historicism. The formulation of modernization is entirely based on its first two attributes that we have called the role structures and the instrumental value system of science. It neglects the role of categorical values in modernization.

An evolutionary universalism in the process of modernization cannot be demonstrated merely by the historicity of a few events. Such treatment is devoid of theoretical validity. A more balanced and scientific approach to this problem, however, we find in the recent writings of Talcott Parsons. His approach is free from the centre-periphery question of modernization and is theoretical in nature.

Modernization, according to Parsons, follows certain structural evolutionary stages in the universal growth of societies through differentiation. Societies grow through a series of stages; they begin with functionally indispensable universals of religion, communication, kinship, social organisation and basic technology. Gradually, the kinship-based homogeneous society is internally stratified through territorial spread, population pressure and social segmentations. Initially, stratification begins with bifurcate class system, with upper-class endogamy, but with the differentiation of rural-urban communities four-class system comes into being with the bifurcation of the upper and lower classes into two urban-rural categories each. Thus, stratification emerges as the sixth evolutionary universal. It has evolutionary advantages for societies since it later creates an autonomous status structure independent of ascriptive base which is essential for the beginning of differentiation and necessary for modernization. Stratification by itself, however, far from inducing may retard modernization if it is not differentiated. Along with stratification follows 'cultural legitimation' the seventh evolutionary universal which reinforces stratification and offers yet another autonomous sphere for innovations.

The above universals only set the stage for modernization which follows through a sequential growth of other four universals—bureaucratic organisation, money and market complex, generalised universal norms and democratic associations. These institutional systems are also causally interlinked and functionally reciprocal, and represent the essential attributes of a modern society.

Parsons' formulation is theoretical and has also been operationalised and tested recently (See Gary L. Buck and A.L. Jacobson: 1968: 343-355). As a theoretical formulation, evolutionary universals constitute a deductive model independent of a particular situation. The Western historicity of modernization is implicit in Parson's frame of reference but it does not foreclose other possibilities of modernising structural adaptations. Parsons writes:

> "Comparatively, the institutionalisation of these four complexes and their interrelations is very uneven; in the broadest frame of reference, however, we may think of them (universals) as together constituting the main outline of structural foundations of modern society. Clearly, such a combination—balanced, relative to the exigencies of particular societal units—confers on its possessors an adaptive advantage far superior to the structural potential of societies lacking it" (Parsons, 1964, p. 357).

The logical implication is that in achieving modernization societies would differ more in terms of scales rather than in quality and also that there is no basic contradiction between tradition and modernity. The institutionalisation at traditional levels is necessary for later differentiation towards modernization. The conflict between tradition and modernity may be more due to a reversal of the logical growth sequence in the evolutionary universals rather than due to the universals themselves.

The study conducted on this model by Buck and Jacobson validates these points fully. It shows not only that even most of the highly modernised countries (such as USA, UK, USSR and Japan) maintain degrees of unevenness in sequential growth of universals but also that the countries which are low on the scale of modernization (such as India, Indonesia and Pakistan) too have high development of one or the other of the four basic universals necessary for modernization. For instance, India is high on the scale of bureaucracy and generalised universalistic norms, and Indonesia has the highest score for bureaucracy comparable to most modernised nations. The real problem in the modernization of these less developed nations is that of the unevenness in evolutionary growth due to the historicity of circumstances.

In Parsons, model emphasis on particularistic development is present by implication only. Directly, the evolutionary universalism in modernization is emphasised. This contrasts with the view of other social scientists who postulate particularistic growth of modernization (See, Bendix *op. cit.*, 8; J.R. Gusfield, 1967: 351-362; S.N. Eisenstadt: 1966: 145-161 and 1965: 659-673). Here the emphasis on the historicity of individual traditions is direct. But their main weakness is lack of a theoretical and logical base except in the theory of multilinear evolutionism. It is exactly at this level that a point of convergence between Parsons' evolutionary model and the particularistic models can be found. The former is, however, preferable for its theoretical power and analytic qualities to explain historicity as well as evolution of modernization.

Historicity of Modernization: Selected Cases

Historicity sets a limit to the evolutionary structural growth of modernization. The relevant problems here are of the stages in growth and acceleration of modernization, and of the similarities and dissimilarities in the modernising experiences of existentially homogeneous and heterogeneous societies. Cases of China, Japan and India may be examined to analyse selected aspects of the above problem. There were many similarities in the social structure and basic values of China and Japan in the initial stages from where modernization started. Both had a predominance of familism, non-mercantile value-orientation in stratification (in both the merchant had the lowest position in social hierarchy), a tradition of xenophobia, a centralised political structure and in both modernization started after the breakdown of the traditional political structure. Still modernization took disparate forms in the two societies. This could be explained by the historicity of other structures which were uncommon in the two nations. We summarise below in a schematic form the major structural variations in the two nations and compare them with India.

Table 5.1: Historicity of the Divergent Structural Forms in Traditional China, Japan and India

	Structural Forms	*China*	*Japan*	*India*
1.	Feudalism	Absent	Present	Present (Partially)
2.	Autonomy of Culture from Political structure	Absent	Present	Present
3.	Relationship of Individual to Authority	Monistic	Dualistic	Dualistic
4.	Recruitment to Class	Open	Closed	Closed
5.	Autonomy of Political Structure from Stratification	Absent	Present	Present

For a smooth and rapid institutionalisation of modern structure it is necessary that the basic elements composing the social system have a degree of internal autonomy along with interdependence. In this sense, the structural feature of the traditional Chinese society differed from that in Japan. In China, the political structure was fully dependent upon the cultural structure, and the system of social stratification too was in identity with the political system. The political elites were also the persons who represented the highest traditional values—the Confucian ethic. Eisenstadt writes:

> "The relation between Chinese political and cultural orders is parallel to that between the political system and social stratification. The most interesting point here is that the total societal system of stratification was entirely focused on the political centre. The Imperial centre, with its strong Confucian orientation and legitimation, was the sole distributor of prestige and honour. Various social groups or strata did not develop autonomous, independent, status orientations except on the purely local level. The very existence of the literati as an elite group was contingent on the persistence of the ideal of a unified Empire" (Eisenstadt: 1965: 661).

This inter-structural congruence among culture, polity and system of stratification was highly detrimental to the growth of a fast differentiating structure of modernization. In contradistinction to China, the Japanese social structure did not have similar degree of inter-structural congruence. Ideologically in Japan too, the political and cultural structures were highly symbiotic, but despite this, there were many autonomous sub-structures to sustain the processes of differentiation through modernization. One autonomous structure was the feudal Shogunate power structure within the symbolic Imperial power structure during the Tokugawa regime. This dualism of power structure was helpful in the modernization of Japan. When modernization necessitated the abolition of the feudal Shogunate structure, the Imperial symbolism could fill the gap in the form of Meiji restoration. In the Chinese system, there was nothing like this kind of dualism of authority and this was further not possible because of the lack of a developed feudal system (M.J. Levy: 1955: 496-503). The coincidence of the political, cultural and hierarchical values of the Chinese society in a single familistic ethic of Confucianism was rather absolute.

Both in China and Japan, the stratification system placed merchants at the bottom of the status order. Since in China the class was an open system, merchants invested their savings in land to climb to the status of nobility; in Japan, as the class was a closed system, merchants invested in modern industries and finally supplanted the power of feudal lords. Moreover, the authority system governing the obligations of individuals was monistic in China; individual was bound to family obligations; he was obliged to Imperial authority only because that institution too was cast in the image of a family order. This monism of authority obligations disturbed the whole locus of rational individual responses when traditional family system began to break down in the initial stages of modernization. There were no alternative centres of legitimation of individual responsibility. This led to rampant corruption and nepotism and finally to the breakdown of the traditional Chinese order.

In the Chinese case, therefore, the breakdown which resulted from the initial stage of modernization during the eighteenth and nineteenth century was a collapse of the elite structure following the collapse of the Confucian system of values. Individuals, liberated from the familistic ethic through modernization of occupational opportunities, did not have an alternative channel of normative conformity and its legitimation. In the second stage of modernization through Communist revolution, therefore, China had to fabricate completely an alternative system of stratification and polity and ideology (See George M. Beckmann: 1962: 515-527). The Japanese experience, on the other hand, was more integrative with only minor breakdowns. Its structural peculiarities *vis-à-vis* China made it possible for some sections of older elites to transform themselves into new middle classes and entrepreneurial roles for sustained modernization. This reveals the primacy of sociological variables to the extent to which structures of modernization could be institutionalised in a society without major breakdown.

This is not to say that societies could completely escape social breakdowns at all stages of modernization. If the structural growth is uneven, such break downs become inevitable. In Japan, following Meiji restoration there took place an uneven growth in the powers of military elites (exploiting the symbolism of Empire) over the industrial and the intellectual elites. The result was the Japanese role in the Second World War, its defeat and finally its radical loss of traditional identities in the new stage of modernization (See Beckmann: 1962:542-580; Eisenstadt: 1965:667).

Comparatively, the historicity of the 'initial stages' of modernization in India was basically different from that in China and Japan. Here modernization began with a colonial heritage which meant the encounter of a traditional society with the modernising West. Despite this, we may note that the basic structural forms in the traditional Indian society were also conducive to modernization. There was a pre-existing high degree of autonomy among the major structures, such as the system of values, the political system and stratification. Traditionally, India offered a fair degree of independence to its policy in relation to the cultural system. The political structure formed the sphere of *Artha*, when the cultural roots were embedded in *Dharma*. The role of king in relation to society was contractual rather than absolute. Dumont writes:

> "This domain (polity or *artha*) is, in the dominant tradition, relatively autonomous with regard to absolute values. In so far as it is autonomous, there is at this stage a rough parallel with the modern Western development, and this leads to a generalising hypothesis, namely that such a domain as we know it necessarily emerges in opposition to and separation from the all-embracing domain of religion and ultimate values and that the basis of such a

development is the recognition of individual" (L. Dumont: 1962:75, No. VI).

This relative dissociation between polity and culture, therefore, provided one very important source of structural autonomy through which political modernization could be attempted during the colonial period without fundamentally breaking down Indian culture structure. At the levels of social stratification and political system too a marked degree of autonomy existed. The caste system had a pluralistic organisation. The villages and townships were relatively independent and the attainment of political power could bring about fundamental status mobility in caste (See Panikkar: 1955, Srinivas; 1966). These facilitated structural tolerance necessary for modernization. The instrumental role was, however, played by the colonial British regime. They introduced an individualistic contractual system of civil rights, bureaucracy, modern education and a modern super-structure of state and economy.

Traditionally in India, the stratification system was closed and hierarchical; the value system was holistic and transcendental; and the political structure was feudal-patrimonial. Although, normatively the autonomy among the political structure, stratification and culture was there, yet the traditional elites represented a congruence between power and stratification. This overall inter-structural conformity co-existing with relative autonomy of each was helpful in synthesising the Islamic impact on Indian culture. The breakdown which might have followed could thus be avoided. Moreover, the Islamic system was itself hierarchical, holistic and transcendental in form by the time it came to India; it had also developed caste-like stratification from Persian influence. It became another segment in the pluralistic Indian tradition. This is vindicated by the fact that the Islamic elite structure too maintained its congruence with the high caste hierarchy; most elites were either high caste Hindus or *Sayyeds, Sheikhs* and *Pathans,* the three uppermost strata of Islam in India. The real challenge to the traditional social structure and value system of India started only with the beginning of the British regime.

As we mentioned above, the British contribution to the modernization in India was primarily in the sphere of developing role-structures. Exposure to education on the Western lines created a new political culture and a tradition of nationalism; the administrative and defence needs became complex, which led to the growth of bureaucracy, and a modern army; industrialisation brought about an entrepreneurial class, and growing technology and education established a new structure of technological, professional and intellectual middle classes. All these structures were relatively autonomous to the Indian cultural tradition *per se*. Their place in the stratification system, however, was congruent with this tradition. Most of the new middle classes, elites and bureaucrats came from the upper castes and by and large there was a congruence between caste status and class status (See B.B. Misra: 1961, Srinivas: 1966) in all these role structures. This development had a dual significance. In terms of role structure, it contributed to modernization but in the matter of stratification it further strengthened the power of the established traditional groups. Thus, colonial modernization in India also partially reinforced the tradition.

As modernization gathered momentum it began to threaten the autonomy of culture. At this stage the emergence of Gandhi represents Indian tradition's orthogenetic response to the challenge of modernization. The Gandhian attempt was to reintegrate the three levels of Indian social system, the stratification, culture and the polity into a reconciliatory pattern which could save the breakdown in the Indian tradition. Gandhi sought to bridge the gap between social stratification and power on the one hand and power and culture system on the other. The first he sought to realise through political and economic decentralisation and the second by universalising the egalitarian norms derived from the traditional moral ethic.

It is an important factor in the historicity of modernization in India that this internal innovation to the challenge of modernization succeeded only half-way (through political Independence) and rapidly wained with the beginning of post-colonial phase of modernization. It would be worthwhile if Indian intellectuals conducted imaginary experiments to reconstruct deductively the consequences of this movement to modernization in India, had it maintained its original force. They could then also compare this movement with the one in China represented by the Maoist reincarnation of the Western ideology of Communism. In this light Gandhism might assume an altogether new dimension unexplored by intellectuals.

As the structural innovations visualised by Gandhi failed to institutionalise, the process of modernization in free India roughly followed the pattern set during the British regime. But, in this phase of development, there emerged many new structural situations leading to stresses and challenges unforeseen in the former days.

Independent India chose to be a federal democracy with adult franchise; development was planned in consonance with the ideology of a socialistic pattern of society; feudal privileges were abolished, states were reorganised on linguistic cultural basis; and in the countryside *Panchayat* institutions were introduced on democratic lines. The network of bureaucracy was, thus, carried far into the villages and was further reinforced by the Community Development Projects. With time, these structural innovations created inconsistencies in the process of modernization.

The autonomy among the structural forms which for the early period was a help to the process of modernization in the new framework has become a handicap. This is because of increase in differentiation without integration. It is a problem encountered by all modernising societies, but in the new nations the stresses are felt far strongly as the processes which in the West took centuries are being compressed into decades. These stresses may be seen at the levels of the elite structure, social stratification, cultural system and political and economic structures.

The elite structure shows an increasing cultural lag between the political level on the one hand and the military, entrepreneurial and administrative levels on the other. In professional training and sub-cultural socialisation, there is greater homogeneity among the administrative, business and military, bureaucratic structures than among the various strata of the political elites. There is also cultural heterogeneity between the political and non-political elites in addition to the different compulsives of their status anxieties. These have resulted from differentiation of democratic association, articulation of regional leadership and the disintegration of one party rule in our polity. The effect that this lag might have on modernization may not be negative. The outcome of these processes so far does on the other hand suggest that despite the heterogeneity of the cultural background among various types of elites, their role is not proved to be of detrimental significance or inconsistent with the demands of modernization (Andre Beteille: 1967, 243; T.B. Bottomore: 1967, 257), and the strains we find existing in the transitional stages are rather symptomatic of structural growth of an adaptive nature necessary for a new equilibrium.

Another new development refers to the increasing degree of contradiction between the structural forms of power and social stratification. This process has gathered a momentum as the democratic forces have grown. Political power has now become a major source for compensating the loss on account of the social stratification. The formation of caste associations and corporate groups (See Y. Singh: 1968, 180-182) based on traditional social networks has become rampant. These new structural forces have twofold implications. On the one hand, these are inevitable for institutionalisation of the structural universals necessary for modernization; the democratic association is one such example; but on the other hand, these also tend to articulate symbolisms connected with the native traditions, caste, and regional cultures. The important point to note here is that these traditional forms (symbolisms) have functions which are basically oriented to modernization.

Here an important theoretical question can be raised: Does modernization in the new nations must of necessity proceed through micro-structural (regional) mobilisation of identities? Are these forces regressive or developmental in nature? To answer these questions, one must recapitulate the factors which have activated them. These factors, however, are none else than macro-structural innovations. This renders these micro-structural inconsistencies not regressive but necessary for modernization. The need is of a new adaptive capacity on the part of the macro-structure to develop viable systems of reconciliation (Apter, *op. cit.*) to rationally integrate these forces of modernization.

The process of modernization in India has today reached a critical point in regard to structural differentiation. The process of segmental modernization that had started during the early British days due to the inter-structural autonomy of culture from political system and of political system from stratification system is now giving way to a more integrated and diffused process of modernization. It should not alarm us if the process causes some breakdown in this process of integration.

Modernization and Tradition

A final question which arises about modernization is that of its relationship with tradition. How far will modernization succeed in an integrative development ? How far will tradition maintain its own identity in the wake of the forces of modernization? These questions are often raised. To our mind the assumed polarity between tradition and modernity is misplaced, and the controversy between the intellectuals who think that a synthesis between tradition and modernity is possible or that it is impossible, is spurious one (Dube 1967: 51; 1965: 43-55). Modernization is an integrative process. It may involve breakdowns of course, which are continual, but finally the process is integrative. Thus, modernization develops through internalisation of norms represented by its role structures. This is not easier, as the values of modernity are never a finished product; they are open-ended, mostly instrumental, and non-categorical. These attributes of modernity lead us logically to conclude that society's categorical values are of necessity to be derived from sources co-existential with cultural structure of modernity. The autonomy of moral values over the instrumental values (modernity) can, therefore, be logically postulated at all stages of modernization in all societies.

The problem of historicity in modernization is, therefore, crucial. Whereas the instrumental values of modernization can be rationally evaluated and would, therefore, sooner or later be uniform in all the societies, the same cannot be true of the categorical or moral values. Societies with different historical traditions in respect of such moral values can always claim a superiority over others, which can never be falsified by science. As such, individual traditions at this level are more likely to coexist with universals of modernization which may, of course, be identical in every society. Modernity might also reinforce tradition (Horowitz: 1966: 308) through its uneven growth. If the role structures grow without a concomitant response from values, modernization may become an instrument in the hands of the traditionally established power groups to maintain the *status quo*. To our mind, the major obstacle in smooth transition to modernization lies in such inconsistent growth which is faced by all societies, but in the new nations the problem is more acute as the economic constraints and aspiration for power give stimulus to populist movements, which may or may not be helpful for modernization.

References

Almond, G.A. and Verba, S., *The Civic Culture* (Boston and Toronto: Little, Brown & Co., 1965).

Andrain, Charles, F., 'Democracy and Socialism', *Ideology and Discontent* (ed.) David, E. Apter, New York: The Free Press of Glencoe, 1965.

Apter, David, E., *The Politics of Modernization,* Chicago: The University of Chicago Press, 1965.

Banifield, Edward C., *The Moral Basis of Backward Society,* Glencoe, Illinois: The Free Press, 1958.

Beckmann, George, M., *The Modernization of China and Japan,* New York: Harper & Row, 1962, pp. 542-580.

Bellah, R.N., 'Religious Revolution', *American Sociological Review,* Vol. 29, No. 3, June 1964, pp. 358-374.

Bendix, Reinhard, *Nation-Building and Citizenship,* New York: John Wiley & Sons Inc. 1964.

Beteille, Andre, 'Elites, Status Groups and Caste in Modern India', *India and Ceylon: Unity an Diversity* (ed.) Philip Mason, London: Oxford University Press, 1967, p. 243.

Bottomore, T.B., 'Cohesion and Division in Indian Elites', *India and Ceylon: Unity and Diversity* (ed.) Philip Mason, London: Oxford University Press, 1967, p. 257.

Buck, Gary L. and Jacobson, Alvin, 'Social Evolution and Structural Functional Analysis', *American Sociological Review,* Vol. 33, No. 3, June 1968, pp. 343-355.

Deutsch, Karl W., 'Social Mobilization and Political Development', *American Political Science Review,* Vol. 55, Sept., 1961, pp. 493-514.

Dube, S.C., 'Modernization and its Adaptive Demands on Indian Society'; *Papers in the Sociology of Education in India* (eds.) M.S. Gore, I.P. Desai and Suma Chitnis, New Delhi: National Council of Educational Research and Training, 1967, pp. 33-51. See also 'Cultural Problems in Economic Development in India', *Religion and Progress in Modern Asia* (ed.) R.N. Bellah (New York: The Free Press, 1965), pp. 43-55.

Dumont, Louis, 'The Conception of Kingship in Ancient India', *Contributions to Indian Sociology* (eds.) Louis Dumont and D. Pocock, Paris: Mouton & Co., No. VI, December, 1962, p. 75.

Eisenstadt, S.N., 'Social Change, Differentiation and Evolution', *American Sociological Review,* (Vol. 29, No. 3, June 1964), pp. 375-386. 'The McIver Lecture: Social Transformation in Modernization', *American*

Sociological Review, Vol. 30, No. 5, October 1965, pp. 659-673, *Modernization: Protest and Change*, London: Prentice-Hall, Inc., 1966.

Geertz, Clifford, 'The Integrative Revolution: Primordial Sentiments and Civil Politics in the New States', *Old Societies and New States*, (ed.) Clifford Geertz, London: The Free Press of Glencoe, 1963, pp. 105-157.

Gusfield, Joseph, R., 'Tradition and Modernity: Misplaced Polarities in the Study of Social Change', *The American Journal of Sociology*, Vol. 72, No. 4, January 1967, pp. 351-362.

Hagen, Everett, E., *On the Theory of Social Change*, Honewood, Illinois: The Dorsey Press, Inc., 1962.

Hempel, Carl G., *Aspects of Scientific Explanation and Other Essays in the Philosophy of Science*, New York: The Free Press, 1965.

Horowitz, Irving Louis, *Three Worlds of Development* (New York: Oxford University Press, 1966).

Lerner, Daniel, *The Passing of Traditional Society* (The Free Press of Glencoe, 1958).

Levy, Jr. Marion, J., 'Contrasting Factors in the Modernization of China and Japan', *Economic Growth: Brazil, India, Japan* (eds.) Simon Kuznets, Wilbert E. Moore, and Joseph J. Spengler, Durham, N.C. Duke University Press, 1955, pp. 496-536. *Modernization and the Structure of Societies*, Princeton: Princeton University Press, 1966.

McClelland, David C., 'The Achievement Motive in Economic Growth', *Political Development and Social Change* (ed.) Jason L. Finkle and Richard W. Gable, New York: John Wiley & Sons, Inc., 1965, pp. 139-156.

Misra, B. B., *The Indian Middle Classes*, London: Oxford University Press, 1961.

Panikkar, K. M., *Hindu Society at Cross Roads*, Bombay: Asia Publishing House, 1955.

Parsons, Talcott, 'Evolutionary Universals in Society', *American Sociological Review.*, Vol. 29, No. 3, June 1964, pp. 339-357.

Popper, Karl R., *The Poverty of Historicism*, New York: Harper and Row, 1961, p. 3. *The Open Society and its Enemies*, Vol. I, London: Routledge and Kegan Paul, 1962, pp. 1-10.

Pye, Lucian W. and Verba, Sidney (eds), *Political Culture and Political Development*, Princeton: Princeton University Press, 1965.

Riggs, Fred W., *Administration in Developing Countries*, Boston: Houghton Mifflin Company, 1964.

Rostov, Walt W., *The Stages of Economic Growth: A Non-Communist Manifesto*, Cambridge: Cambridge University Press, 1960.

Shils, Edward, *The Intellectual Between Tradition and Modernity: The Indian Situation*, The Hague, Netherlands; Mouton & Co. Publishers, 1961.

Singh, Yogendra, 'Caste and Class: Some Aspects of Continuity and Change', *Sociological Bulletin*, Vol. XVII, No. 2, September, 1968, pp. 165-186.

Srinivas, M. N., *Social Change in Modern India,* Berkeley: California University Press, 1966.

Toynbee, Arnold J., *A Study of History,* Vol. 8, London: Oxford University Press, 1963, p. 543.

Weiner, Myron, *The Politics of Scarcity: Public Pressure and Political Response in India,* Chicago: University of Chicago Press, 1962.

6

Perception of Modernization

BINA ROY

Social Perception and Modernization: The Psychological Process

Perception is a psychological "process of information extraction", which is defined as "a superset which subsumes the sub-sets of learning and thinking". Perception, learning and thinking have been traditionally referred to as the cognitive processes because they deal with the problem of acquiring knowledge. In this process, perception is generally defined as the process by which an organism extracts certain information about the environment. Learning is defined as "a process by which this information is acquired through experience and becomes part of organism's storage of facts". Learning modifies the organism so that later perception of the same stimuli will be different. The process of 'thinking', which results from previous learning is the most complex of these cognitive processes; this modifies the organism because new learning occurs. Consequently, the perception of stimuli is modified.

Social perception studies can be grouped as follows:

(*a*) The work of the Europeans has given us a technique for investigating the determiners of the judgment of emotional and motivation expression. Their studies suggest that this judgement is based on configurational principles, such as common fate, radius of action, similarity, proximity, and so on. Whether or not human responses to social aspects of these configurations are innate or are results of learning is still an open question to be answered experimentally, the gestaltists have stated that the gestalt laws operate independently of experience, but would seem reasonable to expect that the social relevance of these laws is probably influenced by social learning, most studies tend to support this expectation.

(*b*) The work of the Americans on social perception points to another type of perceptual learning.

There are theories which postulate that experience produces associative assemblies, increased specificity and differential sensitivity. Thus, perceptual attention is influenced not only by the nature of the stimulus but also by long-term sets resulting from learning. Therefore, such factors as value, anxiety, and the like influence our ability to perceive by affecting our judgement of already perceived stimuli, making us more or less sensitive to certain attributes of the stimulus complex. However, it is hoped that by the process of learning, individuals should be able to respond differently to the potential cues or information even though they may be carried by stimulus complexes which are not very clear.

In the early years of the twentieth century, a great deal of experimental work was done to investigate the nature of association involved in thinking, the method used was mainly introspective analysis of consciousness. One of the greatest outcomes of this group of investigations was the conclusion that "thinking can occur without calling up images for presenting knowledge and consciousness".[1] This was a negation of the structuralist position formulated earlier by Wundt[2] and the structuralists. This controversy has not been resolved yet, but all experimentalists seem to conclude that thinking is usually accompanied by a "state of consciousness".[3]

Noteworthy advances made by other experimentalists include, (*a*) Selz, who made an important advance when he put forward the integrative nature of thought; (*b*) This in turn was criticized by gestalt psychologists who maintained that productive thinking consists of reorganisation of past experience to meet the requirements of the present problem situation. This theoretical advance led to the distinction between the positive and negative effects of sets as they influence the direction of thought particularly as shown in the researches of Maier[4], Dunckar and Luchins[5].

A major advance made in this movement is to be noted in the gestalt laws of perceptual organisation. The investigation of thinking moved away from analysing the contents of thought into studying the act of thought as the process of thinking. This was experimentally more desirable because of the greater objectivity that became possible.[6] The conclusion is that successful thinking depends largely on the individual's ability to group or reorganise problem materials into a more meaningful relationship. Concept formation, therefore, becomes the important basis for problem solving since it provides the categories which the individual will have available for grouping the elements presented in a problem statement.

A problem arises when the correct response expected by the stimulating situation is not immediately available. The result may be described as perception. The relative unavailability of the correct response is determined by the interaction between stimulus presentation and organismic state. Thus, the subject's first task is to extract the relevant potential information from the stimulus. The ability to do this efficiently depends on:

1. "The nature of the stimulus presentation. For example, positive instances usually generate more information than negative instances. This conclusion is related to the principle of contiguity.
2. The sequential relationship of task presentation. For example, reversal-shift learning is more difficult than non-reversal-shift learning. Also, learning sets facilitate subsequent problem solving.
3. The ease with which the subject can assimilate transmitted information. This ability depends on such factors as the presence of relevant sets which the subject can generate to categorize stimuli and the facility of changing these sets as necessary cognitive strain, and risk regulation."[7]

Finally, there are exploratory studies on personalities of creative individuals and the determination of remote associations in these people. This combined with the present trends in the realm of education to increase the learner's sensitivity to a wider range of stimuli leading to creative educational experience is expected to develop social perceptions involving peoples and cultures outside one's own.

In short, this is the process of becoming which has received much emphasis in Indian philosophy. Development of adequate persons who see themselves in the process of becoming holds a great promise for the future. Such a person is open to change and can trust his impulses and values as guides for behaviour in new circumstances, they are most likely to adapt and survive as the environment changes.

The Indian Scene: Attempts at Perceptions of Modernization

The process of modernization in India may be taken to begin consciously in the early years of the nineteenth century when the Indian intellectuals realized the fact of the British conquest of India, with the painful awareness that rigid crystallization of traditional pattern of life caused the Indian society to refuse to accept possibilities of social change. Led by these intellectuals the urge for change to modernization—beginning with the life and work of Raja Ram Mohun Roy continuing through the period of freedom movement, culminating under the actual and (later) moral leadership of Mahatma Gandhi—found final expression in the Constitution of the Indian Union under the leadership of Pandit Jawaharlal Nehru.

Living memory and records testify to the jubilation over our Fundamental Rights and Directive Principles of the Constitution. After 21 years of experimentation with new forces released since political independence for economic and social change, a realistic review of the present scene raises certain fundamental questions on the nature and the process of implementation of the changes envisaged, as well as problems ensuing from the unforeseen changes generated by the complexity of forces operating on Indian society since independence. One also hears questions and comments as to the direction of modernization and motivation of the same.

The discussions in this paper support the findings of the Stage I of the Seminar (Srinagar, June-July 1963) under indicators of modernization (See Background Note, pp. 5-8). Based on these earlier findings of the Seminar, observations are made in a few following examples to indicate only a few problems related to perceptions of modernization in India.

1. *Fundamental Rights*: One perceives a repetitive tendency to state that our Fundamental Rights include much or almost all of the Human Rights postulated by the UN for all mankind. This obviously makes the Constitution very modern. At the same time there is no system to ensure the implementation of the new rights which were non-existent earlier or make a logical attempt to relate consciously our Fundamental Rights with the Human Rights in formulation, adoption and implementation. One has to proceed painfully through the records of the various departments of Government concerned with the subjects to find out which conventions have been ratified and what has been the progress in the effort for implementing these.

In simple psychological term, perception of modernization in this area is made difficult because there does not exist any stimulus in the radius of action of the average citizen. This combined with the current controversy over who has the power to amend (expand or restrict?) these Fundamental Rights brings forth the need to study what should be the true and rational direction of modernization for the citizens of India today with reference to the question of choice[8]—moral, social, or personal—that it should be his right in any modern political system of life.

2. *Social Legislation*: Here again many of our social changes seem to succeed up to the stage of legislation, but then are fated to stagnate for lack of effective administrative and judicial sub-systems. Impact of liberal values of individualism, rationalism and social justice on the educated middle classes provided leadership for many social reforms including those which worked against the rigidity of caste, for social and political privileges for the underprivileged groups such as women and *harijans*, labour laws and for reforms in many of the aspects of social life.

These reforms begin as legislators's dreams, but once the legislation is passed, not much is done to implement them. There is no provision or system for legal aid or action to implement these laws—be they labour laws or those which seek to remove the disabilities of the untouchables, tribes, women or other spheres such as gold control, inheritance laws, etc.

On the other hand one should note examples like Gandhi who needed no law to bring about immediate and effective social change in many of these areas. Law may, therefore, be important but not a necessary prerequisite for social change. What is needed is a temperamental prerequisite, a sense of commitment as part of our value system, for no amount of legislature will deliver the goods if our sense of commitment is weakened.

This goes to show that successful perception of these processes of modernization depend on the interaction of learning and thinking leading to the individual's ability to group or organise problem materials into more meaningful experiences. Motivation for this effort obviously falls short of what is desired.

Perceptual psychologists are of the opinion that all behaviour is the product of the perceptual field of the subject at the time of action, *i.e.*, how a person will behave will be a direct outgrowth of the perceptions existing for him at any moment. To change behaviour in this frame of reference requires that we understand the nature of the individual's perceptual field.[9]

However, studies need to be made in areas such as realisation by the Scheduled Castes on what their organised strength can achieve. Also, there are religious and other minorities forming little islands of obscurantism which need to be demolished from within by development of creative personalities who are open to change and can trust his impulses and values as guides for behaviour in new circumstances. But these communities continue to exist because of protective legislature. The end result is that because of existing perceptions and aperceptions, the forces of traditional life and modernization go in opposite directions and do not meet.

3. *The Educated Minority*: The last statement is best exemplified by the youth and the educated elite. These, normally, should be among the leading and strongest instruments of modernization—being the bulk of the educated population whose grasp of time and space and consequently integrative thought in multi-dimensional aspects should cover a very large radius of action and give them positions of social power today more than what could be enjoyed by the educated leaders of the nineteenth century who lead the vanguard of social reforms.

What we perceive today is that instead of combining forces they too are going in opposite directions creating a vacuum which is more than a gap of generations. A recent observation in this realm has been that the intellectuals have not played their rightful part, partly because there is a feeling of being disinherited because of the power of the 'have-nots'. Thus, some of the potential agents of modernization feel hostile to some who can be main instruments of modernization—the youth, the outcaste and the women. Given enough, these later may be able to accelerate the process of modernization.

Turning our attention to the conceptual level once more, a point was made at the first seminar that with reference to the Indian scene, one should observe two patterns of modernization—those exemplified by (*a*) the free world of Western Europe and America; and (*b*) USSR and those countries which have totalitarian systems of mobilization of resources and regimentation of manpower. The Seminar also noted that Indian identity ought to be preserved in the process of modernization.

The question I raise is, should we give this a second look on the basis of a dialogue between Arnold Toynbee and Raghavan Iyer? Toynbee made a statement that "all the new-Western peoples have had the same experience in modern times; they've all come up against the West and had rather an upsetting experience. That's true of Arabs, other Moslems, that's true of Indians, Chinese, Japanese, Russians.. I think Russia is in the same position as Asia in relation to the West in modern times."[10]

Finally, may I submit to suggest that appropriate studies be carried on or identified which seek to explore the meeting grounds of tradition and modernization.

Notes

1. Forgus, Harold H., *Perception*, McGraw-Hill, N.Y., 1966.
2. Wundt, W., *Outline of Psychology*, Leipzig: Egdman's, 1907.
3. Forgus, Harold H., *Perception*, Mc-Graw-Hill, N.Y., 1966.
4. Maier, N.R.F. "An Aspect of Human Reasoning", *British Journal of Psychology*, 1933.
5. Luchins, A.S. and Luchins, E.A., "New Experimental Attempts at Preventing Mechanization in Problem Solving", *Journal of General Psychology*, 1950.
6. *Ibid.*
7. Fergus, Harold, *Perception*, McGraw-Hill, N.Y., 1966.
8. Apter, David E., *Politics of Modernization*, University of Chicago, 1967.
9. Combs, Arthur W., and S. Donald, *Individual Behaviour: A Perceptual Behaviour: Approach to Behaviour*, Harper, N.Y., 1959.
10. Iyer, Raghavan (ed.), *The Glass Curtain between Asia and Europe*, London, Oxford, 1965.

7

Barriers to Modernization

LEELA DUBE *AND* S.C. DUBE

From the end of the Second World War the story of the *third world*—the developing nations—has been one of hope and despair. In the euphoria of the early years of independence, most of these nations launched ambitious and massive programmes of economic development and technological change. Their ambitions were unbounded and their utopias were unlimited—they hoped to accomplish in decades what Western Europe and North America had taken centuries to achieve. Their uneasy course on the road to modernization, and the many setbacks, breakdowns, and failures experienced by them have generated much frustration and anger. The pay off of the painfully obtained economic inputs has been too meagre to match the prosperity and plenty that were promised to the masses. In consequence, their people are restive and some sections of them at least are attracted towards desperate remedies. The modernising elite itself is confused.

A significant aspect of the programmes of modernization in the emerging nations was that it attempted only a transfer of technology, without effecting necessary institutional changes. In other words, the traditional framework of society was sought to be geared to the tasks of the attainment of the goal of modernization. But modernization, as C.E. Black perceptively puts it, is "the process by which historically evolved institutions are adapted to the rapidly changing functions that reflect the unprecedented increase in man's knowledge, permitting control over his environment, that accompanied the scientific revolution"

(Black, *The Dynamics of Modernization,* New York, Evanston & London, 1966). Many of these societies lacked the necessary infrastructures—education was backward; modern media of communication were poorly developed; transport facilities were primitive; public health standards were appallingly low; and formal organisations with trained personnel to take up the complex tasks of development existed only in an embryonic form. The complexities of the process of development were not adequately understood. As such, both the leadership and the developmental bureaucracy were quite unprepared to meet the setbacks and breakdown. The promises so eloquently made by them were hard to fulfil.

Gaining Wisdom from hindsight an attempt should be made to locate and understand the barriers to modernization. Analysis of the ideological, motivational, institutional, and organisational inadequacies of the developing societies will be a useful diagnostic exercise. It will also perhaps suggest some correctives.

Ideological Barriers

Most developing societies launched their programmes of Modernization with blurred images and conflicting goals. Their nostalgia for the past was a force to contend with, imparting nativistic and vitalistic overtones to their conceptualisation of the future. While the tractor was desired, the ox-plough was idealized. The ideals of democracy, secularism, and socialism were sought to be achieved in *Ramarajya.* The pulls of the past and the desired future, in some situations, were equally strong. The result was confusion and contradiction in the formulation of the goals of change. Such formulations often represented an uneasy compromise between tradition and modernity.

But the aims of modernization—watered down as they were—did not reach down to the masses. This could be attributed to the poor articulation between elite formulation and mass acceptance of ideology.

In this context, we must also consider the lack of fit between the ultimate and the proximate goals. Ideological excesses on the one situational compromises on the other, often led to bizzare results.

Finally, there was a pronounced gap between profession and practice. This often led to puzzlement. The common man did not know what to believe and what not to believe.

Motivational Barriers

Barriers on the motivational level were also many and complex.

The masses had constricted horizons, and low achievement motivation. The belief that the society can and should be transformed and that change is desirable and necessary, was feeble if it existed at all. Little imaginative effort was made to widen mental horizons and to foster the growth of achievement motivation.

Development projects were launched with enthusiasm, but there was no built-in strategy to sustain the effort. Motivational momentum was lost midway. In consequence, few projects showed the desired results.

Lack of social discipline was also a major impediment in the way of successful implementation of the programmes of modernization. Scarce national resources were often destroyed with impunity, while the administration watched on helplessly. This at least partially undid the small gains registered by national effort to ensure economic development.

Torn between parochial and national pulls and between short-run and long-run interests, the masses tended to drift between the two.

Institutional Barriers

The institutional framework of these societies, characterized by ascription, particularism, affectivity, and diffused expectation system, was not particularly propitious for Modernization. It is remarkable how little thought the developing societies gave to structural modification and institutional change. Not much effort was made to understand and reconcile the incompatibilities between the aims of structural units and national objectives.

Sacred emphasis in the thought-ways and work-ways of the masses blocked the emergence of the new attitude complex that is often a pre-condition of Modernization.

Finally, there were incongruities between the political/administrative system and the social system. Consider, in this context, the marriage of caste to democracy in India.

Organisational Barriers

At this level we find an absence of fit between *micro-* and *macro-politics.* The local and national political processes are at best loosely integrated. The reach of administration is limited and is conditioned by a variety of factors. In fact, the legitimacy of the government is not firmly established. The development of communication—political and developmental—leaves much to be desired. Adequate institutions for this purpose have not been built. Many of the planning techniques are still experimental, and show inaptitude and hesitation. The development programme itself lacks a sense of priorities, of timing, and of balance. This is explained, at least partially, by the failure of these countries to evolve effective planning machinery.

These factors, among others, explain the halting and hesitating progress of modernization in developing societies.

8

Modernization and Education

S. SHUKLA

PRELIMINARY

To begin with, the ground must be cleared in respect of certain matters concerning concepts and assumptions.

One assumption implicit in such thought on the question of modernization, or at least encouraged by literature is, as it were, a *gradualist understanding*. It is comparable to what is known in the history of Indian education as the 'downward filtration' theory. Macaulay had argued that Western ideas cultivated by an educated upper or middle class will gradually filter down to the rest of Indian society. Modern thought, taught through the English language, would trickle down to the Indian languages and to groups using them, thereby influencing the rest of society. The assumption was, in the event, unfounded or at least poorly or only partially founded. In any case, it did not work out in the same straight line fashion as visualised. Could it not be that we are, similarly, assuming that if a certain upper or middle or educated or westernised sector of society had adopted modern approaches and values, we expect these to trickle down to the rest of society? Could it also not be that we are similarly mistaken and that the process of modernization might be *dialectical rather than gradual, zig zag rather than linear,* that its dynamics is more complicated—as we shall see presently—than tends to get suggested by the word?

Indeed, precisely as the educated Indian middle class has tended to crystallise out of, and away from the rest of society, the modernised sectors of a society might do the same. In the late twentieth century—a period of increased communication—*the possibility exists that the modern sectors of Indian society will form a more integral part of advanced Western societies than of the ones to which they belong geographically and in terms of the culture of their origin.* The process of modernization of the *whole* of Indian society may, therefore, take a more tortuous path than might be implicit in most of our statements on the subject. The accelerated modernization of the modern sectors might, in fact, lead to a backlash effect *vis-à-vis* the rest of society.

Within the rubric of modernization, we come across value-economic and political elements which need not all march in step with one another. It is, of course, by now well recognised, for instance, that cultural traditionalists may be the instruments of political or the economic modernization. This, in turn, may or may not, lead to cultural modernization at a later stage. This is a statement of the zigzags or dialectics of the modernization process not necessarily extending to the whole of a society, but merely to a certain segment of it. If we extend the zigzag idea to the modernization of the *whole* society, it might involve more revolutionary and discontinuous changes—largely in social structures and their political consequences—some of these accompanied by apparently traditional, cultural or political events.

Further, in a discussion of modernization or other change, one has to take into account the distinct viewpoints of (*a*) *science* (description-analysis), and (*b*) *technology*, i.e., *planned, science-based action*. This, of course, is different from the distinction between the positive and the normative. Even without the induction of values, the scientific and the technological standpoints, the cognitive and the action-oriented approaches can easily be distinguished. For the element of *conscious will* is absent in the former, while it is the main element in the latter. Viewing of past history will, indeed, be primarily of the variety of science. But in analysis of the present and, even more, in the prediction of future an understanding of the factor of will is very much more definitely involved. The role of consciousness in history which has always been ignored by the non-idealist except when they were creative revolutionaries—is important. Thus, we are called upon not only to study the entire range of factors for and against change but to pay special and distinct attention *to the location and institutionalisation of the will for change.* Much more depends on this factor than is common in discussions of all changes including social change and modernization. This, indeed, is no plea for renunciation of science. But it is certainly a call for freeing the human mind from the shackles of social determinism. The issue to determine is: To what extent are institutions or processes—formal education, polity or economy—likely to perform the educative function in as much as it contributes to the development of *will?*

Conventional wisdom in social science has been unable to explore this phenomenon largely because it has not examined the assumptions underlying motivation or will. The drive for wealth or status have rightly been seen as dominant. Nevertheless, the precise contents of concepts of status, reward, etc., vary not only with social classes, etc., but also with individuals. The individuals who are crucial in fashioning the will for change are often motivated by unusual motivations—even more so than the Protestant Ethic appeared to be, when it was noticed by Max Weber. What is more, they seek to fashion new types of instruments, e.g., the Communist Party in Russia or China. The social innovators who fashion these instruments are *entrepreneurs* of the non-economic domain whose psychology and incidence in society require exploration.

Before proceeding much further with this discussion, it may be useful to devote some attention to an aspect of the subject, viz., if one might say so, *sociological growthmanship.* We have been familiar for more than a decade with growthmen amongst economists. But we have also been familiar with the same phenomenon amongst sociologists, who have, however, not hitherto been so identified. The various schools of growthmen in the social sciences may be classified as (*a*) those who deal with modernization as against tradition, or (*b*) those who lay special stress on aspects of social structure related to economic growth. There are variants of each of these. The achievement motivation of McClelland is a conspicuous example of a psychological slant to the tradition-modernity question. By contrast, emphasis on the specific technical or entrepreneurial skills as a factor conducive to growth may be seen as a variant of that school of the study of economic growth which lays great store by social structure.

Now, the place we give to the system of formal education in the process of technical modernization varies considerably with or theoretical predilections. Thus, an emphasis on an achievement motivation (or any other variant of the value orientation approach to economic modernization) appears to suggest that while this motivation is distributed in a given manner, latent motivation can be made manifest—the potential can be actualised. To the extent formal education is effective, existing tendencies can be strengthened through particular forms of curriculum or organisation in education. If, however, we lay store by a belief in the potency of social structure in influencing growth, we shall be very much more concerned about the *incidence* of education, or the recruitment of students. We will be concerned to find out if relevant social strata have been enabled to acquire knowledge and skills functional to their performance of roles in relation to development. Now, certainly, no thinker on the problem of development takes an exclusively either/or position as between these two approaches which are in the nature of ideal types. In fact, it is customary for the proponent of either stance to treat the other variable values or social structure as a dependent or secondary variable which must be taken into account at the point of detailed elaboration of the relationship (One can view communication model of modernization as some sort of a cross between the two positions.).

Conceptual Matters regarding Education

It may be useful to distinguish three facets of the phenomenon of education, viz., as an *institution,* a *function* and a *process.* We need to distinguish these three aspects and analyse education from each of these standpoints at some length as social scientists have, unfortunately, with very few exceptions, failed to do so. Their discussions of the relation of education to social change and economic growth have, therefore, not been free from faulty logic and inadequate analysis. The educative (or educational) function may, by some, be seen to be coterminous with the function of socialisation. The main distinction appears to be that education has necessarily to be *deliberate* or *voluntary* (on the part either of the educator or of the educated or both) while socialisation may be involuntary as well. Even this distinction between education and socialisation is not always accepted. This distinction is different from the one between *intended* and *unintended* consequences of any process or institution.

The *processes* of education as well as socialisation both emphasise an essentially individualistic (or individual centred) aspect of the matter. However, it is possible to take into account the broader social aspects by considering (*a*) *formal* education as an *institution,* and (*b*) the educative (socialising) processes and functions—sometimes unintended, sometimes not-associated with other institutions in the polity and the economy, e.g., the political party, the government, the production team or group, etc. The point of these distinctions is that when we seek to study or to develop educative processes from the viewpoint of their consequences in terms of social change, the part played by institutions other than formal education has to be kept in view.

As an *institution,* formal education performs some other *functions* as well. It is not definitely the case that these other functions or consequences are either *latent* or *unintended.* It contributes, for instance, towards the setting up of an ecological gradient in a society.[1] Some of its sectors perform a role in the recruitment, personality formation and cohesion of elites. It plays a distinct part in the modification of social structure, largely, it seems, through the distribution of education opportunity.

A distinguishing feature of education is its relationship to codified *culture and knowledge* of community. This is to say that formal education cannot be conceived to exist if there were not a codified body of knowledge which it was the function—the manifest function—of education to transmit. Indeed, we cannot neglect, particularly in earlier stages of education and in special institutions, the formation of attitudes and values and the performance, more or less consciously, of an *allocative role* and a concomitant instrumental role in the formation, at an early stage in life, of links between members of the future common stratum coming as they do, in the first instance, from more or less varied backgrounds. However, for most practical purposes, these are *latent* rather than *manifest* functions of education—its unintended rather than intended consequences.

We notice, indeed, a certain ambiguity in all these statements. A consequence not intended by the organisers of a school system could be the consequences intended by individual consumers of education. Conversely, functions which to the consumer are latent, may well be manifest and intended objectives of the organisers of the educational system.

The next important distinguishing feature of the educational process is a necessary age—or generation gap between the educators and the educated, thereby adding certain dimensions to the legitimacy of authority which do not obtain in either the economy or the polity in the same measure and manner.

Viewed from the standpoint of change and Modernization, it is necessary to understand the inherent tendencies towards inertia in any educational system which tend to limit its capacity as an instrument of social change to the extent that changes in the content cognitive or otherwise—of education may be contributing towards social change. Factors contributing to inertia are: (*a*) at the level of the pedagogic process, (*b*) at the level of educational administration, and (*c*) at the level of relationship of education as a whole to its clients—the state and the public. In relatively rapidly expanding educational systems, one sees a phenomenon comparable:

(*a*) *Sanskritisation* at the margin, i.e., the adoption of traditional practice methods and even institutions and options by the newer entrants to the system—both teachers and parents/pupils; and

(*b*) Westernisations—modernization at the apex (i.e., adoption of newer practices and courses by the other clientele). David Riesman has described this process under the *rubric* of the academic procession.[2] The most forward practice of sixty years ago is the common practice of the marginal school today. The advanced institutions have meanwhile moved on the fresh adventures in theory as well as practice. We may also note that the structure of the educational situation from the viewpoint of change has some characteristics, which it shares with (*a*) agriculture—a large industry of small enterprises, and (*b*) some which it shares with industry proper. The degree of centralisation, or otherwise, of change is, therefore, a unique characteristic of each educational systems.[3]

SOCIAL CHANGE AND ECONOMIC DEVELOPMENT

Findings of Conventional Wisdom

The relationship of formal education to modernization has not been systematically enough studies to give us general theories. We have studies which show, for instance, how far adoption of new practices and attitudes, e.g., in agriculture, industry or re-changes of Institutional structure are associated with it. The relationship of education to the formation of certain kinds of *elites* of certain personality qualities, recruiting only very small numbers is more well documented. For example, the use of the Chinese examination sytem and of the British Public Schools to recruit and fashion a closed *elite* of highly able individuals from outside, is well known. In many other cases, however, the formation of an entrepreneurial leadership is not known to be directly associated with university education or even school education. It is known, on the other hand, that the merchants of the eighteenth and nineteenth century England sought to promote themselves in the social hierarchy by organizing education for themselves. It is also known that the working classes as in the Chartist movement started demanding elementary education as a fundamental right.

The relation of education to economic growth has recently been widely noticed and studied. The achievement of 40 per cent literacy has been associated with the period of take off of an economy into sustained growth. Similarly, the period of take off has been located at 30 to 40 years after the growth of post-primary enrolments beyond a certain percentage. In either case, it is easy to assume that some social changes must have been brought about as a result of education which set in tray the process of economic development and in turn was further promoted by the new economic developments.

Many studies of the residual factor in economic growth with a Lernertype stress on communication—in which formal education plays some part, again, bring out, it appears to me, second order, derivative relationship but beg the essential questions which elucidate and explain either economic growth or related social change. The same appears true of McClelland type achievement motivation and other similar theories.

Patterns of Development: Classes and Politics

As we survey the whole field of the relationship between education, social change and economic development, it appears that *the pattern of development* adopted is of crucial importance in determining these relationships. We need, therefore, some typology such as the one proposed by Hoselitz[4], namely, a distinction between *induced* and *spontaneous*, *extrinsic* and *intrinsic*, or *centralised* and *decentralised* patterns. Even this is not sufficiently satisfactory because it tends to abstract from certain *concrete socio-economic factors*, presumably, in a conscious effort to avoid Marxist categories or modes of thought. However, it seems that, irrespective of whether a change is induced or spontaneous, the character of the economic (or technological) base and relationships of the social groups and classes which take dominant part in the process of development is of great importance in determining the futher progress of development itself. The role of formal education is greater in those processes of development in which there is less deliberate and forcible effort to change existing property relationships. In these processes, formal education becomes largely a medium of confirmation of status or achievement of higher status *within the existing status system.* The content—cognitive or skill—attitudinal—of education may remain conventional or may undergo modernization but this appears immaterial to the development process except in as much as it influences the skills and the value orientations of the effective elites.

By contrast, development processes which are characterised by *considerable,* rapid and, more or less, *forcible change in property relations,* the role of organised formal education is *important but nevertheless secondary,* both in a temporal and in a critical value sense. A large effort in this direction of deliberate socialisation as well as communication of ideas is mounted through the political party, the mass organisations and mass media. This is an *educative function* all right. It is, however, not carried out through the *institution* of formal education. The institution of formal education, again, takes over the function of conforming such status as has been ordained by the processes of change in property and other social relationships—very much more political than in other patterns of development—and put under way through the informal education given by other institutions. As, however, formal education has a dominantly knowledge-cum-idea centred image and as this has a content with a bias in the direction of the previously privileged and dominant social groups, two possibilities emerge. On the one hand, the dominant elite which governs the polity and the economy seeks to change the content of formal education in its own image. On the other, it keeps up the institutions and agencies other than formal education as continuously effective instruments of socialisation.

There is, as would be seen, a *mutuality of relationship* between the educative institutions on the one hand, and the dominant elite, on the other. The former is the source of recruitment for the latter and to some extent also, the source of its core values. The latter, has the possibility of influencing the sources of recruitment to formal education as well as its content.

The foregoing description corresponds to the situation in *so-called totalitarian societies.* As builders of a modern national identity from many separate traditional units, the *elite* even in the *"democratic"* developing societies are called upon to perform some of the same functions. This leads, therefore, to one of the two possibilities, viz., (*a*) *The democratic societies will conform more and more to the so-called totalitarian pattern, vis-à-vis,* the relation between education and the polity; or (*b*) they will consolidate a *part of the nation* around the existing state through its formal educational system. This part will, of course, consist of social groups and classes currently dominant in, and profiting from, the state, *viz.,* the big business, the middle class intelligentsia and professionals and the rich and middle peasantry in the Indian circumstance. Recruitment from other strata of the population, into the ranks of these classes will continue to be carried out with the assistance of the educational system. It is not, however, necessary that the educational system itself will spread far beyond actual or aspirant members of these classes. Such a situation would be viable if (*a*) an adequate rate of economic growth, and (*b*) a moderately equitable distribution thereof, makes it possible for the less privileged social groups to remain contended. If this does not come about, the system, as a whole, becomes unviable and may be rocked by major cataclysm.

In contemporary India, one development which is visible is that the emergent middle class and the dominant landed castes in the villages are now seeking to confirm their social status through formal education[5] as also to secure the ways of political power and administrative connections for both economic and political objectives. It appears that while the *general* system of education is giving these classes, the opportunities they seek, the previously educated groups and the top layers of civil services seek, more and more, professional and technical education as well as education abroad partly as means to really *elite* positions and partly in a movement away from this country altogether.

Science, Technology and Formal Education

It is of relevance here to take cognizance of the nature of relationship between science and technology. It is well known that in history, many technical changes took place not under the direct impact of science, but largely as a response to economic and social need, made primarily by technicians whose literacy, personal characteristics and relationship to the economic and social structure enabled them to make these responses. It is not without significance that we now hear of the *second* industrial revolution, which is also called a *scientific* industrial revolution as contrasted to the *first* industrial revolution which does not carry with it this adjective.

In the development of science itself, history in many Western countries appears to show how the established institutions of formal education, the ancient universities, for instance, were less responsive to the development of science and were, in any case, not primarily concerned with the first scientific advances. It is, for instance, the Royal Society in Great Britain and the private laboratories of interested individuals—merchants, gentlemen and so on—which led to early advances in science. The part played by formal education has been largely that of *disseminating* the knowledge and perhaps even the culture—of science *after* it has been developed and promoted elsewhere. Implicit, also, is, of course, the formal learning of the individuals who, in later life, unconnected as they were with the institution of formal education, were in a position to *advance science because,* among other things, they possessed this literacy and formal learning.

This relationship has, indeed, been variable in as much as higher education is concerned. Thus, while the English universities were the most resistant to science, German universities and other institutions of higher and technical education, played, early in the process of technical and scientific development, a significant part in promoting this development. The higher institutes of technology in France and Germany might have been fulfilling functions similar to those fulfilled by the public schools or the ancient universities in Britain in so far as they fostered certain functional non-cognitive elements of socialisation, even as they differed from the British institution in the specific contexts cognitive as well as non-cognitive. In the American context, the German university tradition was borrowed in the nineteenth century in order to develop scientific learning in the universities. Simultaneously, as a response to the needs of expanding industry and agriculture, the Land Grand Colleges in particular an American higher education, in general, took large part in the development of practically applicable technical knowledge and in the dissemination of scientific and technical knowledge so developed. The relatively undermined question here is the extent to which the non-cognitive elements like personal characteristics, attitudes and values relevant to the development of technology were also conveyed through the process of formal education, *viz.*, through the form of the organisation of educational institutions and the scientific values and attitudes cultivated in them in so far as they are relevant to the advance of modern technology.

The place of the school system in this connection is somewhat more obscure. The extent to which the working classes, artisans and industrial workers acquire rudiments of scientific knowledge, skills of the hand and the eyes, and methods of scientific thought, would be significant for the manner and extent of their being either— (*a*) skilled industrial workers, or (*b*) innovators on the bench, as it were. A considerable period of time normally elapses before either the methods of progressive education or the content of science succeed in influencing the curricula and the *regime* of elementary and secondary schools in the direction of the relevant non-cognitive and cognitive outcomes respectively. One should, therefore, look for characteristics of entrance provided by the school system to the system of higher education or to industry in seeking to determine the relationship of education to technical development.

Both schools and institutions of higher education perform the function of bringing together persons from more or less diverse social origins and then (*a*) bring them into a relatively homogeneous stratum with common bonds of acquaintance and intellectual-social culture; and (*b*) allocating them different occupations and social strata. In this process, the role of formal education appears open to enquiry.

MODERNIZATION OF EDUCATION

Unity/Uniformity and Diversification

We may, for purposes of understanding, differentiate education in traditional societies from that in modern, in terms of a number of dichotomies, even at the risk of somewhat oversimplifying the issues involved. The rather generalised statements that follow in this section, by way of clarifying the distinction between traditional and modern education would, as we noted earlier, not provide any straightforward recipes for educational modernization as such. One such dichotomy is *the degree of commonness or diversification* in the education provided to different social groups. With the spread of communication and the formation of national States, a common language and a common minimum of general information with regard to the natural and a social environment characterises the content of education. This commonness tends to cut across the regional or geographical boundaries as also the divisions between different social classes and/or occupational groups. This is particularly the case at the elementary stage. This stage itself becomes longer as a society becomes more prosperous, industrialised and, in general, modern. Thus, in Sweden and the United States, among others, the length of common schooling extends today not only to a primary education of eight or nine years but also in same societies, universal, if not quite common, secondary education. In traditional societies, on the other hand, there has historically, been a tendency to provide a different education even at the primary stage to children of different social groups as, for instance, in the German system of primary schooling. In India[6], in the eighteenth and nineteenth centuries, 'common' elementary instruction was provided in local languages and dialects in different regions while the elementary instruction of the *Brahmin* was actually the learning of the grammar of the classical language *Sanskrit* in quite a different institution. Both of these were different from the *Persian* instruction of the courtly or bureaucratic groups of a slightly earlier period which also continued into this one.

A consequential matter is the very extent to which the whole education of a society is carried on in a formally unified system. In traditional society, the formal institution of the school has not yet fully emerged and the family, clan or other traditional social unit undertakes many educative roles of socialisation skill development, etc. Such schools as exist are not unified in a system with one stage clearly linked to the other and pupils within the stages themselves classified by age, achievement and/or aptitude. The practice of class instruction and of articulation of stages are specifically modern characteristics which grow and develop with the progress of industry and modern economy.

Related to the idea of commonness is the degree to which the *content of education is vocational or general.* It is noticed thus that in the ordinary elementary schools of India in the nineteenth century, the teaching of language and number was itself provided in a vocationally-oriented curriculum. Such characteristics tend to disappear as Modernization of society proceeds.

We might note here that alongside the advance of uniformity in curriculum development with the modernization of society, *a contrary tendency* is also emergent. Greater attention is also paid to *individual differences,* arising possibly from greater worth placed on the human individual differing as this does with specific value systems in different societies. Thus, while the objectives of a common education are more and more recognised, the necessity of providing it through methods and media particularly suited to the ability and personality characteristics of individual pupils also emerges.

Social Function of Education

A further factor calling for a diversification of the content of education, is that as a traditional society changes into modern, the number *of occupations and the types of roles* into which an individual is called upon to function increases. The number of such roles in which codified knowledge and specialised skills are required also increases. At the higher reaches of education, therefore, specialization or adaptation of education to the diversity of occupational and other roles grows. This desideratum coincides with the need for diversification based on individual differences. A modern society thus increasingly develops its educational system *as an instrument of allocation* of individuals to occupational or social roles. Traditional societies, taken as a whole, use formal education primarily for socialisation into roles to which individuals are already assigned on the basis of one or other ascribable criterion.

While, therefore, education even in modern societies largely reinforces the current and existing social structure or stratification, in traditional societies this is even more completely so. Social mobility is much less achieved through education in them than in modern societies. Even as the occupational structure, or other status hierarchy undergoes a change in the early stages of modernization, formal education helps upper and privileged social groups in the traditional hierarchy achieve comparable positions in the new modern hierarchy often by virtue of their early access to modern education itself.

Content and Method of Education

Education in traditional societies also differs from that in modern in the degree to which *the natural sciences and the scientific method* find place in the content of education. In most traditional societies, the knowledge of language and the passing on of tradition which often included much unverified knowledge about the universe and nature itself and considerable normative, value oriented content in social matters find a large place. With modernization, the stress on the natural sciences and their method grows.

Similarly, understanding about society and about the culture in which the individual functions, were inculcated in traditional education, on an *implicit* basis. Thus, existing conditions were taken as given and for granted. The individual was expected to function as if they existed and were *sui generis*. An *explicit* statement regarding society, its institution and culture was not, generally speaking, a characteristic of traditional education nor was the bringing out of the relation of the individual to society and culture. The very fact of making it explicit, is, in fact, a step towards *questioning it*—a characteristic of modern rather than of traditional society. The study of society or at the school level, the curriculum of social studies and citizenship is thus in its formal form a characteristic of modern education. Socialisation for skills and attitudes desired is common to both traditional and modern education. The former, however, makes for much less explicit and conscious internalisation of norms than does the latter. Indeed, this is partly on account of the fact that the functions of education continue in traditional societies to be performed in large measure by family and kinship institutions. The emergence of the school as a distinct social institution with a distinct culture of its own takes time and is actually achieved when schooling is widespread by which time society is also no longer very traditional.

All of these differences are related in some form to *the nature of the pupil-teacher relationships and the media which intervene therein.* Traditional education in China, for instance, has been described as "oral, private, humanistic, confined to nobility and tutorial". That in ancient India, has, again, been described by the same author as "oral, private, semi-aristocratic, basically religious. All practical education was by the apprenticeship method."[7] It is thus seen that pupil-teacher interaction was mediated by the spoken words—or by deed—rather than by the writing. There was a great deal of personal influence leading to the formation of character and personality. Indeed, with the rise of the printed word, the role of the teacher has undergone considerable change.

A further characteristic brought out in the foregoing quotations is *the extent of spread of education.* As, in traditional societies, many occupations, family and other social goals did not require the use of knowledge, the spread of formal education was limited to a small number of pupils in ruling, theological or bureaucratic groups. To these was, thus, given the established knowledge from one generation to another. In the absence of science and its empirical method, there was relatively little scope for change in the content of this knowledge or even skills and personality characteristics. Traditional education has, therefore, relatively speaking remained unchanged over generations in contrast to modern education. There are, of course, other factors as well which explain the greater change-orientation of modern education such as the more open and changing goals of society, the greater availability of scientific knowledge and understanding of the educational process itself, etc.

The spread of traditional education being limited to a small section in society has also resulted in the fact that *the learning of the useful arts* and skills, vocational or professional has largely been outside the purview of formal literary education. This has tended to strengthen the relatively unchanging quality of traditional education. For, it is through empirical experience of, and contact with, nature—such as could have been provided by a practice of the crafts and the arts—that new elements of knowledge might have got incorporated into the formal educational system. Conversely, not informed by knowledge as such and based largely on imitation and skill, the crafts and the arts themselves have tended to remain static. In fact, the growth of science on the one hand, and technology even as it grows through the practice of the vocations in society on the other possess the potential of mutual reinforcement. In traditional societies, this reinforcement has been minimal. The separation has, of course, been carried to its extreme form in societies like the Indian where the caste, as a basis for the choice of occupation as well as marriage has tended to keep the different social groups further apart than in other societies, minimising the possibilities of skills and knowledge interacting with each other or, for instance, in the traditional Chinese society where the learned bureaucrats, once they were selected through an examination system tended to live away from the practice of the useful arts.

It may also be of some interest to see if *the methods and organization of education* can be seen as related to Modernization because it must be recognised that quite aside from the ideational or cognitive content of education, the other content of education, namely, formation of skills, attitudes and values is largely a consequence of the method or pattern of classroom and peer group interaction. The personality of children is some function of the character of their socialisation. In simplistic terms, it appears to be suggested that the bookish and purely knowledge-centred education is associated with a pre-modern society and that active methods involving other elements such as close involvement with nature, explicit emphasis on the development of skills and attitudes is associated with a modern society. The separation of traditional subjects and disciplines not only from actual concrete life but from each other is also seen as a characteristic of education in pre-modern societies. Modern societies are seen to be associated with close integration of the disciplines themselves and with problems and society outside the educational system. This statement is based largely on the Western European, and even more so, the American experience of the rise of 'progressive' education in which a greater recognition of the various capacities of the individual and their relevance to the tasks of industrial and political development was developed over centuries. However, as can be seen from the experience of the Soviet Union and, later, of China, the *pattern* of modernization has much to do with the type of educational methods which are functional to modernization. In a rapid, centrally planned and led pattern of modernization, the traditional interactions in the school are seldom interfered with. They are, in fact, on a long term basis, however, much they may be disturbed during the period of transition, reinforced with a view to achieving certain limited objectives. Other objectives are achieved through para-educational methods.

Quite aside from this major exception, we have also to take into account the relation between educational methods and modernization, on a time scale as it were, i.e., whether modernization precedes or follows new educational methods, which may be more active or more related to society and nature outside education. Again, educational institutions and systems have an inertia of their own. They do not change automatically in a simple response to changes in society or *vice versa.* New educational content has to be internalised through existing institutions, essentially traditional in their character. The educational lag, as it were, is responsible for the co-existence of a traditional education with a modern society or the superimposition of apparently modern education on what is still an essentially traditional society. It is helpful in this connection, mainly as a heuristic device for purposes of explanation, Beeby's stages of educational development[8] in which he distinguishes the "dame school" stage, the orthodox bookish stage, the transitional and the progressive stage. The methods of education appear to grow in any educational system from one to the other in this kind of a sequence. Beeby's theory tends to abstract from broader social change and its interaction with the educational system. Even if, however, we place these in the context of other social change, it appears likely that a certain amount of validity would still be possible for this sequence.

Religion, State and Education

The relations of education to the State have also undergone a similar change as between traditional and modern societies. The modern State is, indeed, increasingly intervening in the development of national educational systems though one could see that there are very considerable variations as between different modern states depending on specific historical circumstances and ideology. Particularly, it is to be noticed about societies which modernised relatively late that the state undertook steps forward rapid modernization. National societies which had been dominated by foreign powers felt the need to develop a national identity through, among other means, education and had often made available to them a nucleus of state apparatus and a vestige of a statist tradition to undertake this task. We see in such cases a close link between State and education. Though in the traditional societies in early phases, the State did not appear always directly related to education.

Religion, in one form or the other, has dominated many traditional societies. However, the degree of direct relationship of education to religion has varied between them. The Hindu social order is an example of a religion without a church. There is, therefore, relatively greater possibility of education being organised by secular agencies such as local community or even the state. There have, however, also been cases in the history of Hindu Civilization where *nathas* have been run on somewhat the same lines as religious foundations in the organised religions. In Islam and in Christianity of many variants, the church has taken upon itself responsibility of teaching the young. In such cases, not only the content of education but also the administration of formal education has been in the hands of religion. In contrast to this, in the modern society, the state or the non-religious communities take up greater role in education. Indeed, the development of autonomous and largely a religious intelligentsia—connected or unconnected with the productive system of industrial society, has taken on the responsibility for governing education. The idea of university autonomy which in an earlier day was intended to protect the religious foundations from the intrusion of the state has now become the institution through which independent modern intelligentsia has the possibility of developing knowledge as an autonomous institution. Certainly, with the financing of higher education coming to the state—and industry in many cases—they would be playing a leading and intimate role. In this, the modern society distinguishes itself from the traditional quite clearly.

Transition from Traditional to Modern Education

The transition from traditional education to education more suited to modern society is likely to take very different paths in different societies. It must, for instance, be accepted that *educational institutions have an inertia*[9] *of their own* and their form, e.g., examinations, methods of teaching, the nature of teachers' authority, etc., change over a very long period of time if they do so at all. This means that modern content have often to be put into traditional institutions such as the older methods of teaching or examination. As, however, the non-cognitive content of education namely, attitudes, skills and values are intimately related to the nature of pupil-teacher interaction and the character of authority experienced by the student, it appears imperative that the forms of educational institutions will have to undergo a change under the pressure of the needs of modernization. This is precisely what we may be witnessing in the twentieth century in the universities of the developed world. However, many societies have attempted other solutions or compromises. Thus, in the Soviet Union, among others, the development of para-educational organisations such as the Komsomol and the pioneer clubs have provided for socialisation and skill development in directions different from that of the formal classroom. The moderniser of education, thus, has the possibility for using institutions other than the established formal education for achieving modern educational goals. In the period of transition from tradition to modernization, this becomes necessary where the resources, efforts and will devoted to the change of education are inadequate for coping with inertia in the established education. The American solution to these problems has, of course, been a straight-forward and simple one, namely, of modifying the formal content and requirements of the school system itself in order to incorporate the new knowledge and skill contents. The American development is, however, in many ways an exceptional one in as much as entirely new society was being created on a continent with an open frontier, in a period in which vast technical modernization was also being developed internally by the society. This situation is not open to many traditional societies modernising today. Practical solutions may arise from *institutionalising* the modernizing functions *vis-à-vis* the educational system. This presents two sets or problems, viz., (*a*) the creation of research and development institutions or other innovating, modernising agencies and arranging for the dissemination of their contribution within the educational system; and (*b*) the institutional arrangements for linking modern and contemporary events or phenomenon with the educational system itself.

Conclusion

As we examine the whole problem of relation of education to

modernization, we are confronted with two major difficulties. The first is, of course, the wooliness of the concept itself. There is no satisfactory statement on modernization which can be used as a reference point. The second problem relates to other areas of our concern. Are we essentially analysts seeking to establish relations between cause and effect as they have already occurred? Or are we actors in the process of social engineering where we seek to derive policy directives? Is our exercise primarily a scientific or normative one?

As we get into the domain of policy formulation we have to clarify the basic assumptions regarding the type of modernization process we are choosing. If it is of the nature of cultural diffusion, in gradualist frame, the solutions would be quite different from those that we choose, if basic changes largely at the level of politics and social structure were envisaged.

Notes

1. C.A. Anderson, "Impact of Education on Technical Change" in B.F. Hoselitz and W.C. Moore (eds.), *Industrialisation and Society*, Mouton & Co. and UNESCO, 1963.
2. David Riesman, "The Academic Procession" in Anderson Flood, and Halsey (eds.) *Education, Economy and Society* (Glencoe, Free Press, 1961).
3. S. Shukla, "Educational Administration for Innovation and Change" in *Education Quarterly*, November 1967 (Delhi, Ministry of Education).
4. Bert F. Hoselitz, *Sociology of Economic Development*, (Glencoe, Free Press, 1962).
5. See for instance, P.C. Joshi, "Literacy and Education in Rural India" (Ajmer, Educational Trends, July 1967) or in *Bhartiya Gram Sansthanik Parivartan aur Arthic Vikas*, (Delhi Raj Kamal, 1966), S. Shukla, *Towards an Educational Policy* (*Political and Economic Weekly*, 29th July, 1967) as also the evidence in Second All India Educational Survey (Delhi, National Council Educational Research and Training, 1967).
6. S. Shukla, "*Educational Development in British India*" (Unpublished doctoral thesis, Delhi 1958).
7. Myers, *Education in the Perspective of History* (Longmans, 1963).
8. C.E. Beeby, *The Quarterly of Education in Developing Countries* (Harvard, ed. 1965).
9. S. Shukla, "Educational Techniques and Educational Planning" in *Educational Sciences—An International Journal*, Oct., 1967 (Oxford).

9

Education as Potent Instrument of Modernization

S.C. DUBE

The complex processes of modernization assume a series of interpenetrating and interdependent transformations. On the level of personality, it is now widely recognised, they envisage characterological changes resulting in the promotion of rationality, empathy, mobility, and high participation. These attributes of modernised personality are promoted and sustained by and, in their turn, they also promote and sustain—institutional and value change on the social and cultural levels. The social and cultural milieu, thus increasingly acquires achievemental, universalistic, and specificity-oriented emphasis. It accepts and produces more innovations, builds up association capability, and sharpens its problem-solving abilities. Absence of fit between the modernised personality and the social/cultural framework would lead to an uncomfortable imbalance. For this reason harmonisation and interlinking of the changes in the personality, the cultural and the social systems is essential. In the context of modernization, these transformations must be viewed as a precondition to the growth of complex organisations that can adequately and effectively exploit and manipulate energy from inanimate sources for human well-being and prosperity.

Three assumptions are basic to this conception of modernization:

1. Inanimate sources of power must be tapped increasingly to solve human problems and to ensure a minimal acceptable standard of living the ceiling of which is progressively rising;
2. This can be done best by collective rather than individual effort—associational capability to operate through increasingly complex organisations, thus, is a prerequisite to at least the middle and higher reaches of modernization; and
3. Such complex organisations cannot be created and run without radical personality change and attendant changes in the social structure and the cultural fabric.

No technique is known to achieve an instant switch from the stone axe to the steam engine. Man's technological progress has been slow and tortuous—some groups progressed more because of their propitious ecological, cultural, and motivational settings, others could first assimilate and adopt the new technology only in limited doses and later made efforts to develop it independently, while still others could accept only its products without being able to master the intricacies of its organisation and techniques. The last category, now an aspirant to a modernised status, constitutes two-thirds of mankind. Far from their being able to take the road to creative innovation, many of these societies are not ready yet even for transfer or adaptation of modern technology. This is accounted for partly by their attitudinal and institutional inadequacies, and partly also by a lack of associational capability in them. They have the desire to enjoy the fruits of modernization, but their institutional-organisational and ideological-motivational framework is not ready yet to adopt modern technology on a large scale. They lack also the infrastructure to adapt foreign technology to their peculiar needs and to innovate in the modern style to meet the challenge of the revolution of rising expectations.

A bound strategy for modernization would appear to include:

1. Directed change in the system of attitudes, beliefs, and values, and also in the institutional complex to enhance the acceptability of modern technology and its organisational and operational framework;
2. Growth of the infrastructure essential to the adaptation

of technology of foreign origin to specific national needs; and

3. Laying the foundation of institutions and organisations which could, in time, assume responsibility for independent innovation and technological growth relevant to the country's needs and problems.

Undeniably, education can be a most potent instrument of modernization. Directly it seeks to promote knowledge and to develop skills, both essential for the furtherance of the goals of modernization. At the same time some of its indirect consequences, such as value and attitude change, are also not without significance. The priority accorded to education in programmes of modernization, thus, is not misplaced: how effectively it is organised and how well it is directed is a different matter.

Some of the ways in which education is functional to the programmes of modernization can now be highlighted thus:

1. By enlarging the cognitive map of those exposed to it, education suggests alternatives to tradition, brings into focus the rewards implicit in them, and indicates—roughly at least—the paths through which the new goals with their attendant rewards can be achieved. It broadens mental horizons, raises expectations, and predisposes people to make experiments.
2. As an instrument of socialisation it can project new images and values. Purposively used, it can be a help in obliterating attitudes and behaviour patterns that are dysfunctional to programmes of modernization.
3. By providing ideological articulation, it can promote development of nationness and help people see their needs and problems in a national perspective. This can stimulate creation of a national consensus at least on major issues.
4. Education provides a highway to elite status. It is not the only source through which personnel to the elite ranks are recruited, but there is perhaps no developing society which does not confer a special status on the educated. The educated provide a reference model to the masses, who, in imitation of the former, take the first steps away from tradition. Modernising elites are almost always the

products of modern or semi-modern school/university systems.

5. Problems-solving leadership—scientists and technicians, management experts and administrators—with requisite knowledge and skills can only be expected to emerge out of the educational system. Large-scale programmes of Modernization demand specialists of several types at different levels, and look to the educational system for a steady flow of technocrats, planners, and managers to operate them.
6. Education is a mobility multiplier. Although its initial impact is on the immobility of thought-ways, in the long run it does alter rigid forms of social stratification. Modernization requires both types of mobility.

In sum, with proper planning and efficient direction education can make a meaningful contribution to the attainment of modernization. It can be harnessed to diffuse attitudes and ideologies required for the adoption of modern technology and its associated values and organisational premises, to provide the personnel to operate and sustain the programmes of modernization, and to create capabilities for adaptation and origination of new technology.

But education is only an instrument, and an instrument, in the final analysis, is only as good as the person wielding it. The efficacy of education as an instrument of modernization would depend largely on its orientation and content as well as on those who impart and receive it. In fact, it is a two-edged weapon—it can serve the aims of the traditionalists as well as the modernisers. Under certain conditions, by generating stresses and strains it may even produce anomic disturbances that are difficult to control and that obstruct ordered movement towards modernization. Therefore, it would be useful to bear in mind some of its dysfunctional aspects also.

1. By enlarging the cognitive map education redefines and resets cultural goals. Up to a point this is necessary and is functional. But cultural goals must bear some relationship to institutional means. Education often becomes dysfunctional when it sets cultural goals way beyond the

institutional means of a society. Inadequacy of the institutional set-up results in anger and frustration, and later in defiance and destruction.

2. While education can project new images and help inculcation of new values, it can also be turned into an instrument for the perpetuation of certain traditional values that run counter to the objectives of modernization. Education does not produce only modernizers, it produces traditionalists also. And some of these traditionists-by-choice are incomparably more articulate and sophisticated than those who may be called "traditionalists who know nothing different". Several types of traditionists can be identified:
   (*i*) Those with whom tradition is a habit of mind because they know nothing better or even different, and whose naive and simplistic traditionalism stands apart as a category by itself.
   (*ii*) Those with a highly selective perception, who identify their culture with its past high achievement in particular fields, ignoring harsh and inconvenient empirical realities both ancient and contemporary.
   (*iii*) The cultural narcissists with unbounded and undiscriminating nostalgia for the past, who find in tradition a compensation for what the society lacks (or is denied) today.
   (*iv*) Those with whom traditionalism is a pose, a mask and a carefully cultivated style, and who only want to stand out from the rest. This category includes also those to whom traditionalism is a convenient political gimmick.
   (*v*) Those who have a vested interest in tradition and who remain attached to it because of its short-term pay-off.
   (*vi*) Pragmatic traditionalists, who are afraid of the uncertainties of modernization and associate it with some of the ills of the contemporary world.

   Traditionalists of the last five categories can easily superimpose their value-attitude systems on education. For political reasons they may even consciously feed the irrational beliefs of the first category. Education, thus, may be promoting conflicting goals.

3. Because of simultaneous operation of push and pull factors in education both centrifugal and centripetal forces may be promoted at the same time. Ideological contradictions in the content of education may weaken nationness and consensus by lending at least partial support to parochialism.
4. Education is undeniably an avenue to status, but when it fails to maintain proper want-get ratio it also results in status denial to many who feel entitled and qualified for it. It may create status aspirations that do not take account of the society's needs and the aspirants' talents and abilities.
5. The foreign models and idiom of education often produce academic and scientific styles that fail to see problems in the perspective of national needs. International styles—including current fashions and even fads—are blindly imitated even though their relevance to national problems is obviously doubtful or patently useless. Intellectual activity thus runs into the danger of degenerating into barren exercises in futility. Problem-solving objectives get blurred and blunted.
6. Vested interests may often seek to utilise education to maintain and sustain traditional forms of stratification. In many cases, it may actually widen the gap between classes and between categories.
7. When education gets to be viewed as an end in itself rather than as means to certain objectives, it becomes an article of consumption and the costs involved in it are considerable. The scarce resources invested into it could be more meaningfully utilised in other sectors of economic growth.
8. Management of the educational explosion is often difficult. The stresses and strains built into the system result in the production of highly volatile and inflammable material that adds to the corpus of problems rather than contribute to their solution.

It is, thus, evident that education, with inept handling, can put societies in reverse motion. The dangers to be guarded against most are—education becoming an instrument of traditionalism, education raising hopes and aspirations whose fulfilment is not immediately feasible and practical *vs.* some education attaining aims and purposes unrelated to modernization and often pulling in an opposite direction, and education creating pervasive discontent and anomic conditions retarding the progress towards modernization.

Strategies of educational planning for modernization are beset with several unresolved dilemmas—national need *vs.* social justice or expanded opportunity, quality *vs.* quality, strategic and selective planning *vs.* operation of market laws of demand and supply, *good* education for some *vs.* some education for all, and consumption-orientation *vs.* production-orientation in education. All too often scarce resources are thinly spread, development of needed skills is subordinated to the requirements of diffused consumption-type education dictated by popular pressure, and substandard teachers working in substandard institutions turn out substandard products. The full potential of education for modernization, thus, is rarely exploited in a full measure. Unless these dilemmas are satisfactorily resolved, it is doubtful if education can make its proper contribution to modernization. It needs focus, direction, and above all relevance.

10

Educated Youths as Promoters of Modernization

Y.B. DAMLE

It is not surprising that the new nations and old societies, such as India, are trying to modernise. Moreover, it is felt that one of the important instruments of modernization would be education. Apart from the glorious scholastic tradition in India in the past, there has been great amount of contribution made by highly educated persons in the task of attaining national independence. Under the stewardship of the late Prime Minister, Pt. Jawaharlal Nehru, India decided upon the path of secularism, rationalism, scientific progress, technological development, etc. In short, there was a quest for modernization and it was also tacitly believed that the process of modernization could be furthered only through advancement of higher education, scientific advancement, industrial and technological revolution, etc. Almost an unquestioning acceptance was accorded to the relationship between education and modernization. As a logical extension of the same premise, it was further felt that if the youth of the country were to receive higher education and advanced training, the process of modernization would be both facilitated and expedited. These premises are written large on the various measures devised to promote higher education and provide facilities for scientific and industrial progress as well as technological development of the country. The proliferation of institutes of learning and research testify to this quest. Moreover, the facilities provided for higher education irrespective of considerations of income and tradition were expected to unleash social change and promote modernization by throwing open facilities of advancement to anyone who could benefit from it. It has to be remembered that this aspiration has not been fulfilled to a sufficient degree to warrant the kind of social change expected, in the sense that even now higher education tends to be more of a privilege.

Another premise which is not explicitly made clear is that education is conceived as an ideal type in the Weberian sense. The role of education tends to be exaggerated and the structural limitations and impediments often tend to be ignored. Thus, it is tacitly assumed that education would promote social mobility and facilitate modernization of the social structure. Moreover, the content of education, the methods of education, the examination system, etc., were expected to undergo a change automatically to suit the demands of modernization. Similarly, teachers were expected to be perfectly proficient and ready to impart education so as to promote rationality, inculcate spirit of enquiry amongst students, as well as to promote autonomy amongst them. Likewise, the recipients of education were also expected to be serious minded in addition to being intelligent and to be dedicated to learning. The purposiveness of education and knowledge was also taken for granted and scant attention was paid to reality which reflects divergence between knowledge and utility. It was felt that knowledge would be automatically used, thereby ignoring the traditional cultural value in this respect. One of the basic assumptions for appointing the Education Commission in 1965 was to emphasize the role of education as a promoter of modernization. It is one thing to make such an assumption and it is quite another to be aware of the structural framework under which such an assumption is least likely to be realised. It was mentioned earlier that education has been conceived as an ideal type without paying due attention to the realities of the situation. Thus, the nature and the quality of education, the competence of teachers not to mention their dedication, the devotion of students and the autonomy of the educational system as well as its purposiveness, etc., seem to have been taken for granted. In the same line, it is assumed that education would promote new attitudes and values congruent with a modern society and thereby promote modernization in the country. All these assumptions fail to take into account the features of Indian culture as well as those of social structure in the country. Education cannot be conceived as an autonomous or a self-contained entity, but has to be viewed in the context of the social structural characteristics and features as exemplified by social institutions like family and kinship, caste, religion, regionalism, etc. Another situation which might queer the pitch would be the differential preparedness and receptivity to education on the part of the new entrants into education. Education could even retard the process of modernization by fostering sectarian loyalties. It is necessary to be very clear about the aims of education and perhaps even more clear about the possibilities of realising such aims. What are the circumstances which are congenial for the realisation of such aims needs to be properly understood. Before spelling out either the aims of education and examining the prospects of education as promoter of modernization, it would be useful to enquire into the nature of modernization which is attempted below.

Characteristics and Prerequisites of Modernization

It is customary to equate modernization with industrialism and economic development. Similarly, scientific and technological development is also interpreted as modernization. Sociologically speaking, however, modernization has to be analysed and understood at three different levels, viz., social system, cultural system and personality system. In this article, it is intended to spell out the characteristics and implications of modernization at these different levels and also to examine whether or not these different characteristics are present in the Indian situation.

SOCIAL SYSTEM

Structural Differentiation

Even before defining modernization, it is necessary to mention the importance of infrastructure for modernization. The infrastructure is composed of an institutional complex and arrangements. It would mean a structural arrangement so that the various aspects of modernization would be facilitated. One of the important criteria of providing the requisite infrastructure for modernization is thought to be structural differentiation.[1] Structural differentiation enables the various sub-system, of society such as economy, polity, pattern maintenance institutions and integrative institutions to function in a more or less independent manner. This is not to suggest that sub-systems work in isolation but only to emphasize that they have evolved to such an extent that a good measure of autonomy can be enjoyed by them. Without such an autonomy which is contingent on development modernization would not be feasible. The relative primary and independence of the sub-systems as envisaged in terms of structural differentiation cannot be said to exist in the Indian situation. In the absence of the relative primacy and autonomy of the various sub-systems in India, the freedom of evolving and development of the various sub-systems is hindered, which in its turn thwarts the process of modernization.

Definition of Modernization

There is a variety of definitions of modernization. However, for purposes of this article it is intended to confine the discussion to a couple of definitions which have been offered by David Apter and Myron Weaner. Of course, while confining ourselves to these two definitions we would be drawing freely on the analysis of modernization as given by Wilbert Moore, Edward Shils, Joseph J. Spengler, *et al.* "At a minimum, modernization means that two conditions are present, neither of which is limited to industrial societies—a social system that can constantly innovate without falling apart, including innovation beliefs about the acceptability of change and, as well, social structures so differentiated as not to be inflexible; and second, a social framework that can provide the skills and knowledge necessary for living in a technologically advanced world, including the ability to communicate in terms of the technology."[2] This definition takes note of both the process of modernization and some of its structural requisites. Apter further observes that "a political religion that can universalize values linked to the widespread desire for better material conditions stimulates modernization by raising material and mundane ends to the level of the sacred."[3] Although this has implications for cultural values it is nevertheless important for the social system in the sense that social systems are upheld by fundamental values.

It is only when an instrumental value is legitimised by cultural value that it can become a part and parcel of human activity. Weiner lays down the essential structural characteristics of modernization as follows: "(1) the scope of government is greater in a 'modern' than in a 'traditional' model that there is a wide range of functions performed which affect the individual citizen; (2) the wider range of activities pursued in a modern state requires a highly developed two-way network of communications between the citizen and the government; (3) secondary associations play a more prominent role in the modern state, and personal, primary groupings and predominant in the traditional state; (4) the legitimacy of authority tends to be sacred in a traditional state, but legal in a modern one; (5) the bureaucracy of a modern state is task-oriented, recruits on the basis of skills, and is subservient to a policy-making elite, while in a traditional model the bureaucracy maintains existing structures, recruits on a particularistic basis and draws no line between policy and administration; (6) traditional politics concern office-holding almost exclusively, while in the modern society greater attention is paid to public policy; and finally (7) the citizens of a modern society have a sense of attachment to the nation as a whole, while in traditional societies ties to kin, caste, and tribe predominate."[4] Apter thus pinpoints attention to structural differentiation and flexibility of social system as well as to the importance of education in respect of providing the necessary skills and knowledge so that the adaptive primacy can be properly taken care of. Moreover, the process of modernization and the underlying lack of finality is also emphasized. Weiner points out the ever increasing scope of government activity in a modern society. He further observes that a highly developed communication network is essential between the citizen and the government. Further, the importance of secondary associations is emphasized. Authority is legal-rational rather than traditional or charismatic. The bureaucracy should be task-oriented and must recruit on the basis of skills. Similarly, in modern society, political must be geared to public policy and should limit itself only to office-holding. There should also be an attachment to the nation as a whole on the part of the citizens. The involvement of the citizens as a whole has been emphasized by Karl Deutsch in his concept of social mobilisation as an essential prerequisite of modernization.

Without asserting that the two sets of definitions of modernization quoted above are the only comprehensive definitions, it can be said that these definitions provide sufficient indicators to adjudge any society from the point of view of modernization. If these indicators are tested in case of India, it is found that the Indian society does not satisfy some of the major canons of modernization. It has already been mentioned that the nature of structural differentiation is not sufficiently advanced. Further, the structural flexibility is also not adequate. There is, no doubt, that there has been development of skill and knowledge in India, although such development cannot cope with the ever-rising problems and situations. There is a proliferation of governmental activity in India. Yet the two way network of communication between the citizens and the government has not developed adequately, not to say that it does not exist at certain levels. Even now the role played by the primary associations like family, kind and caste seems to outweigh the role played by the secondary associations. It is true that legal authority has been established in India, simultaneously there also exists a great deal of both traditional and charismatic authority. The bureaucracy in India seems to be status ridden which partially accounts for its ineffectiveness. Moreover, the recruitment is also not always on the basis of skills. Politics seems to be largely concerned with office holding which is exemplified by the crossing of the floor and political defection as well as the craze for *villy-nilly* holding on to political power. Likewise, the attachment to the nation as a whole on the part of the citizens to be woefully wanting which is characterised by the regional and linguistic squabbles and rivalries.[5] The particularistic loyalties rather than the universalities seem to dominate.

Integrative Revolution

A modern society would be characterised by integration of its discrete units. The various units might be based on regional and cultural differences. Yet the process of modernization would necessarily mean a welding of such units into a composite system. To the extent that the units remain discrete and are not welded, it can be said that the process of modernization would necessarily mean a welding of such units into a composite system. The extent that the units remain discrete and are not welded, it can be said that the process of modernization has been far from satisfactorily completed. It was mentioned earlier that in the Indian context the fissiparous tendencies as exemplified by the regional and linguistic controversies only confirm that the process of modernization has not sufficiently advanced. Similarly, modernization means a proper coordination and relationship between the Centre and Periphery. As Shils[6] observes, "Modern society entails the inclusion of the mass of the population into the society in the sense that both elite and mass regard themselves as members of the society and, as such, as of approximately equal dignity. It involves a greater participation by the masses in the values of society, a more active role of the making of society-wide decisions, and a greater prominence in the consideration of the elite." In the Indian context, it is very clear that the relationship between the Centre and Periphery has been far from well adjusted. Even the relationship between the Union Government and the various State Governments has been far from satisfactory.

Institutional Framework

Modernization necessitates an institutional framework which would be at once flexible and efficient. In the first place, there must be political order and stability which should not be easily disturbed for one reason or another. As observed earlier, modernization must become acceptable to the people through political processes. The elites naturally would play an important role in the furtherance of modernization. It has to be remembered all the same that the elites must not be alienated from the masses of the people. Rather the elites must maintain cultural continuity so that they can work as effective carriers and leaders of the process of modernization. A high degree of urbanisation is also an essential requisite of modernization since it spells mobility and migration. A refashioning of the modes of stratification has also to take place. For instance, stratification should be increasingly based on achievement rather than ascription. Social change should be organised, institutionalised. Work should be organised along rational lines instead of conforming to the traditional patterns. There should be a multiplication of new forms of voluntary associations. It would also necessitate a reorganisation of the family so that it would be conducive to autonomy and initiative. The entire educational programme should be designed to inculcate new skills and knowledge as well as industrial traditions. Inter-generational mobility must be encouraged. There should be an involvement in the market matrix. A new status system should be evolved, which would also facilitate a sense of participation on the part of all members of the society.[7]

In India, it is obvious that the institutional framework is neither sufficiently flexible nor efficient. Every now and then a threat is posed to political stability and the political processes have not succeeded in transforming modernization into a creed. There is no doubt that the elites in India have been playing an important role in modernization. Yet the degree of alienation of the elite from the masses tends to persist and as such the elites have not been able to carry the masses with them. The amount of urbanisation in India has not been of high order to make sufficient impact on the people. The nature and the quality of mobility and migration in India seems to have many limitations. As for the modes of stratification, there has not been a marked change. In the organisation and institutionalisation of social change in India, the progress attained has been haphazard.[8] Even now work has not been organised along rational lines. It is true that a number of voluntary organisations have sprung up, yet such associations tend to have their moorings in groups such as family, kin, caste, region, etc. There has also not been a radical change in the family pattern in the sense that there is a dependency pattern which is far from conducive to modernization. Educational programme even now is largely academic and unrelated to the new needs of the situation. Moreover, the status system in so far as it puts premium on a white collared job may be only clerical has consequences for maintaining *status quo* in the educational programmes. It is true that through the Community Development Programmes, attempts have been made to provide a sense of participation for all. Yet the patent fact about the several limitations and failures of these programmes in respect of (*i*) participation and involvement of the people; (*ii*) inculcation of rational thought and action; (*iii*) evolving of new criteria and symbols of prestige and status; and (*iv*) reducing distance between the various strata do not warrant a great measure of optimism.[9] Even in respect of economic processes decisions are in many a case actuated by political and particularistic considerations, e.g., the establishment of steel factories, oil refineries, etc. Therefore, the requisite organisation which should be characterised by rationality has not been forthcoming.

CULTURAL SYSTEM

In order to promote modernization, the primordial sentiments and ties based on family, kin, caste, language, region, etc., need to be abandoned and universalistic orientations should be developed. There should be a cognitive primacy. Spirit of nationalism must be highly developed so that the primordial sentiments and ties would be neutralised. There should be scientific temper, slant on technological development and its use in day-to-day life. Knowledge should be essentially for use. In the wake of inculcation of rationality, scientific attitude would develop an openness of mind so that the newer modes of thinking and action would not be an anathema. In the Indian context, even now it cannot be said that the primordial sentiments and ties have been even kept in check so that they would not militate against nationalism in the present context treated as universalistic notion. Similarly, the intellectual atmosphere is not permeated by a scientific spirit and temper. Reference must be made to the observations made by Edward Shils on Indian intellectuals. Similarly, there has not been an adequate development of rationality and scientific attitude even on the part of educated persons. Faith in dogmas and stereotyped solutions and the endless prejudices have made it difficult to look for new solutions of the various problems. Both in economic and political policy as well as the management of the system of education, instances of being guided by dogmas, prejudices and fixed stances and postures are too obvious and need mention. Moreover, the phenomenon of age grades dies hard in the Indian set-up so as not to permit democratic and rational conduct of various affairs. Likewise, the value component of the hierarchy also militates against evolution and development of a new status system.

PERSONALITY SYSTEM

At the personality level, modernization would require a flexible personality. There should be latitude for choice and innovation. The process of socialisation should be so designed that it can be conducive to individuation and autonomy development.[10] It is not enough to provide education but to emphasize the freedom of thought and action. Various attributes such as rationality, individuality, achievement orientations, insistence on equality, freedom, social justice, etc., need to be present in the case of the majority of the people. Similarly, secularism also needs to be inculcated. Likewise, a high sense of discipline must be inculcated. An openness of mind and capacity and to arrive at decisions which are out of the ordinary *sine qua non* of the process of modernization.[11] Scanning the Indian scene it has to be observed that some of the most important requirements on the plane of personality do not seem to have been realised, impairing the process and pace of modernization and democracy.

Apart from the definitions discussed regarding modernization, it would be useful to bear in mind the perception of students regarding both modernization and the contribution of education towards attaining modernization. In her study of Indian students, Margaret Cormack mentions that the students conceived of modernity as (*a*) new ways of doing things, (*b*) scientific ideas, (*c*) the secular way of life, (*d*) making one's destiny, and (*e*) the western way of life. Notwithstanding the many misconceptions students had about Westernisation, the rank order which they have given to the various aspects of modernization clearly indicate the importance attached to some of the significant attributes of modernization discussed at lenth. It is significant to note that the same body of students looked upon education as the main instrument of bringing about social change.[12] This perception is further reflected in their response to the question, viz., ways in which the younger generation can lead the older. The response was that it could do so by (*a*) demonstrating modern ways, showing uselessness of tradition, (*b*) scientific rational views and achievement, (*c*) educational knowledge, (*d*) politics based on nation, on all people, (*e*) following the advanced West, (*f*) broad-mindedness, progressive ideas, (*g*) abolition of superstition, (h) creative action intelligent initiative, (*i*) refusing to recognize castes, (*j*) recognising and practising democracy, (*k*) being less religious minded, and (*l*) working hard.

Aims of Education and Requisites for Fulfilling Aims

An important aim of education has been recognised to be training or intellect and development of well-rounded personality. Similarly, successful completion of identity formation has been also recognised to be one of the important aims of education. Development of autonomy and the inculcation of spirit of inquiry, determination in action, etc., are also recognised as important aims of education. It is felt that education would promote initiative, individualism, achievement, motivation, liberalism, humanitarianism, broad mindedness, rationality, etc. In short, education is looked upon as an instrument of modernization. As mentioned earlier, modernization is a complex process and has many facets to it. In order that education fulfils its broad aim of modernization, requisite support must be forthcoming in respect of the development of personality in terms of a type of socialisation which would be conducive to autonomy development and individuation. Cultural values must also be congruent with the aims of education so that change and dynamism would be an accepted value rather than an anathema. At the social structural level, there should be the least hindrance offered to the realisation of the aims mentioned above. It is well known that education is only a social institution which is affected in various ways by other social institutions, economy, quality, prevailing cultural system etc. Education is not mere acquisition of knowledge, but means a deep conviction that action would be guided by the knowledge acquired so that every now and then all types of thought and action would be subjected to severe scrutiny. Education would mean not only sharpening of intellect but also the development of capacity to act fearlessly and without any prejudice. Education should liberate its recipients from dogmatism, narrow-mindedness, particularistic loyalties, etc.

In order to assess the role of education in promoting modernization, due attention will have to be paid to the following aspects of the student body. Youth by itself is no guarantee for rationality, freedom from prejudices and narrow mindedness, initiative, liberalism, etc. Much would depend on the kinds of socialisation the student youth has been exposed to. Therefore, it is very pertinent to enquire into the social background of the students as well as the character of the institutions of learning, methods of learning, examination system, etc. Education has to be analysed from the point of rationality which it promotes or fails to do so. The secular nature education also needs to be enquired into. Whether education promotes achievement motivation or puts a premium on philosophy of denial is also quite pertinent. It is well known that the education *per se* cannot guarantee democracy because the process of education itself may lack democratisation. It has been observed that there is paucity of democratic elements even amongst intellectuals.[13] Modernization signifies integrative revolution and means a reduction of the distance between the Centre and Periphery. How far education succeeds in bridging this distance is very crucial to note. Whether equality is accepted as a value not on the verbal plane but at the level of interaction and relationship would form an important area of enquiry. In the Indian context, age grades, castes, religion, region, sex, etc., provide some of the important foci of inequality and discrimination. In so far as students have not been able to overcome some of these basic inequalities, it has to be accepted that both the aims of education have not been realised and the process of modernization has also been frustrated. Whether rationality is looked upon as instrumented significance or it has become value which percolates all areas of one's activity also needs to be looked into. Education cannot be said to promote modernization unless it sharpens social sensitivity amongst the students. Education must be firmly linked with the occupational system so that education can prove to be useful and meaningful to those who are educated and also to the society. An enquiry into the nature of education imparted, modes and methods of imparting relationship between the teachers and the students, etc., need careful scrutiny.

In a way, it could be said that unless the major aims of education are fulfilled, it would not be possible for the youth to contribute to modernization. As for the aims of education and their being fulfilled, it would necessitate a rehauling of the educational system. The educational system comprises the content and courses of education, the teachers, the students and, of course, the evaluation system, viz., the examination system. It is needless to emphasize that much has to be done to revitalise the courses and content of education. In the Indian context, it is no exaggeration to say that in many cases, the courses and syllabi are at least outdated by 25 years. Similarly, the methods of instruction also seem to be out of tune with the present-day requirements. Too much premium is put on learning by rote. Very little attempt is made to enable students to think for themselves even at the post graduate and research level. Teachers also may either lack the required degree of competence or/and the necessary enthusiasm, not to speak of involvement and commitment to teach. Students also partly because they are not aware of the purpose of education and partly because they do not get the kind of education they would like most, seem to be passive, not to say indifferent participants in the process of education. A great deal of thought has to be given to the institutionalisation of conditions, facilities and atmosphere which would be conducive to the aims of education. This is not to suggest that there is not a silver lining to the dark cloud depicted above. Of course, there are certain institutions where by and large the aims of education are fulfilled and also where the teachers possess a high degree of competence and also have a deep sense of commitment. Similarly, there are some students who are keenly interested in education. As indicated earlier, where education promotes autonomy development and identity formation, the youth can play a major role as catalytic agents of modernization. Under such conditions youth would inculcate rationality and scientific spirit so that they would always tend to revise propositions without exception as and when necessary. This would unleash secular forces and check the forces of tradition. Autonomy development would necessarily spell individuation. Every effort would be made to put knowledge to its maximum use by exploiting scientific and technological advances. Through the generation of competence, attempts will be made to develop overall excellence in various fields—both curricular and extra-curricular. When education becomes purposive and is meaningfully linked up with the occupational structure, the educational system and occupational structure both would tend to become dynamic. Educational system would gain by such linkage since it would be called upon to deal with problems arising every now and then. Similarly, the occupational structure would be enriched since it will directly benefit from advances in knowledge by building up a feedback mechanism between the educational system and occupational structure. Initiative and innovation would receive maximum encouragement. Of course, this assumes freedom of choice of educational courses on the part of the youth as well as that of occupational career. It was indicated earlier that certain types of socialisation would be conducive to individuation. Thus, enlightened and democratic parents, the college system and the peer group can encourage autonomy development and contribute to the training and equipment of the youth so that they can promote modernization. In so far as education lifts one out of narrow mindedness, prejudices, superstitions, etc., education can really be a liberating force. Exposure to various patterns, ideas, beliefs, ideologies would necessarily ensure broadening of the mental vistas of students. There is enough evidence afforded by certain studies such as the study on college youth in Poona that given a proper type of education, the youth can be well equipped to play a major role as promoters of modernization.

The abovementioned study deals with a special group of students. It would be very interesting and instructive to enquire into the general student body.

Notes

1. See Talcott Parsons, *Structure and Process in Modern Societies* (Glencoe, III: The Free Press, 1960).
2. David E. Apter, "Political Religion in the New Nations," in C. Geertz (ed.) *Old Societies and New State* (London: The Free Press of Glencoe, 1963), p. 62.
3. *Ibid.*
4. Myron Weiner, "Political Modernization and Evolutionary Theory", in H.R. Barringer, G.I. Dlanksten and R.W. Mack (eds), *Social Change in Developing Areas* (Cambridge, Mass: Schenkman Publishing Company, 1955), pp. 104-105.
5. See Y.B. Damle, "Formation of Regional States: A Study in De-Individuation", Poona University Teachers' Social Science Seminar 7 (1963).
6. Edward Shils, "On the Comparative Study of New States", in *Old Societies and New States, op. cit.*, p. 21.
7. See Wilbert E. Moore, "The Social Framework of Economic Development", in R. Braibanti and J.J. Spengler (eds.), *Tradition, Values and Socio-Economic Development* (Durham: Durban University Press, 1961), pp. 57-82.
8. See M.C. Sekhar, *Social Change in India: Planning Period* (Poona: Deccan College, 1964) Published doctoral thesis, Deccan College, Monogram Series, M. 39, 1968.

79. See T. Isaac John, *Impact of Community Development on Rationality*, (Poona: Deccan College, 1967), A thesis submitted for Ph.D.
10. See Y. B. Damle, *College Youth in Poona: A Study of Elite in the Making*, (Poona: Deccan College, 1966) Mimeographed.
11. See Y.B, Damle, "Education and Modernization," *The Radical Humanist*, Vol. XXIX, Nos. 4-6, pp. 49-50.
12. Margaret C. Cormack, *She Who Rides A Peacock*, Bombay; Asia Publishing House, 1961, p. 157.
13. Y.B. Damle, *College Youth in Poona, op. cit.*

11

Role of Elites in Modernization

The Context of Value and Ideology

SATYENDRA TRIPATHI

[I]
THE CONCEPT OF MODERNIZATION

The study of modernization is not new. Social scientists have started to study this process since nineteenth century, when industrialisation was accelerated in the European countries. 'Modernization' as a general term describes the process of *rapid* social change and used recently for the understanding of social phenomenon. The word 'modern' denoting the quality of contemporary societies can be traced to late Latin usage of the sixth century. The word was first used in Latin and later in English and other languages to distinguish between contemporary and 'ancient' writers and themes, and by the seventeenth century 'modernity', 'modernisers' and 'modernization' were employed in a variety of more or less limited and technical contexts. Within the past generation 'modernity' has come to be rather widely employed to describe the characteristics common to countries that are more advanced in technological, political, economic and social development, and 'modernization' to describe the process by which they acquired these characteristics.

Economists understand 'modernization' primarily in terms of man's application of technologies to the control of nature's resources in order to bring about a marked increase in the growth of output per head of population. Sociologists and anthropologists have been primarily concerned with the process of differentiation that characterises modern societies. They have explored the way in which new structures arise to assume new functions once performed by other structures and they give attention to differentiation occurring within social structures as new occupations emerge, new complex educational institutions develop and new types of communities appear. Sociologists also studied the dysfunctional aspect of modernization and pointed out the resistances to the same. Political scientists have also been concerned in the remaining analysis of the disruptive features of modernization, but their attention on the problems of nation and governmental building as modernization occurs. They are also concerned how governments increase their capacity to innovate change, respond to demands for change, and cope with social conflicts.

None of the above interpretations leads us to the understanding of the term 'modernization' in a correct perspective because none is sufficiently general to encompass a 'modern' economy, society and polity. Therefore, many scholars have suggested that the starting point of any definition of modernization is not the character of the society, but in the character of individuals (Cyril Block, Arnold Anderson, Edward Shils, David McClelland and others). Some scholars have suggested that the existence of certain modern attitudes is a precondition for modernization and development, for example, D. McClelland mentioned 'mental virus' which psychologists call 'need of achievement'. Other scholars have gone further and suggested that certain traditional societies had within them the seed of modernity. Max Weber, too, has pointed out the same theme in his works. But this position has been opposed by few thinkers like Alexander Gerschenkron who pointed out that Calvinism facilitated development, but that many different value systems seem to exist in modernising societies. To support this argument one might note why Indians have been so much more productive outside their home societies than within. Moreover, values most of us would describe as 'traditional' may hasten development, depending on social context and the use to which these values are put. For example, family particularism need not be an obstacle to modernization, as recent scholarship on the development of family enterprises in modern Japan suggests.

Another view put forth by few academicians, who argue that the effort to justify changes within the context of tradition is itself dysfunctional to change and that a policy of rejecting one's tradition is a more efficacious way of creating in individuals a readiness to change. Revolutionary regimes and societies often take this view and try to replace the present social structure by a new one having its own social system.

Although there are differences among the social scientists as to how values and attitudes can be changed, one school of thought believes that attitudinal and value changes are prerequisites to creating a modern society economy and political system. Other school thinks that the appropriate attitudes, and more importantly, the appropriate behaviour will be forthcoming, once opportunities and incentives are provided. This position finds support among the economists and political scientists.

Modernization does not imply a 'smooth' process of 'balanced' or 'equilibrated' growth. It has always been a *revolutionary* process of undermining and changing the existing institutional structure. But the possibility of successful institutionalisation of an innovating or revolutionary process is never inherent in the revolutionary act itself. It depends on other conditions, primarily the society's capacity for internal transformation.

Generally, modernization is defined "as the process by which historically evolved institutions are adopted to the rapidly changing functions that reflect the unprecedented increase in man's knowledge, permitting control over his environment, that accompanied scientific revolution. This process of adaptation had its origin in the societies of Western Europe, but in the nineteenth and twentieth centuries these changes have been extended to all other societies and have resulted in a worldwide transformation affecting all human relationships. The central problem of modernization can be seen as the ability of any system to adopt itself to these changing demands, to absorb them in terms of policy making, and to assure its own continuity in the face of continuous new demands and new forms of political organisation."

[II]
TRADITION AND MODERNIZATION

In historical perspective, the institutions undergoing this process may be called as the traditional institutions of the societies of the world. 'Traditional' and 'modern' are then, relative terms, but they are used here in a specific sense. For the society of India, the challenge of modernity to the traditional system occurred between the nineteenth and twentieth centuries. Comparable traditional periods before the challenge of modernity may be discussed in all other societies, since the challenge of modernity in the societies that modernised earliest was primarily internal, the process of transformation took place gradually over several countries. In the later modernising societies this challenge has been increasingly external, hence more rapid and even abrupt.

The relations between the traditional and the modern do not necessarily involve displacement conflict on exclusiveness. Modernity does not necessarily weaken tradition. Both tradition and modernity form the bases of ideologies and movements in which the polar opposites (tradition and modernity) are converted into aspirations, but traditional forms may supply support for, as well against, change.

There is an idea of change in contemporary new nations and economically growing societies as one which entails a linear movement from as traditional past towards a modernised future.[1] A significant assumption in this model of change is that existing institutions and values, the content of tradition, are impediments to change and are obstacles to modernization.

In any society the propensity to generate changes and also to some extent to absorb them is built into the traditional structure of modern social system. The capacity to deal with such changes effectively varies greatly among these societies. Therefore, modernization can also be looked as a non-economic process which originates when a culture embodies the attitudes of enquiry and questioning about how men make choices—moral (normative), social (structural) and personal (behavioural). The problem of choice is centred in modern man. To be modern means to see life as alternatives, preferences and choices. The self conscious choice implies rationality. Man will in principle see more than one alternative as plausible. Preferences include the ranking of priorities, and about these reasonable men may differ. Therefore, debate and discussion are characteristics of modernity due to rationality and scientific attitude of mind, and man has controlled nature by making experiment and invention which has changed man's entire outlook. Human affairs could be seen as ultimately explicable. Societies are now able to choose a direction and means of change on the basis of their own choice.

To carry this point of view about one step further, political system becomes a system of choice for a particular collectivity. Government is the mechanism for regulating choice. Different political systems will not only embody different ways of choosing but vary in their priorities. Governments will vary in the ways they regulate choice. Thus, there are systems of choice, and there are choices within the system. One of the characteristics of modernization process is that it involves both the aspects of choice —the improvement of the conditions of choice, and the selections of the most satisfactory mechanisms of choice.

[III]
ELITE AND MODERNIZATION

W.C. Smith has also pointed out that "for men to be modern involves their being aware of the situation in which they stand and the processes in which they are participants, and of the possibilities that are available to them, particularly because of science, and involves their choosing deliberately among these various possibilities—choosing in the sense of actively pursuing their freely selected goal. To be increasingly conscious, and to act in the light of that consciousness, constitutes a person or a society as modern". Therefore, modernization is a process, not a static condition.

The role of elite in modernising traditional societies can be understood in this context. The function may differ on the basis of nature, ideology and resources of the society. During modernization process they have a special role to play, for they are most inclined to respect the culture of freedom. At the same time they remain exceedingly vulnerable to an egalitarian minded public.

The term 'elite' has been used by many social scientists for the understanding of social phenomenon. Pareto had used it to refer to superiority. He had pointed out, "I mean by the elite in a society people who possess in marked degree qualities of intelligence, character, skill, capacity of whatever kind." Gaeteno Mosea in his theory of the ruling class approximated the concept of a ruling elite. For him in all societies, primitive or advanced, two distinct classes of people exist, a class that rules and a class that is ruled. Pareto and Mosea both have attempted to conceptualise the notion of elite, which by implication can be identified as having social class properties in a given nation society. Pareto is flexible enough to accommodate democratic objections by saying that elite is not a restricted self-perpetuating social class of aristocracies, but its maintenance is misused by constant recruitment and sponsorship of superior individuals from lower class. This is what he termed 'circulation of elites'.

Karl Mannheim had used the concept of elite with its relation to the ideology planning and social order. He distinguishes the following main types of elites, the organising, the intellectual, the political, the moral and the religious. His interest was in finding the forces tending to destroy the reality and the prestige of the elite groups. Surprisingly, Mannheim's elite do not interact with the masses directly; but there are mediating social structures between the two groups. He noted, values will differ according to membership in specific sub-groups within a society. There are structurally necessary causes for the special importance which values and value oriented behaviour have for the elites in a society.

A more contemporary usage proposed by the anthropologist S.F. Nadel (in discussing the concept of social elites in the developing areas of Africa) is that an elite is "a stratum of the population which, for whatever reason, can claim a position of superiority, hence a corresponding measure of influence over the fate of the community". When we utilise the concept of elite as Nadel has here defined (rather than as Pareto and other political scientists have done), we immediately see its significance in societies which are either experiencing modern change or are in the process of modernization and development. In a situation of development, great emphasis must be placed on new skills and techniques, and as Nadel notes, "this may mean changes in the whole nation of social superiority, and conceivably the emergence of new elites". The relationship between the old, established and the new emerging elites will always be ambivalent one—at best. When the old elite itself has only very recently moved into first class citizenship following a period of colonial subservience, one can expect even greater intergenerational conflict.

The elite sets standards for the whole society, its influence or power being that of a model accepted and considered worth following. It is in this sense that any established elite has the power to facilitate or hinder new developments and generally, to make new ideas acceptable to the group at large. The elites then communicate values, by enacting them, by demonstration of all that is good or desired or worth being.

The role of elites in modernising autocracy can be understood with the framework of the ideology of state. Their roles differ on the basis of the nature of society—from 'Secular-libertarian model' to 'sacred collectivity model'. Behaviourally, the secular libertarian model consists of units that possess two capacities—the ability to reason and the ability to know self-interest. Structurally, the system must allow maximum opportunity for the exercise of rationality and the pursuit of self-interest. Hence, the emphasis is on a framework that will prevent coercion and provide limited government. Normatively, such a system takes certain fundamental properties as given.

On the other hand, 'sacred collectivity model' contains three elements. Behaviourally, it is made up of units whose singular characteristic is potentiality. Individuals, for example, are perceived as nothing more than potentials. Structurally, the political community is the means of translating potentiality into some sort of reality. Hence, the society is the key to social life. Normatively, the sacred collectivity is an ethical or moral unit. Thus, the morality of the system, which embodies those higher purposes that may be enshrined in kinship, political ideals and so on. This model stresses the unity of the people, not their diversity. It depends less on the free flow of ideas than on the disciplined concentration upon certain political and economic objectives. It claims a 'higher' form of morality, because social life is directed towards the benefit of the collectivity rather than towards that of the self.

Between these polarities there may be many societies which may be having the characteristics of both the models. In secular model, which has also been called reconciliation systems, given values and purposes generate legitimate authority. Conflicts between individuals and groups trying to realise those accepted values give rise to governmental polity. Polity thus reinforces values. In sacred model which is also called mobilisation systems, new values are being created. This means that political elites are trying to work out a moral system of authority. In between these types are some interesting combinations—modernising autocracy, military oligarchy and neo-mercantilist society.[2]

Many mobilisation systems turn into neomercantilist societies in practice, particularly when they employ traditionalist ideologies in an attempt to ritualise authority and change charismatic leadership into a more institutional form.

The most direct impact of modernization on traditional societies is in the formation of new roles associated with the modernising process. Some of the new roles, however, may be only partially new, and outside the context of either accommodationist or traditional roles. As modernization proceeds the hierarchy of power and prestige must be broad enough to encompass traditional, accommodationist, and new roles or a new hierarchy will replace it.

In modernising societies, three types of roles indicated above are to be found in three types of stratification systems—caste, class and status, which often exist side by side. In a society that is modernising, the combination of role type and stratification type produces a situation in which the innovators in the system are status conscious, engaged in role testing and future oriented.

Theoretically, the relationship between role and stratification can be shown in the following way:

Role Type	Stratification Type		
	Caste A	Class B	Status C
1. Traditionalist	A_1	B_1	C_1
2. Accommodationalist	A_2	B_2	C_2
3. Innovator	A_3	B_3	C_3

The combination and permutation of role sets and types of stratification produces some interesting problem for government and can also point out the speed of change. If the combination of A_1 and A_2 takes place by isolating A_3, society will be nearer to the mobilisation system. When A_2 and A_3 combine together, society will direct the changes to reconciliation system. This is also true for the elites of any society. Now let us examine this relationship in the context of India.

[IV]
ROLE OF ELITES IN MODERNIZATION IN INDIA

The Indian society of contact and change consists of three distinct orders of cultural reality—the traditional or conservative Indian, the westernized Indian, and that of Indians in transition. Each of these orders is subject to a specific determinism of its own. At the same time, all three orders or phases are related to or dependent on each other. The impact and initiative come from the organised forces of western educated persons. They are directed into the largely passive rural and tribal resources which respond to contact with adaptation or conflict. This process of reaction, positive or negative—the interaction between traditionalist and westernised covers the field of contact and change between these two boundaries, and there lies the no man's land of change. This is not a narrow strip but really embraces most of what is going on in India.

The western educated elites contribute the initiative and driving force. They largely determine the form of the new cultural realities, and to a certain extent they still control the process of change. They want to modernise the Indian society by changing their own institution of age-long historical growth on the western pattern. But they have not realised that once a change is set going, it acquires a momentum of its own; becomes a process and reality and processes a cultural determinism which is neither Indian nor western but a synthesis.

In ancient India, the problem of bearing of the quality of the population upon social life and change was analysed. According to the Brahmanical theory, in each spiritual age, we can recognise three prominent types of men. There is first mob of those who are pre-occupied with the thought of 'I' and 'Mine' whose objective is self-assertion, but are restrained on the one hand by the fear of retaliation, death or punishment, and on the other by the beginnings of love of family and love of country. These in the main are the 'Devoures' of Blake, the 'Slaves' of Nietzsche. Next there is a smaller, but still larger number of thoughtful and good men whose behaviour is largely determined by a sense of duty, but whose inner life is still the field of conflict between the old and the new Man. Men of this type are actuated on the one hand by the love of power, fame and ambition, more or less noble and on the other disinterested love of mankind. But this type is rarely pan-human, and its outlook is often simultaneously unselfish and narrow. In times of great stress, the men of this type reveal their true nature showing to what extent they have advanced. Finally, there is a much smaller number of great men-heroes, 'Saviours', 'Saints' and *'Avtars'* who have definitely passed the period of greatest stress and have attained peace, or at least have attained occasional and unmistakable vision of life as a whole. These are 'Prolific' of Blake, the 'Master' of Nietzsche, the true Brahman in their own right and partake the nature of superman. Their activity is determined by their love and wisdom and not by rules. In the world, but not of it, they are the flowers of humanity, our leaders and teachers (Coomaraswamy, *'Dance of Shiva'*).

In India, the whole population can be classified on the basis of the characteristics of the individuals as shown below. The most of the Indian population and even leadership is also from second to third category. Indian society can only be modern when it possesses the individuals of third category.

Characteristics of the Individuals

In the study of Indian society, it would seem that it is largely through changed position in the social structure that individuals incorporate value changes and learn new patterns of cultural behaviour. It is also true that individuals will sometimes incorporate new values in anticipation of attaining a different or better place in either the existing social structure or in an anticipated structure. If we see the history of nineteenth century India, it would be clear that the value of some individuals, and of certain social classes, changed as they became members of a new Western educated elite.

It has been in the cities that much of the training for new roles in the elites has taken place. Urban society of necessity began to emphasize achievement in the beginning of twentieth century. However, it should be noted that this achievement was almost entirely limited to persons within specific traditional status groups, particularly the higher castes of Hindu society. In this way, the close correlation of wealth position and caste was carried into the modern period. It is very recently that the doors of opportunity have been officially open to the majority of Indians.

One phenomenon which has gained the attention of sociologists in India is that process is identified as 'Sanskritisation'. Although this process of lower caste groups within Hinduism emulating the Brahmanical way of life reaches into antiquity, it was the "Status-disequilibrium" brought about by economic change in the late nineteenth century which increased the tempo of changes of this sort. Through Sanskritisation lower caste groups having achieved economic progress could hope to establish a somewhat higher position in the ritual and social hierarchy.

At the same time Srinivas discusses, under the term 'Westernisation', the process by which the traditional elites of Indian society adopted modern or western values. In the contemporary period, we see a remnant of orthodox values being learned by certain lower segments of the social hierarchy and an increasing incorporation of modern values by the upper classes. There are certain indicators, however, that a fusion is taking place and that a standard mass culture of modernism is emerging in India. McKim Marriott and Bernard Cohen have discussed in two significant papers the process by which the orthodox and modern values are transmitted through Indian culture. The modern system of communicating cultural values is changing dramatically with the rapid spread of new media, mass education and conscious governmental efforts to propagate a new, modern and pan-Indian culture.

A synthesis of Indian and foreign-inspired values emerged in an important segment of the Congress Party led Independence movement, perhaps best epitomised by Mahatma Gandhi. The "brown Englishman" with their imitation of British styles, etc., were repudiated and a self-consciously created modern image was espoused. To a great extent classes of Indians who had favoured positions in the military and administrative elites, stood apart from the Indianisation process. At the most extreme point these were the "culture-traitors" mercilessly ridiculed by the mainstream. The values of Indianised synthesis included a revitalisation of the traditional Hindu values, injected with egalitarianism, and Western liberal ideology, yet often with a strong revivalist colouring. The post-independence elites are a further amalgam of the Anglicised elites of the past—the senior civil servants, and now elderly British identified interests—plus a greatly expanded sector of the Indianised synthesis.

The most important point here is that positions of leadership in the various sectors of society were taken by men who had often spent most of their lives in positions of subservience to colonial officers. The case with which legitimatised elites played roles of authority and the style of authority role playing depended a great deal upon which pre-Independence tradition they represented. At any rate there is a strong probability that at least a good part of the difficulty in the contemporary university is that authority roles themselves have been debased, questioned and ambivalently played by the "elder generation".

Nationalism is deeply committed to both horns of the dilemma of "tradition and modernity". The effort to define a national heritage in the form of a set of continuing traditions is also a way of coping with the wide gap that separates elite and mass, city and village, region and region in Indian context. It is a compliment to the modernising processes which are involved in the aspiration towards a unified nation. To be modern appears in many new nations, as an aspiration towards which certain groups seek to move the society. 'Modern' becomes a perceived state of things functioning as a criterion against which to judge specific actions and a programme of actions to guide policy.

The desire to be modern and the desire to preserve tradition operate as significant movements in the new nations and developing economies. It is our basic point here that these desires, functioning as ideologies are not always in conflict, that the quest for modernity depends upon and often finds support in the ideological upsurge of traditionalism. In this process tradition may be changed, stretched and modified.

The very process of political egalitarianism and modernization contains the seeds of new ideologies of tradition. Literacy in India not only stimulates a common cultural content but has also led to ideologies of regionalism, extolling the virtues of regional languages and cultures. While such movements impede the development of an all-India cultural consensus, they are neither anti-modern nor specifically anti-India. They do, however, presage the decline of that form of national elite that has been associated with colonial cultural influences. India appears to be approaching and entering a phase in which modernization will be directed and implemented by persons whose loyalties and ideologies are considerably more traditionalised than has been true in the past decades.

[V]
CONCLUSION

To conclude, we can say that the various 'sub-elites'—military, commercial, educational and administrative—each may and probably does have a unique constellation of values, and is a further qualification to the generalisations. Yet our most general hypothesis is that there is a continuity of value orientations from the past into the present in Indian society as in other social systems. Hence, what one might expect to develop as a result of empirical studies of values, are differential arrangements of core values according to social group. One would hope that empirical studies focusing on value of emerging elites would look at the ways in which the traditional values help to define and limit new value orientations in society.

Notes

1. There is a wide literature analysing concepts of tradition and modernity or development. Leading efforts to conceptualise these societal types are W. W. Rostov.

2. (*i*) "Modernising autocracy tends to have a traditionalistic ideology associated with a monarch or king who represents the nation. Authority remains at the top, although, in fact it may be shared through a variety of instrumentalities."

   (*ii*) "Military oligarchy has hierarchical authority and instrumental values, but a military leader takes the place of a king. The curious problem of this type is its inability to deal with politics."

   (*iii*) "Neomercantilist society is headed by a 'presidential monarch'. In order to support authority it uses a mixture of private and public enterprise in which the critical rationale of economic activities is political."

References

Alexander Gerschankren, *The Modernization of Entrepreneurship*, Voice of America.

Apter D. E., *The Politics of Modernization,* The University of Chicago Press, Chicago, 1965.

Black, C.E., *The Dynamics of Modernization,* Harper & Row, Publishers, New York, 1967.

_______, Modernization and Sustained Growth, *World Politics,* Vol. XIII, No. 4, 1964.

David C. McClelland, *The Impulse to Modernization,* Voice of America Lectures on Modernization.

David E. Apter, *Politics of Modernization,* The University of Chicago Press, London, 1965.

Gaetano Mosca, *The Ruling Class,* McGraw Hill Book Co., 1939.

Heckocher, *Mercantalism,* George Allen and Unwin Ltd., 1965.

Joseph Gusfield, "Tradition and Modernity: Misplaced Polarities in the Study of Social Change", *American Journal of Sociology,* Vol. 72, No. 4, January 1967.

Joseph R. Gusfield, "Traditions and Modernity: Misplaced Polarities in the Study of Social Change", *American Journal of Sociology,* Vol. 72, No. 4, January 1967.

Karl Mennhein, *Man and Society in an Age of Reconstruction,* Harcourt Brace & Co., New York, 1940.

Max Weber, *Protestant Ethic and Rise of Capitalism.*

Nedel S. F., *The Concept of Social Elites,* International Social Science Bulletin 8(3).

S.N. Eisenstadt, Social Transformation in Modernization, *American Sociological Review,* Vol. 30, No. 5, October 1965.

Selig Harrisan, India, *Most Dangerous Decades,* Princeton University Press, 1960.

Silverberg, James, "Social Mobility in the Caste System in India", *Journal of Asian Studies* Supplement, 1968.

Smith W. C., *Modernization of a Traditional Society,* Asia Publishing House, Bombay 1965.

Srinivas, M.N., "Caste in Modern India", *The Journal of Asian Studies,* 16 (41: 529-548).

Vilfrade Pareto, *The Mind and Society,* ed., Arthur Livingston, Translated by A. Bongiorno and J.H. Rogers, N.Y. (1935).

Weiner, Myron, *Modernization: The Dynamics of Growth,* Voice of America Lectures, Higginbothams Ltd., Madras.

12

Idea System of Indian Intellectuals

A Model Approach to Tradition and Modernization

H.C. SRIVASTAVA

The Hypothesis: If the history of intellectual ideas in India is conceived in terms of two models—traditional and modernising, elements of continuity in values of the former into the latter system of ideas have infused a trend toward 'structural adjustment' rather than *radical* change (an essential attribute of the process of Modernization). This hypothesis is open to empirical test.

THE CONCEPTUAL FRAME—THE INTELLECTUAL, IDEA SYSTEM, AND BREADTH OF PERSPECTIVE

(*a*) *The Intellectual:* This is an attempt to draw an outline of the history of intellectual ideas of the Indian intellectual class from the ancient to the present day. Professor Baumer has defined the intellectual class as 'not only the comparatively small group of really profound and original thinkers, not only the professional philosophers, scientists, theologians, and scholars in general, but also creative literary men and artists, the popularizers and the intelligent reading public.... And, intellectual history is concerned with the doings, sayings and writings of these intellectuals'. Though Briton would suggest that the job of the intellectual historian is to try to find the relation between the ideas of the philosophers, the intellectuals, the thinkers, and the actual way of living of the millions who carry the tasks of civilization. He has to gather 'material ranging from abstract philosophic concepts to concrete acts of men'. But it is not possible to focus on 'what went on in the heart and head of the man in the street'. It is a task too ambitious in nature. Our problem is to identify the intellectual idea system as explicit in the sayings and writings of the Indian Intellectuals.

'Intellect' is the critical, creative, and contemplative side of mind and 'intelligence' is the capacity to grasp, manipulate, record, and adjust. Intellectual activity is predominantly 'to create'. Intellectuals exhibit "an unusual sensitivity to the sacred, an uncommon reflectiveness about the nature of their universe, and the rules which govern their society". An intellectual is a man who does or tries to do the following:

(*i*) He applies his intellectual faculties to understand and interpret the *world* around him;
(*ii*) As a result of study, observation, and experiment, he formulates conclusions which he believes to be true or, at all events truer than those which were current before;
(*iii*) He communicates his ideas of fellowmen with a view to influencing their mind, life and action.

Intellectuals are interested in all the major currents of ideas, from physics to theology, that influence the times. We have taken only those ideas which are relevant to *status quo* or societal changes. In the Indian context, we shall include intellectuals under the above definition, but in ancient times, the highest caste, i.e., Brahmins, were the intellectuals by whom brain and education had traditionally been devoted to the *status quo*.

(*b*) *Idea System*: Ideas have been recognised as a moving force in the lives of nations and individuals. "Intellectuals are gatekeepers of ideas and fountain heads of ideologies; they create a critical attitude; they tend to scrutinize the received ideas and assumptions of their times and milieu". Themes in intellectual history work on idea systems. By idea system, we understand "the total manifold concrete ideas of means of which an individual or social group defines its reality and guides its affairs". Intellectuals of a society develop a system of ideas that justify and make meaningful its social structure, tradition, and style of life. The idea system helps in defining the situation and choice of alternatives before the collectivity. It provides a kind of 'ideological environment'. "A society moves on the basis and within the limits of the general pattern of ideas available to it.... If that pattern of ideas is false or irrelevant or inadequate to any particular movement, such as one towards prosperity or harmony or modernization, then the society will falter or at least progress slowly in that particular direction, if it does not indeed move in some other". An idea system is invariably linked with the level of technology a society has. It is often covariably with technology and a vehicle in the process of growth through social change.

(c) *Breadth of Perspective to Social Change*: Idea system provides a breadth of perspective to social change. Intellectual breadth of perspective influences social change directly. Breadth of perspectives is the relatively stable 'capacity' of the intellectuals in an era to think of alternative kinds of solution to the problem situations presented to them. "In fact, it is the capacity to see *new* problems in *old* situations by changing the focus of context, by seeing new goals, new means, and new contingencies as relevant...." Warshay regards breadth of perspective a 'covert' rather than 'overt' phenomenon. It is the 'range and variety of angle' or standpoints in solution of a problem. It functions as intellectual variable in the process of modernization because some 'have more of it than others'. Having in view the concept of breadth of perspective to change, we have conceptualised the entire history of intellectual ideas in India in two models—traditional idea system and modernising idea system. The purpose is to see how the value system of the former *continues* in the latter, and consequently, how does it influence the process of Modernization in contemporary India? It constitutes a problem for empirical investigation.

The Traditional Idea System

Indian society was the characteristic of an advanced traditional society. It had a high level technical and an aesthetic perfection, well organised craftsman guild. The village was the unit of social organisation. It was a closely knit and well integrated society based on caste and division of labour and functioning on the basis of self-regulation and self-government. It has agriculture, cottage industry, and services. Implements used were simple and power used was mainly human and animal. The economic activity was predominantly labour-intensive. Indian society, though backward in its economy was advanced in art, architecture, and aesthetics, in polity, religion and philosophy.

It had the sublimating elite group (Brahmins) to direct its culture for creative power. These intellectual elites were responsible for cultural initiative and tradition. Social life was guided by the institutions and rigid norms. The intellectual problems and social problems of Indian civilization went together. The intellectual problem consists in preserving an orthodoxy in the midst of the most bewildering, amalgam of traditions and methods. The social problem was to maintain an integrated social order stable in terms of *dharma* and deliverance (*nirvana*) based on transcendent ends.

Ancient Indian genius conceived nature in terms of personified phenomena and perceived concrete of *Usha*, *Surya*, and *Agni* with whom it maintained direct communion. The central idea behind the deification was of 'paternity'. Main figure, among the mythological cosmology, is *Varuna* the upholder of the physical and moral order, symbolized in *rita*. *Varuna* in the *Rig Veda* is pre-eminently the All-Pervader, the All-Encompasser, the All-Enveloper, as aspect of *Vri* (to cover, or encompass). In Puranas, the old mythological cosmological foundation were added the ritual information, historical memories hymns, simplifying the *Sankhya* and *Yoga* philosophies. In *Mahabharata,* the old gods of the *Vedas* have lost some of their majestic position. Above the gods stands the ascetic, and above human society stands the Brahmin.

For the vast majority of the Indians, the *Manu Smriti* is the basic authority. The material scattered on the subject has the general pattern of the old *Manu Smriti*. Manu (a mental being) is the symbol of ancient 'law giver', and his *Dharma Sastra* is the most ancient idea system of Hindu social organisation. Temperament (ability) and character are the objective characteristics of the occupant who assumes a *Varna*-role in Manu's scheme. The *Varna* roles are arranged in a social hierarchy with Brahmins at the top and Shudra at the bottom. Manu conceives four fundamental *Varnas* (occupational classes)—education and socialising (Brahminic functions), regulative and protective (Kshatriya functions), commercial (*Vaishya* function), and subservience (*Shudric* functions). These are the natural divisions in correspondence with psychological constitution of human beings. Manu's order of primacy is teach, guard, feed, and serve. Life of an individual should be lived in conformity with *dharma* institutionalised in four *ashramas*—for the first *ashrama,* group looks after the individual (*grihastha*) as a trustee, looks after the group. In the third and fourth *ashramas,* the individual, as a training, deinstitutionalises himself in search of the self that hides within the core of his being.

The highest development of Indian wisdom is found in the six principal systems of philosophy. The *Purva Mimansa* is an analysis and a legal code of *Brahmanic dharma*. It is a pursuit of deliverance, through ritual act. The atomism of *Vaisheshika* (early Indian physics), the atom of earth, water, fire and wind constitute the cosmos. Merit (*dharma*) and demerit (*adharma*) make the aggregates in space and time. Man is composed of a soul, having an atomic mind, and a functional organic system. When the soul recognises that it is other than the mind-body complex, it is delivered. *Nyaya* provides an art of reasoning. The *Atman,* by its own effort, makes the mind serve life, and by other it detaches it from life by true knowledge. The *Vedanta* turns towards complete deliverance which consists in judging right, as distinct from appearance; one may realise the absolute in everything and, so far as possible, is being equal to it oneself. Right knowledge undeceives human being.

The common element of Jaina and Buddha teachings is human condition and suffering. Activity (*Karma*) plunges human being into relativity and misery. *Karma* is not an external condition of suffering, but the very fact of life—of becoming. Deliverance (*moksha*) is the cessation of all desires. For Buddha, human existence is made of assemblings, always in flux, and these are of five kinds—material form (*rupa*), pleasant or painful impressions (*Vedana*), perception (*sanjna*), discrimination (*vijnana*) and tendencies (*sanskara*). Jainism and Buddhism are pure systems of metaphysics and also religions like Hinduism. Deliverance (*moksha*) is the cessation of all desires. The nature of their teaching, from the point of society is despair, but optimistic from the point of view of individual liberation. Asceticism is primarily training and knowledge alone liberates the individual. Liberation is to untie the bonds of existence. These philosophical systems decide intellectualism which base deliverance on a certain knowledge of the conditions of human suffering.

Jainism and Buddhism contributed to the renewal or Brahmanism. The popular religions of *Vishnu, Shiva* emerged. Thereby the way is opened for two things characteristic of Brahmanism (Hinduism)—the belief, in a metaphysical first principle periodically becoming incarnate in saviours of the human race, and a pious devotion which connects the relative with the absolute not by knowledge but by sentiment. These religious sects mark the decline of Brahmanic orthodoxy.

In medieval India, the intellectual life was embodied in the teachings of Hindu and Muslim mystic saints. Most of them denounced idolatry, condemned polytheism, and behaved as One God. And what is more important realized the unity of God invoked by various religious sects under different names such as Krishna, Rama, Shiva, Allah, etc. The love of God implied the love of humanity. Kabir (1398), the most popular representative of the age, said, "There was no Turk, no Hindu, no race, no caste." In one of his message poem, he said, "A man may read many books before he dies, and yet not a *pandit,* he is a *pandit* who understands the two and a half letters which form the word love." Chaitanya (1486) laid stress on sincere and passionate love for God as the only way to salvation. He believed in Radha-Krishna cult. Nanak (1469) laid stress on the purity of character and conduct and a high ethical code, rather any dogma or creed of any sect—"abide pure amid the impurities of the world, thus shalt thou find the way of religion". In any case, they failed to modify either the religious ideas and practices or the outward structure of Hindu society to any appreciable extent.

Some of the main characteristics of the traditional idea system can be summarised as follows:

(*i*) It was based on a kind of orthodoxy on traditional teaching. Knowledge of the scripture has been used as a theoretical protective framework.

(*ii*) Deliverance (*nirvana*) remained central, and an individual affair. It evoked no aspiration for greater social justice.

(*iii*) No important attempt has been made to win political freedom for wider rights. Only fidelity to tradition (*dharma*: rights and duties) has been the hallmark of the intellectual idea system.

(*iv*) No progress has been conceived beyond the intact social order.

(*v*) The human intellectual faculties were not placed in service of social progress. The aim was to achieve transcendental ends. To understand the human existence is to free oneself. The dilemma is to have extreme desire to live and also to give it up.

(*vi*) "Where other civilizations unify, mobilise, and level, India tends to divide, to specialise, to arrange in order of rank" (Henri Berr).

The Modernising Idea System

The transformation of the intellectual idea system from tradition to modernization took place under the British regime. The most powerful effect and enduring result of the British rule in India is the intellectual development of the people on an entirely new line, and the consequent changes in their political, social, religious, and economic outlook. It may be said without much exaggeration that during the period of less than a century.... India passed from the medieval to modern age.

Seven hundred years of foreign rule had deprived the Indians (Hindus) of political vitality, national consciousness in whatsoever degree they possessed it. There was no organised Muslim aristocracy in Bengal to place resistance against the British. Hindus and Muslims were divided. Each community knew very little of the other's history, literature, ideas and traditions. The intellectuals of the two communities ran on almost entirely different lines. A scholar of Hindu learning was normally a grammarian, competent to interpret ancient authorities. The social and religious institutions of Hindu society did not go any significant change. So far the Hindu masses were concerned religion meant only as unending series of rituals and ceremonies, performed in strict accordance with scriptual rules.

On the whole, the Indians (of Bengal) looked with favour upon the English community and many appreciated the process of westernisation, though colonization, as a boon. There was a public movement, led by men like Raja Ram Mohun Roy and Dwarika Nath Tagore, to facilitate the permanent settlement of Englishmen in Bengal. There was a general deterioration in the Hindu society due to prolonged lack of contact with the progressive forces of the world. They had an idea system based on 'blind faith' which influenced the mental and moral outlook of men in society.

The British regime introduced political institutions through constitutional adventures in India. Chirol observes, "British rule introduced into India not only a few reign of law and order but the principles of equal tolerance and justice for all which had struck root in our (western) civilization."

Western education introduced the supremacy of reason, critical attitude to religion, and a new concept of social and political justice. A new ideology suddenly burst forth upon the static life, moulded for centuries by a fixed set of religious ideas and social conventions. The upper classes of India were the first to be influenced by English language, literature, journalism and ideas of western society. Western ideas overwhelmed them at the beginning. Fifty years of English education brought greater changes in the minds of the educated Hindus of Bengal than the previous thousands years. It was the period of 'French illumination' which introduced the spirit of rationalism and individualism in the idea system of the intellectuals of the Indian Renaissance.

The foremost positive attitude was taken by Raja Ram Mohun Roy (1772-1833) whose contribution to the process of modernization are as follows:

(*i*) His attack on the existing form of religion; and
(*ii*) His conception of religion through the Brahmo Samaj (1828)— a theistic society.

He revolted against idolatrous practices and other degenerated Hindu institutions like caste system, *kulin* Brahmin polygyny, child marriage and *sattee* practice, etc. He fought against these evils through propaganda, press and vigilance committee. Ram Mohun Roy believed in a universal reason at work in nature and society and religions are the expression of that reason in man. The task of reason today is to disentangle the elements of permanent and Universal truth in each faith from the mass of accretions which has gathered round them and to return to them as the basis of our religious life. But there was no uniformity in the renascent tendencies. These were three groups representing three different intellectual strains—First was the conservative orthodox group which opposed all reforms (Dharma Sabha led by Radha Kant Deb);

second was the Young Bengal Movement led by Derozio, who were the blind imitators of everything Western and like nihilistic and free thinkers they were opposed to traditions. Third group was that of the reformers led by Raja Ram Mohun Roy. Some of the doctrines of the old Brahmo Samaj are significant:

"(111) The Brahmo Samaj believe that the religious condition of man is progressive, like the other parts of his condition in this world.

"(5) They believe in the existence of One Supreme God, as God endowed with a distinct personality, moral attributes equal to His nature, and intelligence befitting the Governor of the universe, and worship Him—Him alone. They do not believe in His incarnation.

"(14) Theoretically there is no distinction of caste among the Brahmans. They declare that all human beings are the children of God, and therefore, must consider them ourselves as brothers and sisters."

Through their newspapers, educational institutions and personal contact, the Brahmo Samajist spread enlightenment among the people and arouse them to new consciousness. They proclaimed modern social values like personal freedom, social equality of man and religion without any distinction of caste or creed, discarded idol worship, freed women from suppression. Ultimately, the new Sadharan Brahmo Samaj merged into the national current of the Indian National Congress.

Swami Dayanand (1824-1883), the founder of Arya Samaj, sought to reform the Hindu society by reviving Vedic rituals and institutions. The Arya Samaj organised relief work in social disaster, organised English education, accepted *Suddhi* (reconversion) and Hindu universalism. The idea system of Arya Samaj can be summarised in two of its official doctrines:

"(6) The primary object of the Samaj is to be good to the world by improving the physical, spiritual, and social condition of mankind.

"(10) In matters which affect the general social well-being of the whole society, one ought to discard all differences and

> not allow one's individuality to interfere, but in strictly personal matters everyone may act with freedom."

The intellectual idea system of the Arya Samaj resisted against the 'inferiority complex' from aggressive Christianity and Islam, and aroused a new national consciousness. The Arya Samaj was at once a religious and a national revival. It sought to bring a new life to India and the Hindu race.... Yet both (Arya Samaj and Brahmo Samaj) were children of the one and the same revolution which destroyed the medieval India ruled by Brahmans and created modern India. But it was the Arya Samaj, which by reawakening the India of the past, did most to prove the way for the India of the twentieth century.

The Theosophical Society contributed to the revival of the eastern faith in her own intellectual potentials. It provided an Indian ideal of education and a liberalising effect on Indian intellectuals through its doctrines:

(1) To form a universal brotherhood of man.
(2) To promote the study of ancient religions, philosophies and sciences.
(3) To investigate the law of nature and develop the divine power latent in man.

It preached the ultimate oneness—one-life which underlies and sustains all phenomenal diversity. Annie Besant favoured constitutional reforms. She was against mass movements. She, therefore, opposed the new political forces in India and was alienated from the political scene.

The religious sentiments both orthodox and enlightened were manifest in the Indian national movement. Lokmanya Bal Gangadhar Tilak (1893) started the celebration of Ganapati and Shiva festivals to instil in the masses a spirit of manliness, discipline, organised action and patriotism. Lord Krishna was the guiding force of action. Tilak said (1897): "Do not circumscribe your vision like frogs in a well. Rise above the Penal Code into the rarified atmosphere of the sacred *Bhagwad Gita* and consider the action of great men." The reawakening of national consciousness revived the ancient idealism of the Shakti cult of Durga and Kali. All these old and traditional gods and goddesses who had lost their hold on the modern mind, have been reinstalled with a new historic and nationalist interpretation on the mind and soul of India. The revolutionaries, who used weapons, practiced the Sakti cult. Their motto was "lay down your life, but first take a life" The revolutionary societies were modelled upon the Russian and Italian secret societies, their mode of operation was to plan and to execute.

The religious trends of the new nationalism produced reaction in the Muslim minority which was led by certain communalists. They laid emphasis on the good graces of the British Government in promoting the temporary interest of their community in stealing march over other communities. Sir Syed Ahmad started the Muslim Educational Conference (as a counterpart of National Congress) to form the attention of Muslim intelligentsia to accept the policy of active cooperation to the British Crown and condemn the criticism of the foreign government as disloyal.

The origin of the Congress gave an intellectual content to the discontent of the masses in India. A.O. Hume founded it in order to avert the imminent danger of a terrible outbreak. He was convinced that starving millions will resort to violence. His attempt was to link the alienated intellectuals to the economic suffering of the masses. His purpose was to promote the mental, moral, social, and political regeneration of people of India. He believed that India could not have a better government than the British. What was needed was an organisation of highly educated men of the nation who could make a resolute struggle to secure greater freedom. The intellectual content of the Congress was in the beginning for political regeneration through reforms. The Indian politicians were to cooperate with the Government for better administration. But soon after that the politically conscious intelligentsia of India began demanding Home Rule for India which was refuted by the Britishers as something 'un-Eastern'. A.R. Desai, who has given a historical account of the social background of Indian nationalism, has divided it into five phases. In the *first* phase (till 1885), the intelligentsia, that has acquired western education and assimilated the democratic and national aspiration of the western culture, conducted socio-reforms and religio-reforms. The *second* phase (1885-1905) was dominated by the liberal intelligentsia (who had faith in British sense of justice), and the extremists (who resorted to boycott campaign). The *third* phase (1905-18) saw the rise of militant challenging ideologies along with the Muslim communalism. In the *fourth* phase (1930-34), direct mass action and civil disobedience were launched. In the *fifth* phase (1934-39), movements of the depressed classes grew steadily.

The National Congress rallied the "high intellectual brilliance of great galaxy of eminent leaders". The idea system influenced not only the Indians but also the Englishmen. The Congress represented the "thinking portion of the Indian people". The contemporary India is in large measure the work of its idea systems under the Gandhi-Nehru leadership. Gandhi's special contribution lies in putting the religious concepts into practice and arousing national consciousness. He combined social reordering and the fight for political Swaraj in a non-violent type of struggle. He tackled problems of untouchability, child marriage, uplift of Harijans and women, basic education, economic self-sufficiency, rural reconstruction and finally non-cooperation with the foreign rule and a movement against them 'to quit India'. Gandhi's success laid in unifying the diverse forces in India. The unique modernising effect of Gandhi was to create, through his ideas and practice, *human conscience* as a social institution, a prerequisite for modernization if it is conceived in terms of moral values.

Nehru introduced elements in Indian political thinking which were outside the mainstream of orthodox Hindu thought. He made experiment with certain forms and ideas "to be realised through a synthesis of the surviving traditional values of India and some of the techniques of the West". His pragmatic, but undefined humanism, inspired an era of intellectual from different realms. Nehru's concept of democracy implies rational consent. For him, freedom and democracy require responsibility, self-discipline, self-reliance, having no room for violence. He believed in *Welfare-statism* that has no place for individualism. Nehru wanted people to develop cooperative attitude against acquisitive attitude. He proclaimed faith in socialism as the only way for economic freedom. His views gained force because of the "alliance of the state with the urge of the people".

In the pre-independence period, the process of modernization was propounded mainly in non-economic terms. It was in the post-independence period that under the leadership of Prime Minister Nehru really began the multifarious modernising process through the Five-Year Plans of development. The intellectuals are exposed to modern intellectual culture being involved in politics, civil service, journalism, law, teaching, research, medicine, and technology. From the literary realm a new humanism has made the hero exist from the fictions and values stern from the common man, not from a conceptual hero-man. A search for authenticity has prevailed over the literary idea system. 'Absurd' movements have become frequent in India. Intense politicisation is not only vocation of intellectual, rather there is dissociation of intellectual class from the political elite. They are being gradually depoliticised. Edward Shils aptly remarks, "Back-benchers and party functionaries will include a very considerable portion of place-holders, and the tasks they will have to perform will not be very attractive to intellectuals, living in the traditions of modern intellectuals." With the growth of Indian economy and creation of institutional framework, the Indian intellectuals well diversified in technology, governmental, industrial, commercial administrative, scientific and scholarly research and many such other sectors. With this diversification, there will be less unity of sentiment, less sense of a common identity among them. In building a modern society, specialisation and diversification are necessary. Critics of contemporary Indian life have marked a decline in intellectual activity. Some of the points raised are:

1. Decline in the standard of education;
2. Total absence of any outstanding intellectual below the age of fifty or rather sixty;
3. More and more imitative nature of Indian thought;
4. The western quarrels are transplanted in Indian situation;
5. The intellectual movement has 'grave internal weakness';
6. Little scope for a wide array of intellectuals because of undiversified nature of society. Activist groups are few, institutions young and relatively underdeveloped. The pressure from authority and the urge to conform are strong. The spirit of protest that challenges every intrusion into freedom and individualism is weak; and
7. It has become a marked destruction among intellectuals to prefer the aristocratic privilege of saying neither 'yes' nor 'no', in order to avoid the necessity of action.

Precocity has been mentioned as one of the major reasons of

decline in intellectual activity. Precocity is the effort to adopt ideas and activities prematurely an attempt to create stir and shock than genuine creation. It often brings "untimely decay in its strain in personal as well as national development". Edward Shils observes that Indian intellectuals are not still "a largely self-sustaining process; they are still intellectually a province of the British metropolis. The culture of a foreign metropolis is the only modern culture he (Indian intellectual) possesses. If he denies that culture, he denies himself and negates his own aspirations to transform his society into a modern society". It raises really a crucial problem for the Indian intellectual from where to derive the content of modernization.

The alternatives are either to borrow the idea system and technology from the intellectual metropolis of the West or to fall back on the sources of traditional culture. About the latter, it is said that modern intellectual tradition consumes the existence of an ego, a concrete individuality and creativity which may not emerge in intellectual traditions and institutions of India. It is an interesting observation that Indian intellectuals when advanced in age are reclaimed to Hinduism, to its orthodoxy and traditional idea system. It is a loss to the intelligentsia. A noted Indian critic has found almost eighty per cent people are attached to the following traditional values of Indian culture:

(*a*) *Universalism:* It is a kind of reinforcement of pantheism and universalism of the Indian idea system. From it springs the doctrine of co-existence—the attitude of human family as one. This value, therefore, still remains a dynamic characteristic unconsciously operative, both among the masses and the intelligentsia.

(*b*) *Intolerant-Tolerance:* There is tolerance due to universalism, but the Hindu does not show any real tolerance to the people of other faiths when some vital challenge comes.

(*c*) *Compassion:* It is an emphasis on tenderness due to the direct result of suffering and exploitation. It allows growth of personality through devotion or enlightenment.

He observes that young Indian intellectuals are bribed and bought out by foreigners to conform with the middle class Western values. The intellectuals, in the post-colonial period, have ceased to be creators of idea system which may influence the consciousness of the time. They have become non-activists. As a class they would find it impossible to live even reasonably well off their gift of mind. Their status is low and their influence on policy feeble. Theirs are not the voices of passionate protest and they themselves are the catalysts of modernization.

Conclusion

Breadth of perspective is a standpoint from which the world is observed and interpreted. This concept, in context to intellectual idea system of a given time-span, is closely related with the process of modernization in a given society. We have framed the history of intellectual idea in two basic models—the traditional idea system and the modernising idea system. Viewed from the concept of continuity, the intellectual idea system of the former has permeated the general intellectual idea system of the modern times. The survival of the following features of the traditional idea system are significant:

1. That human existence is cyclical; it bears the consequences of past actions. In terms of *dharma* (or the cosmic scheme), acceptance of life is fatalistic for what it brings for a given social role in the hierarchical structure of society.
2. That there is a Great Order, a spiritual reason or purpose; there should be harmony between man, nature, and supernatural conflict and violence are to be avoided.
3. That the concept of social responsibility is particularistic, being limited to family, caste, region, or community. For a limited interest, the interest of the larger society is ignored.

The social reforms and political action, influenced by these ideas, were oriented mainly towards *structural adjustment* in society. The religico-political idea system, in the post-colonial era, is exploiting certain Hindu ideals for competing with the state influence on people and acquiring power. The literary and artistic trends have shown considerable variation in the so-called modern techniques at the cost of meaningful content.

Marxism, which is the only idea system outside Hindu tradition, made a remarkable influence on Indian mind. The socialistic ideas of the right and left wings showed a considerable deviation from the ancient cultural tradition. In fact, it were the pragmatic humanism and welfare-statism of Nehru which have brought certain positive modernising strains in Indian politico-administrative and economic systems.

Of course, the solution of many of the problems of contemporary India depends upon political issues and the Indian scientists have been contributing well, but they also lack a common platform for cross-fertilisation of scientific ideas. Indian scientists have still "to make of life a dream, and to turn the dream into reality" (Marie Curie). The Indian intellectuals are failing to create the image of the future society. A society which has a re-negative or pessimistic image of the future is likely to be disorganised and its image of future is all too likely to be fulfilled. On the other hand, the society which has an optimistic image of the future, even though this image may be quite unrealistic, will be well organised and will go forward into some future, although not necessarily the future of its image.

References

A. Rahman, 'Indian Science Congress—A Need for Change', *Science Today*, Jan. 1969.

Briton, *Ideas and Men—The Story of Western Thought*, Prentice-Hall, 1965.

Chaudhari, N.C., *The Intellectual in India*, Vir Publishing House, New Delhi, 1967.

Chirol, Velentine, *India: Old and New*, Macmillan & Co., London, 1921.

Coser, Lewis, *Men of Ideas—A Sociologist's Views*, The Free Press, New York, 1965.

Desai, A.R., *Social Background of Indian Nationalism*, 3rd edition, Popular Book Depot, Bombay, 1959.

Levincow, *Idea System in Individual and in Society*, Zollschar and Hirsch (eds.), *Explorations in Social Change*, Routledge, London, 1964.

Majumdar, R.C. (ed.), *The Delhi Sultanate—The History and Culture of the Indian People*, Bombay, 1967.

_______, *British Paramountcy and Indian Renaissance—The History and Culture of the Indian People*, Part II, Bombay, 1965.

Paul Masson and Others, *Ancient Indian and Indian Civilization*, New Delhi, 1967.

Rao, V.K.R.V. *Some Problems of Confronting Traditional Societies in the Process of Development*, Popular Bombay, 1956.

Shils, Edward, 'The Intellectuals in the Political Development of the New States, Kantsky (ed.) *Political Change in Underdeveloped Countries*, London, 1962.

Shils, Edward, *The Intellectual and the Power, Comparative Studies in Society and History*. Glenoo Free Press, 1958.

Smith, W.C., *Modernization of a Traditional Society*, Asia Publishing House, Bombay, 1965.

Srivastava, H.C., *The Intellectual between Tradition and Modernity: The Indian Situation*, Unpublished Ph.D. thesis, B.H.U., Varanasi, 1976.

Vyas, K.C., *The Social Renaissance in India*, Vora & Co., Bombay, 1957.

Warshay, Leon, *Breadth of Perspective and Social Change*, Zollschar and Hirsch (eds.), 1961.

13
Political Participation and Modernization

YOGESH ATAL

[I]

With the onset of the era of newly independent states, forces designed to "change" the structure of society and to ensure economic "development" and political stability have been set into operation. Concern for development appears to be a universal phenomenon. The ruling elite, bereft of the unifying force, provided by the rallying cry of "independence" during the colonial period, are avowedly busy in the task of "Nation-Building", "Modernization", and "Development".

Use of these new slogans, though less powerful than the call for "freedom-fight", had policy implications. Attainment of the goal of modernization requires a rationalist programme of concerted action. An era of directed culture change has been ushered in. While each nation has decided, or at least claims to have decided, for herself the direction of this change, some authors tend to think that the process of modernization "is a secular trend unilateral in direction—from traditional to participant life-ways" (Lerner, 1965 : 89).

The simplistic analogy of unilinear evolution provided a basic dichotomy of "Tradition" and "Modernity". "The scale is anchored on one end by an aggregate cluster labelled 'tradition', and on the other by a similarly clustered group of characteristics judged 'modern'" (Wilcox, 1968: 27).

Doubts have been expressed in regard to the utility of such a model. Thus Wilcox writes:

> "The assignment of scale rankings makes data amenable to linear or curvilinear portrayal, but the making of ordinal rank and verbal category introduces more confusion than clarity" (*ibid.*, 2).

It is doubtless admitted by the students who follow the linear model indicated above that many elements of "modernity" in any "changing" society *arrive* not through the womb of its own culture, but they *diffuse* from other cultures. As a part of the nationalistic sentiment they may reject the idea of "owing a debt" to any external source, but they welcome the journey towards modernization. Implicit in this line of argument is the moral that the process is not evolutionary or orthogenetic in nature. The heterogeneity of factors accounting for the modernization process in any society may seriously handicap the universality of generalisations. Availability of a trait alone, according to this argument, cannot be taken as an indicator; the meaning assigned to it by the participants is of crucial significance.

Happily, we have a set of scholars who considers the two poles as purely analytical categories, as "one-sided accentuations" of traits and who believe that all concrete societies fall somewhere in between the two ends of the continuum.

Symptomatologies of the two ends—tradition and modernity—are, as it were, not universally agreed upon. It is not our intention to examine the whole range of differences in regard to the traits to be included in either end of the continuum. What we propose to do, however, is to examine the relationship between political participation—a category having a set of definable and, perhaps, less disputable characteristics—and modernization.

Three approaches are available in the current social science literature indicating the relationship between participation and modernization.

One set of authors considers participation as one of the attributes of modernization. Thus, the authors of the *World Handbook of Political and Social Indicators* (Russett, Alker, Deutsch,

& Lasswell, 1965) identified *five* stages of economic and political development on the basis of nine variables, including percentage of voting. The model of analysis (classifying societies along these nine variables as (*i*) Traditional Primitive, (*ii*) Traditional Civilizations, (*iii*) Transitional, (*iv*) Industrial Revolution Societies, and (*v*) High Mass Consumption Societies) is longitudinal in character. Similar is the case with Lerner (1965) who mentions urbanisation, literacy, media participation as successive stages, each accelerating the pace of modernization. Lerner's contention is that "rising media participation tends to raise participation in all sectors of the social system. In accelerating the spread of empathy, it also diffuses those other modern demands to which participant institutions have responded: in consumer's economy *via* cash (and credit), in the public forum *via* opinion, in the representative polity *via* voting" (Lerner, *Ibid*., 62).

A diagrammatic presentation of this model would be like Chart 13.1 this:

Chart 13.1: Modernization Process

I. Stage: Urbanisation.
II. Stage: Literacy.
III. Stage: Media Participation:
  (*a*) Consumer Economy,
  (*b*) Opinion Range, and
  (*c*) Voting.

There are others who separate political participation from modernization and believe that modernization serves as a precipitating agent for political participation. Thus, Weiner believes that a set of factors—among which modernization is one—create conditions for increased participation in politics. His reasoning can be summarised in the form of a chart (Chart 13.2).

Chart 13.2

A. Growth of Urban Labour Force.
B. Unevenness in Modernization.
C. Minority *Vs*. Majority in a multiethnic Society.
D. Expansion of Governmental Activities.
E. Rift between State and Religion.
F. Growth of Mass Communication.

A careful look at the chart would, however, indicate that the factors listed as "casual" can be subsumed under the broad category, "Modernization". Factor A is a consequence of Industrialisation and urbanisation, Factor F is just the another name for media participation, Factors B, C, and E indicate the extent of empathy, awareness, and opinion. Factor D has a direct reference to polity which seeks to *involve* more and more people.

One may as well argue and suggest that there is no basic difference between Lerner and Weiner on this score. What Weiner does is to define the goal of modernization in terms of Lerner's stage 3 and treat the latter step as a by-product of modernization.

A third approach to the problem seems to be a deserving candidate for further exploration. According to this approach, political participation is viewed as a *precipitating* factor for modernization. Once the stage is set for modernization the two may serve as reinforcing mechanisms for each other. What may differ is the character of participation rather than the fact of participation. The prescription-prone, ideologue analysts take a limited view of participation, that which takes place in a democratic frame and finds expression in "inputs" of various forms, and 'lament' on a disturbingly low rate of participation.

The term participation can be defined in specific or highly diffused terms. Lerner describes a person "participant" when he learns to "have opinions" and "the more numerous and varied the matters on which he has opinions, the more participant he is" (*ibid.*, 71). The above definition is much broader and goes beyond the mere fact of *physical* participation. *Empathy,* understood as psychic participation, is an index of participation for Lerner.

Considering voting as an index of participation emphasises the fact of physical participation. This, being a more visible index, defines the terms rather more specifically. An advantage in accepting this definition is that it provides an opportunity to examine the relationship between empathy and its translation into action.

[II]

Indian setting provides an excellent testing ground for the relationship between the two sets of variables, viz., political participation and Modernizations. India during her pre-independence era was by all standards a "less-modern" society. On all indicators (urbanisation, industrialisation, literacy, and media-production and consumption) her record was poor. Mobilisation of Indian population with a view to putting a fight against the British was intense despite slow rate of modernization on other fronts. Even participation in the democratic framework was initiated in the country long ago. The Act of 1935 envisaged an electorate of 18 per cent of the total population in contrast to only 2-8 per cent in the Dyarchy electorate under the 1919 Act (*c.f.* Tinker, 1962).

That there was heightened political participation in the pre-Independence period, particularly the last 40-50 years, cannot be denied. Even after the Independence the participant political culture has been gaining in strength. "All groups in India crucial to the success of the inherited participant economic and political culture—entrepreneurs, labour leaders, bankers, judges and barristers, bureaucrats, soldiers, legislators and party bosses—at all levels of the society—national, state and local—have grown in strength, size and confidence in India" (Wilcox, *ibid.*, 12).

The participation of the people in the democratic politics of the country is rapidly increasing. One who witnessed the political scene in the year preceding the fourth General Elections would unhesitatingly certify to the effect that Indian masses are fast politicising themselves. Politics of agitation characterised the Indian polity. The "middle class" came to the forefront with its demands and widespread movements. In terms of expressive symbols, the new vocabulary of Indian political culture includes *Gherao, Band, Anshan* and *Atma Daah* (self-immolation).

That political participation of the people has increased can be measured in several ways.

Take the voting population. With the increase in population size, the voting public has also grown over the years. Thus, 173 million people were eligible to vote in 1952, 193 million in 1957, 212 million in 1962, and 245 million in 1967. Though polling has never been hundred per cent, it has shown an ever-increasing trend in the past four elections. This is shown in Table 13.1.

Indian voting population has thus grown in the past twenty years by 72 million. In the current elections, 33 million fresh voters were registered. These persons are largely from the age group 21-25. They represent, therefore, that segment of Indian population

Table 13.1: Electorate and the Polling Percentage

Election Year	*Electorate (in millions)*	*Votes Polled*	
		State Assemblies	*Lok Sabha*
1952	173	37.1	45.7
1957	193	46.6	46.6
1962	212	51.1	55.4
1967	245	57.0	61.0

who have spent most of their intelligent lives in independent India. Since there is major concentration of literate population in the younger age groups it can be believed that most of the new voting public is literate and, as such, more exposed communicationally and more informed politically. In terms of voting we find that whereas in the first General Elections *less than* 50 per cent of the people did exercise their franchise, in the Fourth Elections 61 per cent voted, thus registering an increase of 15.3 per cent. If this rise is caused by the younger voting public, the next elections may show a still higher polling rate.

If we were to take the contestants as indicator of participation, we notice that in the 1952 elections about 17,000 candidates contested for various seats. In 1967, this number went down to 10,438, the average number of contestants per seat being 3.6. There are two implications of this datum—one, that decline in the number of contestants can be interpreted as a trend toward the consolidation of party strength. In the third elections, the number of independents was reduced considerably, but in these elections it again showed a rising trend in some States. For example, in Rajasthan about half the contestants were without an explicit party backing; two, from the point of view of the electorate, a larger number of candidates means a bigger battery of political workers and intensive campaigning, both congenial for political socialisation.

Growing maturity of the democracy is also exhibited by the increasingly decreasing number of days in the conduct of polling. It took more than two months to complete the polling during the first General Elections; the second election was completed in 19 days; the third took only 10 days; and the fourth one was finished in a record period of four days. The Election Commissioner hopes to accomplish the task in one day in the next elections.

Elections on such a massive scale, completed without many problems are surely a ray of hope, more so because of the revolutionary changes wrought by the recent election on the political map of the country, so silently and in such an unanticipated manner.

Compared to the increasing rate of political participation, progress in the rates of urbanism, literacy, industrialisation and use of mass media, is strikingly low; this notwithstanding increase in each of them by several hundred times. A brief review of the process of modernization is in order.

The rate of urbanisation has been very slow. Only 18 per cent of the 439 million people inhabit the urban centres. The literacy rate is somewhat faster. While only 0.7 per cent people were added to the urban population in the decade ending in 1961, 7.4 per cent were added to the literate category. Through literacy, thus, some of the urban traits have reached the village.

The "Mobility Multipliers", to use Lerner's phrase, have definitely shown a remarkable growth rate over the decade 1951-1961. In various channels of communication the index of increase has varied between 650 and 104. The mean index of growth is 221. In media consumption, the mean index of growth is 266; the indices ranging between 511 and 139.9. It must be said that while the index shows a very high rate of increase, the coverage even after this increase is very little. For example, the index of increase in electrification is 650 but only 4.27 per cent of the settlements had been electrified. Similarly, while the index of increase of radio licences was 316.7, only 0.46 per cent of the households have been covered. However, there seems to be a concentration of modern traits in urban centres. We find that all the settlements have more than 50,000 population have been electrified. Even among those falling between 10,000 and 50,000 of population range all but 15 per cent have been electrified while only 20 per cent of the rural population is literate, the literacy percentage among the urban population is 47.5.

Improvements in transport facilities are expected to enhance geographical mobility. By 1961, 705 thousand kilometres were covered by road, 57 thousand by rail-road, and 47 thousand by air. 1712 million passengers travelled through the railway in 1961 which is about 39 per cent more than the number of passengers travelled in 1951. The passengers travelling by buses and cars will be much more than this figure. In the past few years, organisation of pilgrim specials, pilgrims carriages, or tourist buses has become a business proposition. Tourist traffic has increased considerably. Though we have not collected the migration statistics, yet it can be surmised that increase in passenger traffic is bringing more and more people into close contact. Avenues of employment outside one's place of residence accelerate the migration process. The migrators serve as a link between the community of their orientation and the community of their migration. With such a slow rate of growth of urban population, however, it cannot be assumed that migrations have been a powerful trend. Perhaps travel has increased; temporary migration have a higher rate; daily communities is more than permanent settlement.

Postal, telegraphic, and telephone facilities have increased a good deal. In 1961, there was a post office for every 5,353 persons, a telephone for every 1,000 persons. On an average, there is a transaction of 9.71 letters per individual. Telegraphic and telephonic communication is still very little. However, there has been a sizeable increase (index being 511.2) in the number of trunk calls. This is a significant trend. Increasing communication between communities is an advance towards integration and towards training in *empathy*.

Electrification leaves much to be desired. Only 4.27 per cent of our settlements have electricity. This means that industries, mass media, and other amenities are largely located in a small number (23,969) of settlements. The radio-listening habit is likewise limited to a very minor segment of the population.

In terms of accessibility to important amenities, this is the picture of India in 1957-58 (India, 1964: 149).

Table 13.2: Average Distance from Villages to Important Amenities

Amenity	*Average distance in miles*
Primary School	1.4
Post Office	3.8
Police Station	8.2
Hospital	8.8
High School	10.2
Telephone Office	11.5
Railway Station	20.2

[III]

An effort was made by the author to trace the relationship between political participation and modernization with a sample of 215 persons drawn from three distinct communities—differentially developed communicationally and ranging from rural to urban. The communities form part of the Etah District in Uttar Pradesh. Of the 215 persons, 120 were drawn from the large urban community called centre-of-centres community (COC), 65 were chosen from a large-sized village (a Link Community—LC), and 30 belonged to a small rural community (SC). The sample constituted a panel which was interviewed thrice, twice before, and once after the 1967 elections. Questions pertaining to exposure, awareness, opinion and political participation were asked the sample and changes in their indices over a three-month period were recorded. The mean scores for the three communities on exposure, awareness and opinion showed this pattern (Table 13.3):

Table 13.3: Mean Scores of Exposure, Awareness and Opinion

		Exposure	*Awareness*	*Opinion*
I Panel Wave	COC	1.8	1.9	2.2
	LC	1.2	1.6	2.3
	SC	0.9	1.2	1.8
	Total	**1.5**	**1.7**	**2.2**
II Panel Wave	COC	1.6	2.7	2.7
	LC	1.6	2.5	2.6
	SC	1.6	2.2	2.6
	Total	**1.6**	**2.6**	**2.7**
III Panel Wave	COC	1.5	2.0	1.7
	LC	1.3	1.6	1.6
	SC	1.2	1.1	1.1
	Total	**1.3**	**1.7**	**1.6**

A review of Table 13.3 would suggest that the indicators of Modernization in this region place it much below the mark. While during the second panel wave, when the electioneering campaign was at its peak the mean scores on each of these variables show increase and the differences in the three communities tend to be minimal, they return to their normal pattern soon after electioneering is over.

During the second wave a set of five questions was included in the schedule to elicit people's sense of political efficacy (for details of this exercise, see Atal, 1969: 171-78). It was discovered that 23 persons had high SPE (sense of political efficacy), 104 had medium, 40 had low, and the remaining 48 could not be placed on the SPE rank.

How do the people having various EAO (exposure, awareness and opinion) as well as SPE, scores rank in terms of political participation? Without going into the details of index-construction we may list the scores of people in terms of participation in various panel waves (Table 13.4):

Table 13.4: Political Participation Scores

	I Wave	*II Wave*	*III Wave*
High	20	20	10
Medium	95	118	36
Low	85	150	138
No	15	27*	31**

* Including 17 who could not be interviewed.
** Including 12 who could not be interviewed.

Panelwise mean scores of various communities on Political Participation (PP) are shown in Table 13.5:

Table 13.5: Mean Score on Political Participation

Communities	*Panel Waves*		
	I	*II*	*III*
COC	1.53	1.71	1.27
LC	1.66	1.77	1.08
SC	1.44	1.80	1.03
Total	1.55	1.74	1.18

It is evident from Table 13.5 that the communities do not form a continuum as is the case for the other variables (EAO). It is also significant to observe that the index shows a decline during the third panel wave. One thing must be said here. In the third wave, political participation was measured not only in terms of voting; questions regarding participation in processions and meetings were also included. A question on voting alone would make the entire analysis misleading. The percentage of voting in the sample population was as high as 89.

To avoid complication, we may take the data of second panel wave when questions on SPE were also asked. This was the period when a rise on all indicators was registered.

Combining the scores on exposure, awareness, and opinion (EAO) we get a consolidated score on modernization variables (distributed community-wise). People having High, Medium, Low and Very Low scores on EAO have the following PP scores:

Table 13.6: Political Participation Scores (PP)

EAO Scores		*H*	*M*	*L*	*N*	*Grand Total*
H	COC	9	59	14	2	84
	LC	8	24	8	1	41
	SC	3	16	0	0	19
Total		20	99	22	3	144
M	COC	0	5	8	2	15
	LC	0	10	10	0	20
	SC	0	4	4	1	9
Total		0	19	22	3	44
L	COC	0	0	3	2	5
	LC	0	0	2	0	2
	SC	0	0	1	1	2
Total		0	0	6	3	9
N	COC	0	0	0	16	16
	LC	0	0	0	2	2
	SC	0	0	0	0	0
Total		0	0	0	18	18
Grand Total		20	118	50	27	215

Giving 3, 2 and 1 weights to the frequencies of COC, LC and SC respectively the distribution shows this clear pattern:

Table 13.7: PP Scores for EAO Scores (Weights for communities)

EAO	*H*	*M*	*L*	*N*	*Total*
H	46	241	58	8	353
M	0	39	48	7	94
L	0	0	14	7	21
N	0	0	0	50	50
Total	46	280	120	72	518

Note: Index of Association taking rows as independent variable (*i.e.,* given EAO, the PP) is .30; the Index of association taking columns as independent variable (*i.e.,* given PP, the EAO) is .25; the no-variable prior Index of Association is .28.

Analysis of the relationship between Sense of Political Efficacy (SPE) and Political Participation (PP) shows that the index of participation of various SPE categories does not form a continuum; the mean participation scores computed for each of the categories also support the conclusion. This is the case in all the panel waves. However, it appears that the past political participation shapes the present SPE, and the latter sets the course for future participation. Index of efficacy computed on the basis of past political participation shows that the higher a person's political participation, the higher is his sense of political efficacy. Treating SPE as the independent variable, the PP index for the third wave is compared likewise (see Atal, 1969: 178).

Simple comparisons between political participations and EAO, taken individually bring out the following pattern:

Table 13.8: Mean Scores on Various Indices in Three Waves

	Exposure	*Awareness*	*Opinion*	*Participation*
I Panel wave	1.5	1.7	2.2	1.5
II Panel wave	1.6	2.6	2.7	1.7
III Panel wave	1.3	1.7	1.6	1.1

Higher indices are to be found in case of opinions to be followed by awareness. Participation would come third. It appears that opinions are expressed even when people possess distorted and incorrect information. Expression of opinion (taken as an index of "participant person") does not necessarily lead to active participation. Taking voting as the sole index of participation we would arrive at a conclusion that participation is relatively much higher than EAO indices taken individually or together.

[IV]

The analysis brings out the following points:

1. Political participation defined narrowly as voting shows a very high rate for the country as a whole. The number of people who participated in voting even in the first General Elections held in 1952 (45.7%) was much higher compared to other indices of modernization. In 1961-62, when

urbanisation was only 18 per cent, literacy was 24 per cent, newspapers were read by 1.29 per cent, and radio was owned by 0.46 per cent, a total of 55.4 per cent, participated in voting. Voting performance of India has been much better than some of the Middle-East countries who are high on other indices. Thus, while much behind in urbanisation compared to Turkey, and having just half its literacy rate, India had a higher voting rate; in Turkey, 36 per cent people voted in 1950; in India, 45.7 per cent voted in 1952. Jordan had 20 per cent literacy (when India had in 1951 only 16.6% literates) but polling there was only 14 per cent.

The three communities of the U.P. district under study are very low in terms of urbanisation and literacy, compared to all-India pattern, and yet their voting rate has been fairly high.

2. It is true that the nature of political participation in the pre-Independence period was different, its intensity and mass character cannot be denied. A decision to oust the foreign rule and its implementation through "direct action" of "non-cooperation" was a participation in the movement—the revolution. Participation in voting may indicate a positive orientation, as helping the political "machine". Not only the rate of voting has increased over the years, Indian masses have also begun participating in the political system in a variety of ways: protests, strikes, challenge to the hegemony of the ruling party, etc. No doubt, such occurrences are still minimal, and many people do not actively participate in them; awareness about them and opinions on them are on the increase, however.

   In the three communities studies, voting rate has been quite high but the three are differentially developed. A composite index of participation prepared for them does not show a linear relationship—lower in SC, medium in LC, and high in COC. In terms of awareness and opinion this trend is much clear.

3. If we accept Lerner's definition of the word "participant" then in all the three communities, irrespective of differential modernization, we find remarkable similarity

during the second wave of interviews, when electioneering was at its peak. If we separate awareness and "having opinions" from their translation into action then we discover that the channel for most of them is voting alone.

4. The analysis also indicates that past political participation develops the sense of political efficacy in the participant and this sense of efficacy moulds, to some extent, future pattern of political participation.

It may be argued that without regard to urbanisation and literacy and media use people can be mobilised to participate. The fact of participation may widen the scope of awareness and opinion-formation. Rather than involving in the chicken-egg polemics, one can view them as mutually reinforcing processes.

References

Almond, Gabriel A. and G. Bingham Pawell Jr., 1966 *Comparative Politics: A Developmental Approach,* Little & Brown Co., Boston.

Atal, Yogesh, *Indian Democracy: A Sociological Appraisal,* Extension Lecture, University of Saugar, 1967.

(*i*) *The Modernization Process in India,* Seminar on Rural Change & Planned Development organised by Institute of Social Sciences, Agra University at Simla, 1969.

(*ii*) *Citizen's Sense of Political Efficacy, Economic and Political Weekly,* Annual Number, Vol. IV, Nos. 1 and 2, Bombay.

Deutsch, Karl W. and William J. Foltz, *Nation Building:* Atherton Press, New York, 1963.

Lerner, Daniel, *The Passing of Traditional Society,* Free Press, Glencoe (Paperback), 1965.

Russett, Bruce M., Hayward R. Alker, Karl W. Deutsch and Harold D. Lasswell, *World Handbook of Political & Social Indicators,* Yale University Press, New Haven.

Wilcox, Wayne, *Political Modernization in South Asia,* the Rand Corporation (p. 3845), 1968.

14

Modernization among the Tribes of the North Eastern India (Assam)

S.M. DUBEY

[I]

Despite their wide popularity in the contemporary literature of the sociology of development, 'tradition' and 'modernity' are still vague terms. Recently, a group of social scientists[1] has either attempted to define them or to develop their 'ideal types'. In this process, modernization has covered a wide field which includes a number of other concepts such as development, westernisation, industrial urbanisation, Sanskritisation and transformation.

'Tradition' and 'Modernization' are often used as polar opposites in an evolutionary theory of Social Change. In this approach, the basic hypothesis is that the social structure of traditional societies is simple, homogeneous, static, close and dominated by customs and traditions. These societies are less differentiated—with primitive agrarian economy and ascriptive system. Just contrary to the 'traditional model', 'modernity' represents rationality, emphasis on achievement, complex social structure, industrial urbanism, scientific outlook and complex organisations like state, party, corporation, etc. According to Daniel Lerner[2], "Modernization includes disquieting positivist spirit, a revolution in communication, increasing urbanisation, economic and political participation, social mobility and achievement. He prefers to use the term 'Modernization' in place of Westernization. Rostow thinks that the traditional societies are dominated by kinship and pre-conditions of science and technology. Their economy mainly depends on agriculture, which often suffers from fluctuations depending on the natural conditions.[3] According to him modernization starts with the 'take-off, which is the 'break' from tradition.

On the other hand, Gusfield[4] does not consider them as 'polar opposites'. In the light of Indian and other materials on development, he presents seven fallacies in this connection and points out, "It is incorrect to view traditional societies as static, normatively consistent, or structurally homogeneous. The relation between the traditional and the modern does not necessarily involve displacement, conflict or exclusiveness. Modernity does not necessarily weaken tradition. Both tradition and modernity form the bases of ideologies and movements in which the polar opposites are converted into aspirations but traditional forms may supply support as well as resistance for change. In his paper, Modernization is almost equal to 'Westernization' and he stresses in this respect it has been impossible to divorce 'modernization' from some processes of 'westernisation' which may be characterised with adoption of western way of life, liberal thought, parliamentary democracy, secular ideals and modern bureaucracy and industrialisation."

According to Srinivas[5], " 'Sanskritisation' and 'Westernisation' are the two aspects of social change in the context of India. Sanskritisation is the process by which a 'low' Hindu or tribal or other group changes its costume, rituals, ideology and way of life in the direction of a high and frequently 'twice born' caste. Generally such changes are followed by a claim to higher position in the caste hierarchy than that traditionally conceded to the claimant caste by the local community."

In connection with the present theme, this concept in the case of lower castes indicates towards the departure from the traditional custom, ritual and way of life and the adoption of the way of life of the higher castes. According to Prof. Srinivas, this practice has always been going on in India and this implies that the 'caste system representing tradition did not restrict mobility and change'. Srinivas thinks that "the term Westernisation unlike 'Modernization' is ethically neutral"[6], and it includes British way of life in India, Christianity, new technology, education, high income, urbanisation and secularisation and nationalism.

Social change in India, in the form of 'Sanskritisation' emerged out of tradition and as regards 'Westernisation'—a traditional modern continuum did exist. Srinivas thinks: "This continuity exists in a double sense—first, some members or sections of the traditional elite transformed themselves into the new elite and second, there is a continuity between the old and new occupations."[7]

In a Seminar recently held at Srinagar to discuss "Tradition and Modernization—their processes of continuity and change in India"[8], it was concluded: "Tradition and modernization should not be taken as one against the other.... they may be distinguished for analytical purposes, but in reality there is no exclusively traditional or modern society."

In the light of the above discussion and keeping in view the Indian situation in general and the tribal situation in Assam in particular, for the purpose of the present chapter and future field work, I would like to formulate my tentative generalisations:

1. Instead of emphasising only on the theoretical concepts, relation between "tradition" and modernity should be decided on the basis of the experience and conclusions drawn from 'field situations'.
2. For the analytical purpose, tradition and modernity are two different concepts and to understand the process of social change in the developing world these are very helpful 'categories'. As regards their relationship, in some 'field situations' there may be a continuity between 'tradition' and modernity, as for example, in the case of comparatively advanced section of Indian society and the developing world, but in the case of tribal population, 'modernity' is quite different from their traditional social structure, economy and political structure.
3. As a process of change, 'Modernization' may be regarded as a 'broad category' which includes 'Westernisation', 'Sanskritisation' and 'development', whereas 'Westernisation, in India is the result of the impact of external forces, 'Sanskritisation' has emerged out of Indian tradition but due to this process also lower castes and tribes have adopted a new way of life which may be

different from their traditions and customs and 'development' is the result of the planned change—particularly initiated by the State. Agents and instruments of these three processes are different from each other which will be clear by *Paradigm.*

4. In the context of the tribes of Assam, process of 'Westernisation' and 'Sanskritisation' have been going on since long and now the process of development has also started and their social implications are different from each other.

On the basis of the observation and historical facts, it may be concluded that there are chances of the 'traditionalisation' of 'modernization'. It happened so in the case of the Indian resurgence in the nineteenth and twentieth centuries and the same process has been repeated to a large extent in the case of hill tribes in Assam.

[II]

Let us now consider the case of tribes in Assam. It should be clear at the very outset that since times immemorial, tribal, Indo-Tibetan, Mongol, Vedic and Islamic cultures have been fusing together in Assam. That is the main reason why tribal as well as plain people were influenced by each other. An analysis of the social structure of Assam, will show that:

(*a*) the caste-system was never so rigid in this part of India—as it was in the North and South India in matters of untouchability and intercaste relations.

(*b*) a comparative freedom and equality were always enjoyed by the women of this part since there was no '*purdah* system' and still there is no system of dowry. Probably these are the results of tribal impact.

Ordinarily, Assam is divided into two parts—hills and plains. Population in the hills is mainly tribal whereas in the plains the major section of population is non-tribal but even save plain tribes which have accepted Hinduism and thus sanskritized are found.

According to an old arrangement, the tribal areas of Assam[9] are divided into two parts as below:

PART A

1. The United Khasi-Jaintia Hills District (Tribe Khasi)
2. The Garo Hills district (Tribe Garo)
3. The Mizo district (Tribe Lushai or Mizo)
4. The Naga Hills district (Tribe Naga with many sub-groups like Angami, Sema, Ao, etc.)
5. The North-Cachhar Hills (Tribe Cachharis)
6. The Mikir Hills (Tribe Cachharis and Mikirs)

PART B

1. North Eastern Frontier Tract—including Balipara and Tirap frontier tracts and Abor and Misimi Hills districts
2. The Naga Tribal area.

Paradigm									
Modernization (External Impact)				*Sanskritisation (Emerging out of tradition)*				*Development (Planned and induced change)*	
Agents				*Agents*				*Agents*	
Christianity	Modern Education	British Administration	Modern Political Organization	Impact of the caste	Urge to raise one's status	Change of religious sect	Change of traditional caste customs and the adoption of the rituals and customs of higher castes	State Bureaucracy	Developmental activities
A (In this model tradition and modernity may exist side by side and in some cases there may be traditionalisation of modernization.)				B (In this model tradition is replaced within the orbit of the old tradition.)				C (Transformation of the old society with emphasis on Socio-economic development)	

Among these tribal areas, an important process of modernization is the adoption of new administrative pattern. Now the Naga hills district has achieved the status of a complete Statehood while a new State is to be carved out of Assam, consisting of the United Khasi-Jaintia Hills district, the Garo Hills district and the people of the North-Cachhar Hills have to opt whether they would like to join the new State of 'Meghalaya' or would like to remain in Assam. The areas covered by Part B fall within the NEFA administration. From a political point of view, the tribes of Assam fall within the five political units as below:

(1) Assam, (2) Nagaland, (3) Manipur; (4) Meghalaya, and (5) NEFA

In this connection, it is noteworthy that in Assam there is a considerable number of 'Plain Tribes'[10] and they may be classified as given below:

1. Miris—mostly living in the districts of Sibsagar and Lakhimpur.
2. Cachharis—in the districts of Sibsagar, Lakhimpur, the Mikir Hills and the North Cachhar Hills.
3. Bodo—in district Goalpara and Lower Assam.
4. Deori—upper and central Assam.

For a sociological analysis, these tribes of Assam may be divided into three parts as given below:

1. *The South Western Hill Tribes:* consisting of the Khasi, the Garos, the Cachharis, the Mikirs, the Lushais and the Bodos, etc.
2. *The Naga Tribes:* The Naga Tribes can be classified into five major groups, consisting of the Rangpan and the Konyak in the Northern; the Rengma, the Sema and the Angami in the Western; the Ao, Lhota, Phom, Chang, Santam and the Yimstsungar in the central; the Kacha and the Kabui in the Southern; and the Tangkhul and the Kalyo Kengo in the Eastern sections.[11]
3. *The Plain Tribes:* consisting of Miri, Kachhari, Deori, Bodo and others.

These three tribal groups are characterised by different standards of social organisation, culture and language, development and social problems.

[III]

The next aspect of consideration now is the nature, extent, causes and consequences of modernization among the tribes in Assam. We have pointed out earlier that the tribes of Assam are at different levels of development and modernization. In paradigm we have divided modernization into 'Westernisation', 'Sanskritisation', and 'development' and these three models may very easily be applied to understand the process of change which has taken place among these different tribes. This does not mean that these three processes are quite independent or completely isolated from each other. On the other hand, these are overlapping categories.

Some social anthropologists have recently tried to explain the nature of social organisation of the different tribes in this part of India and the forces of change which are operating among them.[12] On the basis of the existing materials and systematic observation, the following three models of 'modernization' can be developed regarding these tribes.

Model 1: Westernisation

In the first model, the process of modernization is more westernised. In this model for a considerable period 'developmental activities' were secondary and even today there may be some resistance to the planned change in some areas. 'Sanskritisation'[13] is an insignificant process in this type and, at times, forces of conflict and separation appear to be more dominant.

Tribes: This type of 'Modernization' has mainly taken place among all the Naga Tribes, the Khasis, the Garos and the Lushais. We find a paradoxical situation among these tribes. On the one hand, these tribes are more westernised than even the most advanced sections of Indian community; percentage of literacy is the highest among the Mizo Hills in Indian and English is the official language of the State of Nagaland; the political awareness is very much developed; on the other hand, tribal values and loyalties are extremely strong.

Modernization has been 'transplanted' here from the outside and we find the 'traditionalisation' of modernization. The British Administration in India played a dual role regarding the status of the Naga tribes. On the one hand, foreign Christian missionaries were encouraged to work among them and on the other hand, they were kept "isolated" from the main current of Indian life. Organisations of the Nagas with British orientation were encouraged and when the Simon Commission visited Kohima in January 1929 members of the Naga Club (an organisation founded under the official patronage) submitted a memorandum to it demanding that the "Nagas should be excluded from the proposed reforms and kept under direct administration to save them from being overwhelmed by the people of the plains".[14]

The following quotation will indicate that they are not only 'westernized in dress, religion and education but ideologically too. Mr Gadogan visited Kohima in 1935 when freedom for India was just within the range of vision and he delivered a speech in the House of Commons, "they (Nagas) said 'we hear that a black king is going to come to rule over India. If that is so, for goodness sake, do not let it to be a Bengali'. They ended by saying that they much preferred Queen Victoria."[15]

Agents and the Indicators of Modernization

For a future empirical research in this model, the following forces may be regarded as the agents and the indicators of modernization:

1. Christianity,
2. Modern Education and a high percentage of literacy,
3. English language,
4. British administration,
5. New political organisations (The Naga National Council—now divided into many functions and the present ruling party in Nagaland and All Hills People's Party working for the creation of Meghalaya),
6. Westernised dress and food,
7. Modern Schools, Hospitals and postal service,
8. Urban growth (Shillong and Kohima are within the tribal areas),
9. Modern means of transportation and communication,

10. Money economy,
11. Improvement in agriculture and cottage industries, and
12. New political system and the separate statehood.

The main problem before the sociologists and the planners in India regarding some of these tribes is to analyse and understand the root causes of the 'separationist tendencies' and to integrate them with the main current of Indian life. As Barua points out, "It will be indeed an interesting spectacle to see how the hill groups with their basic Christian orientation (westernization) and a more or less undecided attitude to the western way of life (as it seems now) grow side by side with the traditional Hindu India."[16]

Model 2: Sanskritisation

In this model, modernization in the form of change in the tribal way of life, customs and rituals have enlarged out of the impact of Hindu traditions. The second process in this model is 'development' and 'westernization' is not so significant here.

The second model (Sanskritisation) is applicable mainly on the plain tribes, viz., the Cachharis, the Miris, the Deoris, the Ahoms and the Bodos, etc.

Agents and the Indicators of Modernization

1. Adoption of Hindu rituals, customs and names;
2. Impact of the 'Vaishnava' movement led by Sri Sankaradeva;
3. Adoption of Assamese language in the place of the different tribal languages;
4. Social reform movements and the National Movements;
5. Modern education, schools and hospitals;
6. Modern means of transportation and communication;
7. Tribal blocks and the community development;
8. Reservation of seats in legislatures and Government services;
9. Modern dress; and
10. Improvement in agriculture and cottage industries.

In these tribes process of 'integration' and identification with the national life is quite strong.

Model 3: Development

In the third model the process of 'Modernization' is taking place in the form of 'development' through a planned effort of the agencies of the Government. In this model, the tribal tradition is deliberately being preserved though attempts are being made for raising the standard of living, productivity and to provide facilities for better and modern education to the tribal population.

Agents and the Indicators of Modernization

1. Governmental agencies,
2. Bureaucracy,
3. Community Development,
4. Tribal Welfare,
5. Modern education: schools and hospitals,
6. Introduction of new political system,
7. Improvement in the techniques of agriculture,
8. Tribal voluntary organizations and Ramakrishna Mission,
9. Money economy,
10. Modern means of transportation and communication, etc., and
11. In some areas, due to the impact of Buddhism, we find the process of Sanskritisation also.

In these tribes, process of modernization in the form of development has strengthened the process of 'integration'.

Finally, for a proper understanding of change and 'modernization' among the tribes of the North Eastern India, it is essential that there should be emphasis on the comparative studies since 'modernization' itself is a relative term and the different tribes in this region are not on an equal level of development.

Regarding the development of the NEFA tribes, a middle path between 'assimilation' and 'isolation' is being followed.[17]

References

1. W.W. Rostow: *Stages of Economic Growth*, 1960.
   D. Lerner: *The Passing of Traditional Society*, 1958.

C. Geert. (ed): *Old Societies and New States*, 1963.
Apter: *The Politics of Modernization*, 1965.
Joseph R. Gusfield: *Tradition and Modernity: Misplaced Polarities in the Study of Social Change*. 'Economic Development and Cultural Change', July 1965, pp. 385-393.
S.N. Eisenstadt: *Modernization—Protest and Change*, 1967.

2. Daniel Lerner, *The Passing of Traditional Society*, Glencoe III 1958, pp. 45-49.
3. W.W. Rostow, *Stages of Economic Growth*, 1960, Cambridge University Press.
4. Joseph R. Gusfiel, 'Tradition and Modernity: 'Misplaced Polarities in the Study of Social Change,' *American Journal of Sociology*, Vol. 72, 1967, pp. 351-362.
5. M.N. Srinivas, 'Sanskritization' in *Social Change in Modern India*, 1966, p. 6.
6. *Ibid*., pp. 52-54.
7. *Ibid*, p. 69.
8. S.K. Srivastava (Discussionist), 'Different approaches to Tradition and Modernization'. Presented in the Seminar held from 29th June to 3rd July 1968 at Srinagar (Kashmir).
9. P.K. Bardoli: "Social Structure of a village in Upper Assam" (dissertation for M.A. examination—Dept. of Sociology, Dibrugarh University, 1968) under the supervision of the author of this paper.
10. Report of the Commissioner for Scheduled Castes and Scheduled Tribes, 1956-57.
11. Two plain tribes namely Miris and Cachharis were selected for study by the students of the Department of Sociology (1968), Dibrugarh University and the report will be finalized in near future.
12. B.S. Guha, "Indian Aborigines and Who They are 'in Adivasis'". The Publications Division, Government of India (Revised edition, June 1960), p. 32.
13. These works of Verrier Elvin are very important. A Philosophy for Nefa (1957), *Myths of the North East Frontier of India* (1958), *The Hill People of North-East India* (1960).
    Furer-Haimindrof: "Naked Nagas" (second revised Indian edition (1962).
    Sachin Roy, *Aspects of Padam Minyong Culture* (1966).
14. Verrier Elwin, *Nagaland*, p. 49.
15. *Ibid*., p. 50.
16. Dr Dilip Barua's paper, "Socio-Economic Development and its Cultural Interaction—with particular reference to the North Eastern region of India", read out at a seminar sponsored by the Department of Sociology, Dibrugarh University (January, 1969).
17. Verrier Elvin's book, *A Philosophy for NEFA* (Chapter II: The Fundamental Problem, pp. 29-60) throws a light on this point.

15

Some Thoughts on Tradition and Modernization

R.N. SAKSENA

Modernization, as a phase of and consequent to economic growth, has recently attracted much attention of sociologists, mainly from those who are concerned with analysing and conceptualising social change. In various contexts modernization includes certain ideals, which provide the base for the ideology of the politically alert, articulate and active part of the population—particularly the intellectual elite. Consequently, the judgements that follow refer to the opinion of these groups. The inclinations of the broader strata of the population, who are not yet touched due to lack of awareness, represent the masses who resist and create obstacles. This has given rise to the recent intellectual exercise of building up concepts regarding tradition and modernity. In fact so far as the ideology of a developing society is concerned, it represents a dichotomy. But it is worth analysing, for purposes of scientific study, the essential attributes and the factors that lead to these ideals.

The sponsors of this series of seminar have to be congratulated for having brought out a number of interesting reports on various themes and aspects of modernization, based both on thematical and empirical investigations which have great relevance to our society. But I suggest improvement of the host of undesirable conditions in the social system that have perpetuated a state of underdevelopment. Planning represents the search for a rational coordinated system of policy measures that can bring about development.

(*a*) *Rise of Productivity*: It is generally assumed to be achieved primarily by improved techniques and increased capital intensity in all branches of production and by an improvement in what is generally called modes of production.

(*b*) *Rise of Levels of Living*: This represents the main object of planned development. In a developing society, the levels of living are already low and naturally this constitutes emergent area. But it is possible that substantial improvements in levels of living may be postponed for some time to come in order to permit capital accumulation and even higher productivity.

(*c*) *Social and Economic Equilibrium:* In India this ideal has, on the general level of valuations, been carried to the point of widespread acceptances of such radical policy to formulate as "a socialistic pattern of society" and the "classless society". Naturally, this ideal implies a radical change in social and economic stratification.

The magnitude of the problem can easily be seen by the sharp reaction of eminent Indian sociologists to the inequalities resulting from the social gaps and handicaps created by the present system of social stratification in our country. At the end of his book, *Social Change in India,* M.N. Srinivas has allowed his personal feeling to come to the surface after an excellent macro-sociological study of the subject when he writes: "Finally, my stressing of the importance of the Backward class movement and of the role of caste in politics and administration are very probably the result of my being a South Indian and a Brahmin at that. The principle of caste quota for appointments to posts in the administration, and for admissions to scientific and technical courses produces much bitterness among Mysore Brahmins. Some of these were my friends and relatives, and I could not help being sensitive to their distress as well as to the steady deterioration in efficiency and the fouling of inter-personal relations in academic circles and the administration—both results of a policy of caste quotas. As one with a strong attachment to Mysore, I could not but be affected by the manner in which conflict between castes prevented concentration on the all important task of developing the economic resources of the State for the benefit of all sections of its populations."

That these reports may be consolidated into a single report highlighting the following points:

(*i*) What are the trends and salient features of modernization that has taken place in Indian society;
(*ii*) To what extent has Indian society been modernised;
(*iii*) How far has induced change been successful in accelerating modernization; and
(*iv*) What are the additional values that have provided resistance to Modernization and to what extent have they proved to be helpful in this process?

However, modernization must be understood not only from the economic point of view. A society may be highly mechanised, yet experiences no change in attitudes and social structures. Just as modernization cannot be identified with industrialisation or economic growth it cannot also be identified with the development of democratic institutions. As Gunnar Myrdal observes: "All countries of South Asia began their independent existence by declaring their ambition to become democratic nation-states; they gave themselves Constitutions, or began to work on Constitutions, on the pattern of those recently evolved in Western countries, with representative assemblies founded on free elections and universal suffrage. They also attempted to establish legal guarantees for civil liberties and to give these a very inclusive interpretation. As these ambitions were thwarted in some countries in the region and their full realisation curtailed or endangered in all of them, certain alternative ideals.... compatible with the genius of the country were substituted for the original Western ideals.... Yet it may be doubted whether this ideal of political democracy—with freedom of assembly, press, and other civil liberties should be given weight in formulating the modernization ideals. This is not because the ideal is at present not very fully met, and may not be met in future...but experience has shown that, unlike other value premises this ideal is not essential to a system comprising other modernization ideals. National independence, National Constitution, changes in institutions and attitudes and equalisation, rise of productivity, rise and redirection of consumption, and more generally, planning for development can be attained by an authoritative regime bent on their realisation. On the other hand, the substitution of an authoritarian regime for a more democratic one gives no assurance that policies will be directed towards the realization of those ideals, or that, if so directed, they will be more effective."

But success of any social and economic planning programme in a poor society depends essentially on popular cooperation and joint responsibility in local and sectional communities within it. This represents the core of democratic planning and is sometimes called democracy at the grassroots. In a traditional society, this imposes a kind of social discipline and implies various institutional changes and derived value premises.

In the Indian context some changes that are likely to occur from a traditional to a modern society are:

1. Age-old agricultural implements and methods give way to tractors and fertilizers.
2. Health improvement through more varied food and public medical care.
3. Distances are shortened by the speed of improved means of communications and mechanised transport.
4. Printing and other media of mass communication supplement the reliance on oral communication.
5. All interdependence comes into being between the communities that previously were separated from an independence of one another.
6. Population shift from the countryside to the towns and urbanisation takes place rapidly.
7. Money is used more commonly as a medium of exchange and replaces the unwieldy barter system.
8. Sustaining economic growth begins to occur.
9. A taste of consumer goods becomes more diversified.
10. Formal school replaces tribal initiation. By and large, ascriptive status tends to give way to achieved status or those with ascriptive status school to compliment it with achieved status.
11. Occupations become more skilled and specialised.
12. Salaried employment in industry and elsewhere begins to spread and more impersonal labour relations dominate.

13. Civil liberties, established according to rational and universalist norms, replace the slow-going personal administration of royal courts and village elders.
14. Sharper distinction arises between work and leisure.

Not all these processes may work at the same pace and may even become a problem with respect to extent of temporal sequence and length of tolerable variation. Thus, modernization should be understood not only with reference to its economic implications; but more important are its social implications, particularly so far as they concern attitudes and social structures.

Thus, modernization may be said to have main characteristics: a temper for science, reason and rationalism, secularism, and a growth-oriented economy. The necessary concomitants of Modernization may be stated as: significant changes in production, urbanisation and industrialisation, individual freedom and a social system based on contract and not status. There are certain prerequisites of social change also, which are essential for modernization:

(*a*) An awareness of preparedness with an eye to the future and a sense of urgency;
(*b*) An infinite variety of opportunities and roles;
(*c*) An intellectual understanding of and an emotional preparedness of self-imposed tasks and sacrifices; and
(*d*) The elevation and emergence of a dynamic and determined leadership.

However, in this context we cannot ignore the fact that Indian society has been tradition-bound to such an extent that it has practically become an immobile society. In a society of high mobility which has been toward an 'open society' a person can change his position freely, utilising his abilities and opportunities which came his way. In an immobile or 'closed society', on the other hand, no individual would be able to change his personal social fate; by 'change' is meant the extent of invention and innovation which take place in the institutions, ideas when it is encouraged, and the idea of change is itself a positive value of a culture, what results is a society that may be characterised as mobile and modern. When change is slow and infrequent, when it is discouraged by the institutional or ideological structure of a society, and when quietism rather than change are the evident value of its culture, such a society may be characterised as 'immobile'.

The Indian caste system is an extreme example of immobility. In urban areas, caste system is undoubtedly shedding its rituals. But the vast rural areas remain very much as before. Even in cities there is no evidence that caste, as a system, is losing its grip. The change is rather in the attitudes of the castes, which now work to improve themselves and to raise their social standing; it is not in the direction of dissolving the system as such. In some respects, caste-consciousness has become even more acute. Many people, stimulated by their in-group feeling, want to preserve caste system all the more tenaciously. Each tries to organise itself for social, economic and political purposes. Even elections are being fought on caste lines.

In the process of modernization, the problem India faces is whether caste and democracy are campatible. Obviously not. It is perhaps still too early to predict whether democracy or caste will win ultimately in India. What we are witnessing at present is that we have the outer form of democracy, but the inner content is of caste, which may ever be called 'casteocracy'.

16

Tradition and Modernization Dichotomy

M.N. SRINIVAS

The tradition and modernization dichotomy is an extremely popular with sociologists these days. It may be said to be part of their "conceptual baggage". So much so that the two concepts are taken for granted, and it is usually thought superfluous to ask the question how far they refer to existential situations. Obviously, in the twentieth century, no society is either wholly traditional or wholly modern. For instance, England, which may be described as a country where some events and processes which are universally regarded as part of modernization had their origin, has several extremely "traditional" areas. To quote but one example, dining arrangements in an Oxford college—at least as I knew them some 22 years ago—are governed by tradition and ritual. The dining hall reflects the academic hierarchy in the college. The dons dine at the "high" table, which is on a raised platform in the hall while the students' tables are on a low level. The latter are again distinguished on the basis of their seniority and scholarly record. There are separate tables for the first, second and third year students, and for those who have won scholarships, to the college, and the lowest student table is farthest away from the high table. The dons enter the dining hall by a separate door leading from the Senior Common Room where they smoke and drink port after dinner. The Rector or Master presides over the high table and the food served there is better than the food served to the students. Once the dons retire to their Common Room, the Rector ceases to be Rector and assumes the role of merely a fellow of the college. The seating arrangement around the fire in the S. C. R. is again hierarchical, with the oldest fellow occupying a place closest to the fire, while the junior most fellow has the duty of passing around cigarettes, cigars and port. In brief, dinner at an Oxford college is a highly traditional and hierarchical affair.

Before World War II, the public schools as well as Oxford and Cambridge gave some preference in the matter of admission to the sons of their former students. In fact, among the upper sections of British society it was common to send up the name of a son soon after birth, to the public school and college where the father had been a student. In other words, "ascriptive" considerations were given a certain weight by these institutions. Entry into these institutions facilitated entry into the "Establishment", a term which was appropriately invented in Britain several years ago. I shall not elaborate on this further but merely conclude this point by saying that when I was a student in Oxford I heard several dons bemoan the fact that the people had become, in contrast to their younger days, are very serious place where students, many of whom were married and had returned after war service, only concentrated on their studies with a view to securing jobs and settle down. Gone was the *old joie de vivre* of Oxford, and the student who enjoyed himself and gave free rein to his individuality.

If a "modernised" country such as England had until very recently (and perhaps even now) areas of social life which are "traditional", and if customs and laws are changing rapidly in a "traditional" country such as India, how far is it meaningful or heuristically useful, to characterize entire cultures as traditional or modern? Are we using this dichotomy merely because it is academically fashionable? Do we find here only a desire on the part of Indian sociologists not to be left out of the academic bandwagon?

I shall now mention a central difficulty with the concept of "modernization". It does not merely refer to a cultural and social process but also involves the value-judgement that modernization is good and desirable while traditionalism is bad and undesirable. Yet another assumption which seems to be present, though rarely articulated, is the idea that modernization is inevitable, however long drawn out the process, just as traditional cultures are on the way out. Sociologists who discuss tradition and modernization make certain that they are betting on the winning horse. I have rarely found anyone of them standing up for tradition and against modernization.

There is yet another difficulty. How can one be sure that something is a part of modernization? The experimental method of science and modern knowledge can certainly be included under modernization but what about a great many things which seem to have no necessary relationship with modernization such as fashions in clothing and recreation? Are pop music, art and the taking of psychedelic drugs—to mention but three things—parts of modernization? If they are not, then only some things and aspects of the culture of the industrially advanced countries of the West are subsumed under "Modernization" while others are not. If so, what are the criteria by which we identify events, processes, techniques and objects as modern?

An external symbol may be easily identified as modern but the inner attitudes and values that accompany them may be something else. A highly educated and efficient business manager may be consulting astrologers about his personal and factory problems. Workers in Indian factories, even those working with sophisticated machines, are known to make the same gestures of reverence which they make to their deities, before beginning the day's work. And during the Dasehra, machine, cars, cycles, etc. are cleaned, washed, decorated with vermilion and garland.

I suppose a strong nationalist movement would be regarded as part of the modernization process as it generally means the increasing participation of the people in the political process. But nationalism can transform itself into chauvinism, xenophobia and militant expansionism, and lead to courses of action which may result in national suicide. How does the student of modernization cope with this problem? What are the criteria by which social goals are characterized as rational or irrational? Even the public discussion on these goals which occurs in a democracy does not guarantee their rationality. Democracies can also be in the grip of national hysteria especially in these days when governments have control over powerful mass media. And, in the last analysis, the question has to be asked whether rationality can at all be predicted of the ends of social action. Social goals are essentially non-rational in character.

It would be profitable to dilate a little on the question of rationalism: When self-consciousness comes to a people it comes at every structural node and not merely at the apex. But politicians and nationalistic historians like to stress the growth of nationalism, and belittle, ignore and bemoan the simultaneous emergence of lesser group identities. But the sociologist has to take a more scientific view of the phenomenon. Along with nationalism there emerges a host of lesser identities, and in a poor and illiterate country, for the majority of the people the lesser identities may seem more immediate than nationalism. Further, once the central aim of the nationalist movement has been achieved, the lower identities may increase in strength, and pose a threat to the new nation which has come into existence. Such new identities are emerging, for instance, in the north-eastern hill regions, and while a concern at what is happening in this strategic part of the country is only natural, it should not be forgotten that the process is essentially similar to that which happened in the mainland of India several decades ago. It is understandable that in a country of the size and heterogeneity of India, self-consciousness comes to various groups at widely different points in time.

Yet another point. A well-known characteristic of Indian society today is the fusion of cognate sub-castes or *jatis* to form bigger groups or categories which occasionally cut across a few states. I have used the term "horizontal solidarity" to describe this process, and the infrastructure for this process was provided by the development of communications—railways, roads, post and telegraph and printing. These emergent castes are essentially different from the *jatis* of pre-British India which were part of a local system of interdependent units. It is very likely that there has been systemic change in the caste system as castes or caste sections get increasingly freed from the local multi-caste frameworks to form the horizontal entities which act as political and economic pressure groups, and provide facilities for mobility for their members. These castes are in a relation of competition with similar other castes for political and economic power.

This brings me to another point. It is not only in the caste system that changes of a fundamental character are occurring but also in religion. The Arya Samaj, Brahmo Samaj, Ramakrishna Mission and other similar movements, all represent attempts to reinterpret Hinduism and provide it with new institutional systems. This is how such an acephalous entity as Hinduism has tried to adopt itself to the forces and challenges of the modern world. I do not have the time to go into the details but broadly this reinterpretation involves an attempt to distinguish the "essence" of Hinduism from its historical accretions. Even when there is an open call to go back to the *Vedas* what is really involved is an attempt to rid modern Hinduism of many of its most obnoxious features which it acquired in its post-*Vedic* history. Paradoxically, a call to return to the pristine past is really an attempt at marching forward.

The new Hinduism is also characterized by an emphasis on social and political action. It has increasingly displayed a concern for the weaker sections of the society, the Harijans, women, and the poor and the sick.

Among the western-educated intellectuals or folk popular Hinduism has been interpreted as a concession to the ignorance of the uneducated and the poor, and philosophic Hinduism, especially as expressed in the *Upanishads, Vedanta,* and the Six Systems, has been given the pride of place. Indian intellectuals take a great deal of pride in their philosophical and spiritual heritage, and the exposition of Indian thought reveals a strong streak of nationalist pride.

Finally, the institutions on which Hinduism is dependent such as caste, village and the monastic and family systems are all changing in significant respects, and this cannot but have repercussion on the religion as a whole.

All that I have said so far should not, however, be interpreted to mean that there are no genuine problems in the empirical region denoted in the tradition/modernization dichotomy. The attitude of a great many Indians to time and work, their sensitivity to urban and industrial hazards, and their levels of organisation, is all characteristic of a rural civilization which is in varying stages of transition to an industrial meritocracy. For many years to come, a good deal of our research work will lie in this enormously untidy and complex but fascinating area. It requires a great deal of painstaking analysis. We should take up small areas for research and put together the results for individual industries, professions, etc., in order to get some idea of the nature of the intermeshing of the diverse and complex forces which are active.

PART TWO
The Emerging Features of Tradition, Modernization and Globalization

17

Globalization with Multiple Modernities

YOGENDRA SINGH

The social science debate on Globalization is at present highly fragmented. It is mainly due to the increasing ideological and emotional ruptures on this issue on a global scale. The euphoria about modernization and Globalization which existed in the mainstream thinking at one point of time (during the early 1950s) has undergone radical reorientation. Now, social scientists show near unanimity in believing that the course of modernization would not be in the singular but manifest plural forms. It would reflect and incorporate the specificities of each culture and its basic characters. It would, in general, follow an adaptive rather than transformative path in bringing about social, political and economic changes in different societies. Several new counter ideologies which not only interrogate or challenge but also reject the notion of Globalization have gained prominence. The concept of modernity and the process of modernization are now domains of thought which inspire both hope and disenchantment.

What are the reasons for this disenchantment? What social and ideological factors have gone into the shaping of this phase of rationalisation and counter-rationalisation of issues? What epistemological and philosophical questions arise from the viewpoint of its theoretical analysis? These and a few associated aspects of the problem deserve our attention. Here, we would examine some of these contemporary questions. These may be classified as: (1) epistemological questions of theory and ideology;

(2) issues of identity and culture; (3) social structural problems of political economy, levels of development and political and social equality-inequality and marginalisation.

Epistemological and Ideological Issues

The epistemological and ideological anchorage of the notion of modernity rests in the Enlightenment philosophies of the West which deeply influenced the paradigms of social sciences. It is reflected in the focus upon reasons and humanism. The normative legitimation of secularism was its logical consequences. The contemporary debate on 'reason *versus* faith' in the discourse on modernity and post-modernity has its antecedents in the past European history of differentiation of the relationship between Church and State, the institutionalisation of the principles of legal rationality in polity and economy, recognition of the right of the individual 'citizen' and consequent republican revolution. It is also reflected in the revolutionary structural transformations in European society through phenomenal technological, scientific and economic progress. This scientific and technological advancements led to the celebration of reason, individualism and faith in linear progress ideologies. Individualism and market rationality contributed to the rise of capitalism, new class structure in society, colonial expansion of European empires and markets in Asia, Africa and Latin America. The expansion of international trade and migration of labour during this phase of colonial capitalism is treated by some historians as the precursor of Globalization.

Epistemologically, positivism and methodological individualism are two main features of the theories on which the concepts of modernity and Globalization have been traditionally founded. Faith and values which could not be justified on the rational-pragmatic principles of utilitarianism are to be rejected from scientific discourse. Universal and uninterrupted social progress seems to result as an axiomatic consequence of such theorising. The dominance of this paradigm continued in the European thought well up to the end of the nineteenth century. Thereafter, serious challenges to the axiomatic belief in universal reason began to emerge because of a series of historical contradictions of capitalism, imperialism and colonialism. Both the notions of universal reason and that of primacy of individual as a unit-component constituting society were seriously challenged by Karl Marx and Sigmund Freud (see, Singh Y. 2004). Both of them rejected the assumption that human institutions and actions were universally guided by principle of reason. Marx elaborated upon how capitalist economic system which apparently functioned as a goal-optimising rational institution of profit and capital accmulation contained in itself the seeds of self-destruction which intensified in its course of advancement due to structural and historical class contradictions. Freud wrote extensively on how human actions and choices were not always governed by the utilitarian rationality or hedonistic calculus. Such actions were often motivated by deliberate choices which were irrational and out of the ken of the pleasure principles.

Several cataclysmic crises that the Euro-American society went through during the early nineteenth century, such as the Russian Revolution of 1917, the First and the Second World Wars, the rise of national liberation movements in the colonies which led eventually to the collapse of colonial empires, reinforced an intensified rethinking on the paradigm of rationality. The rise of Nazism and Fascism as racial and cultural ideologies which perpetrated the "holocaust" and mass murders of the Jews shook the foundations upon which the philosophies of universal rationality both in the domains of social and cultural choices as well as application of modern sciences and technology were embedded. This led to the emergence of "critical theory", uses of phenomenological and interpretative social and cultural paradigms for the study of different societies and cultures in respect of both modernization and techno-economic development. The rise of post-modern philosophy and its interface with the social science theories is a consequence of these socio-cultural developments. But such theories in their mood of disenchantment have generally erred in respect of meaningful integration of the objective principles of scientific methods with the post-modern models of their social science explorations (see, Singh Y: 2004). However, the acceptance of the presence of 'multiple modernities' now by the mainstream sociology and social sciences marks a major epistemological shift in the studies of Globalization and modernization.

Issues of Identity and Culture

The presence of multiple modernities recognizes the relevance of the issues of identity and culture of societies with dissimilar heritages and civilizations. Most discussions on this problem have recently confined themselves to a distinction between "faith" and "reason", in other words, the specificities of cultures and societies with dissimilar religious belief systems. Its premises are adequately supported by empirical facts. The response of different faith-communities at the global scale has demonstrated a variety of patterns of both Globalization and modernization. We have witnessed unprecedented rise of conflict and violence based on misconceptions about religion and faith recently. It continues to baffle us since the perpetrators of such violence make full use of the technological and financial instruments of Globalization which they paradoxically perceive as a threat to their faith. Evidently, most such violence based on the paradigms of faiths arises from more complex set of issues of identity, social structure and culture. For instance, can the totality of the 'identity' of a community or society be reduced to religion or faith of its members? Does religion, any religion of the world, justify the kind of violence being witnessed in most parts of the world as a call of its basic religious principles? Can faith and reason be reconciled?

There is massive literature based on empirical studies which suggests that community's identity is formed by multiple sets of cultural, historical and social determinants of which faith constitutes a vital component, no doubt, but is only among several other factors. These factors may include historical antecedents of contacts with other cultures, the compositeness of culture, ecological and geographical locations, levels of economic developments and differentiation of work and occupation. Not all these factors which enter into the formation of identity of a particular community or religious group can be subsumed by faith. "...cultural identity is linked to the dynamics of culture as constituted by its need to rationalize either on account of factors which are *sui generic* or are results of intervention from outside. The perception of the 'other' in terms of one's own culture energizes the construction of identity. The processes of 'development', which are sponsored by the state, by the social groups or classes wielding power within society or the outside agencies invariably impact upon people's self-consciousness of their own culture, its symbolic significance and resilience and symbolic power to withstand the challenges of change and development." (see, Singh Y: 2007: 196-97).

Obviously, the rational factors among others influence constitution of identity due to the imperatives of the uses of science, technology and other tools of capital, money and market, etc., so essential for a community's well-being in the modern world. A large part of these cultural attributes has a global character of sharing and interdependence. A significant residual part of such institutions, no doubt derives its flavour and style which are grounded in local realities. That is why today Globalization proceeds along with localisation. Faith and reason, therefore, are bound to coexist in contemporary world of high uses of technology, massive and large-scale migration of people of different faiths and communities all-over the world and their coming to terms with problems that humankind faces today threatening its very survival, such as ecological disaster and global warming etc. These are common threats to all those living on earth despite the differences of faith, culture and identities.

Social Structural Issues in Evaluation of Globalization

The presence of 'multiple-modernities' in a globalising world recognizes the significance of the social structural issues as well as those related to the cultural identities of nations and communities. It contends the hypothesis of optimists like Friedman who pronounces that Globalization has made this world 'flat' or that it overrides the social and cultural differences and inequalities. The theoretical appraisal of Globalization has differed both in theoretical and substantive terms on account of ideology such as the liberal *versus* Marxists, or on account of its substantive perception in segmental or holistic terms. The deeper social structural and historical interface of institutions of each individual societies or cultures in terms of their initial conditions while coming into contact with the forces of Globalization are often overlooked. J. Stiglitz, for instance, in his *Globalization and Its Discontent* as well as in *Making Globalization Work* critiques Globalization mainly in terms of the role that international agencies or policies of the developed nations have to play in making it a success. Most other economists too have focused on the centrality of the economy and market institutions in their assessment of this process. For an objective appraisal of Globalization this needs to be supplemented with a holistic perspective rather than a segmental one. This has relevance to both the theoretical and structural analysis of this process.

Segmental Evaluation

Most substantive and theoretical treatments of Globalization are based on a selective, often singular factor in their studies and appraisal. Such treatment remains segmental. A segmental evaluation Globalization process is self-limited in its critique or prognosis. There are several varieties of segment theorising on Globalization, but amongst them the 'political economy' approach anchored in the Marxist discourse is the most prominent. This approach gives centrality to the economic factors. These include flow of capital, technologies and market linkages on a global scale from the metropolitan developed countries to the developing nations at the periphery. It is assumed that beneficiaries in this process are the multinational capitalist corporations. They benefit from the low wages and skilled human resources available in these countries. The capital investment is for optimisation of profit, extension of market access and a new form of control on economy of the developing societies. Most advantages from Globalization, according to them, are unilateral rather than reciprocal. Globalization reinforces or only replaces the traditional form of dependency of the poorer nations over the rich in a new incarnation. The Brettonwood institutions and WTO, etc., are designed to reinforce this iniquitous exchange. Globalization, therefore, enhances rather reduces poverty and creates social structural asymmetries in the receiving countries. Its impact is often socially schismatic. It may create enclaves of prosperity for a few in some sectors of economy, but it does not contribute to reduction in poverty of the people at large, such as the peasantry, the working classes and the marginalised communities in villages and towns.

According to the Marxist approach, this form of Globalization also subverts the ability of the state to pursue autonomous policies of social welfare. It hinders rather than helps the state in creation of avenues of empowerment for the peasants, working classes and the marginalised groups through independent initiatives. It binds the state-sector into ties of agreements with the global institutions such as the WTO and a variety of regional blocks with terms of trade which enhance its vulnerability and circumscribes its autonomy for taking initiative for the welfare of the poor. Globalization, therefore, according to the Marxist or the neo-Marxist theory exemplifies several features of neo-imperialism or neo-colonialism in relation to the institution of state and public policies in the developing societies. In substantive terms, it enlarges social cleavage, expands the nature and scope of national dependency on global capitalism whose priorities belong to maximisation of profit rather than reduction in social disparities in the developing societies.

The 'political economy' approach to Globalization, in logical terms, has no doubt elements in its theory which can lead to a holistic study of this process. But in practice, its evaluation of Globalization process is self-limited as it equates Globalization entirely with global capitalism and underpins its evaluation with ideological nuances whose relevance today is hugely debated. It is true that spur to global dynamism comes from capital investment, its flow or expansion of markets and trading activities which come from corporate capitalism originating in the rich societies. But it is yet to be established that such investment in the developing countries adds to their social structural inequities. It also remains to be established that states lose their initiative or autonomy on policies as Globalization gains momentum. In fact, the recent Human Development Report of the World Bank argues in favour of more rather than less initiatives from the states for removal of economic disparities, empowerment of the weak and overall development of less developed societies. The Marxist and neo-Marxist critique of Globalization focuses only upon a selected segments Globalization processes, such as foreign sources of capital and its investment for profit, exploitation of low wage human resource in the developing countries and promotion of adverse terms of trade, intellectual property rights and right to work, etc. Even though some of its inferences may have validity, it is no longer true that corporate capitalism is confined only to the rich countries; several developing countries, including India are witnessing a growth of local multinational corporations with global investment of capital. The iniquitous terms of trade are under continual negotiation and fiscal policies of countries, such as India, remain cautious without being inflexible. The same is true for labour policies and intellectual property regimes. The Marxist approach perceives Globalization merely as an instrument of dependency of the poorer countries over the rich. It overlooks, however, a variety of areas in which Globalization is creating social, cultural and economic space among societies to become interdependent.

The other variety of segmental approach to Globalization is reflected in the ideologies of a variety of new social movements. These movements take up various issues of contemporary social concern in right earnest and organise protest movements against Globalization from time to time. From Seatle to Bombay, the champions of these new social movements have been agitating against the institutional framework of Globalization and also its policies. They perceive Globalization process and its ideology as being instrumental to perpetration of countless new ways of exploitation of the weaker and marginalised sections such as the women, the working classes, the peasantry, the artisans, the refugees and the displaced communities and the small traders. Unlike the Marxist, the new social movement does not consider exploitation perpetrated through Globalization to be asymmetric. It perceives Globalization as a universal phenomenon both in the poor countries at the periphery as well as the rich ones in the metropolis. The activists engaged in the new social movements focus upon human and civil rights, protection of environment, right to health care and protection of ethnic cultural identities of the minorities, tribes and ethnic groups, etc. They view Globalization as a mindless pursuit of market for profit, production to promote consumerism and growth without generating employment. They reflect a range of interest groups and are organised on these lines. Each interest group offers a critique of Globalization from its own segmental perspective. But taken together, these movements exemplify a collective manifestation of disenchantment from the contemporary processes of Globalization. Only the irony is, that new movements have to utilise the instruments of Globalization such as the new information technology, computers, internet and telephony, etc., to first globalise their movement and then protest against

Globalization. This only proves the efficacy of Globalization and its social contradictions.

To what extent is the disenchantment from Globalization justified? One reason for disenchantment is the Globalization impacts in unexpected and dissimilar ways on different societies and on different sections of people in the same society. Its influence is mediated by specificities of history, social structures, economy and culture. Globalization in the developed world engenders anxieties among members employed in professions, among working classes and retail traders, etc., for various reasons: it contributes to growth without generating commensurate employment, there is constant fear of sudden unemployment due to continual structural changes in the economy and outsourcing of jobs, and finally, Globalization also brings in workers from other cultures due to higher demand and short supply of labour in an ageing population in the rich societies which at times becomes a cause for cultural dissonance or even conflict. Michel Chossudosky calls the latter as the "third-worldisation" of the western cities. The developed nations faced environment problems due to unfettered industrialisation much earlier. They have successfully brought about technological and social adjustments to overcome this problem; they are at present engaged in strengthening the civil society. However, each interest group leading new social movement against Globalization looks at it from a segmental perspective. The disparate worries of several interest groups, such as the trade unions, environmental and gender activities, etc., in the rich countries find a common ground with those in the developing societies where too there is disenchantment with Globalization for similar or different reasons. Together, it has generated a global debate about the impact of Globalization on the welfare of human societies.

The criticism of Globalization in the developing countries follows a different historical and social structural trajectory. Social inequalities, poverty and lack of political and cultural empowerment of the marginalised and the poor are some of the most urgent and specific issues here which dominated the discourse on Globalization. And yet, there are issues such as the degradation of ecology and environment, the destruction of biodiversity, the issues of gender and human rights which are common between these societies and the rich ones. The historical and social dimensions of the perception of problems may be different but the disenchantment and anxieties are universal. It is, therefore, obvious that analysis of the social, economic and political consequences of Globalization in the developing societies and its conceptualisation would have to be not only innovative but also holistic in perspective. A segmental approach may not be able to capture the complexity of the issues that the processes of Globalization trigger in the social structure, polity and economy of the developing societies. A holistic approach is required.

A Holistic Evaluation

The lack of a holistic approach to understand Globalization arises out of several misconceptions about it. First, Globalization is not located in proper historical perspective; it is treated as a temporally discontinuous process. Hence, false dichotomies of eastern and western civilizations as cultural borderlines of Globalization are drawn. Globalization is not entirely a product of the western civilization; it has been long in the making and most societies and major civilizations both of the east and the west have made contributions to the myriads of technological and intellectual endowments which in totality have today evolved and converged into the processes of social and cultural changes which we define as Globalization. Secondly, Globalization is a multidimensional process founded as it is on the revolution in information technology such as computers, Internet, telephony and multimedia, etc., which converge in strengthening its reach; Globalization impact is not only seen on economy but also on culture, social structure and polity. There is a viewpoint with which I am inclined to agree that Globalization is a process which may lead towards the birth of a new society, known as the "information society". The information society would inaugurate radical transformations in the basic principles of governance and in the structure and function of a range of institutions of a contemporary societies when fully evolved. For instance, the information society may resolve the limitations of the electoral politics of the representative democracies of today through widening the base of "participatory democracy". This may be possible by empowerment of people with new information technology, education and reduction of their social and economic deprivations. It would make "participatory governance" possible. Its corollary would be the growth of a strong civil society to overlook and audit the working of the state and other vital economic and social institutions of society.

Similarly, it would introduce radical changes in the structure of economy due to the inevitable changes in the mode of work, concept of labour and occupational mobility. Also, it may bring about reform in normative and objective orientation of corporate capitalism. The growing strength of civil society and its sensitivity to the market situations in a variety of social and economic settings are most likely to put pressure on corporate capitalism to become socially responsible in its own self-interest. A variety of new models of capitalism in the age of Globalization are now in circulation. We might mention here the debate on "inclusive capitalism" in India. It implies a collaborative effort by corporate capitalism and the civil society to involve the poor and the marginalized in productive activities that are beneficial to them and which are also linked to an assured market profitable for capital investments by industrial concerns. Eventually, the strength of the civil society is bound to exert pressure upon the functioning of economy and its institutions such as banking, trade, and market as it may call for increased transparency of information, participation of people in governance and in policy formulation. The civil society may also achieve the power of networking, quick feedback and retrieval of facts in case of deviation from expected norm. Expectedly, the process of Globalization should release social forces which serve as correctives to its pitfalls and help in ethicising its economic, social and cultural consequences.

The information society model might also make new structural and cultural changes inevitable for a host of vital institutions of society such as family system, gender inequalities, primordial relationships of tribes, ethnic groups and communities and identities both of individuals and groups. The higher quality and wider range of empowerment, accruing simultaneously both to the individual and collectivities may be a result of the revolutionary changes in the models of production and the scale of freedoms that information society may render accessible to people. It may offer varieties in the choices to people in matters of lifestyle, modes of work, occupation, marriage, belief systems, customs and rituals. The fear about the loss of identities of local cultures, ethnic groups or nationalities is unfounded. It has been noticed that despite multicultural impact that Globalization may have on communities their local cultures in India continue to have vitality and their cultural identities, indeed become stronger than ever. These identities are being strengthened through technologies and opportunities that the processes of Globalization sets into motion such as the mass media, external and internal migration, electronic media of entertainment and social mobility. Due to the influence of migration and media several religious customs, rituals and festivals which once were localised to a few regions or were confined to a singe state have now spread across regions or have become pan-Indian or even global. The traditional producers of cultural objects, folk artisans, artists and religious functionaries which for long had only a local presence are now increasingly being brought within the network of global space with the help of media and market. Studies show that the Indian Diaspora too is not culturally displaced from its roots, rather its native cultural identities are only strengthened following emigration. There are endogenous forces that reinforce cultural identities. But exogenous factors emanating from Globalization are also making an impact. We notice increased incidence of branding of ethnic culture, culinary practices, fashion designs, artistic and aesthetic objects, etc. Their exposure to global market through new institutions has increased as never before. New facets of tourism which are oriented to global market such as religious and health tourism or eco-tourism have gained momentum. The consumer industries such as hotels and restaurants and other institutions of recreation focus increasingly upon ethnic styles, a variety of Indian culinary heritages. On the other hand, there is fusion on global cultural styles, practices and forms, such as in music, dance, culinary practices and other artistic creations. Increasingly, the multinational consumer industries have had to bend to the Indian cultural sensitivities in branding and marketing of their products. If, on the one hand Globalization strengthens identities, it also on the other increases the space for inter-cultural global reciprocity and inter-dependence.

It is, however, true that the hypothetical information society is yet to come to full bloom anywhere in the world. Towards this end, it is not clear as yet how the increased pace of Globalization would impact upon nation-states, cultural identities of nationalities and ethnic groups. What is obvious so far is that Globalization contributes to modernization or hypermodernization in only selected domains of economy, polity, culture and social structure. Its influence is confined to those sectors of society which are closely linked to instrumental or technological aspects. In matters of the fundamental values such as those of multiple civlizations or religious systems and ideologies the principle of 'multiple modernities' remains still valid. Any effort to efface such multiplicity can be fruitless or even schismatic to the process of Globalization itself. The fear of clash of civilizations in the West, the rising incidence of communal conflict in Europe between the emigrant and the native population and global fear of terrorism are only some indicators of the unintended consequences of Globalization. The world also stands at the thresholds of new technological innovations and discoveries, such as in genetic engineering, biotechnology, nano-technology and exploration of space. These are sure to add impetus to the forces of Globalization but would at the same time create new domain of uncertainties, contradictions and anxieties. A holistic understanding of Globalization is, therefore, necessary to face up to the challenges and opportunities that it offers to us today.

Multiple-modernity and Globalization in India

What are the challenges that Globalization poses for the Indian society? How is it related to the problem of poverty in India? Does Globalization compromise the autonomy of our state? How far is the new economic policy of the state an endogenous commitment or an outcome of Globalization? Does Globalization threaten our cultural identity and the identities of local cultures, and ethnic groups? To seek answer to these questions we may have to explore the nature and extent of Globalization taking place in India. It also may necessitate an objective evaluation or analysis.

India throughout its history has maintained active economic, cultural, scientific and social contacts across nations and societies. Its cultural traditions, religions, science, art, aesthetics and trade have had contacts across civilizations for centuries, and also through such it has enriched its own cultural heritage. India is the home of numerous racial groups, communities and tribes who have emigrated to its land and enriched its diversity through plurality of customs, lifestyles and traditions. Over a period of time, India has successfully evolved a unity of inter-civilizational consciousness without compromising its own identity or the identities of a variety of local cultures and diverse ethnicities rooted in religion, language, region, caste and tribes. It has, therefore, traditionally been familiar to a kind of proto-Globalization ever since its history. The contemporary processes of Globalization, though qualitatively different do not add up to being entirely unfamiliar or unexpected to the people of India.

Yet, the processes of contemporary Globalization have implications for societies which are entirely unique in history. A product of new innovations in information and communication technologies and modes of production, Globalization impacts upon economy, society, polity and culture of societies leading to irreversible revolutionary consequences. Its reach is universal, and for nations now to pursue a policy of economic autarky or cultural and social isolation is impossible. Globalization does not impact in a uniform manner in all societies. Historical antecedents, specificities of social structure, culture on the one hand, and on the other the nature of the economic and social policies pursued by nations in their encounter with Globalization make a major difference in the ways that Globalization impacts upon societies. Also, Globalization is not a single but a set of heterogeneous processes and not all its processes may impact in a similar measure in each society. For instance, India has moved much faster in the sphere of Globalization of information technology and services but has been cautiously slow in other sectors, for instance, in its economy.

The processes of Globalization imply a variety of elements. Its first element is the revolutionary changes in information technology, such as computers, Internet, telephony, multimedia and space technologies, etc. Secondly, Globalization leads to the emergence of new economy and mode of production which radically change the traditional role of capital, labour, money, banking and market. The scope of these are extended, as never before. Thirdly, Globalization implies active partnership of multinational and multilateral institutions such as the World Bank, International Monetary Fund and World Trade Organization and the regional blocks for trade and economic cooperation. These play a role in formulation of policies and strategies. Fourthly, Globalization gives impetus to international migration and emigration of working population which intensifies inter-cultural contacts, creates new spheres of cultural identities and, may lead to problems of inter-cultural conflict or tensions. Finally, Globalization ushers in a cultural revolution on an international scale as never before. Increasingly due to Globalization cultural personnel, products, cultural symbols, festivals and ceremonies at the local level come into contact with other cultures all-over the world. Simultaneously, the local cultures are exposed to the challenges from the market forces, corporate capitalism and mass media. This brings a threefold consequence, firstly, inter-cultural consciousness and contact increases, secondly, local cultures become more conscious of their identities and thirdly, cultures face a new threat by becoming a commodity and come into the realm of the market forces and market economy. Globalization, therefore, impacts upon cultures in contradictory fashion; it empowers local cultures by extension of their space and at the same time poses challenges to their identities.

From 1991 onwards when India started economic liberalisation and gave up the import substitution model of economy, the space of Globalization has moved cautiously and in a controlled manner. India joined the multilateral institutions of Globalization, but unlike several of the pacific nations, it did not open its economy to the floodgates of structural reforms recommended by the World Bank and IMF, etc. It remained conservative in respect of monetary, banking, fiscal and trade policies. Its negotiations with WTO on agricultural subsidies continue before opening the agricultural sector of economy to global competition. On the issue of Intellectual Property rights India remains vigilant in negotiations. Many sectors of the Indian economy, such as reform in labour policy, insurance, banking and foreign investments etc., have yet to be opened up to global standards. Correspondingly, the rate of foreign investment in India has been slower but its rate of economic growth has remained almost stable at 6 per cent and is now rising. India has thus been able to avoid the social cost of the structural adjustment in its economy which almost invariably worsens the condition of the poor and weak in society.

India has, however, globalised relatively faster in communication and information and services sectors of economy. Its impact is visible in our culture, lifestyle and social institutions and practices. The presence of a substantial section of influential

Diaspora attracts more and more tourists from all-over the world and consumption and marketing of the Indian cultural products, skills and knowledge are expanding fast across the globe. The identity of local cultures has in this process shown a new resilience. Together with this we also notice increased incidence of fusion of cultural styles, forms and products. The teledensity in India is increasing at a faster pace. Now, the cellular telephony has surpassed the landline telephones. Access to computers and Internet though limited at present is on a growth trajectory. It does create a digital divide but if there is a convergence of efforts by the state, the non-governmental organisations and support from an inclusive corporate capitalism, this gap could not only be bridged but converted into a potent instrument for increasing literacy, health care, productivity and market access to the peasants and workers in the remote parts of India. Globalization, using technologies in a flexible manner, may contribute to the diversification and modernization of the rural economy by networking of information about markets, institutions of research and upgradation of technologies.

Globalization as such does not hinder but may help in reduction of poverty. A wide variety of experiments on this issue in various parts of India are currently going on. But the most effective manner in which Globalization helps in reduction of poverty is by creating employment opportunities for the poor, increasing their productivity and quality of life. This is achieved by infusion of capital investment, creation of jobs and improving the quality of governance. Multinational institutions and foreign capital contribute to this end not alone but in partnership with the nation-state. There is a crucial role for the state and the democratic institutions in the determination of policy and the pace of implementation of Globalization policies. Though belatedly, even the World Bank has realised this fact and now supports state initiatives in this regard. We notice that in the cultural and social spheres, Globalization is no longer considered to be a threat to cultural and social identities in India; rather its processes are increasingly being Indianised.

Globalization is not a single process nor is it a homogeneous phenomenon. It is a step towards irreversible social, economic and political evolution of human societies made possible by new innovations and revolutions in technology. Its impact on societies is variable with their initial historical conditions and in the manner that societies of adaptive responses which depend upon several factors, such as the nature of state, its initiative, the role of civil society and also corporate capitalism. Globalization may help in the emergence of a world order conducive to global growth and peace, but it may not lead to either the irrelevance of the state or the nation-state. Globalization manifests many universal attributes but it is highly civilization-specific. Multi-modernities will, therefore, survive despite the successes of Globalization.

References

Singh, Yogendra, *Ideology and Theory in Indian Sociology*, New Delhi, Rawat Publications, 2004.

______, "Composite Culture, Community and Identity: Interface with Social Change in India", in Bipin Chandra and Sucheta Mahajan (ed.), New Delhi: Pearson Longman, 2007.

18

Tradition, Modernization and Globalization

Conceptual Shifts and Ideological Constraints

S.M. DUBEY

In the Indian sociology, since 1950s, there have been much discussions on tradition, Sanskritisation, westernisation, development and modernization. The concepts and theories of development and modernization were evolved in the Western academic world. The concept of Sanskritisation was an Indian version of acculturation. The process of westernisation was the byproduct of the joint ventures of the colonial rule and the spread of Christianity in Asia and Africa. Now, in Indian sociology there is as much talk of Globalization as it was regarding modernization in 1960-70s, without much realisation that these two concepts are the refined extensions of the original notion of westernisation. The sequential genesis of these three concepts primarily indicates only conceptual shifts, without much alterations in their contents and they are constrained by the ideological baggage of the western polity and economy.

In the post-Second World War period, a group of western social scientists took keen interest in the study of the relationship among society, economy, polity in 'newly independent states' of Asia and Africa. Much earlier, Karl Marx, Emile Durkheim and Max Weber had already laid the foundation for the future debates on development and modernization. Lewis (1955), Parsons (1960),

Hoselitz (1960), Rostov (1960), Hagen (1962), Myrdal (1968), were concerned with the relationship between society and economy, with special reference to economic growth, development underdevelopment, poverty. While discussing the relationship between society and polity, in spite of divergence in their approaches, the focus of Deutsch (1953), Shils (1960), Lipset (1963), Geertz (1963), Smith M.G. (ed. 1968), McCord (1969), Bendix (1969) Gabriel and others (ed. 1960) was on nationalism, political development, new states in old societies, pluralism in Africa, evolution of developing societies, nation building and politics. The 'new states' after their independence have started the twin processes of nation building and economic development. There was a natural interest in understanding how the primordial social order, traditional value system and conservative mindset of the old societies are taking a modern shape. The works of Lerner (1958), Parsons (1960), Shils (1961), McClelland (1961), Smelser (1964), Smith W.C. (1965) Eisenstadt (1966) and Apter (1966), promoted studies on modernization.

These studies raised a number of issues pertaining to relationship between tradition and modernization, whether they are polar opposites or there is a continuum between the two (Gusfield: 1967), universal structural ingredients and normative aspects of modernization (Parsons: 1951), psychological motivating factors in modernization (McClelland: *ibid*), context specificity and historicity of modernization (Levy Ir.: 1955; Myrdal: 1968).

Conceptually, the notion of modernization was *ad hoc* and historically of limited time frame. That is the reason why within two decades, there were constant shifts from growth to development, from development to modernization, from modernization to post-modernization and then to Globalization. The term 'underdeveloped' earlier used for the Asian, African countries was considered to be impolite and, therefore, a more acceptable term 'developing' was coined. The earlier division of the world into 'east' (traditional/backward) and 'west' (developed/ modern) was replaced by 'north' (rich, prosperous, modern) and 'south' (traditional, underdeveloped, poor). In the cold war polemics, the world system was classified into the 'first world' representing democracy—capitalism—consisting of Western Europe and North America, the 'second world' of the communist Soviet Russia, Eastern Europe and the 'Third World' of Asia, Africa and Latin America (Horowitz: 1966) which was supposed to be non-aligned to the power blocks. The concept and the structure of the 'second world' collapsed. Today, the USA is the only superpower. The world system is based on the market economy. The concepts of modernization and now Globalization are not free from the context-specificity, Euro-US-centric ideology, western democratic liberal value system and the ethos of capitalism rooted in the free market and open competition.

In contrast to the liberal-capitalist approach, Marxist scholars talked of modernization in terms of the historical-materialistic stages of development from feudalism to capitalism, from capitalism to communism, proletarian revolution, rule by communist party, social-economic equality, classless society, co-operation and scientific socialism. After the Bolshevik Revolution in 1917, the social, political, economic experiments started by Lenin (Christopher Hill: 1977) in Soviet Russia worked as a model for these scholars. In 1960s to a group of Marxists, the Soviet Russian model appeared to be 'revisionist' and they were enamoured by the Chinese path of modernization–based on peasant revolution, one party rule, 'great leap forward', 'cultural revolution' and socialism as interpreted and led by Mao (Philip Short, 1999) in China.

A critical appraisal of modernity and of its expanding process has been made by a perceptive sociologist of the late twentieth century (Zygmunt Bauman: 1987, 1989, 1991) who had rare experience of the 'modernity' in the fascist, communist and the capitalist systems. As a Polish Jew, he had first-hand understanding of the inhuman acts committed by state under the Third Reich. He had an insider's knowledge of the totalitarian, socialist modernization in Soviet Russia as a student, as a soldier of the Red Army in the Second World War and as a staunch communist who was later on thoroughly disillusioned by the working of the communist system in Soviet Russia. As a revisionist emigrant settled in the West, he is a keen ob server of the liberal capitalist modernization suffering from the 'guilt' and 'dethronement' after the collapse of the Western European imperialism.

To Bauman, modern age has a history and it began in Europe sometime in the late sixteenth century. Modernity represents constant change, latest ideas and technical kits more advanced than the previous versions. At the heart of modernity is the struggle for betterment between ideologies. In the modern age, the nation-state, science and capitalism are three key players. The ideologies of social Darvinism, *laissez-faire*, democracy linked with Keynesian welfarism; fascism and communism assign roles to state, science and capitalism. The people select their ideologies in accordance with their choices and preferences.

Bauman is considered to be a leading analyst of post-modernism but he is of the firm view that modernity as a value system and modernization as its process have not ended. Following the footsteps of the post-modernists, he offers a critic of the European modernization represented by the 'great narration' of fascism, capitalism, communism and pinpoints their betrayal to the people. In between the two World War period, the German state guided by the ideology of national socialism under Hitler, succeeded in economic and technological modernization with a 'civilizing mission' which ultimately led to the most catastrophic war and the most inhuman 'Holocaust' in human history (Dennis Smith: 1999). Bauman's analysis of Hitler's Germany may be helpful in understanding the fallout of 'modernization' started by European powers in the South-North America, Asia and Africa. Under the garb of 'discovery' and the Christian 'civilizing zeal' millions of original inhabitants were killed in the Latin and the North America in the post-Columbus phase. The people of Asia and Africa were enslaved by the modern, capitalist, western European countries. They started colonial rule, exploited resources, violated human rights and enforced imperialism in the name of western values and modernization. In the communist countries, the basic human rights and freedom were denied to the people in their notion of modernization. The so-called civilizing policies practised by the imperialist powers all-over the globe and the zeal of imposing their brands of modernization by fascists Hitler-Mussolini in Germany and Italy, by communists Stalin-Mao in Soviet Russia and China and the autocrat Shah in Iran led to the cruel death of millions of innocent people.

In the process of modernization associated with industrialisation, technological progress, large-scale production, mass consumption, market economy, democracy, European languages, culture, there is an implicit 'dependency' relationship between the core/centre/metropolis/promoters of the images of modernity and the fringe/periphery/province/colonies/latecomers who try to imitate these images (Richard: 1987). Modernization in Latin America unfolded as a process of Europeanisation. Later on, there was greater influence of the USA. In India, as indicated by Marx, the image of dependent modernity was provided by England. Similarly, the other colonial powers like France and Portugal imposed their economic interests, language and culture on their colonies.

Simon During (1993) thinks that the process of westernisation/ modernization in the third world represents economic, technological and cultural domination of Europe. In his view, the concept of post-modernity has been intentionally evolved to wipe out the possibility of post-colonial identity. In the place of the post-modernism, there is a need for the concept of 'post-colonialism' to achieve an identity uncontaminated by Euro-centric images.

The Euro-centric modernization was based on industrial revolution, the nation-state and its energy sources were steam, electricity and petrol. The 1960s were the period of optimism, growth, development modernization, central planning, social welfare, whereas the 1970s were dominated by oil crisis, limits to growth, a mood of pessimism and the decline in the classical industrialism as discussed by Durkheim and Max Weber (Krishan Kumar, 1955). In 1960-1970s several sociologists talked of transition from industrial to the post-industrial phase of society (Toffler: 1970, Bell: 1973) and from modernization to post-modernization. Computer, new information technology, electronics, nuclear power and the digital devices brought about a great deal of change in techniques of production, information channels, concepts of time space, social-economic relationships and the international system. There was a split in the communist bloc led by Soviet Russia and China. Later on, communist system collapsed in Russia, central Asia and the eastern Europe. The rise of multinational companies, large corporations and the regional organisations have weakened the nation-state. The last quarter of the twentieth century is branded as information society, post-modern society, post-Fordism and the phase of Globalization.

In developing concepts in social sciences, first of all, there must be a rigorous analysis to understand the relationship between the concept and the social structure. Secondly, a clear demarcation is required between a context-specific term of limited usage and a concept which may be universally applicable. Thirdly, a sophisticated distinction has to be made between normal social change and societal transformation—leading to paradigm shift in social relationship, mode of production, economy, polity, technology, communication, ideas, symbols, and either a break or a smooth transition from traditional-customary ways of life. The liberal and Marxist models of modernization are equally burdened with the context specificity, conceptual shifts and ideological constraints.

[II]

The process of industrialisation and modernization in Europe in the second part of the nineteenth century found their powerful critics in John Ruskin (1860, 1871, 1874) and Leo Tolstoy. Their emphasis was on simplicity, nearness to nature, rural life and the dignity of labour. They tried to pinpoint the ill-effects of the modern economic system with a moralistic tone... Ruskin preached that men should not seek greater wealth but simpler pleasure; not higher fortune but deeper felicity.

M.K. Gandhi (1910) was influenced by Ruskin and Tolstoy. He raised doubts regarding the validity of the premises of the western industrial civilisation, education and political institutions. He offered an alternative framework for the reorganisation of Indian society on the foundations of truth and non-violence. In conformity with this moralistic overtone, mixed with political insight, he chalked out programmes of social reform, regeneration of village industries, decentralisation of polity-economy, basic education, rightful place of mother tongues, Hindi as a national language, constructive work, uplifting the status of depressed castes and tribes, civil disobedience (*satyagraha*) against foreign rule and injustice. It was some sort of a counter-culture-negating westernisation. Gandhi evolved his political weapons of *satyagraha*, fast, *hartal* out of the practices rooted in the Indian cultural traditions.

Before the rise of the theories of modernization, there was debate on tradition and the modern civilisation by people like Rene Guenon and A.K. Coomarswami who may be regarded as 'traditionalist'. In Coomarswami's view, the modern civilization is neither human, nor Christian. It is a murderous machine with no conscience and no ideals. The essential feature of the traditional society is 'order' (Coomarswami: 1919, 1946) which is absent in modern society. Among the Indian sociologists, A.K. Saran (1962, 1964) in conformity with Coomarswami, pleaded to develop social sciences on the 'First Principles of Traditional Wisdom'. The European critics of the industrial system and the 'traditionalists' in Europe and Asia could provide only a critical perspective to examine the pitfalls of modernity. Saran's focus is on examining the limitations of the positivist, evolutionary, Marxist theories and their methodologies. On the whole, their analysis is only of academic value. Contrary to them, Gandhi combined his theoretical understanding with political activism. Applying traditional techniques of mobilisation, he not only succeeded in overthrowing the British rule in India but through his insights, experiments, struggles and practices offered an alternative path of development in contrast to the western notion of modernity.

In the debate on tradition-modernization in sociology, traditional social structure is generally used as opposite to modernity. It is associated culturally with customs, mores, folkways, beliefs, practices; socially with family, clan, kinship, village, tribes, peasantry, low levels of literacy-urbanisation, less differentiation, mechanical solidarity; economically with poverty, backwardness, underdevelopment, tribal forms of production, barter system, agriculture, handicraft, localised small volume of trade, lacking rational means-end relationship; politically with small, local units such as territories of tribal/feudal chiefs, kingdoms, or large empires, command and authority confined to a single person, inheritance of political power by dynastic principle or by might and non-participant political behaviour.

In the course of his study of Mexican communities, Redfield (1955-56) developed the concepts of 'Little' and 'Great' traditions. Little tradition is represented by folk and peasant communities with their small role performers whereas the Great traditions in the peasant structure is represented by epics, classics, mythologies, literati, ritual leaders—performing superior roles and occupying high status. These concepts were applied by Milton Singer (1955-56) in the Indian context. According to him, villages, tribes, castes in different regions have their 'Little Traditions'. The 'Little' and 'Great' traditions derive a great deal of rituals and practices from each other. There is a cultural continuity between the two.

To D.P. Mukerji (1958) 'tradition' comes from the root 'traders' which means 'to transmit'. Traditions are supposed to have emanated from a source which may be scriptures, sages, mythical heroes with or without names. The historicity of traditions has to be recognised since they are quoted, recalled and esteemed. Mukerji feels that the first task for Indian sociologists is to study traditions. This should precede the socialist interpretations of changes in the Indian traditions in terms of economic forces.

Among the Indian sociologies, contributions of Srinivas (1966), S.C. Dube (1965, 1967) and Yogendra Singh (reprint: 1988) on modernization may be specially mentioned. Srinivas tried to understand the undergoing process of change in Indian society through 'Sanskritisation' and 'westernisation'. The first denotes the adoption of upper caste practices and rituals by the lower castes to upgrade their social standing and to claim the status of upper castes. By taking help of census reports between 1911-31, he shows how lower castes in different regions of India claimed the status of Brahmans, Kshatriyas and Vaishyas on the basis of rituals, puritanism and the nature of their work. During the same period, a movement, led by lower caste leaders, opposed to the upper caste rituals, practices and domination was going on in South India. Srinivas could not properly assess its impact on the mobilisation of lower castes. Westernisation, as generated by the British rule, indicates the imitation of western education, dress patterns, food habits, lifestyle by the upper section of Indian society. It is almost synonym to modernization in Srinivas's analysis.

Dube, characterizing modernization as the combination of social, psychological, political and economic factors, tried to evolve integrated idicators of modernization such as empathy, mobility, political participation (borrowed from Lerner), interest articulation, interest aggregation, institutionalised political competition (taken from Almost-Coleman: 1960), achievement orientation (from McClelland) rational means-end relationship (Weber and Parsons), faith in change, risk work culture, motivation for savings and wealth creation.

Singh treats modernization, as a dimension of the process of social change. He agrees with Milton Singer that there is the continuity of orthogenetic changes in Great (classical, Sanskritic, elite) and Little (folks, peasants) cultural traditions in India. Modernization in India, on the one hand is the result of indigenous factors and on other hand it has been influenced by Islam and the west. Macro-structural changes such as migration, urbanisation, industrialisation, roles of elite, industrial workers and the micro-structural changes in family structure and village community have accelerated the process of modernization.

In 1968, a project was jointly chalked out by the Department of Sociology, Benaras Hindu University and the U.S. Educational Foundation in India to undertake a three-phase study of modernization in India. At the theoretical level in the first-two phases, the main themes to be explored were relationship between tradition and modernization, conceptual framework, historicity, agents and indicators of modernization. The third phase was to be devoted to the field studies. Now in 2006, Prof. S.K. Srivastava, the main architect of the 1968 project, plans to revisit the question of tradition-modernization in India in the context of present-day Globalization. He has asked the original participants along with some younger sociologists to ponder over the theoretical and empirical aspects of tradition, modernization and Globalization. He wants a linkage between the two phases of his plans. In this context, a brief personal note wil not be out of place.

[III]

In 1968, I joined the Department of Sociology, Dibrugarh University. We were almost the first department in the country to start a post graduate course on the 'Sociology of Development' in which there was a major component on 'modernization'. The contributions of Daniel Lerner, E.E. Hagen, Marrion J. Levy, David McClelland, Talcot Parsons and Gunnar Myrdal on modernization were hot topics of discussions in classrooms and seminar halls in those days. Karl Marx was already included in the post graduate 'sociological theory' course. The North-East India is the home of so many tribes with their exclusive habitats. I developed a keen interest in understanding the society, economy, polity and the level of development among the tribes in the region. In that background, I was inivited by Prof. S.K. Srivastava to join a group of Indian sociologists, engaged in the study of modernization in India and the specific project given to me was 'Modernization among the Tribes of the North-East India'.

The second stage of Seminar on modernization was organised at the IIT, New Delhi. There were three main points in my paper 'Modernization among the Tribes of North India'. First, the relation between tradition and modernity may be decided by the experiences of the different societies and from the field situations in the context of the research project undertaken by the group. Second, modernization is a part of the broad process of social change. Third, 'sanskritisation', 'westernisation' and 'development' are the three visible agents and indicators of modernization/ transformation in the tribal context of the North-East India. In different historical periods, they were instrumental in starting a 'break' from the traditional-customary ways of life and in introducing changes in tribal communities. The first point was much appreciated by Prof. M.N. Srinivas in his valedictory address. In the course of informal discussion, some Marxist participants asked me how Sanskritisation can be an agent of modernization? A few other participants, trained in western-liberal tradition, thought that modernization was linked with industrilisation and, therefore, in the non-industrial tribal communities, how modernization could be thought about?

For the proper understanding of modernization as envisaged in the western liberal tradition, we must keep in view its context specificity, historicity, pre-modern and post-modern structural conditions. Modernity cannot be defined by the visibility of a few piecemeal attributes. There must be simultaneous social, economic, political and technological transformation in a particular historical epoch. A particular society may appear to be modern in some areas but in some other areas, it may be mores-bound. Therefore, mere presence of industrialisation, democratic government in the domestic field and urbanisation cannot be the real indicators of modernization as it is normally understood.

In the late eighteenth century, England was the centre of the Industrial Revolution and mother of the parliamentary democracy but it did not allow political participation of women in the democratic process and denied franchise rights to them till the beginning of the twentieth century. Political revolution took place in France and the USA in the late eighteenth century but they remained predominantly agricultural till the late nineteenth century. France did not allow franchise rights to women till 1945. Countries of the Western Europe and the USA were engaged in large scale lucrative slave trade till the last part of the nineteenth century. On the suspicion of being witches, thousands of women were burnt alive in the nineteenth century Europe. The basic human rights of gypsies are even today denied in Europe. Normal civil rights to the blacks were granted by the American laws in the late 1960s. France did not allow franchise rights to women till 1945. Over and above, England and France were champions of imperialism till the later part of the twentieth century. The annihilation of aboriginal people in Australia-New Zealand by the British immigrants and the treatment meted out to Vietnamese-Algerians by France during 1950-60s was inhuman.

Going much beyond rituals, multi-dimensional sanskritisation (perhaps may be substituted by a more appropriate term), specially the growing contacts with the Hindu peasantry had far-reaching impact on social mobility, achievement orientation, state formation, permanent settled village community, permanent cultivation, new tools, use of plough, human energy supplemented by the use of animal (bullocks) energy in agriculture, bilinguism, script, symbols, myths and legends of the Indian tribal communities in general and of the North-Eastern tribes in particular. In this context, starting from the eighth century A.D. to the twelfth century A.D., the structural transformation which took place among Gonds (central-south India), Bhils (central-western India), Kunabis (Gujarat-Maharashtra), Bodos, Koch-Rajbansis, Kachharis, Ahoms, Tripuris, Meiteis, Khasis, Jayantias (North-East India) and Chakmas (Buddhists, majority of them living in Bangla Desh) are of tremendous sociological significance. In that historical phase, Europe was passing through the 'dark age'. These epoch-making changes—indicating shift or break from 'tradition' can be effectively explained by the concept of 'transformation' which is free from the ideological bias, more objective and expansive than modernization.

The hill tribes in the North-East India came in contact with the British rule and Christianity in different decades of the ninth century. They were converted to Christianity. A few English medium schools were opened in tribal areas. A few tribal men and women adopted western dress but their tribal structural base remained intact. They were subjugated and they lost their political power. The plain tribes like Rajbansis, Bodos and Kachharis during the phase of sanskritisation experienced upward social mobility and succeeded in carving out their own kingdoms. With the advent of the British rule, they lost their royal status and dignity. But the process of sanskritisation, continued unabated, encouraging upward social mobility among them—passing through the status of Sarania, then to status of Koch and finally to the status of Kayastha—next to Brahmans in Assam. The early impact of westernisation among the hill tribes with the advent of the British rule, Christianity, stray English education and a few lower level government jobs led to 'structural duality' whereby a Christianised superstructure was imposed on the deep-rooted tribal social-economic base. In the post-independence period, constitutional safeguards, developmental activities and political reorganisation offered them reservations in educational institutions, government jobs, state assemblies and the Union Parliament, accelerated the process of modernization, granted them statehood, provided them autonomy and offered them full opportunities for political participation.

[IV]

In 1970-80s due to increasing oil crisis, the pace of growth was restrained in the western world. It was realised that the industrial system, dependent on petrol to a great extent, has limits of growth. The conservative ideologies were upswing and the welfare programmes of social democrats were under attack in the western world. The economic policies were dominated by 'Thacherism', 'Reaganism' and 'Degaulism'. In this period, a group of sociologists started talking of 'post-industrial society' (Bell: 1973) which is regarded as the conceptual product of the right wing ideology. The Marxist scholars disagreed with the idea of the 'post-industrial' and they preferred to use the concept of 'post-Fordism'. It was soon followed by the debate on the 'information society' which fits in the liberal tradition of the western thought (Krishna Kumar: 1955).

Alvin Tofflier talks of the 'Third Wave' (1980) of the social transformation which is different from industrialisation and modernization. This phase of momentous social change is articulated through the concept of information society which is post-industrial and post-modern. The latter two are having an ideological tilt but the knowledge-based 'information society' is a neutral social reality—equally acceptable to the left and the right.

Industrial society with its heavy machines, large factories was a goods producing society and it passed through the phases of steam, electricity, petrol, and the first phase of modern communication system such as electric telegraph, telephone, radio, cinema, TV. Toffler talked of post-industrial society in his book *Future Shock* (1970) and the change was so rapid that only within a decade, he introduced the concept of 'information society' (1980), based on electronics, super computers, digital devices.

Since then, the revolution in the field of information technology (IT) and unthinkable speed in the field of communication-transport have turned the globe into a village. The large scale multi-national corporations, plastic money with highly sophisticated banking system, unprecedented migration-mobility at the international level, large volumes of international trade unknown earlier in economic history, international organisation such as the World Bank, IMF, WTO have accelerated the emergence of a new form of economic-commercial Globalization.

There is a great deal of confusion regarding the historicity of Globalization. Thomas Friedman (2005) thinks that when Columbus reached America in 1492, opening trade between the Old World and the New World, that was the beginning of Globalization. In his view, there are three eras of Globalization. The first lasted from 1492 to 1800 which depended on muscle, horse, wind and steam powers in a sequence. This era was dominated by religion, imperialism, mercantile trade and large sea going boats. The period from 1800 to 2000 is the second era of Globalization which witnessed the beginning of industrial revolution, steam engine, rail road, tele-communication, and maturation of global economy. In this era, the multinational corporations became the driving economic force. It was interrupted by two World Wars and the Great Depression. The post-2000 era is the third phase of Globalization which is characterised by software, global fibre optic network and from size small to size tiny.

As regards the original source of Globalization is concerned, Lechner and Boli (ed. 2004) point out that in the opinion of many writers, the sixteenth century Europe may be regarded as original source of Globalization due to the increased travel, trade and exploration of new routes. But in their view, after the World War II, improvement in communication and transport led to better connectivity among groups, institutions and countries. At the end of the twentieth century, Globalization became an all-purpose catchword in public and scholarly debates. In Toffler's analysis, the process of social development has passed through 'Three Waves'. The 'First Wave' was of agricultural development consisting of around 10 thousand years, followed by the 'Second Wave' of industrial revolution and mammoth industrialisation. The post-1980 phase is represented by the 'Third Wave' with features of knowledge of industry and information society which have accelerated the process of Globalization.

Like development and modernization, the historicity of present-day Globalization, as discussed above, is narrow, Euro-centric and shows the ignorance of the available ancient and medieval evidences. During the last five thousand years, there were constant endeavours in different civilizations to explore and to integrate the world through voyage, trade, migration, empire building, religion and cultural exchange. There are several archaeological evidences, historical records and linguistic features of pre-Christian era which demonstrate widespread influence of Indian trade, culture and polity on the South-East Asia, East Asia, West Asia and Europe. The economic, political and cultural contacts of India with Rome and Greece are well-known. Indians *via* South-East Asia succeeded in crossing the Pacific and reached Mexico. A recently found record indicates that in July 923 AD an Indian explorer reached Mexico in his trade ship (*The Hindu*: 1985). The Romans and Greeks in the ancient period succeeded in integrating almost the whole of Europe, North Africa and West Asia with their empires. The Mongols in the medieval period could overpower Central Asia, East Asia, South-East Asia, West Asia, East and Central Europe. In the medieval period, the influence of Indian trade, polity, religion and culture was deep-rooted in South-East Asia which is visible even today. The religious preachers of Hinduism, Buddhism, Christianity and Islam tried their best to propagate their religions in different parts of the globe. Capitalism through liberal democracy, private enterprise, market economy and communism through proletarian revolution, abolition of classes, state control, planning tried to build international systems in their own mould.

Berger and Huntington (ed. 2002) talk of many Globalizations, mainly based on cultural diversity. According to Lechner and Boli (*ibid.*), there are economic, political and cultural aspects of Globalization. In economic sphere, there is integration of the world market. In political, sphere the viability of the nation-state is being questioned and there is a serious attempt to reorganise the world in the western democratic framework. Two trends are visible in the cultural field. First, there is likelihood of the greater homogeneity which is being augmented by media and communication networks. Second, is the rise of the religious fundamentalism, opposing the liberal ideology. In Berger's analysis, Globalization has led to the core-centre/periphery-dependency relationship as it happened in the case of development in 1950-60s. In this relationship, America is in the vanguard of Globalization.

Discussing the cultural dynamics of Globalization, Berger thinks it has influenced both elite and popular cultures. The vehicle of elite culture is what Huntington calls the 'Davos culture' on the basis of the annual meetings of the world leaders to discuss politics, economy, industry, business. In the area of popular culture, food, dress, fashion, language, films, TV, theatre, art forms are being influenced by Euro-American culture. In the era of Globalization, as discussed by Craig and King (2002), the question of global *vs.* local culture has prominently emerged. They explain the nature of political, ideological and spiritual tensions in Asian popular culture by examining the contents of Chinese music, drama and TV programmes, moral advertising in Malyasian TV, cult and popular media in Thailand and revisioning of Japanese religiosity. They indicate that the imported cultural forms have been reinvented in local popular culture. In reality, in the name of the 'global' the North American culture has spread all-over the world. The local cultural forms are only the pale imitation of this so-called global culture.

There are two opposite assessments of Globalization. Its advocate like Thomas Friedman (*ibid.*) argues that the twenty-first century will be remembered not for military conflicts or political events but for a whole new age of Globalization, a flattening of the world. The explosion of technology, knowledge pools and resources have connected all parts of the globe with each other. Due to the software, open-sourcing, in-sourcing and in-forming, the world has become flat—levelling the playing field as never before. Though, he casually mentions 'crisis' and 'untouchables' in 'Globalization, yet in his flat thinking the complexity of terrorism, rising fundamentalism, crises of nation-building in Asia, tribal wars in Africa, dictatorship, death, disease, hunger in Africa, poverty in South Asia, rising cases of AIDS in Africa and Asia, denial of freedom and human rights, growing inequality are no problems.

On the other side, the critics of Globalization have looked into the growing economic, social and regional inequalities in the age of Globalization, eclipse of territoriality, weakening of sovereignty and gradual decline or demise of the nation-state. Commenting on the annual meeting of the World Economic Forum held in Davos in January 2006, Mei Xinyu, in his article, 'A Developing Inequality', (2006) agrees with the point of robust growth in world economy in the recent years, but at the same breath he points out that inequality has grown in the phase of Globalization. Oppello Jr. and Rosov (2004) have examined the nature of the ancient, medieval, modern territorial states, modern liberal and anti-liberal states in a historical perspective. The present state of states is passing through a crisis and the new global order has posed a challenge to the nation-state. The unprecedented global representations at the conferences of the World Social Forum, as an alternative to the World Economic Forum, demonstrate the growing opposition to Globalization. Since 1999, thousands of protesters gather every time to resist the ill effects of Globalization at the time of the meetings of the World Trade Organisation, an international UN body championing the case of Globalization.

With the spread of Globalization and the shrinkage of the nation-state, as indicated by Toffler, there is emergence of a global economy and 'planetary consciousness'. Two other trends— formation of regional groupings and the rise of ethnic identities are also prominently visible in this global phase. In the first category, the European Union and ASEAN have taken a formidable shape. The countries of South Asia formed the South Asian Regional Cooperation in 1985 but due to rivalries between India and Pakistan, cross-border terrorism, insurgency in almost all South Asian countries, it has not made expected progress. The inner contradictions within the nation-state, political-economic interests of the big powers, transnational corporations' interest in raw materials, energy, cheap labour, profit-making market have encouraged conflicts and weakened nation-states. There are separatist trends in England, Canada, Spain, Russia and China. A former province of Indonesia has already seceded. India, Sri Lanka, Pakistan, Bangladesh, Myanmar, Thailand, Philippines are facing insurgency. In this process, the global economic system and the local-ethnic sentiments are getting strengthened at the cost of the well integrated states as middle level units as it happened in the case of the Soviet Union and Yugoslavia. Perhaps, the same story is to be repeated in the case of Iraq also.

In the dynamics of human civilization, every epoch in human history experiences change and transformations. It is not correct to say that the inventions of man-driven Potter's, bullocks driven cart's or horse driven chariot's wheels were less revolutionary than the steam engine's wheels. Agricultural systems, with its techniques of production, feudal organisation and social values, was a global reality in which India and China were at the top in territorial integration, state formation, production and trade. The Industrial Revolution was an epoch-making phenomenon. From the western world, it was taken to colonies by the imperialist powers along with its imitative education, language, dress, religion, culture to serve their economic-political-cultural interests. By the middle of the twentieth century, the colonial system was dismantled and the industrial system became obsolete. The electronics, software and digital devices in the late decades of the twentieth century have revolutionised production, trade, economic organisation and communication. This phase has tilted political and economic balance in favour of America.

In Marx Weber's and Durkheim's theories, epoch-making historical events have been termed respectively as 'historical individuals' and 'social facts'. Capitalism is projected as 'historical individual' by Max Weber with its ideal types of economic rationality and bureaucracy. To Durkheim, 'division of labour' is one of the social facts, characterised by organic solidarity and complex social diffferentiation. The prevailing social-economic conditions in Western Europe and needs of German and French society are reflected in their thought process. Similarly, the rise of European imperialism and the spread of colonialism to Asia, Africa and Latin America were epoch-making historical events. The exploitation of economic resources in colonies, utilisation of their cheap labour force in agro-based industries, mines, railways, shipping, transport, taking labour from one colony to other to serve in plantations, trade barriers on the finished goods of colonies, imposition of unequal treaties on the rulers of the colonies and slave trade made Europe's nations politically powerful and economically prosperous. The relationship between the colonial powers and the subjugated colonies was based on hegemony and dependency. Under the yoke of political subjugation and economic exploitation, colonies became poor and the self-confidence of their proud people was subdued by defeatism.

Westernisation, in the form of European system of administration, languages, dress patterns, food habits, lifestyle, fashion, recreation, sports, beliefs, festivals, music, was the cultural-ideological vehicle of colonialism. In the post-colonial period, there were conceptual shifts from the hegemonistic notion of westernisation to more sophisticated and palatable concept of modernization. Under the ideological constraints, the traditionalists and the Marxists disagreed with the liberal, Euro-centric, capitalist contents of modernization. The Indian sociological works on westernisation do not reflect the efficacy of movement to counter it and the deep impact on the Indian psyche of the nationalist ideology—symbolised by the ideals of *swadeshi* (national products), *swaraj* (home rule), *swawalamban* (self-sufficiency), *swabhasha* (mother tongue, national language) and *swabhiman* (self-respect) during the independence movement. The modernization studies moved around the early western works. In these studies, the pre-colonial India is projected as a traditional, custom bound, backward, underdeveloped society which experienced reawakening with the introduction of the British rule, new light with the expansion of westernisation and a new direction towards modernization with English education, English laws, incipient industrialisation, transport, communication and social reform movements. They are oblivious on the one side of colonial exploitation, destruction of Indian agriculture, handicrafts, industries, schools, urban centres and on the other side, of the available data/records of the highly developed system of production, trade, business, technology, network of schools, integrated community life, dignified social relationship in villages and cities around guilds-castes, large-scale spatial and upward social mobility, large cities as centres of administration, production, trade, business, religion and active people's participation in social work and decision making through common gatherings and Panchayats in pre-colonial India. At the conceptual plains, the Indian tradition encouraged the idea of *Bahul* (plurality), *Udar Charit* (liberal mindset) and *Vasudhaiva Kutumbakam* (globe as a family) since the time immemorial.

This does not mean that I am pleading for a traditionalist approach, rather my emphasis is on developing a social-historical perspective for the understanding of the pre-colonial and the colonial phases of India. The traditionalists speak of 'order' and 'first principles' and ignore the dynamic nature of society concentrate their analysis on a golden past or on a transcendental reality. In their narration, there is no place for empirical data and historical facts. Even a Marxist like D.P. Mukerji explains significant sources of traditions in terms of scriptures, sages and mythical heroes, but he pays little attention to the equally vital roles played in it by generations of common people, their folk beliefs and practices. During and after the First World War, apart from the Marxists and the Fascists who were critical of the modern capitalist, western civilization mainly on economic grounds, there were sociologists like Sorokin, Spengler and several church leaders who considered it decadent and opposed it on moral grounds. In India, traditionalists like A.K. Saran outrightly rejected western modernity, philosopher like Radha Krishnan and sociologist like Radha Kamal Mukherji supported synthesis between the modern scientific knowledge of the west and the traditional wisdom of the east were equally influenced by this moralist logic. In this context, we have to remember that as in the name of modernization, capitalism, fascism and communism created several problems, similarly overdose of traditionalism, religious conservatism and cultural dogmatism have posed a new global crisis in the form of fundamentalism and terrorism.

[V]

In the 1970s, serious doubts were raised regarding the future of industrialisation and the industrial system by Toffler (*ibid.*), Galbraith (1970), Bell (*ibid.*) and Lipset (1979). Galbraith pointed out that there are a lot of discussions on the future of capitalism but little discussion on the future of industrial system. According to him, industrial system is the product of vast technostructure and autonomous corporations—with their much power and reach. But there is a vast change in the industrial system. Large corporations have removed themselves from the control of the stockholders. They have acquired their own internal sources of capital. There are large changes in relationship with workers and the state. Two opposite tendencies are visible in the capitalist and the communist industrial systems. In the capitalist industrial system, the role of state is increasing in the field of regulation, taxation, education, trade and supply. In communist system, the large, autonomous, technocratic corporations have gained ground. In spite of ideological differences between the two systems, they now have similar technology, large-scale production, heavy requirements of capital and similar organisations. Thus, ideology is now of little value and there are strong tendencies of convergence between the two systems which are meeting with each other in the post-industrial system. This is a clear shift from the traditionally opposite capitalist and communist industrial systems and post-Mao China is the best example of this emerging trend of convergence.

Lipset thinks that in her third century, America is a post-industrial society. He is concerned with the future of the post-industrial society. He asks—can its future be predicted? The nature of the post-industrial society is global but the opposite trends in the form of the rise of ethnicity in the western, communist and developing societies are emerging. He talks of the inadequacies of the economic, political, sociological and Marxist analysis in coping with the global post-industrial society, ethnic challenges and limits of growth discussions.

There are tendencies of convergence and it appears that the ideological differences are declining but in reality the global market economy with a liberal face of capitalism is dominant all-over the world which is being termed as 'Globalization'. Going beyond traditional industrialism, modernization, this is another conceptual shift with heavy ideological baggage. In the starting decade of the twenty-first century, the academic debates and policy discussions are effused with the idea of Globalization. It is another major inevitable historic event—economically an extension of capitalist market economy and culturally it is rooted in the attributes and the value system of westernisation. Westernisation and modernization were primarily Euro-centric concepts, whereas the current process of Globalization is more US-centric.

The rapid expansion of Globalization has posed a number of questions. Where does Ideology stand in this era? Does Globalization offer opportunities to the poor countries? Is the twenty-first century, as it is often repeated, a century of Asia? As the technology of industrial age was supposed to be ideologically neutral and it was equally applied by the capitalist and the communist countries, similarly, the technologies of digital device and software are also neutral. There were two repercussions of the collapse of communism in Russia. First, America remained the uncontested single superpower in the world. Second, liberal democracy, market economy and capitalism proved their superiority over communism. The social democratic parties in Europe had conceded to capitalism much earlier. After the death of Mao, China and after 1991 India embraced economic reforms, market economy and capitalism. Undoubtedly, forces of Globalization have blurred sharp ideological divisions but in practice the supremacy of capitalism has been accepted by the governments at the global level. The only remaining islands of dissent are in some Latin American countries.

The other two questions are interrelated. The amazing progress in the field of electronics, computer, software, digital device, bio-technology and the new methods of manufacturing based on them are supposed to offer tremendous opportunities to the entire mankind. They may be powerful engines of equitable global development by creating wealth, by their proper distribution, by removing poverty, and by possible elimination of inequality. But unfortunately, it is not happening. In the era of Globalization, the gaps between the rich/poor nations and the rich/poor population within the nations are rising. A most recent UN report found that world's richest 2 per cent own half the global wealth. As per this report, to be among the most affluent 10 per cent of adults required $ 61,000 in household assets. Of them, around 25 per cent lived in the United States, 20 per cent in Japan, 10 per cent in Germany, 7 per cent in Italy, 6 per cent in Britain, and 4 per cent each in France and Spain. The report did not measure income from salary, pension and other benefits (UN Report: 2006).

In the post-Second World War period, there was remarkable economic development in Japan, South Korea, Taiwan and Hong Kong. In academic areas, the 'Japanese model of development and modernization' was much highlighted. During 1980-95, Singapore, Malaysia, Thailand and Indonesia known as 'Asian tigers' made significant progress. It was considered as the result of the 'Asian Values' comprising strong family bonds, enterprise, hard work, thrift and savings. There was a sudden jolt in 1997 and the economy of the Asian tigers collapsed. Now, there are strong trends of revival. The discovery of oil brought much wealth and prosperity at the macro level in the West Asian countries. The rise in oil prices in 1970s was one of the factors for the decline of the industrial system, growing importance of electronics and the rise of the post-industrial-post-modern system which was ultimately termed as Globalization.

Today, China and India—the two largest countries in population, along with Vietnam—are the fastest growing economies in the world. Due to their cheap, skilled labour force, excellent opportunities for investment and profit, they are attracting foreign multi-national companies for investment. They are experiencing the impact of Globalization at the macroeconomic level. There is unprecedented growth in GDP, increase in foreign currency reserve, rise in the number of foreign companies and their investment, growth in trade, jump in the share market and parade of increasing number of millionaires. China is still far ahead, India is moving fast and Vietnam is also catching up. Their combined population is around two and a half billion, almost 40 per cent of the world population. Due to rise in prosperity in the East and the West Asia, rapid development in the South-East Asia, fastest economic Growth in China, India, Vietnam, India's spectacular achievements in software and China's performance in hardware, the twenty-first century is being called the Asian century.

As we have observed earlier, the conversion to Christianity and westernisation created 'structural duality' among the hill tribes in North-East India; similarly, market economy and Globalization have created ideological and structural duality in China, India and Vietnam. China and Vietnam are officially communist countries, ruled by their respective communist parties but they are following capitalist path of development. In the preamble to Constitution, India is a socialist country but she has adopted the policy of economic liberalisation and market economy. In spite of the shining macro-level economic indicator, Globalization has increased social-economic inequality, regional imbalance and social tensions in China and India. In both the countries, the acquisition of land for industries, new townships, special economic zones, construction of river dams have made millions of peasants landless—leading to tensions and conflicts. The large industries and their mass production have led to the destruction of small scale and home-centred industries. The emergence of big malls with their marketing emphasis on internationally reputed brands have done great damage to the local products, millions of small corner shops and to the livelihood of their owners. The stress on wealth creation, trade, business, profit has undermined required investment in social sectors. The trick of the trade mentality and deep-rooted profit motives have dropped traditional ethical practices into backyard. As a consequence, crimes, malpractices, illegal trade and different forms of corruption are rampant.

[VI]

The current Globalization, as a product of micro-electronics, computer chips, atomic and renewal sources of energy, information technology, knowledge industry, unprecedented speed, multinational corporations—productivity, trade, money exchange related with them, has revolutionised the world in the same manner, as it was done by the Industrial Revolution linked with machines, factories, steam, electricity, petrol, mass communication, imperialism, capitalism or by the Bolshevik Revolution inspired by the ideas of Karl Marx, with a dream to establish an international communist system. As there were inherent contradictions in the industrial system—capitalism, similarly, Globalization also suffers from numerous inconsistencies and contradictions. The benefits of Globalization are not being adequately distributed throughout the world. Today, America as a single superpower, the Group of G-8 as rich nations, the five permanent members of the UN Security Council have economic-political leverage in the emerging global system. The process of Globalization is prominently visible in trade and commerce, otherwise, the non-global, non-inclusive, separatist, ethnocentric sectarian, fundamentalist, terrorist forces have risen with great strength and ferocity in the phase of Globalization. The rise of multinational corporations and separatist-ethnocentric forces are undermining the status of the state as a middle range political organisation in the emerging global system. In many cases, disintegration of the state is providing momentum to the strengthening of the non-inclusive, fundamentalist forces. In this process, the harmony among the global (world system) and of its sub-systems—the national (state) and the local (ethnic) are disturbed—leading to conflicts.

In the current phase of Globalization, there are unresolved questions. Can a real world system based on equitable principles be created? Is there any wayout to liberate the process of Globalization from the clutches of rich and powerful countries? Can it be turned into an opportunity for the entire humanity? How can the growth of fundamentalist, terrorist forces be checked in effective, persuasive, democratic manner? How can harmony be established among a well established world system and its national and local sub-systems?

In Alvin Toffler's book, *The Third Wave,* there is a chapter entitled as 'Gandhi with Satellites'. In his view, modernization related with industrial civilization 'left behind a world in which one quarter of the species lived in relative affluence, three quarters in relative poverty'. This myth, that the poor countries should also follow the Second World strategy of industrialisation as it happened in the west, was exploded in the 1960s when industrialised countries faced the crisis built up by the deprivation of their colonial resources, waves of strikes, blackouts and crimes in their home fronts. Experiencing the widening gaps between cities and villages, shortage of capital for heavy industrialisation and unavailability of modern technology, there was a sudden emphasis on the First Wave strategy of rural development and labour intensive production. Toffler thinks that the 'labour intensity is also subject to the charge that it is self-serving for the rich'. By remaining in the First Wave conditions, the poor countries will remain at the level of low productivity and cannot complete with the rich countries. As a remedy, he talks about the Third Wave alternative strategies consisting of micro-electronics, computer chips which can be operated with less capital, will help in saving factory space, office accommodation, possibilities to work from home and saving travelling time.

Gandhi's plans for the renewal of Indian society and economy may be divided into immediate, context-specific strategies like the use of spinning wheel, encouragement to traditional occupations and long term directions of permanent value—such as truth, non-violence, civil disobedience (*satyagraha*) against oppression-injustice, equal regards for all religions, respect for plurality, decentralisation of power and economy, deurbanisation by stressing on the rural life, developing villages as the centres of production, preservation of nature, renewable energy and appropriate technology. These long-range strategies were successfully applied by Gandhi in his life time and he left their legacy for posterity. Toffler equates some of these features with the First Wave and suggests to combine them with the features of the Third Wave to create a harmonious, equitable and prosperous world.

As westernisation and modernization along with scientific-technological achievements, indusrialisation, urbanisation and several forms of governance were afflicted by conceptual shifts, Euro-centric ideological constraints, western domination, conflicts, wars, economic depressions, environmental degradations, the current phase of Globalization along with these pitfalls suffer from serious inconsistencies and contradictions as discussed above. Globalization as a process may be utilised for building a world system—a much higher order than Globalization. This is the real need of today's world. The prerequisites of such a humanitarian, all-inclusive, equitable world system are freedom from poverty, exploitation, domination, wars and having global equality, prosperity, peace, environmental protection, harmony among man, nature, science and preserving a proper balance among global, national, local aspirations.

References

Almond and Coleman, *The Politics of Developing Areas*, Princeton, 1960.

Apter David E., *The Politics of Modernization*, The University of Chicago Press, Chicago, 1965.

Bendix Reinhard, *Nation Building and Citizenship*, John Wiley & Sons, Inc. New York, 1964.

Bauman Zygmunt, *Legislators and Interpreters* (1987), *Modernity and Holocaust* (1989), *Modernity and Ambivalence* (1991). Dennis Smith' book: 'Zygmunt Bauman: Prophet of Post Modernity' Policy Press and Blackwill Publishers, 1999, is an excellent work for the understanding of Bauman's contributions to sociology, post-modernity and his criticism of modernity.

Bell Daniel, *The Coming of Post Industrial Society*, New York, 1973.

Berger Peter and Huntington P. Samuel, *Many Globalizations: Cultural Diversity in the Contemporary World*, Oxford University Press, New York, 2002.

Coomarswami A.K., See, *The Bugbear of Literacy*, Dennis Dobson, London, 1919, and *The Dance of Shiva*, Asia Publishing House, Bombay, 1948.

Craig Timothy J. and King Richard, *Global Goes Local: Popular Culture in Asia*, Hong Kong University Press, 2002.

Deutsch Karl W., 'Social Mobilisation and Political Development', *American Political Science Review*, Vol. 55, Sept. 1961, pp. 493-514.

Dube S.C., *Modernization and Its Adaptive Demands on Indian Society*, Papers in Sociology of Education in India (ed.) M.S. Gore, I.P. Desai and Suma Chitnis, NCERT, New Delhi, 1967.

During Simon, 'Post-modernism or Post-Colonialism Today' in Docherty Thomas (ed), *Postmodernism: A Reader*, Columbia University Press, New York, 1993, pp. 448-70.

Eisenstadt S. N., *Modernization: Protest and Change*, Prentice Hall, Inc. London, 1966.

Friedman Thomas, *The World is Flat* (A Brief History of the Globalized World in the 21st Century), Allen Lane—An imprint of Penium Books, London, 2005.

Gabriel A. Almond and James S. Colomen, *The Politics of Developing Areas*, 1960.

Galbraith John Kenneth, *The New Industrial State*, Penguin Books, Reprint, 1970, pp. 389-400.

Gandhi M.K., *Hind Swaraj*, first published in 1910, reprınted in 1938, Navajeevan Press, Ahmedabad, 1938.

Geertz Clifford (ed.), *Old Societies and New States*, The Free Press of Glen, London, 1963.

Gusfield Joseph R., 'Tradition and Modernity: Misplaced Polarities in the Study of Social Change', *The American Journal of Sociology*, Vol. 72, No. 4, January 1967, pp. 351-362.

Hagen Everett, E., *On the Theory of Social Change*, Honewood, Illinois, The Dorsey Press, Inc. 1962.

Hill Christopher, *Lenin and the Russian Revolution*, Penguin Books, 1977.

Hoselitz R. F., *Sociological Aspects of Economic Growth*, 1960.

Horowitz Irving Lous, *Three Worlds of Development*, Oxford University Press, New York, 1966.

Krishan Kumar, *From Post-Industrial to Post-Modern Society*, Blackwell Publishers LTD., Oxford, 1995.

Lechner Frank J. and Boli John (ed), *The Globalization Reader*, Blackwell Publishing, Oxford, Second Edition, 2004.

Lerner Daniel, *The Passing of Traditional Society: Modernising the Middle East*, The Free Press of Glencoe, 1958.

Levy Jr. Marrion J., *Modernization and the Structure of Societies*, Princeton University Press, Princeton, 1966.

Lewis Arther, *The Theory of Economic Growth*, 1955.

Lipset S. M. (ed), *The Third Century: America as a Post-Industrial Society,* Kalyan Publishers, Calcutta, 1979, pp. 1-36.

McCord William, *The Spring Time of Freedom: Evolution of Developing Societies,* Oxford and IBH Publishing Co., Calcutta, 1969.

McClelland David C., *The Achieving Society,* Princeton University Press, Princeton, 1961.

Mei Xinyu, *A Developing Inequality,* Beijing Review, Feb. 16, 2006, pp. 10-13.

Mukerji D.P., *Indian Tradition and Social Change* (1955) in D.P. Mukerji, 'Diversities', People's Publishing House, New Delhi, 1958, pp. 228-241.

Myrdal Gunnar, *Asian Drama: An Enquiry into the Poverty of Nations,* Three Volumes, Penguin Books, Middlesex, U.K. 1968.

Parsons Talcott, *Structure and Process in Modern Societies,* The Free Press, Glencoe, 1960.

Opello, Jr Walter C. and Rosow Stephen J., *The Nation-State and the Global Order: A Historical Introduction to Contemporary Politics,* Leinno-Reiner Publishers, London, 2004.

Redfield Robert, 'The Social Organisation of Tradition', *Far-Eastern Quarterly,* Vol. 15, 1955-1956, pp. 13-21.

Richard Nelly, 'Postmodernism and Periphery' in Docherty Thomas (*ibid.*), pp. 463-70.

Rostov W.W., *The Stages of Economic Growth: A Non-Communist Manifesto,* Cambridge University Press, Cambridge, 1960.

Ruskin John, *Unto This Last: Four Essays on the First Principles of Political Economy,* Harper, New York, 1860.

Saran A.K., *Traditionalism and Transcendentalism in Indian Sociology* (1962) in G.C. Hallen 'Sociology in India', Vol. 1, New Delhi, 1988, pp. 336-349. His another paper 'The Indian Tradition' (1964), presented at the Social Science Conference at Patna, explains his traditionalist point of view.

Shils Milton, 'The Cultural Patterns of Indian Civilisation', *Far-Eastern Quarterly,* Vol. 15, 1955-56, pp. 23-36.

Short Philip, *Mao: A Life,* Henry Holt, & Co; New York, 1999. A recent book by Jung Chang and Jon Halliday *Mao—An Unknown Story,* Jonathan Cape, London, 2005, Part-5 of the book provides an insightful account of Mao's growing rivalry with Stalin (1947-49), his attempts to undermine the position of Khruschev (1956-59) and China's growing differences with Soviet Russia.

Singh Yogendra, *Modernization of Indian Tradition,* Rawat Publications (reprint), Jaipur, 1988.

Smith W.C., *Modernization of a Traditional Society,* Asia Publishing House, Bombay.

Smith M.G. (ed.), *Pluralism in Africa,* 1968.

Srinivas M.N., *Social Change in Modern India*, California University Press, Berkeley, 1966.

The Hindu, September 27, 1985.

Toffler Alvin, His three books, 'Future Shock', Broadley Head Ltd., London, 1970, 'The Third Wave', 1980 and 'Power Shift', 1990 paved the way for the development of 'futurology' in social sciences. In his words, they respectively deal with the process of change—how change affects people and organisations, the direction of change—where today's changes are taking us and the control of changes still to come—who will shape them and how.

19

Globalization and Persisting Cultural Diversity

YOGESH ATAL

> The notion of world civilization can only be accepted.... as a sort of limiting concept or as an epitome of a highly complex process. There is not, and can never be, a world civilization in the absolute sense in which the term is often used, since civilization implies, and indeed consists in the co-existence of cultures exhibiting the maximum possible diversities. A world civilization could, in fact, represent no more than a worldwide coalition of cultures, each of which would preserve its own originality.
>
> **[Claude Levi-Strauss]**[1]

Of the several lessons that we learnt while reviewing the development experience of the past six decades the most significant is that forces of Westernisation and Modernization could not erase the creative cultural diversity of planet Earth. The homogenisation project of the development paradigms—capitalist or communist—failed miserably. Communism in Eastern Europe collapsed and the Capitalist West admitted of deficits in its social development. The world continues to be pluricultural.

Predicting the clash of civilizations, the celebrated American author, Samuel P. Huntington, acknowledges this fact in no uncertain terms:

> Non-Western civilizations have attempted to become modern without being Western. To date only Japan has fully succeeded in that quest. Non-Western civilizations will continue to attempt to acquire the wealth, technology, skills, machines and weapons that are part of being modern. They will also attempt to reconcile this modernity with their traditional culture and values. Their economic and military strength relative to the West will increase. Hence, the West will increasingly have to accommodate these non-Western modern civilizations whose power approaches that of the West but whose values and interests differ significantly from those of the West. This will require the West to maintain the economic and military power necessary to protect its interests in relation to these civilizations. It will also, however, require the West to develop a more profound understanding of the basic religious and philosophical assumptions underlying other civilizations and the ways in which people in those civilizations see their interests. It will require an effort to identify elements of commonality between Western and other civilisations. For the relevant future, there will be no universal civilization, but instead a world of different civilizations, each of which will have to learn to coexist with the others.[2]

While Huntington closes his article with a hint for developing strategies for co-existence—and hence derivatively for a "dialogue"—the tone of his entire essay remains militarist. He seems to be worried about the rising power of non-Western civilizations and, therefore, he has justified the need for the West "to maintain the economic and military power". It is clear that Huntington is not happy at the loss of Western hegemony, and is, for that reason, prescribing preparations for a conflict. Of course, he is careful to declare that his essay "is not to advocate the desirability of conflicts between civilizations". But he is of the view that the earlier "conflicts between princes, nation-states and ideologies were primarily conflicts within Western civilization" in which non-Western civilizations were only "the objects of history as targets of Western colonialism", and that they only now "join the West as movers and shapers of history".

For a person coming from, what Huntington calls, a non-Western civilization the clash of civilization hypothesis appears not as a possible scenario but a dangerous prescription; or an expression of frustration caused by the failure of the Western paradigm of development in not being able to create a world civilization. Huntington did not acknowledge the enormous role that other civilizations have played in the past in enriching the world—through ideas, philosophies, and other material and non-material cultural products.[3]

The difficulty with Huntington is that he has made civilization a non-specific term using it for all kinds of entities—a country (Japan), a religion (Islam, Hindu, etc.), and a multicultural kit emanating from a geographical region (China, which for him is "a civilization pretending to be a state"[4]). These illustrations contradict the definition of civilization given by him: "A civilization is the highest cultural grouping of people and the broadest level of cultural identity people have short of that which distinguishes humans from other species. It is defined both by common objective elements, such as language, history, religion, customs, institutions, and by subjective self-identification of people." Such a definition is not applicable to any cultural identity.

In the emerging reality of a multicultural world, aided by the powerful forces of Globalization, there is a need to change the vocabulary of our discourse. The word "civilization" belongs to the vocabulary of the bygone era. It made sense when people talked of humanity's transition from savagery to barbarism to civilization. It was still useful when the peoples of the world lived in relative isolation and had several overlapping identities—of birth place, language, religion, common history. But all this has changed due to a long record of culture contacts between different societies. Such contacts made first the concept of "pure race" a myth with continuous production of hybrid progeny; later they also affected the pristinity of cultures. What we witness today is not only racial miscegenation but also cultural miscegenation. In earlier period of cultural expansion there occurred a conglomeration of local cultures with universalisation of parochial traits and also parochialisation of received traits. Such a cultural expansion was the feature of the indigenous civilizations that crossed local, parochial boundaries. They were then described with the prefix of "pan"—Pan-Indian, Pan-Islamic, etc. Such spread enclosed many contiguous regions and different regimes. Belonging to a common civilisation, in this sense, did not rule out clashes between states, and between people following the same religion or living the same culture. However, the clashes have never been at the civilization level; they were always between two groups, be they societies as a whole or parts of it. The fact is that all societies are characterised as "cooperation crossed by conflict".

Sociologists analysing processes of cultural contacts between outsiders and insiders have talked of four phases, namely, competition, conflict, accommodation, and assimilation. Initial resistances and even conflicts give way, in due course, to processes of accommodation which enlarge the arena of culture—outsiders become insiders, outside traits are selectively allowed entry and given a suitable location in the cultural fabric, inside traits get redefined and re-evaluated. It is these processes of attrition and addition that go on changing the profile of living cultures, and yet cultures maintain themselves by selectively accommodating, and finally assimilating outside elements. It is only the non-resilient cultures that get dissipated or absorbed by other cultures. Human history has seen death of several cultures, and disappearance of several cultural traits.

Language: A Good Example

The Atlas of the world's languages lists 6,796 languages that are currently spoken. Many fear that several of these are likely to disappear in the next 20-25 years. To be sure, this number is far too smaller than the number of languages spoken 10,000 years ago. According to Michael Krauss' calculation, some 10,000 years ago, there were about 12,000 languages. And he predicts that "during the next 150 years it will decline to between something like 3,000 for the best scenario I can imagine, to about 300, a scenario I fear is more likely."[5]

What is more significant is the fact that 96 per cent of the currently live languages are spoken by only four per cent of the world's population, and 80 per cent of these languages are confined to single countries. There are only 20 languages that have their speakers in millions and spread over several countries. Given such a scenario, the fear is expressed that majority of the languages that have few speakers—and these languages have their high concentration in the Asia-Pacific region—are likely to disappear in the next century. *UNESCO Courier* of April 2000 has recounted the following forecasts:

- In Africa, more than 200 languages have fewer than 500 speakers each and may soon die out.
- In North America, the biggest threats are to indigenous and Creole languages. With the exception of Navajo, Cree and Ojibwa, the 200 Amerindian languages of USA and Canada are endangered.
- In Latin America, nearly 50 per cent of the 500 Amerindian languages are in danger.
- In South East Asia, the future of 40 of the 600 to 700 languages depends on government policies. On the other hand, only six languages out of North East Asia's 47 have any real chance of survival in the face of the Russian.
- In Europe, of the 132 languages spoken, nine are nearly extinct, 26 are seriously endangered, and 38 are endangered.

According to *Millennium Family Encyclopaedia* (Dorling Kindersley, London 1997), half of the world uses in everyday life one of the planet's eight most widespread languages that include Chinese (1.2 billion), English 478 million), Hindi (437 million), Spanish (392 million), Russian (284 million), Arabic (225 million), Portuguese (184 million), and French (125 million). If we were to combine the figures of those for whom a particular language is second language with the mother tongue statistics, then the figure for English goes up to 1,000 million, and for Hindi-Urdu to 900 million.

This makes it obvious that a common language is not going to be a defining characteristic of a culture, much less of a "civilization" in the sense in which Huntington uses the word. In fact, most of the people are becoming bilingual. And yet the multiplicity of cultures will remain a distinguishing feature of the world.

Emergence of Plural Structures

The phenomenon of plural structures is, in a way, associated with colonialism. In the re-colonial era, there existed three types of societies—(*i*) small primitive cultures, leading a relatively isolated life; (*ii*) indigenous civilizations, consisting of several regional regimes but following a common complex culture; and (*iii*) culturally homogeneous large nation-states (of Europe, for example).

Opening of apertures to the neighbouring societies initiated the process of culture contact in the prehistoric times. Arrival of adventures and armies of other regimes to expand their empires created situations of conflict and ultimate accommodation of the outsiders. These happenings introduced the phenomenon of coexistence of cultures in a given society, and making the culture of that society a complex culture. India is a good example of a complex culture. Some anthropologists have called it an indigenous civilization that is composed of several subcultures—of the autochthones and the later settlers.

Such societies got enlarged through the process of inclusion. The small primitive cultures—the autochthones—coming in contact with relatively advanced neighbours identified themselves as subgroups and began following cultural practices, including religious rituals; and the outsiders coming as invaders got settled in the new environs maintaining their individual group identity and yet mutually sharing some of the cultural traits. Attempts at empire building led to reorganisation of some of the regional regimes, but did not fully succeed in creating a larger political unity despite a commonly shared cultural unity.

It is with the arrival of the colonial era that a political unity at a level higher than the regional entity could be established in such countries. Different regional regimes coming under a single colonial umbrella constituted the country. And since these entities signified different subcultures, including religious affiliations, the constitution of the emerging political unity came to be described as "plural society" by the Western scholars. The phrase had two connotations—it was plural *compared* to the society of the colonizer that was "single" and homogeneous; secondly, it was plural in the sense that the constituents of the colony were "not one" single homogeneous whole and that different societies were joined together to become a plural society with a common administration. The colonizers emphasised the distinctness of the constituents and fostered their separate identities to keep them divided and yet to ensure their allegiance to the Crown. The policy known as "Divide and Rule" promoted the concept of plural society to emphasise heterogeneity and separateness and undermine the emerging unity amidst diversity. Thus, the colonial rule consolidated the regional regimes into a larger political unity but tried to create fractures in the evolving unity of a complex culture by highlighting the differences and fostering them.

The end of the colonial era brought new challenges. The former colonies had the important task of transforming the "plural societies"—that is the "divided" subgroups—into a multicultural society by breaking the insulations planted by the colonial powers and opening out apertures of interaction between the various groups to create an atmosphere of amity and congeniality. This task was named "nation building", the main plank of which was to foster national integration.

Post-colonial era also brought about changes in the structure of the societies of the former colonizer countries. As a result of the process of reverse migration, people from the former colonies began migrating to the countries of the North. During that colonial phase such migrations were highly restricted. Chosen individuals from elite families had the privilege of going to the colonial capital. That was an instance of a single aperture model for outside contacts. In the post-colonial era, multiple apertures were opened for the people of the independent country to get exposed to the outside world. Migrations meant arrival of people from different lands to the country and departures of the country's citizens to different lands for visits and work. The departures created plurality not only in the former coloniser country but also in other host countries of the developed world.

In the post-colonial era, the world has seen new forms of migration that have changed the structure of societies of the West. Rapid advances in the technology of transportation and communication have greatly aided the phenomenon of migration. People migrate not only for education—a feature that was characteristic of the colonial era and confined mostly to the select few—but also for work, and for final settlement. The collapse of communism in Eastern Europe caused loosening of the control and created a pool of 450 million potential emigrants. Social dislocation caused by current period of economic transition in that region, and the growth of ethnic tensions encouraged people to look for better prospects in the free world. Add to this the number of refugees who were driven from their home countries because of natural calamities or civil conflicts or mass persecutions. In the early years of the 1990s, there were as many as 16.25 million such refugees that were officially recognised; those not qualified but seeking refuge were an additional seven million. One estimate suggested that in 1993, the number of people—including economic migrants and refugees—living abroad was around a 100 million.[6] Most of these migrants went to the United States[7], Canada, and Australia, and they came from Latin America and Asia. Immigrations are also increasing in Italy and Spain, which had earlier seen emigration of their people to other European countries. Germany has been the recipient of immigrants from Eastern Europe, and France from North and West Africa. In Eastern Europe, Hungary, Poland, Czech Republic and Slovakia have become destinations for people migrating from the former Soviet Union. Another destination for migration has been the Middle East. Though a region with only 0.4 per cent of the world population, it has been recipient of 13 per cent of the total migrant population. In Africa, Nigeria, Cote d'Ivoire, and South Africa attract migrations from the neighbouring countries. In Latin America, Argentina and Venezuela have become new homes for the Latino migrants. In Asia, Japan claims to have around 3,00,000 illegal immigrants. The Republic of Korea, Taiwan, Singapore, Thailand and Malaysia have also emerged as host societies. The problem of illegal migrants from Bangladesh is faced by India; but India is also a major exporting country of both skilled and unskilled labour to the Middle East and to several destinations in the West. The new trend of migration includes illegal migrants, and also increasing number of female migrants.

Notwithstanding the nature of migration, the recent spurt in migration with its destination to Europe and North America has remarkably affected not only the economies of these countries but also their social structures. These societies that claimed to be homogeneous in terms of culture, though part of a vaguely defined "Western Civilization", have been converted into "plural" societies. Unlike the colonial era, when the individuals from the colonies used to temporarily migrate for education and training, now people with families, and in large numbers, are moving to work and settle in them. A larger presence has given their parent culture a distinct visibility, and helped them retain their identity. Such migrants live simultaneously in two cultures—that of the host society and of the parent society. In the process they evolve a sub-culture taking the parent culture as the base and mounting on it adaptable characteristics of the host culture. I have named these sub-cultures as *Sandwich Cultures.*[8]

Multiculturalism, as it is employed now is a plea for amicable living together of the various cultures in the same setting. Some scholars use it only for the changing structures of the developed societies where people of different cultures lead a migrant life but freely interact with the host culture. The pressures of host culture and the parent culture cause the creation of a *sandwich culture* for the migrant group. Thus, the developed countries of the North are becoming a composite of several sandwich cultures coexisting with the host culture. Unlike the countries of the Third World, such as India, these countries do not face the crisis of "nation building". They are faced with the challenge of accommodating the arriving sub-cultures and extending the delivery system to respond to needs of the migrant communities. The impact of migration on the economy, and on the existing social services has created new strains. Also there is worry of an unwelcome reaction by the natives against the arriving (not invading) cultures demanding an equal treatment.

Creation of such composite cultures, thereby making all societies—of the North and the South—multicultural, is a phenomenon that can be called one of the distinctive features of Globalization.

Globalization: A Sociological Perspective

While everybody now talks of Globalization, the word connotes different meanings to different people. There is a need for conceptual clarity. Most talks about Globalization are in the nature of the perceived "ill effects" of this proccess on the cultures and societies of the developing world, and laying blame for all this to the countries of the North, as if they were to derive all the benefits from this process by extending their markets, locating their industries, killing local enterprises, and engulfing national cultures.

All these criticisms sound familiar. This was being talked in the past decades when the countries of the so-called "Third World" adopted "Western paradigm" of development. As long as the countries are pursuing that paradigm, even when the processes of Globalization have begun impacting, perhaps the criticism may remain valid. But that should remain the criticism of the continued paradigm of development rather than of Globalization. If the latter is a new process, it is too early to assess the damage wrought by it; the fears expressed may only serve as a caution, but need not be taken for the truth.

I am of the view that what Globalization signifies is a major turning point in development. Broadly speaking, one can say that change goes through three phases—namely, endogenous change influenced by the outside as a one-way traffic, and the reciprocal processes of change. It is true that as long as change was only from within, it was not so noticeable because of its slowness. But once societies came in contact with each other, the pace of change became faster. The colonial period was characterized by this kind of change when the colonizing countries were influencing their colonies and bringing about radical changes in them through imported system of administration, introduction of modern education, improvements in transportation and communication, etc., to make these societies "similar" to the cultures of the colonisers. Since there was more of a give by the colonisers, it was a one-way traffic with the colonies at the receiving end. Anthropologists called this process a process of *acculturation*. Even after the attainment of independence, this process continued with the difference that developing countries identified more than one reference group outside their cultures and had the possibility, at least in principle, to decide what to receive, from where, and when. Colonisation and acculturation gave way to development and modernization, but still keeping the developing countries at the receiving end most of the time. But the development that has taken place in the past four to five decades has changed the scenario and created conditions for the new phase, which is now called Globalization.

To sum up, it can be said that the precolonial phase was a phase of *self-dependence*—of endogenous or orthogenetic growth with minimal of addition from the outside world. The colonial phase can be characterized as a period of *dependence*—colonies heavily dependent on the colonial master and hegemonised by the outside culture from a single source (single aperture model of interaction). The post-colonial phase that lasted for about five decades was a period of *independence*—colonies becoming politically independent and making choices for the receipt of outside elements from a wide variety of sources (multiple aperture model) generating an ambivalence between tradition and modernity while pursuing either the Western paradigm of development or the socialist-communist mode of growth, or a mixture of the two; it was the phase of *modernization* and *Westernisation*. With the collapse of communism in the Eastern Europe and the end of the era of cold war, the world has entered the phase of *interdependence* that is characterized by the process of *Globalization*. As Huntington admits, societies became "modern" without being "western". But this phase is not the phase of "West *versus* Rest", as Huntington makes it out to be. All the societies are engulfed in this process of mutual give and take. The globe is entering in each of the cultures and each of the cultures is entering in different ways in every culture. And the globe as a whole is experiencing problems that are common—environmental pollution explosion, violence and crime, deficits in social development as exhibited by rising rates of poverty, expanding unemployment, and threats to the integration of societies. It is this fact that has brought the cultural variable to the centre stage. Common problems need uncommon solutions. Each culture has to work out solutions to the problems that it confronts. Leaders of society are to think globally and act locally.

Globalization can be understood as a process of making the world a "global village" in the sense in which Marshall McLuhan used the concept. Geographical distances notwithstanding, communications playing their role in bringing closer different parts of the globe as an interacting and communicating community. The essence of this is that things happening in any part of the world influence, albeit in different degrees and in different ways—positive and negative, all the parts of the rest of the system. In other words, isolation of individual, communities and countries is broken. Thus, not only India is affected by what happens in the US or in Singapore, but Singapore and the US are also affected by what happens in India. This is how the process of Globalization has brought the entire world to India and taken India to different parts of the world. And this is made possible by advances in the technologies of transportation and communication. Even when individuals remain stationary in their homesteads, the information technolgoy—technology of the mass media—transports them to distant lands. This revolution has taken away the monopoly of information from the State by opening alternative channels of information. In the 1970s, some of the authoritarian states used to censor all the arriving mail and the printed magazines and books. Today, one can ignore the postal system and get the mail and magazines through the electronic medium. The happenings at the Tiennamen Square and the brutal military attack on democratic protestors in Thailand were witnessed by people all around the world because of the presence of the foreign media. The fact that they were banned on the national channels did not serve the intended purpose of the state to withhold information. I tend to believe that the IT revolution was responsible for the collapse of communism in Eastern Europe as it opened apertures to the outside world, which the state was unable to prevent.

The Challenge of Managing Diversity

Since multiculturalism is now a universal phenomenon, there is a need to distinguish the different manifestations of multiculturalism. Broadly speaking, we can speak of three sets of societies—societies of the First World; societies of the now collapsed Communist World (or the Second World, now usually referred to as "Countries-in-transition"), and the societies of the so-called Third World—so-called, because with the disappearance of the Second World, one cannot talk of the Third.

Multiculturalism in the first set of societies is caused by the arrival of people in substantial numbers from different cultures, particularly from the societies belonging to the second and the third sets. Such arrivals are not new, what is new is the fact of migration in large numbers and their ghettoization in the arriving countries that has allowed them to live their sandwich cultures. Earlier these migrations were of individuals or of individual families, who led a transient life and returned to their homeland or, in some cases, decided to stay back and adopt the host country as their domicile. In the former colonizing countries, such as France and the United Kingdom, the new migrations became a group phenomenon. Thus, UK has now distinctive colonies of the people from Bangladesh, Pakistan, India, and Sri Lanka. In France, similarly, there are groups of people from Pondicherry, and from several former French colonies in Africa. The United States, itself a country of migrant settlers, has been recipient of people not only from its former colony of the Philippines but also from Thailand, India, Pakistan, Korea, etc., not to talk of people from Latin America, particularly Mexico, Cuba and Puerto Rico. Presence of these cultural groups is so large that they are no longer monolingual. Their metropolises have become cosmopolitan in the real sense with restaurants serving different cuisines, and stores selling items drawn from different cultures, and media bringing in messages and cultural programmes from a wide variety of sources. Migrants in these settings live in two cultures—that of the host country and their own parental culture. The media and IT have bridged the distance; geographical separation has not caused cultural isolation. The mainstream media continue to play their role in attending to the needs of the mainstream society, and the other channels cater to the needs of the diaspora communities. Watching a CNN programme in the United States one can get all one wishes to know about the US but very little about the rest of the world. So is the case even with the prominent dailies like the *New York Times*; one finds very little of India, for example, in it barring some unusual happening. To know more about things happening elsewhere one has to read the "International" edition of the *Hearald Tribune*. An American or a French exposed only to his country's media is likely to be ignorant about many things outside of his country. This process has been described by some as a process of "dumbing down"— literates remaining largely ignorant about the wider world, despite the growth and exposure to the media. Of course, those interested in knowing can now take the help of the Internet and surf; they know where to go to look for the needed information, but they do not encumber with all the available information nor is it possible. With more and more information produced less and less is used by any single individual.

Morris Berman, in his book *The Twilight of American Culture* makes a prophetic examination of Western decline through a "dumbing down" process. Berman has provided ample evidence of the collapse of American intelligence. He makes the startling revelation that the number of people reading a daily newspaper in the US has halved since 1965. Many people deposit the bulkier dailies to the dustbin without even opening them. For an outsider visiting that country, there is very little by way of news in them; the only purpose they serve is to tell the reader about the places where goods are on sale, or to compare prices. Communication media in that country have insulated the people from the wider world whereas in the developing countries, the media have served the function of opening the apertures to expose people to the outside world and to broaden their cognitive horizons.

How insulated are the American children can be guessed from Berman's book. He quotes his experience at the Charter High School for Black Teenagers in Washington D.C.: "...some of them, at age sixteen or seventeen, had never heard of the Atlantic Ocean, did not know what 1999 meant, historically speaking, or thought the Civil War had taken place in the 1960s. One student thought that Washington, D.C. was in the Midwest, and was not able to locate New York, Florida, or Texas on a sketchy map." Berman does not regard this as mere "cultural deprivation; it is cultural massacre."[9]

To further cement his argument, quoting other sources, he reports that:

> Forty-two per cent of American adults cannot locate Japan on a world map, and according to Garrison Keillor (National Public Radio, 22 March, 1997), another survey revealed that nearly 15 per cent couldn't locate the United States.
>
> A survey taken in the October 1996 revealed that one in ten voters did not know who the Republican or Democratic nominees for President were.
>
> The 1995 article in the *New York Times* reported a survey result according to which "40 per cent of the American adults (this could be upward 70 million people) did not know that Germany was our enemy in World War II". Another survey (1996) reported that 84 per cent of American College seniors couldn't say who was President at the start of the Korean War (Harry Truman). Fifty-eight per cent of American high school seniors cannot understand a newspaper editorial in any newspaper, and a US Department of Education survey of 22,000 students in 1995 revealed that 50 per cent were unaware of the Cold War, and that 60 per cent had no idea of how the United States came into existence (*Ibid.*: 34-35).

Berman feels that all this is an evidence of "steady lobotomising' of American culture. Such lobotomisation, making people sluggish, seems to be a real danger not only for American culture but everywhere. The task of managing diversity in the context of these societies is to promote the values of multiculturalism in their native population, which had been socialised to live in a single culture society. Socialisation of the young will now have to have a multicultural dimension so that they learn to co-live with people coming from other cultural stocks. They have to broaden their cognitive horizons to acknowledge the existence of a larger world beyond the confines of their country. Simultaneously, the children of the migrant families would require such socialisation that they do not just remain oriented to the culture of their origin but also imbibe the elements of the culture of their adoption.

In the region of Eastern Europe, the collapse of communism meant a certain breakdown of multiculturalism. The Soviet Union got spilt into a number of new nation-states. In some other countries of this bloc partitions took place along ethnic lines and the post-communist phase witnessed a series of ethnic conflicts. The ideology of communism that fostered solidarity gave way to a different kind of ethnic nationalism, which fractured this unity and unleashed forces of ethnic cleansing. The warring groups took advantage of the media to propagate their respective stands; but the international media broadcast the carnage and invited attention of the world community to such an onslaught on the humanity. It is the reach of the media, breaking the national barriers that contain such upsurge.

In the countries of the Third World, as has been said earlier, the tradition of multiculturalism received a renewed emphasis as part of the nation building. The task was to destroy the insulations created by the colonial powers between ethnic and religious communities. That continues to be a stupendous task.

In all the cases, the first necessity is to locate the sources of diversity, and also to find out the factors that continue to foster separateness rather than unity. In this context, the concepts of *insider* and *outsider* can be helpful. A multicultural society, by definition, consists of several subcultures. Membership to these cultures divides people into subgroups and creates a distinction between those who are members and who are not. Those belonging to a particular subgroup identify themselves as *insiders* to distinguish the non-members as *outsiders*. In relation to that group, the outsiders are a heterogeneous lot consisting of people belonging to different subgroups. Each set of such outsiders *vis-à-vis* the group under reference is a group to which these outsiders are the insiders. However, all these people may become insiders of a larger entity to which these subcultures belong. Thus, a reigon may consist of several subgroups with exclusive memberships, but in the context of a regional grouping all the people will be a single membership group. Without further elaborating these twin concepts, let me say that in a multicultural society, any individual or a family enjoys membership to several groups, and at times the boundaries of the two groups may overlap or intersect. As a result, a person becomes insider in one context and outsider in the other.

This usage of the outsider concept is somewhat different from the one used by some scholars who employ it only for the migrant individual or the group, or for the people belonging to the minority group to suggest its location outside the "mainstream" of the majority group. It is wrong to think that the main task of managing diversity is to transform the outsider status into the insider status. This is, to my way of thinking, a wrong formulation. Because the consequence of such an effort will be to *erase* the diversity, which is different from managing it.

Managing diversity does not mean erasing diversity. The challenge is to locate bonds of unity in an ocean of diversity. Neither is the recipe of absorption of the outsider groups into the mainstream of society, nor the prescription for installing insulations between the communities and encourage them to secede and close their shells a workable proposition. Both attempts have proved futile and dysfunctional. The rise of fundamentalism has the seeds of its own destruction in it. When communism as an ideology became religious and fundamentalist, it created iron walls all around. But these walls fell through in due course of time. Communism collapsed under its own weight. Religious fundamentalism, which has now taken the form of international and cross-border terrorism, is universally decried. What happened in the United States on September 11, 2001 was condemned by the entire world barring the fanatics. The aftermath was not an attack on any religion, but on the so-called *Jehadis* who wanted to disregard diversity and hoped to impose their ethics over all. Such clashes need not be defined as instances of clash between civilizations. The present war in Iraq is not a war between Christianity and Islam. Many Christians in the US and the UK have decried this assault on a sovereign state. And not all Muslim states are on the side of Saddam. In the fight against the Taliban and the Al Qaeda it is the Islamic state of Pakistan that was on the side of the United States. Terrorism is publicly condemned by all religions. A small group of fundamentalists in any religious formation cannot become the mouthpiece of the entire community of followers. Putting them in the conceptual cage of civilization would mean ignoring the prevailing diversity. In this regard, I would like to quote with approval what Kenichi Ohmae has to say in his celebrated book, *The End of the Nation State: The Rise of National Economies:*

> Huntington's argument ignores the fact that, even within the same civilisation, people have often fought against each other. From the outside, the differences between the Catholics and the Protestants in Northern Ireland do not seem like a good reason for intense hatred. But for political leaders and mass agitators, they are good enough. Again, from outside, it is difficult to tell Hutu from Tulsi in Rwanda. But they have mutually created...one of the bloodiest clashes in the world. People usually fight when their political and/or military leaders inflate minute differences so as to stir up latent—not when "civilisations" clash. If leaders are enlightened, they can make their people believe in the power of working together. This is the case today with the multiple races and cultures linked peacefully by Lee Kwan Yew in Singapore and Dr. Mahatir in Malaysia (and was true in the Yugoslavia of Josip Broj Tito and the India of Mahatma Gandhi and Jawaharlal Nehru after World War II). It is not civilisations that promote clashes. They occur when old-fashioned leaders look for old-fashioned ways to solve problems by rousing their people to armed confrontation."[10]

Ohmae forcefully argues that clustering cultures in broader supranational entities—either a product of the process of epigenesis or creation of analysts—do not erase underlying differences. For understanding economic activity, he does not regard them as "meaningful aggregates".

> ...Think, for a moment, of ASEAN countries. In what sense is it useful to talk about them as a single, culturally defined area? As they affect local patterns of work, trade, and industry, the internal differences among their Buddhist, Islamic, Catholic (in the Philippines and the Sabah State of Malaysia), and Confucian traditions are every bit as large as, if not larger than, the differences separating any one of these traditions from the dominant business cultures of New York or London or Paris.[11]

Ohmae also reminds that the "particular dissolution of bipolar 'great power' discipline that so greatly affects us today is not taking place in the 1790s or 1890s, but the 1990s. And that means it is taking place in a world whose peoples, no matter how far-flung geographically or disparate culturally, are all linked to much the same sources of global information". A "nanosecond migration of ideas and innovations" facilitated by the revolution in Information Technology has changed the very platform of dialogue. Today, the practitioners of Indian sandwich culture in the US do not have to travel to India to get exposed to Indian culture. These sandwich cultures have created mini-Indias in strange lands. Cultures have began to travel with the migrants, and they are establishing dialogues with the host cultures. Such a conglomeration of cultures defies compartmentalisation in terms of civilization. A return to roots does not require a geographical migration back to the parent culture. IT has made possible an emphatic journey. Glorification of the past is an exercise of the mindless fundmentalists who believe in re-living the past through re-entry in the corridors of history. Sandwich cultures have changed the cultural cartography of the world. And the people have focus on the future with the reigning culture of peace.

Final Comment

As we review the past developments, we come to the conclusion that progress on the path of modernization does not mean death of the tradition. It is interesting to note that with the onset of the process of Globalization, there is a return of the concern for culture. In the earlier phase of modernization and development, culture was equated with tradition and the entire emphasis was on bringing "developed" elements from outside and implanting them in the traditional cultures. All failures of innovation as were attributed to cultures and traditions and all efforts were directed at changing them or discarding them in favour of modernity. Carried out in the 1990s, the review of the past development efforts led people to acknowledge the role of cultures. Culture was brought back in the developing dialogue not as an easy scapegoat, but as an essential factor in development. The demand for cultural identity grew with the growth of literacy and successes on other indicators of modernization and economic development. It was agreed that while the societies are coming closer to each other, they are not getting homogenised. The global village will have to be multi-cultural and polyglot. Solutions to common problems will have to be sought differently for different cultural settings. What may work in given context may completely fail in another.

Notes

1. Quoted from the *Report* of the World Commission on Culture and Development. UNESCO, p. 29.
2. Samuel P. Huntington, "The Clash of Civilizations and the Remarking of the World Order", *Foreign Affairs, 1993*, Vol. 72, No. 3, Concluding paragraph.
3. The idea of a world civilization was wrong dream. I have famous French anthropologist Claude Levi-Strauss on my side to whom I have quoted in the beginning.
4. A quote from Lucien Pye.
5. Krauss, Michael, "The scope of the Language Endangerment Crisis and Recent Response to it" in *Studies in Endangered Languages* (ed. Kazuto Matsumura), ICHEL Linguistic Studies 1998, Vol. 1, p. 105. Tokyo, Hituzi Syobo.
6. S. Castles and M. Miller, *The Age of Migration: International Population Movements in the Modern World.* Mac Millan, London, 1993, p. 4.
7. In the late 1980s, 90 per cent of the immigrants to the United States were from the Third World countries.
8. See Yogesh Atal, "Outsiders as Insiders: The Phenomenon of

Sandwich Culture" in *Sociological Bulletin*, Vol. 38, No. 1, March 1989, pp. 23-41.

9. Morris Berman, *The Twilight of American Culture*, New York, W.W. Norton & Co., 2000, p. 11.
10. Konichi Ohmae, *The End of the Nation-State: The Rise of National Economics*. London, Harper-Collins, 1996, pp. 10-11.
11. *Ibid.*, p. 14.

20
Globalization
Towards an Alternative View

D.N. DHANAGARE

During the past decade and a half, no other concept, with perhaps the solitary exception of 'gender', has stirred a major discourse in social sciences as the term 'Globalization' did. It is not just an accident that the term came speedily into academic parlance following almost on the heels of Dunkel Agreement that finally led to the formation of the World Trade Organisation (hereafter WTO). This synchronisation of social science discourse on Globalization and the institutionalisation of WTO is a striking instance of how developments in the world economy keep impinging on societal processes and institutions, induce new patterns of change and necessitate reassessment of the adequacy of concepts and approaches in social sciences for understanding complex social reality.

The term 'Globalization' refers to the growing economic integration at international level based significantly on the activities of multinational corporations (hereafter MNCs). These activities involve financial exchanges, evolving production strategies, marketing rights and responsibilities across boundaries of nation-states and, of course, accelerating growth by deploying the new information technology. Although not an entirely new phenomenon, the Globalization process in the 1980s and 1990s led to surging of international trade and investments mostly centred around and dictated by the advanced industrial capitalist economies. Because of the intensification of the economic integration process, more recently many developing countries have chosen to get more closely integrated into the network of global economy. In their anxiety to rebuild their economies, most developing post-colonial countries perceive such integration as a short cut to realising their long-cherished developmental dreams. By the standards of the industrially developed countries of the West, however, the process of Globalization in several developing countries, including India, remains at an incipient stage.

The Globalization debate in general is focused largely on more recent developments, whose impact is not confined either to a single nation-state, continent, or subcontinent. Consequences of the global economic integration are seen spread over a wide range of non-economic spheres of life all-over the world. It is commonly understood as a process that rapidly transforms an otherwise disparate and heterogeneous world into a compressed, but not necessarily homogeneous entity and yet at the same time it 'intensifies consciousness of the world as a whole' (Robertson, 1992: 8). It is generally claimed that Globalization accelerates and reinforces interdependence of markets, peoples and their cultures and nation-states. Therefore, some sociologists approach the problematic of Globalization *via* considerations of modernity. In his model of the global system, Giddens (1990: 64), for example, defines Globalization as "intensification of worldwide social relations which link distant localities in such a way that local happenings are shaped by events occurring miles away and *vice versa*. He emphasises four dimensions of Globalization—the nation-state system, the world capitalist economy, the world military order, and the international division of labour. Each of these four, according to him, is an extension of societal modernity and an offshoot of its basic institutional features. He, therefore, postulates modernity as inherently globalising and hence today's Globalization is no more than the fundamental consequence of the modernity project of the West" (*ibid.*, 52-63, 177). However, cultures are not and, in fact, cannot be, obliterated by modernity because "features of Globalization and modernity relate specifically to the separation and recombination of space and time that are so crucial to the dynamism of modernity" (*ibid.*, 20-21, 59-71).

The claim by Giddens that Globalization does not involve any dismemberment or dissolution of non-Western cultures (the 'other' of the West) practically borders on optimism with utopian futuristic streaks. As we shall see later, this use of 'modernity prism' for understanding Globalization is really not very common among contributors to the contemporary debate. Today, the concept of 'Globalization' revolves mainly around social consequences of integration with world economy *via* the market and multinationals. The thrust of the current debate is as much on understanding the devastating effects of global economy on less developed countries as it is on revealing mechanisms that monopoly capitalism deploys to perpetuate its domination. These concerns are discussed emphatically by economists and by other social scientists alike. It, however, needs to be emphasised that although theoretical relevance of 'Globalization' is being taken seriously by all social scientists (including those of the Marxist and neo-Marxist persuasions), the debate as yet has not gained maturity and sophistication as a major social science discourse (Sengupta, 2001: 3137).

The origin of the concept of 'Globalization' is usually traced to Marshal McLuhan (1960) who first introduced the idea of what is today called 'global village'—a notion that implied a sort of compression of the world intensification of consciousness of the world as a single entity. This shrinking of the world, in the early 1960s was then attributed to the growing impact of media revolution, more specifically to the television. The visual medium and its multi-channels abetted market invasion on peoples and cultures. Their influence on human experience has been so deep and all pervasive that it became a part of our being, our consciousness and our very existence.

It is necessary to explicate the notion of Globalization first. While oversimplifying its meaning, Friedman has defined Globalization as "the integration of everything with everything else". This nominal definition tends to hide more and reveal little about the meaning structure. Globalization involves a process of change that is too simple and yet paradoxically too complicated to grapple with. "It is a process of integration of markets, finance and technology, especially information technology (hereafter IT) in a way that shrinks the world to a miniature in size and enables people from different parts of the globe to reach around the world faster, deeper and cheaper" (Friedman and Kaplan, 2002: 64). This characterisation of Globalization, however, projects it as if it is confined to the sphere of market and economic activities alone. Anitat (2002:4) has talked of Globalization as "the process through which an increasingly free flow of ideas, people, goods and capital leads to the integration of economies and societies". Exuding his confidence about what Globalization has fetched for humankind, Anitat argues that such global integration has boosted growth and incomes and has thereby helped to raise general standards of living in less developed and underprivileged parts of the world. With Globalization not only sophisticated technologies have become available to developing countries, but also marked improvements in average literacy, quality of health and general life expectancy and above all greater integration have taken place and these have promoted human freedom. This has been possible because information sharing and market expansion now provide increasing choices to people (Anitat, 2002: 4).

The growing interest in 'Globalization' has to be understood in the context of developments since early 1960s that mark an important watershed in world history. After the World War II, the Berlin Wall had been erected signifying the bipolar world as well as the ideological divide between two super powers that mothered their respective spheres of geo-political influence. The world economy was clearly divided between two blocks represented by 'free market economy' and 'administered economy', between capitalism and socialism. Only modern communication system—the media—contributed to 'global consciousness'. Nonetheless, the term 'global community' was seldom used since the media then fully acknowledged nationality and autonomy of a particular media system. In other words, despite the emergence of a new global awareness, increased communication had not overshadowed or obliterated the remnants of identities of nation-state, ethnicity, caste, religion, race, language and region even within a nation-state, let alone across nation-states. Their insularity was consciously protected by the 'Berlin Wall', 'Iron Curtain' or a 'Warsaw Pact' and by protective tariffs. Behind these walls and fences nation-states could preserve their own unique forms of cultures, traditions, lifestyles and politics, not just their economies.

The nature of interrelations and economic linkages leading to cultural influences came to be understood within two dominant theoretical paradigms, namely 'modernization-modernity, and 'world systems theory'—the latter one as cogently articulated and propounded by Wallerstein (1980). These two conceptual apparatuses practically kept the social science scholarship preoccupied from the 1960s till 1990s. Contributions of neo-Marxists like Paul Baran (1957), Samir Amin (1982, 1997), Hanza Alavi (1982) and Andre Gunder Frank (1978, 1982) to theories of development and underdevelopment, are replete with concepts like 'core', 'centre-periphery', 'international division of labour', 'capitalist world economy', 'monopoly capitalism' and the like that are found in Wallerstein's writing abundantly. Without going into the details of these two paradigms, it should suffice to note that they are precursors of the present day discourse on 'Globalization'. Quite surprisingly though, Wallerstein (2000: 19-35) considers Globalization as no more than a buzzword that describes the current situation in which the end of the 'Cold War' has led to emergence of a unipolar world with an unassailable supremacy of the United States of America both in global economy and geopolitics. To him, Globalization is meaningless as an analytical concept. It is being given legitimacy by spokes persons of the neo-liberal creed that ideologically sustains the pro-global regime. The concept only serves primarily as a political prescription (or exhortation) for the developing world to opt for all kinds of short cuts to integration with the capitalist global economy (*ibid.*).

Nature of Integration through Market

The current debate on Globalization focuses on the role of international trade and market as a cohesive force mainly assisted by modern media and IT. It would, therefore, be necesary to examine the nature of the global integration that is taking place today. John Kenneth Galbraith, an eminent economist, was once asked whether Globalization is truly metamorphosing economy in any fundamental way, and his reply was: 'such a reference to a *new* economy is just short of fraudulent' (Galbraith, 2001: 10). He was only suggesting that forms of expressions change more frequently than does substantive content to which they refer. What was once termed 'capitalism' is now being called a market economy or corporate system. Such euphemistic change, however, does not alter the quintessence of capitalism and its ultimate goal, that is, profit maximisation through monopolies at any cost, that was, and continues to be, the hallmark of capitalism. But then the new expression 'market system' is preferred because it is seen as a more bland, ideologically neutral and yet a sophisticated way of describing the gory side of capitalism. Globalization is, thus, yet another way of putting the fact that capitalist regime gets extended beyond political boundaries of nation-states. Systems of formal governance are relegated to the status of subordinate partners while the business, dominated by MNCs and their managerial class, controls decision-making process and occupies a pre-eminent position in global economy.

The rapid changes in the transnational business world are usually attributed to the revolution in the new digital technology and IT. It is often said that information superhighways are the routes through which Globalization process takes deep and firm roots. The high-speed digital technology is its principal vehicle that enables Globalization to change economies and societies—their norms and rules of game, especially those of the transnational business world. The unstoppable speed of the new IT has thus accelerated the process of integration of the world economies. It is seen in the ever increasing exports of goods and services on the one hand, and the growing trend of cross-border investment flows, mergers, and acquisitions of manufacturing companies on the other.

More specifically, far-reaching Globalization of the financial sector in recent history has been facilitated by electronic communications. All financial and market transactions (transfer of money, bank accounts, loans–lending and borrowing, securities, investments, sale and purchase of stocks of companies, etc.) can now be conducted from, and transferred to, any part of the world in practically no time. Thus, IT has enabled principal companies and actors in the international market to organise themselves as global enterprises. Banking, the backbone of finance sector, for instance, has also become a substantially global phenomenon. According to one estimate, "the world's total bank deposits owned by non-residents of a country rose from $ 20 billion in 1964 to $ 7,900 billion in 1995. Electronic payments through the Society for worldwide Inter-bank Financial Telecommunications (SWIFT) has itself arranged more than $ 5 trillion worth payments per day in 1999" (Scholte, 2002:22-23). The magnitude of these financial exchanges on a global scale is simply mind boggling.

Global financial governance, however, seems to have a weak structure and an arbitrary system of decision making. Apart from the fact that the global financial system is haunted constantly by anxiety over stability of currencies and security of investments, the system clearly favours the North as against the South, big corporate players than upcoming entrepreneurs, and developed industrial capitalist countries more than their developing counterparts. "In the absence of strong civil society initiatives, this global financial system tends to function in a partisan manner while its governance is insufficiently participatory, consultative, transparent and publicly accountable" (*ibid.*, 3). A study conducted by the Organisation of Economic Co-operation and Development (OECD) comprising of some 29 highly industrialised countries worldwide has revealed that "the value of cross-border mergers and acquisitions by US-based MNCs grew sixfold from 1991 to 1998. Similarly between 1990 and 1999, the number of international business alliances (for sale, marketing, and development agreements) rose from just over 3,000 to almost 60,000" (Ferranti, 2000: 1-2). Such an exponential growth in financial transactions in the developed capitalist world is not, however, seen in their exchanges with the less developed countries.

Such research findings on rapid integration of economies within a global space present only a partial picture of reality. They tend to create an impression as if a unified one world—a global community—has arrived not only in economic terms but also in social and political terms. Truth claims of such assertions, often made more tacitly than explicitly, need to be scrutinised with great care and caution. Triumphalists of Globalization always paint a rosy picture of a transnational business class as a cohesive and unified entity. The fact that transnational corporations (hereafter TNCs) have truly become global institutions in structural and functional terms is often overstated. An impression is thus sought to be created that the corporate business world is fast shaking off the national anchorages, nostalgia, attributes and obsessions of its constituents. Sklair's (2001) thesis on Globalization is a good example of such an overstatement. While suggesting the active constructors of the global system, following many a predecessor systems theorist, Sklair has highlighted three analytical divisions between the economy, polity and culture that TNCs dominate the economic sphere, while their cultural ideology of consumerism—

the chief driving force in the sphere of culture and ideology—plays the role of a surrogate of market force. The transnational capitalist class takes over the control of the political sphere (*ibid.*, 20-55). This theoretical position is founded on the assumption of transcendence of not only nation-state boundaries, class interests defined primarily in terms of ownership of means of production (in the classical Marxist sense), but also of cultural tastes, habits, choices and practices. In the event of the latter happening, with the extension of the TNCs, the transcendence would entail a near complete homogenisation of culture and ideology.

The core of Sklair's argument is that a transnational class is rapidly emerging. It comprises of (*a*) TNC executives, (*b*) globalising bureaucracy and politicians (whose services are lent by nation-states, who occupy decision making positions in international organisations or structures of governance—such as the United Nations, UNESCO, UNDP, IMF, World Bank, European Union, Commonwealth and SAARC secretariats, and the like, (*c*) globalising professionals (such as IT specialists, and finance and management consultants), and (*d*) merchants and media. Some of these research findings and statistics do establish the fact that in recent decades this transnational class and the corporate groups they preside over are inclined to go for direct foreign investment in the form of collaborations, or financing subsidiaries to begin with, followed by gradual mergers and takeovers. Sometimes, it is also seen that the TNCs thanks to the ingenuity of their executives and management experts, are effectively dealing with two major crisis facing the global society today, namely, the crisis resulting from extreme form of class polarisation and the environmental crisis. The crises are handled so adroitly that some TNCs are now actively advocating the notion of 'sustainable development', production of environmentally safe commodities and services, and are championing the cause of social justice by selectively appropriating the language as well as rhetoric of non-governmental organisations (hereafter NGOs), primarily to pre-empt or ward off any activist intervention.[2]

Sklair's thesis raises more fundamental questions: whether Globalization has really resulted in increasing free international competition, whether production processes and outputs are getting internationalised—leading to a quantum jump in international labour migration, whether new forms of global governance are really crystallising, and whether or not Globalization process would finally disintegrate nation-states and obliterate cultures and civilizations. In other words, does Globalization truly lead to the formation of a world community and foster at least a *quasi gemeinschaft* solidarity across nation-state boundaries and corporate business class? To answer this question, it would be instructive to examine whether the TNCs—the prime catalysts of Globalization—are really moving in the direction of internationalisation of capital ownership and development of a genuinely transnational business community. Recently, Carroll and Fennema (2002) have studied some 176 leading MNCs in the world economy over a period of two decades between 1976 and 1996. This important empirical study, using a longitudinal research design, found that most of the world's largest business corporations continued their operations within boundaries. Although some financial flows, investments and production activities did go beyond national corporate networks, nearly three quarters of their business linkages were domiciled in the same country (*ibid.*, 413-14). Even a transnational network, developed around large financial institutions too, was found to be no more than a mere superstructure that rests on resilient national institutions. Thus, Wallerstein's (1980: 1-36) argument 'that capitalism has essentially been a world system all through history' stands substantially undermined because MNCs and their so-called corporate forms of governance seem to operate predominantly within national networks. Thus, neither in corporate ownership nor in forms of governance, a truly global framework seems to be emerging in structural and functional terms. This is not to suggest that barring its euphoria no transnational corporation or business class is emerging. Some interlinkages are developing, no doubt, but they are seen operating on a moderate scale only. Financial markets have become global and more integrated but the governance of MNCs whether from the North America or from Europe, remains firmly embedded in national and regional structures and cultures (Carroll and Fennema, 2002: 403-09).

The Future of Nation-States

The present Globalization discourse also touches on the issue of the future of nation-states under the condition of global financial integration. The triumph of TNCs and their finance capitalism over microcosms of nation-states raises the question whether Globalization will strengthen or weaken nation-states. Two diametrically opposite views are advanced. A more optimistic vision is that Globalization actually strengthens the state by redefining its role in changed economic conditions resulting from global integration *via* market and finance capitalism. The other more pessimistic view is that the Globalization process will not only weaken but will also hasten the demise of nation-state. On a more optimistic side it is argued that once a technology-driven Globalization sets in, it starts shrinking the world. As people used to reaching around the world faster, deeper and cheaper, they also start thinking globally. The logic is very simple. Technology builds capabilities, and capabilities create human intentions 'to act globally' regardless of whether or not a formal structure of global governance (like WTO) exists. When declining costs and increasing returns entice people, companies and institutions to tie up with foreign collaborators for maximising their profits, their increasing global interactions create a semblance of disorder. Nation-states then start using primordial and cultural identities as instruments to assert choice of staying in or out of global trade and market competition as and when it suits them. The situation is also conducive for breeding a sense of insecurity and business instability. As the need for morality of order gets reinforced naturally then everyone is willing to give up a share of one's independence of the sake of 'world government' (Friedman and Kaplan, 2002: 65). The scenario reminds us of famous arguments of 'contract theorists' about the origin of the state as a regulating institution.

Today, not few social scientists think that a 'world government' is round the corner. In fact, some theorists go even to the extent of visualising nation-state as no more than a bubble that would soon evaporate in the face of the emerging world community and a global system of governance. It is argued that historically nation-state developed only through the growth of civil bureaucracy, an army and diplomacy that catapulted in the formation of a nation as an 'imagined community'.[3] The bubble of nation-state actually results from modernising initiatives of industrial capitalism. Usually nationalist elites, supported and bolstered up by the national bourgeoisie, often resort to evoking primordial, ethnic and cultural-symbolic roots and identities of people (see Gellner, 1983; Anderson, 1991; Smith, 1991).[4] Globalization is that final phase of capitalism when it completes the entombment of sovereign nation-states. Kaplan (see Friedman and Kaplan, 2002:67) has cited the example of the European Union (hereafter EU) emerging out of the coal and steel consortium in the early 1950s with only a few nation-states but later gradually developing in a superstructure of EU. Kaplan, therefore, argues that the state is weakening in Europe with the formation of EU.

In the context of growing anxiety over the future of nation-states, it is significant to note that Martinelli (2002:9-11) views Globalization process as eroding the very foundation of sovereignty and autonomy of nation-states. This is largely because global finance capitalism compels nation-states to adopt neo-liberal economic policies to stay in the competitive world market. Sovereign states have, therefore, no option but to come to terms with gradual loss of sovereignty and erosion of their power. Martinelli also thinks that EU is a step towards global governance. He is, however, not arguing that nation-states disappear altogether under the bulldozing impact of global economic system. He is only saying that 'they undergo a deep transformation'. In other words, it amounts to saying that nation-states are not demised, but they get reconstituted or reconstructed. Projecting EU as a model of supranational system of governance, Martinelli is simply highlighting the EU experiment as a convincing demonstration of how the two concepts of autonomy and sovereignty have been rendered obsolete and redundant by the Globalization process (*ibid.*, 13-14).

Quite surprisingly, Martinelli takes no cognizance of Amin's position on the true nature of 'so-called' European integration under Globalization. While discussing changes that capitalism goes through during Globalization, Amin has stressed the need to separate the grain from the chaff. He has almost drawn up a balance sheet of what the European Economic Community (hereafter EEC) has not been able to achieve by way of economic integration through the market. He draws our attention to the fact that what truly holds the European community together is the fear of revival of Germany as a major industrial and military power. This shared fear is the motive force underlying the other member nation-states voting for European unification. Beneath the facade of unity of

EU there have been ideological pulls and counter-pulls on the 'right' (that is, pro-USA) and on the 'left' of the political spectrum. The latter position is obviously 'pro-Russia' as a checkmate for the United Germany. Certainly, nationalism and national priorities have had an overwhelming influence on the member-states of EU since its formation (Amin, 1997: 108-12). Economic gains of EEC in the form of visible growth have been attributed by Amin (*ibid.*, 113) to a kind of social compromise between capital and labour in post-War Europe. Quite paradoxically, the success of EU is largely because national policies built around Fordism and welfare state, have been determining the extent of individual nation-state's participation in the EEC experiment. Notwithstanding the triumphalists' discourses around the united European community, the fact remains that "Europe has not made itself an irreversible history", and that the future of its integration as yet remains an unsettled issue. To prove his point Amin (*ibid.*, 118-19) has cited four examples of how the member-states of EU have steadfastly kept four sensitive issues of national economic interest outside the purview of the European Union:

1. Research and development policy, being closely linked to development of military capacities, is still guarded as an exclusively national responsibility of each of the EU members.
2. Transparency in economic policy and practice, on which rests a truly competitive market, is readily discarded. Basic principles of a free market are often bypassed owing to pressure of national interests and policy preferences.
3. Though active partners in the European economy, MNCs still have to operate only within the bounds of national commercial laws of respective member-states of EU.
4. Media (movies, TV. etc.), that is, 'culture' has been completely excluded from the sphere of fierce commercial competition within EU.

Therefore, EU has really not achieved even truly integrated economic governance, except in areas marked out and approved by its sovereign member nation-states.

What is often glossed over in the discourse on Globalization is the fact that the concept presupposes construction of an effective global production system. Advocates of global integration share a faith that the Globalization process is indeed leading to disintegration of national productive systems that they consider as both necessary and desirable often the domineering presence of MNCs in a national economic space is taken as an unassailable proof that global productive system has come to stay. Economic, mainly financial, integration through the market may have accelerated the pace of exchanges between nation-states and their principal corporate actors. However, to assume that such frequent exchanges necessarily lead to shaping of a new global society—civil, economic and political—appears to be a far-fetched idea. It is as much an unattainable dream as it is a historical viewpoint simply because a community or society needs a shared vision, values and sentiments. Just shared economic interests, pursued with the calculus of balance of payments, trade deficits and profits, do not suffice. That shared vision is possible only when commonality of interests transcends pure economic interests or financial integration. As things stand today, centrifugal tendencies do operate quite visibly even within EU and other formations like the Group of 7/16/20, Commonwealth, ASEAN, SAARC and similar other regional formations. 'Fear of the other' seems to be a common running undercurrent of all centrifugal activities and initiatives within such formations.

It is necessary to emphasise that Globalization is the ideology of capitalist superpowers that harbour "a utopian vision of running the world like a market."[5] On a more political and pragmatic side, it involves an exhortation for the less developed economies on the one hand and a project to effect disintegration of nation-state entities on the other hand, to fragment power and achieve social disaggregation, even ruthlessly if necessary. The final aim of this project is to render nation-states as economically parasites, politically powerless and socio-culturally faceless before bulldozing power of the market with MNCs driving from the back seat. Protagonists of the Globalization thesis, who assume that the process is inevitable, often miss the fact that global hierarchy or ascendancy remains perpetually unstable or shaky due to vicissitudes of a world market occasioned by a combination of devaluation of currencies, costs of production and collapse in commodity prices. Today, a developing country with fragile economy may lack the capacity and resources to compete in the world market, but a decade or two later the same country may realise its development potential fully. It needs to be stressed that a hierarchical structure founded on the pedestal of market, commodities and financial power is not irrevocable. Japan and Germany at the end of the 'Cold War' are not the same as they were at the end of the World War II. Hence, though a market-centred vision of Globalization legitimises hierarchy, it is not very conducive for sharing of community sentiments. The market is only an institutional mechanism for one-sided accumulation. Furthermore, it has no history of being very poor-friendly. In the economic history, no economic theorist has ever claimed markets to be pro-poor institutions. Although competitors in the market might have contributed to infrastructure development and to some welfare measures here and there through aid, credit (soft loan) or through foreign direct investments, generally the market tends to polarise societies not only in the relative but also in absolute terms. Therefore, financial integration of world economy through market mechanisms is neither necessary nor sufficient condition for developing a truly sustainable 'world community'. This dictum is true as much for national regional and local levels as it is for the global scale. Hence, Globalization *via* the market is incapable of inculcating a sense of identity, history and social purpose among people. Such a 'we' feeling can alone generate moral strength and survival instinct among social aggregates in times of crisis.

Developing Countries, the Poor and Globalization

What impact the market-driven global integration is having on the less industrialised developing countries and their vast population, especially those belonging to the disadvantaged, weaker and marginalised sections—such as the small and marginal farmers—that is, primary producers, agricultural labourers and more so the women in India? Considerable attention is now being paid to this question in the debate on Globalization. Policy makers, development administrators and international funding agencies, besides, of course, NGOs are presently preoccupied with searching for a viable and more sustainable alternative for the developing countries. More recent debates have tended to zero down on minimum food security for the poor in less industrialised countries in the face of Globalization. The need to launch some kind of 'stop global and shop local' campaign is underscored by such debates. Because, the most important manifestation of Globalization process is that it inevitably leads to increased international trade, including trade in food, across the world that is really avoidable. Besides, economic Globalization tends to turn agricultural farms more capital intensive. This change is conducive to corporate controlled agriculture that is spreading to countries where the great bulk of farmers is poor with small and marginal holdings. Once global agri-business and biotechnology corporations are allowed to penetrate and destroy local economies (in the hope that the free market economy will make food cheaply available to the needy), incomes of small-farm owners in the developing countries start declining (Shiva, 2000: 15-16). The Globalization of non-sustainble industrial agriculture (often promoted in the form of mono-culture) gets established; it creates perpetual dependence among small farmers from developing countries making it impossible for them to survive. This has risked their minimum livelihood.[6]

Generally, increased international trade is justified by the WTO on the grounds that it can promote economic development, that it is the solution to world poverty, and that it has a built-in guarantee of minimum food security to the poor in developing countries. In reality, however, the WTO has promoted an unnecessary trading and export-import activity involving foods and cereals. Moreover, the WTO is unable to control unfair trade practices of some developed nations against developing countries effectively. The idea that farmers, whether small or big, can make more profits by growing food (cereals, fruits, poultry, etc.,) for market, especially for export, is theoretically sound. However, things just do not work out that way. The ground realities have shown time and again that once small farmers get drawn into the vortex of export-import activities under the WTO regime, they are forced to drop prices of their produce if they wish to compete with capitalist farm producers from the developed world. In a sense small producers from developing countries have to compete with rich farm producers from the developed countries as unequals, because the level of farm subsidies given by the latter can never be matched by the former, that is, countries like India.[7] China, for instance, presently supplies about 80 per cent of the demand for green tea in the international market. Anticipating an upsurge in demand from the Western developed countries for green and organic tea (that is reported to have health-promoting properties), China is now getting ready to meet the increased demand by flooding the world market with tea at rock bottom prices to push out potential competitors like tea producers from India and Sri Lanka (Hines *et al.*, 2002: 40). The latest victim of this global competition is the edible oil industry in India. It appears to be nearing the threshold of extinction because of low import duties that have led to highly subsidised soya and palm oil imports from Malaysia that are flooding the Indian domestic market today.[8]

Any attempt by developing countries to project their small farm producers by putting trade barriers and tariffs are stoutly opposed by the corporate business lobby using the WTO sanctions effectively. In conformity with the WTO norms, India had to remove some of the trade barriers on foods by the year 2000 following a complaint by the USA. Consequently, the prices of export items like coconuts, coffee and pepper have plummeted by 80, 60, and 45 per cent respectively (see Hines, *et al.*, 2002: 38). Even the gap between the industrial-urban economy and the rural farm setting is getting widened. For example, corn as an ordinary cereal is sold for Rs. 15 per kg, but the processed cornflakes produced by the cereal company Kelloggs are sold for Rs. 200 per kg. Integration with the global economy, thus, accentuates disparities, and polarises sections of a society and also nation-states. It produces a strange paradox that increased economic growth through global commerce entails absolute deprivation and denial of minimum food security to the poor and vulnerable sections, and threatens sustainability of the local economy (see Shiva, 2000: 17-19; see also Bagchi, 1999).

Champions of Globalization often gloss over the fact that 'food security' is quintessentially a poverty problem. It simply means that lack of food is due to the lack of means to acquire or buy it. Invariably, lack of food is not due to a shortfall in food production but because the poor who need the security badly lack purchasing power, a fact highlighted by the familiar findings of Nobel laureate Amartya Sen from his studies in China and India. Therefore, despite economic Globalization and growth in international trade, in general 'protectionism' continues to be a serious problem that subverts the sustainable agriculture sector in developing countries (Schuh, 2002: 15-16). This explains why Globalization process has failed to capitalise on international trade as a means to ensure food security to the poor from developing countries. Experience of the past decade suggests that the WTO modalities are rapidly pushing small-farm producers into the ranks of the poor in developing countries.

Conditions of working class, in both organised and unorganised sectors, in developing countries seem to be no better under a globalising economy. Throughout the history, working class movements and trade unions have always sought to influence and humanise capitalist system within the nation-states framework. In the Globalization phase of capitalism, however, MNCs and TNCs have rendered economic borders more permeable. They have thereby undercut the capacities of national governments to regulate them, particularly in developing countries (Ross, 2000: 1-2). India is no exception to this trend. Consequently, the labour is facing a new problem under Globalization, as markets keep expanding in their reach as well as in their power beyond labour organisations' will and capacity to affect MNCs. Secondly, in a developing economy like India's, organised non-agricultural industrial labour is only a fraction of total workforce and a great bulk is found in the unorganised sector. Here the transition to a free and organised labour market has been exceptionally slow. Furthermore, different parts of India are unevenly developed—a fact that tends to weaken labour and especially the bargaining power of their unions because of intra-labour competition.

Indian experience with MNCs is that they are willing to pay handsome wages—more attractive than wages offered by their Indian counterparts. While enticing the labour with better wages, greater job security and further prospects, MNCs successfully seek cooperation of workers and their unions winning them away from the national government. Almost compelled to move rapidly in the direction of economic reforms—deregulation, privatisation, liberalisation, and patronisation to foreign direct investments, etc., the national economy is already finding itself in the tentacular global capitalist system. Therefore, the most important challenge Indian labour is facing as a result of Globalization is that the traditional industrial working class is practically pushed into the background and is likely to become invisible soon because of four processes, namely, tertiarisation, feminisation, casualisation and precariarisation.[9] These processes unleashed by Globalization are adversely affecting labour and their unions that hitherto depended on the traditional support base of orgnised 'blue-collar workers'.

As regards effects of Globalization on female labour in India, studies have come out with diverse, at times even conflicting, findings. According to some researchers, liberalisation and opening of avenues for international trade can offer opportunities and provide employment to women workers. If India's share in world trade is expanded, then increased export-import activities can provide income-generating opportunities to women who are currently found mostly in the unorganised sector. Mehta (1999: 70-71), for instance, has pointed out that exports in handicrafts and hand-made carpets (its share in export being 20.41%), textile fabrics and manufacturers (its share being 23.28%), and agricultural and allied products (such as tea, spices, and fish processing, their total share being 17.61%) are some potential areas of more opportunities for women's employment that Globalization is opening up. But then, effects of increased international trade, women as products and consumers, can be both positive and negative. If sectors having employment potential for women are identified and if, side-by-side, sectors where women's employment is getting drastically curtailed are also spotted, then alternatives can be found through planned development. In the event of that happening, women workforce too can readjust itself with forces of Globalization. Theoretically it sounds both valid and convincing. However, the ground realities of unorganised labour market and weakening bargaining position of workers, especially female labour in a developing country like India, do not bear out this optimism. To cite only one example, the textile industry in Mumbai was a strong forte of women workers until the 1920s. As unions managed to get security for labour under various industrial Acts and labour laws, their numbers started declining. In 1985, there were 2,50,000 textile workers in Mumbai. Their strength has come down to just 40,000 in 2000-01. In 1950, 40 per cent of textile workers were women. It is less than one per cent today. Similarly, the Mumbai based industrial plant of Hindustan Levers—an MNC—had as many as 1,600 workers during the 1960s decade of which 600 were women employees. The total number of workers came down to just 800 in 1993, with only three females among them (Dewan, 2002: 1-3). Some studies have even reported that sex-based division of labour persists in India to the disadvantage of women workers in various fields, that women remain under-represented in government services and great bulk—92 per cent of total working women in India continue working in informal and unorganised sector (Jain, 1996: 405-08). Therefore, the general feeling shared in the developing world is that gains from Globalization are going to be negligible and the only visible impact is likely to be negative for female workers. Some also fear that Globalization can further accelerate the pace of feminisation of poverty that in turn will deepen miseries of women, particularly from the underprivileged sections of Indian society.[10]

Cultural Impact of Globalization in a Unipolar World

An unintended but important consequence of modernity and aggressive modernization projects, assisted and funded by developed Western countries, is that people in the developing world have started seeing their identity or even reinventing their tradition—whether religious, ethnic or cultural—is a rallying point. Assertions of such identities often lead inevitably to enmity and conflict. During the Cold War years, the world was polarised with friends on one side and enemies on the other. In contrast 'under Globalization world tends to turn friends and enemies into competitors' (Friedman, 2000: 12). Nonetheless, fierce conflicts and warfare seem to be tormenting our contemporary history. Conflict becomes unavoidable, according to Huntington (1996: 20), because cultural identities are basically civilisational identities and the most dangerous enmities are occurring today among cultures lined up on two sides of the great divide between the Western and non-Western civilisation. The conflict is getting further accentuated by the way market-centred Globalization is making deep inroads into local and regional cultures that feel their very survival is threatened.

The Western worldview has been 'universalistic, positivistic, generalising and even totalising' (Singh, 2002: 40-41) especially during the colonial era. It tended to treat local, regional and parochial cultures and their traditions in the non-Western world condescendingly at best and disdainfully at worst. With the emergence of the unipolar world under the domination of Western capitalism, cultural impact of market and trade relations is further intensified. Culturally, Globalization involves some kind of homogenisation that basically means Americanisation (Friedman, 2000: 9). From the 1980s, particularly from the early 1990s, since India joined the WTO, her economy is being rapidly drawn into the global economic network. As consumerism spreads, changes are visible in people's lifestyles, cultural tastes, food habits, dress codes and choices, and in modes of entertainment; changes even in norms and values are quite striking. Market mechanisms and media is the armoury with which global capitalism successfully demolishes all walls of resistance to its expansion. Revolution in electronic communication (such as radio, TV, cinema, telephone, fax, email, Internet, etc.) has produced an indelible impact on local, regional and national cultures because these media can now reach swiftly even the remotest corner of any country. It should not be an exaggeration to say that in every Indian village beer-bars and McDonald's fast foods will become available earlier than potable drinking water. For more authentic news on casualties in accidents, cyclonic storms or communal riots, India's elite switches on to channels like BBC or CNN. This situation is often characterised as a 'cultural invasion' that global capitalism plans as an offensive without the inconvenience of resorting to traditional warfare. Aggressive marketing and consumerism are thus clearly precipitating a serious conflict of cultures.

As stated earlier, the conflict emanating from Globalization is essentially a civilisational conflict. As Huntington (1996: 20-21) has argued, after the end of the Cold War, as influence of the West is waning, the balance of power is shifting clearly in favour of Asian civilisations. The new world order is emerging in which societies sharing cultural and civilisational attributes, affinities and history have started reaffirming their own cultural identities and values.

Such assertions perhaps constitute a defence mechanism against the onslaught of Globalization. In this scenario, the United States has to keep blowing hot and cold. On the one hand, she has to advocate Globalization ideology less by choice and more by compulsion of the market. On the other, she has bluntly to resort to brutal warfare against those non-conformist nation-states or 'super-empowered individuals' (like President Saddam Hussain of Iraq, Col. Gaddafi of Libya or Osama bin Laden)[11], because they not only challenge the very notion of a unipolar world but also question the legitimacy of the United States to preside over it.

Since the end of the Second World War, the USA has been consolidating her control over the resources and assets of the developed capitalist industrialised world and over the oil-rich Middle East. After the collapse of the Soviet Union in the early 1990s, capitalism has practically trounced its principal ideological and political rivals—such as fascism followed by communism and socialism. The USA's top priority then shifted to bringing all the former colonies shared by different empires (British, Dutch, French, Portuguese, Spanish, etc.) under one roof and to remove politico-administrative barriers to her financial empire. The USA thought she alone had the will, capacity and ability to keep all the former colonies tied to the global economy. For this integration, some visible growth and economic development were promoted in the developing world through aid, soft loans and foreign direct investments, and by deploying modern technology on a large-scale. Furthermore, to meet any exigency or challenge to her domination, the USA had to be prepared militarily with latest technology, including nuclear armaments of mass destruction. To complete the 'end of history' project, the media and Cyberspace networks are now being used for legitimising the Globalization ideology and a network of new NGOs has also been created.[12] Fukayama (1992) calls it as "the triumph of liberalism and market capitalism".

To understand the cultural impact of the Globalization process better, the distinction between 'internationalisation' and 'Globalization' would be quite pertinent here. Before the World War II, the imperial powers, to a certain extent, promoted international understanding and tried to encourage transnational and cross-cultural solidarity with a broad liberal humanistic vision. In doing so, however, cultural autonomy of colonies was seldom harmed. Today, Globalization has only one-point agenda namely, to make markets truly global by fostering commodification of everything including all forms of cultural creativity. Very attractive products of local cultures (ethnic, tribal, indigenous, etc.) are now wrapped up in beautiful packages and sold globally. Whether it is a Madhubani painting, an ethno-medicine, a folk dance, embroidery of a bridal dress, a *dalit's* autobiography, or even a food recipe, everything is produced locally but marketed globally. Therefore, whether Globalization constitutes a threat to local and regional cultures becomes a moot question that Indian discourse on the issue must address itself to. In his two recent essays, Yogendra Singh has admitted that local cultures are coming under tremendous pressure of Globalization, market economy and the media power reinforced by IT. Yet a robust faith in cultural resilience of Indian local communities makes him optimistic about the ability of local cultures, tribes and castes to engage themselves with Globalization creatively and then try 'refractory and pragmatic adaptations'. Being optimistic about India's positive cultural response, Singh (2002: 62-65) holds that adaptive reconciliation with the forces of Globalization would eventually strengthen, instead of weaken or threaten, local or regional cultures and identities. However, to say that 'for traditional local artisans, craftsmen and artists, Globalization is a friendly process because it creates spaces for their economic empowerment and social mobility' (*ibid.*, 103-04), and to argue that Globalization would enhance cultural consciousness of local, regional and ethnic communities, amounts to either overstating the case or glossing over the ground realities, if not to expressing a pious hope.

Such hopes are betrayed by everyday experiences in recent decades. The overstated virtuosity of Globalization notwithstanding, its record so far has been far from unblemished. While Globalization means greater interdependence, it seems simultaneously to cause increasing fragmentation of the world. The Human Development Report too has stated that "economically and politically, frustration in developing countries about the skewed distribution of global power has seldom been greater" (UNDP, 2002:101). The bulldozing on-march of Globalization has provoked strong reactions especially among the youth from countries that have been at the receiving end of the global capitalist and market-dominated network (Bhagwati, 2002:2). Despite the triumph of global capitalist system, both as economy and as an ideology of governance for domination *via* the market, the fact remains that it could not realise goals of social justice in appreciable measure. This limitation of global capitalist system, even under its corporate incarnation, is being realised increasingly both by its core-insiders and by peripheral-outsiders. Hence, in the Globalization phase, capitalism produces anti-capitalist critics who tend to respond to the global integration more with passion than with reason. One of more recent additions to enemies of Globalization has two faces—religious fundamentalism and international terrorism that are acting in unison as if they are two sides of the same coin.

Most of us remain dimly aware of the fact that fanaticism, fundamentalism and ethnic strife have been on the rise for many decades all-over the world, not in the Islamic part alone. Secondly, it is not historically correct to trace the origin of these fundamentalist and terrorist tendencies to the happenings of 11 September, 2001, when terrorists exploded the twin towers of the World Trade Centre in New York and to the series of events that followed. According to the Initiative on Conflict Resolution and Ethnicity (ENCORE) Organisation, a variety of ethnic strife has affected as many as 43 countries around the world (Norberg-Hodge, 2002: 36). Therefore, the growing trend of ethnic conflicts and religious fundamentalism has to be understood primarily as a repulsive response to the pernicious impact of the global consumer culture on diverse, even unique, local cultures. Local communities feel both unstable and unsafe in the face of global market forces—bolstered up by media that too are controlled by MNCs. The media impact on local communities and cultures is so shattering that the consumer culture has pushed them to the threshold of extinction. Local economies are being swallowed gradually by the global capitalism and traditional cultures are being displaced by the ever-expanding global market and consumer culture. Local communities in the developing world are silently, and somewhat helplessly, watching that their plentiful raw material and natural resources are getting depleted and these are replaced by scarce imported materials produced by TNCs. At the same time 'local communities are experiencing a steady and systematic undermining of their self-esteem' (Norberg-Hodge, 2002:37-38). While introducing new brands and products of MNCs/TNCs, their professional advisers and marketing consultants inflict a sense of shame on the people about their local products, customs and food habits, etc., quite subtly and suggestively through commercial advertisements.

This kind of erosion of local cultures by the process of homogenisation, and particularly by the promotion of global monoculture, has disastrous consequence. To achieve development at any cost, many developing economies are pressurised to make structural adjustments, introduce neo-liberal measures, reduce social sector spending and undertake massive programmes of infrastructure development that is unsustainable in the long run (Mahendra Dev and Moosi, 2002:8). Much of the development initiatives in developing countries is geared to serve the needs of global capitalism to exploit their cheap labour, material resources and vast markets. Development under Globalization gets heavily concentrated in urban industrial, metropolitan cities and tends to leave out rural hinterlands to fend for themselves, to face acute problems of poverty, unemployment and even drinking water. It is this kind of impact of Globalization that prepares a breeding ground for religious fundamentalism and for terrorist activities. In fact, decentralised development is a precondition for nurturing local cultural diversities because that development is not only adapted to local cultures but it is also sustainable.[13]

There is some room for optimism, as Friedman has suggested, that Globalization system can still be sustained without letting any major cultural conflicts, without competitors, being perceived as enemies. Having its own power structure, Globalization has to build itself around three sets of balances that overlap and affect each other. First is the traditional balance between the nation-states. With the emergence of the United States as the superpower without any rival, this balance has, however, been upset considerably. In the second place, "the balance between the nation-states and global market" – which implies that investors from all-over the world must have a sense of security of their investments if the global economy is to maintain its efficiency and profitability. The third balance has to be between individuals and nation-states, particularly because in certain historical situations 'super-empowered individuals' become larger than life size for their nation-states (Friedman, 2000:13-14). However, these balances are often beset by powerful nations, like the USA, and their political leadership that keep subserving the interests of their own MNCs and aim at perpetuating asymmetrical relationships between nation-states and the global market. That defies all principles of equity, social justice, autonomy and sovereignty. Erosion of local cultures and national sensitivities—a logical corollary of the global market—then results in conflict inevitably.

Towards an Alternative Vision

The foregoing, somewhat extensive, review should suffice to show that effects of Globalization are taking away from people in local communities even their basic rights to life and livelihood. For India, it took her nearly half a century since the adoption of the Republican Constitution to turn people's entitlements into rights. These very basic human rights now appear to be threatened by a totally market- and commodity-centred Globalization. The situation, therefore, calls for a debate on the possibility of an alternative vision of Globalization. In our view, such an alternative can be traced and rediscovered in the Indian tradition. It would be worthwhile to explore how best we can draw selectively upon the history of India's past collective experiences and achievements. Indian philosophical traditions, spiritual resources and civilisational wisdom contain a global vision—a vision that is neither commodity nor market-centred, nor is it focused on material calculus of gains and losses, profits or deficits purely in material-monetary terms. Such an alternative vision is best encapsulated in ancient sayings like: '*vasudhaiva kutumbakam*' (Let the whole globe be our family), '*aa no bhadraha kratavah yantu vishwatah*' (Let noble thoughts come to us from every side) and '*krunvanto vishwa-maryam*' (Let us make the whole world *Arya*, that is, let us equip people's minds with noble thoughts, ideals and actions all-over the world).[14] To realise this vision, neither any commercial or military war has to be fought, nor conquests of others' territories are necessary, nor external markets need to be captured through media aggression and offending advertisements. It is a humanistic vision that predicates autonomy to individuals, groups, communities and nation-states, freedom of choice of a development path and is also founded on the principles of brotherhood, peace and coexistence.

Such an alternative vision comes very close to the principles enshrined in the Constitution of India. Nonetheless, while searching for a globalising vision in the ancient Indian tradition and civilisational history, a caution is necessary. Often it is suspected, and rightly so, that such a search will entail revival of traditional brahmanical ideas, ritual practices and cultural domination. It must be remembered that *varna* caste distinctions, associated with a spectrum ranging from ennobling to debasing actions, discrimination and injustices based on purity and pollution were justified using the theory of *karma* and *punarjanma* as an ideological tool of the brahmanical order and its hegemony.

However, a careful glance at some Indian philosophical traditions, such as *Vedanta* (mostly contained in rich upanishadic literature), would reveal that the concept of *advaita* (non-dualism or monism), suggests that *atman* and *paramatman* (self and the supreme consciousness) are not two separate entities; rather the 'other' is very much an integral part of the 'self' while the self is inseparable from the *Brahman*. Such traditions contain elements of a truly secular, humanistic, non-hierarchical and non-discriminatory worldview.[15] Yoga is yet another tradition—involving theory and practice—that is now accepted as a scientific way of establishing, or bringing back, harmony with one's true self—a precondition for lasting happiness and peace of mind, and for achieving 'liberation' in existential sense, if not for attaining spiritual purpose or bliss in life.

It is not being suggested here that facts like elitist character of the sacred knowledge and learning in the brahmanical order, resulting in alienation of the toiling and illiterate masses, should be ignored. On the contrary, it needs to be emphasised that knowledge subsequently became the chief source of temporal power superior to the power of the sword. The knowledge of Vedanta (mostly written in Sanskrit—a language unintelligible to the masses) became the main instrument for stabilising the cultural power of the few. However, it is also noteworthy that this domination of ritualised knowledge power did not go unchallenged. India's long history is replete with a series of pan-Indian and grassroot level people's struggle and protest movements against the brahmanical orthodoxy. From Lord Buddha down to Mahatma Phule and Dr. Ambedkar, and from Mahavira to Narayan Guru, and to Mahatma Gandhi, everyone contributed richly to these protests and sought to build a non-discriminatory egalitarian society.

Considering the whole world as a manifestation of the supreme consciousness requires some kind of spiritual realisation that has some streaks of mysticism. However, Swami Vivekananda gave that pursuit an existential meaning and a social purpose. In this worldview[16], real salvation comes only through a selfless service to the needy and all religions are similar. Indian religion, chiefly Hinduism, has always treated all religions to be true. It has taught the world both tolerance and universal acceptance. In an obvious reference to the famous 'Colombia'—Liberty Statue (that stands at the Hudson Bay, New York)—Swami Vivekananda (1989, Vol. 1:

20), in his Chicago speech back in 1893, offered the following advice to the American people:

> Hail, Columbia, motherland of liberty! It has been given to thee, who never dipped her hand in her neighbour's blood, who never found out that the shortest way of becoming rich was by robbing one's neighbours, it has been given to thee to march at the vanguard of civilisation with the flag of harmony.

These words of wisdom have been either forgotten or their meaning misread by the American superpower. To dominate the unipolar world, today, the United States, assisted by her MNCs, is doing exactly the opposite. Likewise, the record of protagonists of *Hindutva* in contemporary India is no different because they have either banished the ethos of tolerance and universal acceptance or have consigned it back to history. Religious fanaticism and market fanaticism are not only flourishing simultaneously but are also competing with each other in the current phase of Globalization. Swami Vivekananda's message in the closing part of his famous speech at Chicago has still some relevance to the Globalization debate today. To him each of the world religions must assimilate the spirit of the others and yet preserve its individuality and grow according to its own law of growth: 'Help and not Fight', 'Assimilation and not Destruction', 'Harmony and Peace and not Dissension' (*ibid.*, 24). If this message is carried beyond religion in the domain of economic integration, it has the potential to provide an alternative global vision.

Globalization *via* the market has brought humanity at the crossroads of history today as "social systems and secular order are simply crumbling down under the weight of ideologies". Therefore, social scientists need to "traverse beyond the realm of concepts and clouds of despair". As Romano Prodi has put it: 'The proper response to Globalization is not to build protective barriers or walls to insulate economies and societies from each other, but to harness the forces of Globalization and make them work for the good of all the countries—rich and poor' (2002: 8).

In this essentially normative statement, Prodi only suggests that Globalization rests on an effective system of global governance that is possible only when as partners nation-states adhere to the agreed rules and operate within a transparent, participatory and an accountable set of institutions. Global order is, or has to be, a moral-ethical order. Powerful nation-states will have a tendency to pressurise the weak and less developed ones and thereby to perpetuate their domination. Growing polarisation between affluence and poverty, between overconsumption and malnutrition, and the ubiquitous distribution of power in global system is then glossed over. Whether science and technology or systems of production and market, they must be founded on ethical values of human dignity, freedom and equity, and must honour minimum rights of life and livelihood. Otherwise, Globalization would be no more than a shibboleth for reinforcing unipolar domination through global market and finance capitalism. For Indian society, that is still trying to get over response; similarly mystifying it will provide no answers to the problems it precipitates. This should be a sufficient pointer to the task of critiquing the present Globalization phenomenon and its demystification that should preoccupy sociologists everywhere in years to come.

Notes

1. Presidential Address delivered at the XXVIII All India Sociological Conference, Indian Institute of Technology, Kanpur, 18-20 December, 2002.
2. Some professional NGOs in developing countries are financially supported by leading international funding agencies and organisations from the developed world. It is estimated that between 1,00,000 and 5,00,000 NGOs were actively doing development work at the grassroots level in India in 1999-2000. During the 1990s' decade foreign funding to some of these NGOs increased by 13.5 per cent per annum, and every year on an average Rs. 2,200 crores worth of foreign exchange came in to support some of these NGOs (see HIVOS, 2002:53-54; see also Dhanagare, 1993).
3. The phrase 'imagined communities' was introduced in social science discourse by Benedict Anderson (1991).
4. Wallerstein (1986:56) has argued that nationalism in general, including in India, in historical terms is a relatively new concept and it is clearly a product, indeed a late product of world capitalist system. Any nation-state serves the purpose assigned to it within that system and hence its existence is contingent upon that purpose.

When that function is over, the existence of that nation-state cannot be guaranteed or taken for granted indefinitely.

5. This expression has been taken from Amin (1997:128).
6. A graphic description of the disastrous effects of monoculture on the ecosystem with rich biodiversity in Latin America is available in Baran (1982: 195-204).
7. For disparities in levels of agricultural subsidies received by farm producers in the developed and developing countries, see Dhanagare (1999: 250-54).
8. Nearly 70 per cent of India's demand for domestic consumption of edible oil is met by such imports (see Hines *et al.*, 2002: 38-40).
9. Some of these terms have been reported in more than one study (see Sethi 1999, particularly the essays by Mahanto and Sonowal (16-61) and by Gawari and Singh (187-88) in that volume, and Sangari and Chakravarty 1999.
10. Similar views and findings have been reported in more than one study (see Sethi 1999, particularly the essays by Mahanto and Sonowal (160-61) and by Gawari and Singh (187-88) in that volume, and Sangari and Chakravarty 1999.)
11. The phrase 'super-empowered individuals' is taken from Friedman (2000: 14-15).
12. For a more elaborate statement of this argument or reasoning, see Ahmad (2001: 25-27).
13. For a detailed exposition of this point of view on sustainable decentralised development of local cultures and economies, see Norberg-Hodge 2001.
14. The term *Arya* came to acquire a rather devious connotation of an ethnic/racial identity, particularly during the British period, to mean *"people of superior social origin with specific pheno-typical features"*. Originally, in the epic literature *Arya* was used as an honorific while addressing a person of noble disposition, enlightened thoughts and actions. In *Ramayana,* for instance, Sita repeatedly addresses Rama as *Arya*.
15. See, for instance, Aurobindo's (1996: 1-13) 'Introduction' to his celebrated commentary on the *Upanishads*.
16. This is taken from Swami Vivekananda's address to the World Parliament of Religions at Chicago, on 11 September, 1893 (see Vivekananda, 1989, Vol. 1:3).

References

Ahmad, A. 2001. 'Globalization: A society of aliens?' (An article originally published in *Frontline,* and its translation in Marathi by Nalini Pandit appeared in *Thinkers' Academy Journal,* 10(2): 24-31.

Alavi, H. 1982. 'The structure of peripheral capitalism', in H. Alavi and T. Shanin (eds.): *Introduction to the Sociology of Developing Societies* (172: 92). London: The Mac Millan Press.

Amin, S. 1982. 'The disarticulation of economy within developing societies' in H. Alavi and T. Shanin (eds.): *Introduction to the Sociology of Developing Societies* (204-09). London: The Mac Millan Press.

Amin, S. 1997. *Capitalism in the Age of Globalization.* Delhi: Madhyam Books.

Anderson, B. 1991. *Imagined Communities.* London: Verso.

Anitat, E. 2002. 'Surmounting the Challenge of Globalization', *Finance and Development,* March: 4-7.

Aurobindo, S. 1996. *The Upanishads: Texts, Translation and Commentary.* Pondicherry: Sri Aurobindo Ashram.

Bagchi, A. 1999. 'Globalization, liberalisation and vulnerability: India and third world', *Economic and Political Weekly,* 34(45): 3219-30).

Baran, P. 1957. *The Political Economy of Growth.* New York: Monthly Review Press.

______ 1982. 'A morphology of backwardness', in H. Alavi and T. Shanin (eds.): *Introduction to the Sociology of Developing Societies* (195-204). London: The Mac Millan Press.

Bhagwati, J. 2002. 'Coping with anti-Globalization: A trilogy of discontents', *Foreign Affairs,* January-February: 2-7.

Carroll, W.K. and Fennema. 2002. 'Is there a transnational business community?', *International Sociology,* 17(3): 393-420.

Dewan, R. 2002. 'Gender and the dominant development paradigm: A conceptual note' (A paper presented at a seminar on 'Globalization and the Academia: Challenges and Prospects' at K.C. College, Mumbai, 22 January, 2002).

Dhanagare, D.N. 1993. 'NGOs and foreign funding', *Man and Development,* 20(2): 133–46.

______ 1999. 'The new farmers' movement in Maharashtra and its response to new economic reforms', in F. Oshikawa (ed.): *South Asia under the Economic Reforms* (JCAS symposium series 6) (247-61): Osaka: Japan Centre for Area Studies, National Museum of Ethnology.

Ferranti, M. 2000. 'Globalization tidal wave', *Infoworld,* 23(48): Item No. 3819925: 1-2.

Frank, A.G. 1978. *Dependent Accumulation and Underdevelopment.* New York: Monthly Review Press.

______ 1982. *On Capitalist Underdevelopment.* Bombay: Oxford University Press.

Friedman, T. 2000. *The Lexus and the Olive Tree.* London: Harper Collins.

Friedman, T. and R. Kaplan. 2002. 'States of discord' (A debate), *Foreign Policy,* March-April: 64-70.

Fukayama, F. 1992. *The End of History and the Last Man*. New York: Free Press.

Galbraith, J.K. 2001. 'What happened to the good society?' (An interview recorded and transcribed), *Current*, July-August: 5-13.

Gellner, E. 1983. *Nations and Nationalism*. Ithaca, NY: Cornell University Press.

Giddens, A. 1990. *The Consequences of Modernity*. Stanford, CA: Stanford University Press.

Hines, C.; Lucas, C. MEP and V. Shiva. 2002. 'Local food, global solution', *The Ecologist*, 32(5): 38-40.

HIVOS. 2002. *HIVOS Annual Report: 2001*. Bangalore: India Regional Office.

Huntington, S.P. 1996. *The Clash of Civilisations and the Making of World Order*. New York: Simon and Schuster.

Jain, L.C. 1996. 'Cooperatives: An appropriate vehicle for women's empowerment', in N. Rao *et al.* (eds.): *Sites of Change: The Structural Context for Empowering Women in India* (400-20). New Delhi: FES and UNDP.

Mahendra Dev, S. and J. Moosi. 2002. 'Social sector spending in nineteen nineties', *The Hindu*, 1 February: 8.

Martinelli, A. 2002. 'Markets, government, communities and global governance' (Presidential address delivered at the XV World Congress of Sociology, Brisbane, 7-13 July, 2002: 1-26).

McLuhan, M. 1960. *Explorations in Communication* (ed. E.S. Carpenter). Boston: Beacon Press.

Mehta, A.K. 1999. 'Globalization and women', in R.M. Sethi (ed.): *Globalization Culture and Women's Development* (55-67). Jaipur: Rawat Publications.

Norberg-Hodge, H. 2001. *Ancient Futures*. Rider Publications.

______ 2002. 'Globalization and Terror', *The Ecologist*, 31(10): 36-39.

Prodi, R. 2002. 'Heal the world: EU and India have a moral duty', *The Times of India* (Pune: 23 November): 8.

Robertson, R. 1992. *Globalization: Social Theory and Global Culture*. London: Sage Publications.

Ross, G. 2000. 'Labour *versus* Globalization', *Annals of the American Academy of Political and Social Science*, Vol. 570 (July). pp. 12\4 and 78 as abstracted by the American Information Resource Centre, New Delhi.

Sangari K. and U. Chakravarty (eds.). 1999. *From Myths to Market: Essays in Gender*. Shimla: IIAS./Delhi: Manohar.

Scholte, J.A. 2002. 'Civil society and global finance: Contributions and challenges', *Work in Progress* (A review of research activities of the United Nations University), 16 (3-Pacific Affairs Section): 22-24.

Schuh, G.E. 2002. 'Global food security', *Economic Perspectives* (An Electronic Journal of the US Department of States), 7(2): 15-17.

Sengupta, C. 2001. 'Conceptualising Globalization: Issues and implications', *Economic and Political Weekly*, 36(13): 3137-43.

Sethi, R.M. (ed.). 1999. *Globalization, Culture and Women's Development*. Jaipur: Rawat Publications.

Shiva, V. 2000. 'Globalization and poverty', Ruth Lecture, *Resurgence*, 202 (September-October): 15-19.

Singh, Y. 2002. *Culture Change in India: Identity and Globalization*. Jaipur: Rawat Publications.

Sklair, L. 2001. *The Transnational Capitalist Class*. Oxford: Basil Blackwell.

Smith, A. 1991. *National Identity*. London: Penguin Books.

UNDP. 2002. *Human Development Report: 2002*. New Delhi: Oxford University Press.

Vivekananda, S. 1989. *The Complete Works of Swami Vivekananda* (Vol. 1). Calcutta: Advaita Ashram.

Wallerstein, I. 1980. *The Capitalist World Economy*. Cambridge: Cambridge University Press (Paris: Editions de la M.S.H. Reprint).

______ 1986. 'Does India exist?' (Paper presented at Session: Historical Sociology in India, XI World Congress of Sociology, New Delhi, 18-23 August: 1-6).

______ 2000. 'From Sociology to Historical Social Science: Prospects and Obstacles', *British Journal of Sociology*, 51(1): 19-35.

21

Globalization

A Conceptual History and Contemporary Cultural Trends

T.K. OOMMEN

[I]

There is no consensus about the starting point of Globalization although many agree that the process had accelerated with the demise of the tripartite division of the world occasioned by the dismantling of the Second World. A large number of authors locate 1500 A.D. as the starting point of Globalization. There are a few who pitch it at 1800 A.D. and still others aver that Globalization began as recently as the 1960s with cultural planetarisation. But these views imply that the history of modernity/Globalization began with the history of the West and, therefore, these views are not only geographically narrow but also historically shallow.

It is not my purpose to settle the dispute on the starting point of the 'Age of Globalization' through this address but to identify certain factors associated with the process of Globalization which started in the sixteenth century. Therefore, it is necessary to recall that there existed a different mode of Globalization prior to 1500. For example, Anthropologist Eric Wolf argues that a survey of the world in 1400 shows that there existed well-formed civilization not only in the Orient but also there existed of states and polities in Africa as well as in the America and they existed in interconnections.

What is relevant for my argument is not the fact of connectivity between societies in the pre-1500 world, but the quality of connectivity. Thus, historian Abu-Lughod argues that the world economy of the thirteenth century contained no single hegemonic power; in fact there were eight circuits in that. My present concern is to understand as to how this interdependent equitous-world was transformed into a dependent-inequitous one; how horizontality is replaced by verticality. We need to take a long term view to appreciate how the phase of Globalization which started with sixteenth century colonialism created inequality.

I suggest that three mechanisms were/are invoked for perpetuating hegemony. These are—stigmatisation, regulation and elite incorporation. Needless to say the specific manner in which these mechanisms were/are applied vary across the three phases namely, civilizing mission of the colonial era, modernization project of the Cold War phase and the present ongoing process of Globalization. This is to say that the hegemonic intent of Globalization which started in the sixteenth century continued with appropriate adaptations in spite of the changing attributes of the 'Others'.

With the discovery of the New World—the Americans, Australia and New Zealand—the Wild Man, the Savage Other or the Primitive Man surfaced. The inhabitants of America were 'wild', 'savage', 'barbarous' and 'beastial' as well as 'simple', 'peaceful', 'innocent' and 'uncorrupted by the evils of civilisation'. Although noble, being a people without history, religion and state they needed to be civilized. If they resisted, physical liquidation was the answer.

One looks in vain in the entire New World for a 'nation-state' governed by the Noble savage—they have been physically liquidated/reduced/dispersed; politically and culturally emaciated, notwithstanding the fact that a full-blooded native had become President of Bolivia in 2005 for the first time in Latin America. The civilizing mission had hardly left any trace of the 'Savage Other'. Their conceptual liquidation is complete and hence regulation is irrelevant. They are utterly powerless and have been incorporated into the 'world system' with pariah status.

The story of the Black Other is somewhat different and greatly complicated. First, Africa, the Dark Continent, was not only a part of the Old World, it was also fairly well populated unlike the New

World. Second, part of Africa was encapsulated within the ancient Egyptian civilization region. Third, the colonizer's religion, *viz.*, Christianity had to face stiff competition from Islam, another world religion, belonging to the Semitic trio. Therefore, two identities had to be stigmatised—racial (Black) and religious (Islamic). Finally, there were two Africas—Pagan and Arab—the former 'primitive' and the latter 'civilized'.

Convinced that the Africans were incapable of self-rule, Europeans apportioned Africa at the Berlin Conference held in 1885 in the most haphazard vein completely shattering the integrity of the 'nations' of Africa. The notion of national self-determination by the people was inapplicable because being a 'people without history' they were not nations in colonial Europe's perception. Having accepted the western anthropologist's certification that African Society was stateless, the colonizers had set out to plant modern states in Africa.

Invoking the Weberian notion that state is the only institution endowed with the authority to handle public violence, European colonizers appropriated the right to control the African people. But the paradox that the colonial state is a wholly illegitimate institution was ignored by the European colonizers. To cope with this difficulty local tribal chieftains were incorporated into the lower of state administration.

Three factors have facilitated to gain control over Muslim Africa—(1) the belief in the higher Christian material civilization; (2) the claim regarding superiority of the moral system of Christianity; and (3) the application of a double standard of judgment.

The strategy of othering had to be different in the case of the Indian civilizational region. They could not have been dismissed as peoples without history; they had a long and enduring civilization. The Aryan myth further complicated the situation because it claimed a shared ancestry between the Indians and Europeans. Admittedly, a new set of factors needed to be invented to stigmatise Indians. The institutionalised inequality of caste system, the oppression of women and the presumed inadequacy of Indian knowledge system came handy.

It is necessary to recall here that the 'standard of civilization' in international society, a step towards Globalization was fixed by the West. These standards reflected the norms and values of the

European civilisation rooted in the mores of Christendom. To accept these standards the non-western peoples had to ignore and marginalise their own standards.

However, the Globalization which started in 1500 recognised the strong, those who were willing to fall in line or those with some strategic value. The non-European states to be recognised first as having the requisite standard of civilization were—(1) the two strong states: the Ottoman Empire and Chinese state, (2) Japan and Siam (Thailand) which undertook the required internal reform (Siam was not colonized also because it was kept as a buffer state between the British and French colonies to minimise conflicts), and (3) Abyssinia (Ethiopia), a centre of pre-colonial Christianity, the only African country not colonized during the scramble for Africa at the end of the nineteenth century. It seems that to escape colonialism one had to possess appropriate resources—the capacity to pose threat, willingness to adapt European norms and values, of strategic value to avoid conflict between European states and/or shared religious sentiments.

Colonialism ended with World War II, and the Cold War persisted barely for forty-five years, that is, during 1945-1989. We find a shift from the old strategy of constructing Others, a shift from specific social categories such as Savages, Blacks, Muslims, Africans, Asians, Orientals and the like, a movement from several dichotomies to one trichotomy—the First World, the Second World, and the Third World. If civilizing mission was the motto of the colonial era, modernization became the motif during the Cold War. Here we come across a new complication because there is a contestation between two modernities; that of capitalist democracies, of the First World, and that of socialist people's democracies of the Second World. The Cold War provided the context to annex the modernising Third World into one of these modernities.

Why is it that such a contestation was necessary? Because capitalist democracies claimed that their modernity was 'natural' and socialist one-party regimes insisted that theirs was 'enlightened'. One can discern two constructions here—'we' of the First World and 'they' of the Second World and 'those' of the Third World. The Second World was partially good—technologically efficient and advanced, but they did not have multi-party democracy, civil society, or competitive market. As for the Third

World, it was negative in all respects. That is, as we come to the Cold War period, there is a new construction; others of the colonial period have either been completely deconstructed as in the case of the Savage Other, or have been reconstructed as in the cases of the Black Other, and the Oriented Other. Instead, the three worlds were put in a hierarchy, the first at the top, the second in the middle, and the third largely unmodern at the bottom. And inequality between them continued unabated.

With the dismantling of the Second World, the world has become one; there is but one modernity, the capitalist modernity, and everybody can be equal. But to become equals the inhabitants of the erstwhile Second World and Third World should endorse certain values and adopt certain institutional arrangements. The Structural Adjustment Programme (SAP) wherein there ought to be a minimal state, a free market, and a vibrant civil society is the new prescription. Today's ideal society is one in which the state, the market and the civil society co-exist and a division of labour between them should be accepted. If a country, nation or people do not accept this prescription, they remain marginalised or excluded. Therefore, one no more hears about the civilising mission of the colonial times or modernization project of the Cold War era but only of good governance. During the colonial times, the stigmatised others were told that they were incapable of self-government and hence the justification of the colonial state. During the Cold War, the Third World democratic polities were castigated for their states being 'soft' and hence the need to establish modern 'hard' states. But now what they need is minimal states so that they can globalise swiftly. To globalise is to catch up and there is no possibility to opt out.

The chief agent of this advocacy is the First World and within it the only surviving superpower, the United States of America. The U.S. is aided and abetted by the Bretton Woods institutions. In this project the real deficit of the Second World was the absence of multi-party democracy. One party rule or "peoples' democracy" was stigmatised as totalitarianism. To be sure, structural differentiation, a prerequisite for modernization was indeed absent in the Second World. As for the Third World, its real maladies were primordial collectivism, casteism, communalism and corruption. But all these persist in the First World also although their manifestations differ.

As is well-known, Islamophobia is rampant and discrimination against Asians and Africans persists, not to speak of gender oppression. The point I want to make is that negative attributes are not exclusive or inherent feature of a group, community or civilisation. But it is a matter of labelling by powerful and the dominant, through a process so that they can be excluded from the mainstream and inequality can be perpetuated. This is the long macro-picture of Globalization which started in 1500, the central tendency of which is domination by a few hegemons. This version of Globalization perpetuates disparity and discrimination; brings about displacement and distress for the majority of the world population.

[II]

Keeping this sort of conceptual history of Globalization in mind, let us look at the ongoing cultural trends. Globalization, as other "izations", has both negative and positive consequences. In what follows I shall identify four interrelated and interacting cultural processes—homogenisation, pluralisation, traditionalisation and hybridisation—in terms of their positive and negative social impact and through that the challenges faced by Globalization.

The revolution in transport and communication did bring about a certain degree of homogenisation in cultural patterns and institutional arrangements right from the time of colonialism. While modernization accelerated this process, homogenisation seems to be climaxing with the onset of Globalization. The more visible aspects of homogenisation manifest in the cultural context through common lifestyle and consumption pattern—dress (*e.g.*, jeans), food (*e.g.*, McDonalds), music (*e.g.*, popularity of Michael Jackson). Yet it is not true that this consumption pattern and lifestyle have become or fast becoming universal. Generally speaking, these are confined to the urban population and within that those who live in metropolitan centres, which is a minority. But this minority is the most visible groups in the contemporary world population and the similarity in their lifestyle leaves a deep social impact. Notwithstanding this, to argue that Globalization brings about homogenisation of lifestyle and consumption pattern is to mistake the part for the whole. The majority of world's population is still untouched by the process of homogenisation; cultural heterogeneity obstinately persists.

However, homogenisation is more visible in certain other contexts—nuclear family, monogamous marriages, parliamentary democracy, private property and western technology. Here again, some of these institutional arrangements (*e.g.*, parliamentary democracy, private property) have a near-universal endorsement as compared with other institutional patterns. For example, joint family ethic has not disappeared from Asia and monogamy has not yet become the normative pattern in most Muslim societies. The homogenisation process in these institutional arrangements was initiated during the colonial era and gained momentum during the Modern Age.

The process of homogenisation assumes the effective functioning of displacement syndrome, that is, the belief that the old is necessarily displaced by the new. But this is not a correct perception regarding the dynamics of social transformation. It is true that some of the old elements/aspects are displaced but some others are retained and new elements are added to the existing stock of the old. Further, retention of the unique elements in the national heritages while incorporating exogenous elements facilitate 'Globalization'. These processes—displacement, retention, accretion, Globalization—conjointly produce pluralisation.

Pluralisation concedes and commends the co-existence of a variety of consumption and institutional patterns. To go back to the examples I have used along with McDonalds, other varieties of junk food (*e.g.*, pizza) and along with Michael Jackson's other recent styles of popular music (such as rap by Eminem) come to be accommodated. Not only that, several of the old patterns in food, dress and music persist with vehemence; cultural revivals are indeed common in contemporary world. This partial change and partial persistence gives birth to what I have designated as pluralisation.

I have already hinted above the possibility of pluralisation in the institutional realm. Witness the arrangements of 'marriage' that exists today from simple temporary cohabitation without any legal or moral binding to highly committed and life-long marriages. Similarly, what are designated as 'families' range from ephemeral dwelling units of couples to long term cohabitation of a wide circle of kin. Even as private property and parliamentary democracy are endorsed in form, their content varies across societies. The democratic pattern varies from two-party systems to multi-party coalitions. Property forms vary from exclusive ownership, to joint-stock companies to co-operatives and collective enterprises. Even in the case of technology, the distinction between simple (traditional), intermediate and advanced (complex) technologies is not merely conceptual but is of robust empirical possibility. That is, pluralisation is a fact of contemporary social reality.

I must add a caveat here. It is not my point that Globalization causes pluralisation. But I want to suggest that because of the processes of accretion and retention, pluralisation comes about as Globalization proceeds. That is, Globalization cannot be and indeed should not be homogenising in its tenor which was the central tendency of modernization. Pluralism does not reject a cultural item or an institutional device based on the locale of its origin, because it recognises and respects other cultures. But generally speaking, the non-west accepts many more of the western cultural items and west reluctantly takes to things non-western. Globalization which should imply flow of goods and ideas in multiple directions actually results in their flow in one direction, from the west to the non-west, from the centre to the periphery and hence hegemonising in its tenor and orientation. One of the challenges of Globalization is to reject this unilinearity and consciously move towards reciprocity.

The hegemonising tendency of modernization gives birth to a loss of meaning and an erosion of identity to the non-west. This leads to the revivalist syndrome, the resurrection of roots, a search for identity, a process I designate as traditionalisation. However, this tendency is not confined to the non-west. Americanisation is resisted even by Europeans, particularly the French. Different nations even as they modernise and globalise want to retain their 'national' heritages. Sometimes response to Globalization takes the form of cultural revival and results in the reinvention of tradition both as religious fundamentalism and also as religious reforms. If fundamentalism is invariably a literal interpretation of texts ignoring the changing contexts, reform is a creative reinterpretation of the text taking into account the change in the context. When traditionalisation relapses into the search for cultural purity, it engenders cultural relativism, the belief that one's culture is the purest and it needs to be maintained in its pristine purity.

Globalization has to meet the challenge of containing fundamentalism and accelerating reform.

Tradition, however, is not a monolith; plurality of tradition is widely recognised. Given the plurality of tradition, the tendency of one or another strand of tradition to establish hegemony over other traditions cannot be ruled out. Generally speaking, the conflict between tradition and modernity is a conflict between the traditional hegemony and the homogenising tendency of modernity. Dominated traditions do not have the power to challenge modernity and hence they tend to succumb or acquiesce. If modernity succeeds in successfully challenging the hegemonic tradition, homogenisation will occur. But this is unlikely to happen in all parts of the world with equal intensity as hegemonic traditions and their strength varies across the globe. This is evident from the persistence of fundamentalism/revivalism—religious, political, economic and/or cultural—in different parts of the world.

The plurality of tradition that I am referring to has another dimension—its verticality. Thus, one may distinguish between Little and Great Traditions. The latter, generally speaking, obtains at the civilisation level often transcending nations and states. Little traditions exist essentially at the level of communities—some big, others small; some territorially anchored, others spatially dispersed. The confrontation between Great Traditions resurfaces in the context of Globalization, designated as 'clash of civilizations' to recall Huntington's phrase. The intensity of clash across these great traditions depends upon their proximity or distance to the process of Globalization. Thus, one may postulate a continuum with globalising great traditions on the one end and those great traditions which resist the process of Globalization on the other. All the same, Globalization produces self-awareness and dignity about one's heritage and culture.

The clashes between great traditions transmit their tension vertically leading to conflicts at the level of local communities. These manifest in a million mutinies between religious, linguistic and tribal communities as well as racial and caste groups over a period of time. The clashes between these little traditions are based on the specificities of their situations whether they occur in Ireland, Bosnia, Basqure Land, Kashmir, Burundi or Los Angeles. These are not 'clash of civilisation' as such but are their local expressions which have a bearing at the macro level. Further, these local clashes feed on each other because of Globalization, through the agency of communication, particularly electronic media.

It is not my intention to suggest that Globalization only intensifies the clashes between little traditions; it can also and often it does prompt communitarianism. The mass media often instils in their audience sympathy and concern for the victims of different types of disasters. Humanitarian work and charity result from this. Thus, Globalization does produce fellow feeling, fraternity and altruism.

There is another aspect of communitarianism that merits reference. Modernity's emphasis on homogenisation tends to destroy the specificities of local communities. Therefore, people soon discover the deficits of modernity—anonymity, impersonality and bureaucratisation. These render them rudderless creatures and they often yearn for the 'return of the community'. New associations of friendship—clubs, eating jaunts, entertainments, picnics, excursions, tours and the like—come into vogue. Neighbourhood associations and other voluntary associations get established to meet instrumental and expressive needs. There occurs a resurrection of localism as a reaction to globalism resulting in the return of community.

The cross-breeding of the traditional and the modern, the local and the global, gives birth to hybridity. Hybridisation creates new cultural elements and social patterns which are neither traditional nor modern, neither local nor global. Hybridisation is different from pluralisation in that it is neither co-existence nor elaboration. It is an effort to innovate, to break out of cultural and social dead ends. It is a product of the mutation syndrome. It is simultaneous engagement with both tradition and modernity and local and global. This is evident in contemporary institutional arrangements and consumption patterns.

If in the traditional societies living in joint family was the norm, in the modern society nuclear family came to be accepted as the standard. But it was realised that nuclear family with its aggressive individualism neglects not only the aged, the imbecile and the physically handicapped but even the 'normal' child. An appreciation of eastern family ethic gradually developed in the West. Inter-family arrangements to look after children intermittently are gradually emerging (*e.g.*, in Scandinavian countries) instead of vigorously pursuing the 'professionalisation of mother role', the refrain of modernity. Acute sexual division of labour which prevailed in the wake of modernization is gradually being replaced by sharing of domestic chores by husband and wife. The possibility of lodging the aged parents in houses and flats proximate to those of adult children is being explored instead of their being dumped into Old Age Homes, which are invariably run with a commercial motive. In all these institutional arrangements of the Global Age, one sees mutation of the traditional and the modern.

The mutation between the local and global too leads to hybridisation as is evident in music, art forms or food items. Vegetarian hamburger, Indian rap music, European curry, Japanese pasta, and numerous other examples suggest the relentless march of hybridisation. And yet, it ought to be noted that there is a hierarchy here. Generally speaking, the cultural elements from the affluent and dominant 'nations' dominate over the cultural elements from weak, small and/or dominated 'nations'. There is an unfortunate tendency to value positively everything from the dominant groups—be they political institutions, economic organisations, family patterns, or eating habits and stigmatisation of those from dominated ones. Nullification of this tendency is an important challenge before Globalization.

[III]

The four processes—homogenisation, pluralisation, traditionalisation and hybridization—that I have referred to above are resultants of the revolutions in transport and communication leading to ideational, spatial, social and cultural mobilities. Precisely because Globalization contributes to the acceleration of these processes, it is extremely unlikely that the world will become one socially and culturally. True, a commonly shared social and cultural layer is emerging and getting universal endorsement. But even as this layer is likely to be similar in its form, it is likely to be different in its contents in different locales. To wit Indian democracy, the 'biggest' in the world functions differently from the American, the most 'successful'. Italian Catholicism is 'conservative' as compared with the Brazilian one which is 'radical'. Indonesian Islam is 'syncretic', if Iranian Islam is 'puritanic'. Thus, beneath the common homogeneous layer there lies many uncommon and differing layers. This is so because of the different histories and traditions of these societies which impact on the processes of modernization and hence Globalization differently through cultural mutations and social hybridisations.

The four processes operating independently and in interaction give birth to a world society which is much more complex than the protagonists of Globalization would have it. It is not a movement from tradition to modernity, simplicity to complexity, heterogeneity to homogeneity. But it produces new permutations and combinations giving birth to diversity. The challenge of Globalization lies in welcoming and celebrating this emerging diversity instead of opting for the engineered homogeneity of the Modern Age. Diversity as a social fact existed since the hoary past and modernity tried to destroy it through Project Homogenisation. The challenge of the Global Age is to endorse diversity as a value, that is, transform diversity into pluralism. Globalization is not uniform but regionally and nationally variable.

22

Modernity, Post-Modernity and Global Development

P.N. PANDEY

Auguste Comte (1798-1857) perceived a rationalist progression of society from theological to metaphysical to scientific stage.

Henri de' Saint Simon (1760-1825), the master of Auguste Comte and one of the founders of 'Sociology' initiated his quest in 1816 when he began publishing, irregularly, the periodical *L'Industrie* (popularising there the word Industrialism) and describing in it the society of the future. Past society, said Saint Simon, had been military society in which the chief figures were priests, warriors and feudal lords, the parasites and consumers of wealth. The new industrial society, he said, would be ruled by producers—the engineers and the entrepreneurs the "coming men" of the times.

Writing in 1840 Alexis de Tocqueville (1996: 666-667) predicted the possible outcome of the new mass democracy he saw emerging in modern society. Thirty years later the historian Jacob Burckhardt (1871: 151-158) observing the transformation of German society wrote a letter mentioning that the military state would be turned into "industrialist". Forty years after Burckhardt, Thorstein Veblen (1963: 4) returned Saint Simonian theme, *i.e.*, 'Revolution in the Twentieth century', he said, 'could only be on "Industrial overturn"'. He also observed in his "The Engineers and the Prince System" (1963) that if a revolution came in the United States of America, it would be led by Production engineers who were indispensable "General Staff" of the industrial system.

One skeptic Clifford Geertz has remarked that the category "Transitional society" may become a permanent category in the social sciences. As a matter of fact, we began using the term transitional society since the end of the World War II (1945) and fifty years after we still prefer to denote our society with the same adjective.

For Ralf Dahrendorf (1959: 272-276, 301-303), we are living in a "Post-capitalist Society". It was authority not ownership that counted in industrial society. With the denunciation in legal ownership of means of production there is a break between economic and the political order. In post-capitalist society relations to the instruments of production no longer decide dominance or power or privileges in society. No doubt, economic and property relations still generate their own conflicts but they no longer become the centre of conflict in society. Who constitute the ruling class of post-capitalist society? Our answer to this is that it is head of bureaucratic hierarchies, the authorised ones who give the directives to the administrative staff. Outside the portals of an industry, a manager (Administrative staff) is simply a citizen while a worker of the factory may happen to be a member of the parliament and a minister and here lies the authority of direction.

According to George Lichitheim (1963: 194), the contemporary industrial society is increasingly "post bourgeois". The Nineteenth century class struggle is ending with institution of private entrepreneurship on which it was pivoted because of social welfare legislation, human rights legislations and income distribution which are getting associated with the operation of market economy.

For Amitai Etzioni (1968: 8), we are in a "Post-modern era". It is from his book *The Active Society* that we find a heralded pronouncement of "Post-modernism". A new conceptual reference to connote the unprecedented transformation of the societies of West, particularly the U.S.A., Germany, France, Italy, the U.K. and other western European societies. He says the modern period has ended with the radical transformation of the technologies of communication, knowledge and energy that followed the Second World War. Now the societies have moved on towards super technologies, computer, electronics and wonderlands of knowledge and ideologies. The so-called post-modern societies are conducted, controlled and geared up by technocrats, knowledge elites, and computer scientists, electronic and nuclear experts.

Modernization, Modernity and Modernism

Frequent expressions of modernization, modernity and modernism have been synonymous in common parlance. Modernization and aspiration to modernity are probably the most penetrating features of the contemporary scene. Most nations are nowadays caught in the web of becoming modern. Historically, modernization is a process of change towards those types of social, political and economic systems that have developed in western Europe and North America from the seventeenth century to the nineteenth century and have then spread to other European countries and in the nineteenth and twentieth centuries to the south American, Asian and African continents (S.N. Eisenstadt, 1969: 1-2). It is a process of change, a total transformation of traditional or post-traditional societies proceeding with techno-economic changes which necessarily produce changes in the socio-political order.

Modernization is essentially a process—a movement from traditional or quasi-traditional order to certain desired types of technology and associated form of social structure, value orientations, motivations and norms (S.C. Dube: 1969: 33-45). Two other terms are sometimes used almost synonymously with modernization. They are—westernisation and industrialisation. But, modernization denotes a broader perspective and scope than westernisation. The west and things western do not have entirely happy connotations for most of the developing societies. Many of these countries have gone through an intense anti-colonial phase, and have lingering memories of ruthless domination and exploitation by the west. The choice of the new world order of international goodwill and welfarism requires a less emotionally charged term, like modernization. The term 'modernization' in such a situation soothes their healing. Further, the westernisation seems to be direction bound, limited and releasing generally a smell of British colonialism and imperialism. There are several western models with British model overshadowing. modernization is neutral, direction-free and keeps the choice open. Thus as a concession to the sensitivity of developing societies and as an aid to conceptual clarity, modernization is to be preferred to westernization. Modernization too, has several models. Japan and South Korea and recently China have developed their own indigenous models. The advancement in Japanese technology and electronics are superseding all-over the world and rank matchlessly in the western markets. As regards industrialisation, it is an important part of modernization; it does not encompass the entire process. The connotations of industrialisation are overtly technologies. Social and cultural processes are considered under it only by implication.

Modernity denotes the common "behavioural systems" historically associated with the societies of Western Europe, North America as well as those of Japan. In a sense, thus, modernity refers to the state and situation of having been modern. It denotes common behavioural systems historically associated with urban, industrial, literate and participant societies of Western Europe, North America as well as those of Japan. Modernism, on the other hand, is a wave, a trend of tendency towards adoption of contemporary style of life and systems of developed societies of the west. It has been an overwhelming choice, a contemporary scenario, a call of the people, a taste of the time as well as a pronouncement of the present era. A number of brilliant analyses in the works and writings of particularly Deniel Lerner (1962), Almond and Coleman (1960), McClelland (1963), S.C. Dube (1968) appeared in regard to the process of modernization during the end of the sixties. Now the period of full fledged modernization has already reached its saturation point during the first half of the twentieth century in the western world. Now these societies are showing an upward march beyond modernization to be termed in this present discourse as post-modern.

In the process of modernization both the developed and developing societies are apprehensive of their identity loss and that is why they attempt to put their attentiveness on the agenda of modernity. If we look in the context of the developed countries of the west, we find that the European Union presently a federation of 27 European countries has a common economy, polity and social structure and is showing a collectivist identity of the western Europe. Despite the emerging new scientific attitude, the national objectives and goals and the evaluation of the policies of science and technology are done on the basis of purposive rationality as against communicative rationality in terms of Habermas' perception.

Most of the classical sociologists were engaged in an analysis of the critique of modern society. Such analysis is clear in the work of sociological theory of Marx, Weber, Durkheim and Simmel. All were working on the point of emergence of modernity. In the perception of Marx, modernity was defined by the capitalist economy.

To Weber, the most critical and the defining problem of the modern world was the expansion of the formal rationality at the expense of the other types of rationality, for example, practical rationality, substantive rationality, theoretical or intellectual rationality. In Durkheim's view, modernity was defined by its organic solidarity and the weakening of the collective conscience. George Simmel has been both a modernist (Frisby, 1992) and a post-modernist (Weinstein and Weinstein, 1992). Frisby accepts him as the first sociologist of modernity (1992, 59). Simmel is seen as tracing out modernity into major sites—the city and the money economy.

The city is where the modernity is concentrated or intensified. The money economy involves extension and expansion of modernity. The detailed description which Simmel has made in his *Philosophy of Money* (1975), where Simmel perceives modernity as 'Epiphany'. Simmel deals with the powerful effect of money on modern society, especially, alienation. This, in turn, brings us back to the central issue in Simmel's sociology of modernity, that is, "tragedy of culture", the growing gap between objective and subjective culture or as Simmel put it, "the atrophy of individual culture" and "hypertrophy of objective culture" (Frisby, 1992: 69).

Giddens defined modernity in terms of four basic institutions—the first is capitalism, characterised by commodity production, private ownership of capital, properties as labour and a system of class based on these characteristics. The second is individualism which involves the use of inanimative power to source and machine to produce goods. Industrialism is not restricted to only work place, it affects others such as transportation, domestic life and communication. The third institution is surveillance capacity. It refers to the supervision of the activities of subject population in the political sphere and the final institutional dimension of modernity in military power or the control of the means of violence.

Anthony Giddens has described the modern world (its origin in seventeenth century) as a juggernaut. More specifically he is using this term to describe an advanced stage of modernity—

radical, high or late modernity. Among others is Ulrich Beck, who perceives modern society in terms of "risk society" (1992). Beck has perceived a perspective of modern society. He wants to explain that modenity is followed by industrial society which emerged by eliminating the 19th century feudal order of society. Now he perceives that it is a new phase of modernity. Beck perceives this risk society in terms of new modernity as a reflexive project in which the modern society is getting rid of the structural web work and allows the people to develop their personality according to their choice and they are making the society also reflexive. His ideas are quite akin to the ideas of Giddens. To Zigmunt Bauman, modernity is associated with holocaust where he describes how the so-called modernised Nazi German society caused the genocide of the Jews during the World War II. The machinery and technology of the modernity with all their systems and programmes were applied by the German Nazis to weed out the Jews. They were transported by the military, police authority and the railway officers in a planned way to the gas chambers of the factories and were reduced to ashes. In other words, it was application of irrationality of the rationality. What he means to say is a negatively planned application of apparatus, machinery and resources of modernity to bring an end to a specie of humanity. Jurgen Habermas (1987b) described modernity as an unfinished project implying that there is a move to return in modern world before we can think about the possibility of the modern world. The progressive stage of modernity to him appears as a colonization of the life world by the system.

From Modernity to Post-Modernity

The very concept of post-modernity or post-modernism has emerged as a wave of change or an ideology of impression from western modern developed societies, *viz.*, the USA, France, Germany, Italy and the U.K. The post-modern development, as a matter of fact, refers to the changes emerging in these societies which have attended the zenith of their urbo-industrial development. Zbegniew Brezezinski (1970) observes American society as the first 'technetronic society'. The so-called post-modernity refers to the unprecedented changes that have been brought about in the form of culture. Malcolm Waters (1992) defines post-modernity in terms of 'Post-Cultural Development'.

The contemporary debate on post-modernity is thought provoking with contradictory remarks. The intellectuals, the architects, the cultural entrepreneurs—all have shown their concern about the unprecedented changes that have emerged in modern society as a result of excessive bureaucratisation, computerisation and commodification of knowledge. Most of the social theorists perceived this trend of change as an emerging cultural practice. There are others who perceive this phenomenon as objective discussion. In contemporary writings, the concept has emerged as a warm game or as a dazzling point of debate. Kellner (1989b2), Lemert (1994: 42) perceives this phenomenon as an extremely hot subject.

The post-modernism can be seen as a dazzling variety of styles that can be mixed and matched with various packages. To Lyotard, this post-modernity refers to a historical epoch that is generally seen as following the modern era. J.F. Lyotard characterises post-modernity as changes in the structure of feeling and sensitivity of the human beings. He starts with his working hypothesis that the status of knowledge is altered as society enters what is known as post-industrial stage and culture enters what is known as post-modern stage. Lyotard basically involved himself in the study of post-modernity with reference to art, literature and problem of communication and cybernetics. To him, post-modernism is incredible to metanarratives and grand theories.

Fredric Jameson characterises post-modernity as a cultural logic of late capitalism (1984). He describes this new formation as cultural dominant. It may also be considered a new systematic cultural norm. It is made up of quiet heterogeneous elements (Jameson, 1984: 7). In Jameson's understanding, this post-modernity can be characterised by superficiality and lack of depth. It is depthless, a historical, timeless and immediate. It conceives of the social world as technological entity. It is more concerned with simulacrum. This post-modernity ignores historicity and, therefore, this loss of historicity tends to random cannibalisation of all styles of past (Jameson, 1984: 65-66). The results lead us to another key term in post-modern theory, i.e., pastiche. Since, it is impossible for historian to find the past. It is assumed that God is dead and the latter is alive. Jean Baudrillard in his *Mirror of Production* (1975) characterises post-modernity as a shift from mode of production to code of production and more to speak he adds number of inputs as against adjectives as implosion, seduction, simulation dedifferentiation and hyper reality. Baudrillard is an extreme post-modern theorist. Jurgen Habermas observes it in terms of colonising the life world of individual by the system, ascendancy of purposive rationality (In Weberian term Zweckrationalitat), over communicative rationality (In Weberian term Wertrationalitat). There are some theorists who characterise post-modernism as a chaotic mass mediated individual preference based phenomenon. David Harvey (1989) characterises post-modernity with fragmentation, ephimerality and discontinuity.

Debate on Modernity and Post-Modernity Not Ended

The debate on modernity and post-modernity has not ended. There are proponents of post-modernity as well as defenders of modernity. Among the defenders of modernity mention may be made of Anthony Giddens, who perceives the existing situation as advanced modernity that is radical, high or late modernity. Zygmunt Bauman and Ulrich Beck are the other theorists of this group. Habermas is another name who observes modernity as an unfinished project. Zygmunt Bauman characterises in a different way. Instead of discussing about post-modernity he is using the term 'Liquid Modernity' and more to say the present trend of modern development as 'Posthumous Modernity'. Among the proponents of post-modernity, the names of Kellner (1991), Lemert (1994), Lyotard (1984), Jameson (1984), David Harvey (1989) and Baudrillard (1975, 1983) may be cited.

Unfortunately, there is no discussion of the technologies of communication, knowledge and energy or a clear specification of what exactly; post-modern societies are in the discussion of Etzioni. No doubt, he talks of continued increase in the efficacy of knowledge and technology as a central characteristics of modern period. So, the post-modern period or society is not a discussion, but only a question in his book. He is skeptic in his views. He says the efficacy of the technology of production and ever growing super systems of technology pose a challenge to the primacy of values they are supposed to serve. He fears to predict about the future whether the society is to be the servant or the master of the instruments it creates.

Similarly, Sam Bear (1969:426) talks of 'post-collectivist' politics. He feels the collectivist model of British politics which was partly divided feudalist society and as oriented to the welfare state may be coming to a close. The post-collectivist tendency is a "reaction to the increasing scale and intensity of rationalisation in both government and society".

And so a debate moves with the above prologue on 'post modernism'. It used to be that the great literacy modifier was the word 'beyond', *e.g.*, beyond tragedy, beyond culture, beyond society. But we seem to have exhausted the 'beyond' and today the sociological modifier is the prefix 'post' (Bell, 1974: 53). Sydny E. Ahlstram, (1970), a theologian, has described the religious scenario in the United States in 1960 as 'Post-Puritan', 'Post-Protestant', and 'Post-Christian'. Lewis Feuer has sub-titled his work on Marx and intellectuals as a 'Set of Post-Ideological Essays'.

John Leonard (1970: 26) in the *New York Times* has talked of the 'Post-Literature culture' as being heralded by McLuhanite age. For S.N. Eisenstadt and Eric Hobsbaum (1970, 1971: 36), the new states have become 'Post-Tribal Societies' for though they are no longer bound by the norms of the past and they seek consciously to change, they live in a suspended world with little approximation to the modern societies of the West. Eric Hobsbaum has obviously written about 'post-tribal societies'. Similarly, Roderick Seidenberg (1950) foretelling the victory of rationalism had described a 'Post-historic man' in which we move from periphery in which instinct dominated intelligence through the transitional period in history into post-history in which intelligence dominates instinct.

Daniel Bell (1974: 54) observes that the concept of 'Post-Industrial Society' emphasises the centrality of theoretical knowledge as the axis around which new technology, economic growth and the stratification of society will be organised. Empirically one can try to show that this axial principle is becoming more and more pre-dominant in advanced industrial societies. To Bell (1974: 112), the post-industrial society is a continuation of trends unfolding out of industrial society and many of the developments were foreseen long ago.

Since the phenomenon of the so-called Post-Modernism and Post-Industrialism are evolving and continued, no scientific parameter can be applied to bifurcate the modern from the post-modern and the industrial from the post-industrial be made in absolute sense of distinction.

As it has been discussed in the preceding pages, the essential division in modern society is not between those who own the means of production and an undifferentiated 'proletariat' but the bureaucratic and authority relations between those who have powers of decision and those who have not in all kinds of organisation social, economic and political. The basic attributes of post-industrial societies can be observed as: (*i*) a change in the economy denoting a shift from good producing to service economy, (*ii*) pre-eminence of a professional or technological section, (*iii*) centrality of theoretical knowledge as source of innovation towards control, (*iv*) Modern technology and technological assessment, and (*v*) creation of a new 'intellectual technology' for decision making.

Zbegniew Brzezinski (1967: 1821) is one of the contemporary social scientists who has made his observation of American society in regard to post-industrial development and has pointed out that America is in the midst of transition, that is both unique and baffling and is being shaped to an ever increasing extent by technology and electronics and thus, is going to be the first 'Technetronic society'.

Sociologically, it appears that the theoretical knowledge of modern technology, electronics, nuclear resources and computer science formulate the very edifice of the post-industrial social structure of societies in the western world. Daniel Bell (1967: 24-39, 102-119) in his study of the post-industrial society stresses on the functional significance of the knowledge derived in the areas of techno-electronic resources in the system of economic production and shift from manufacturing economy to service economy.

Observations and Postulates

In order to proceed in the interpretation of the subject matter we have formulated certain sociological postulates as follows:

1. The concepts of post-modernism and post-industrial society as referred to social and economic structure of those industrially developed capitalist societies which are being conducted, regulated and controlled by

technological, electronic and computerised machines, instruments and resources. Such societies in the writings of social socientists like Alain Louraine, Daniel Bell, Albrecht Wellmer, Zbegniew Brezezinski, Stephen Crook, Jan Pakulski and Malcom Waters (1994) and Robert Holinger are termed as post-industrial societies.

Our postulate in this regard is that the more the application and dominance of technologies and electronic resources, the greater shall be an upper hand of dominance by technocrats and knowledge elites and they will emerge as experts and 'house ideologues' in the service of the ruling class.

2. The perspective of the post-modernism and post-industrialism is limited and cannot at the same time be applied to societies or nations of the Third World.
3. Our observation in regard to super industrial societies is that there is still the dominance and importance of property ownership in such societies but the capitalist class has failed to continue its dominance as it did in the industrial societies because of the emergence of technocratic elites as an important component possessed of a power-oriented mentality in these societies.

The Indian Context

India is an old society but a new nation which is a living example of multi-cultural pluralism comprising all major religions, languages, castes, cultural, sub-cultural, ethnic and parochial networking. Religion in India has played a pivotal role from times immemorial. Therefore, all the scientific developments and technological innovations had to be associated with religion and morality. Religion without science is lame and science without religion is blind. Therefore, modern technology has to be associated with the values of tolerance, righteousness, and morality otherwise it will create catastrophe in society. The social, economic, cultural and political systems in India have evolved out of its traditions.

Therefore, the application of technology of the developed societies without indigenous concerns will impede the growth. The traditional bonds in India are such that we are not ready to put one step forward without looking two steps backward. The process of social transformation in India is ongoing and, therefore, modernization of the country requires a well-organised national endeavour. But in the process of modernization, we perceive that the situation is elusive and full of dilemmas, for example, *dharma, karma,* rebirh, spirituality, caste system and secularism, universalism and particularism, ascription and achievement can be taken as dilemmalic situations. It can be said that such dilemmas have not emerged in India only but in the other developing societies as well. They are facing the dilemma of tradition *vs.* modernization. On the other hand, there is the lure of ascription while on the other, there is a craze of achievement. Similarly, the dilemma of universalism *vs.* particularism, self-interest *vs.* collective interest, affectivity *vs.* affective neutrality can also be traced. In addition to above, the concept of *dharma,* rebirth, the notion that this world is a mirage, happen to be major constraints in the implementation of the national programmes of modernization. If we look at the programme of family planning and population control through medico-technological resources, we can easily perceive that religious sanctions and cultural taboos in certain sections of society create major constraints.

Modernization proceeds with secularisation, rational outlook, and accelerates the democratic values. At the same time, the age ridden iron laws of caste impose the bars of stratification. Westernisation and the articles of western origin in India might have created temptations to adopt them but their pronouncement and appreciation by civil and intellectual society are not very much appreciable because they bear the smell of last 200 years of British colonial and imperial domination and exploitation.

In such a situation, undoubtedly, a neutral process like modernization happens to be more acceptable and soothes the healings of the past. But the problem is that there is no single model of modernization before India. Most of the western developed nations, *viz.,* the USA, France, Germany, Italy and the UK in the west and Japan, Korea and China in the easternland have developed their own models of modernization. In such a situation, India has also to evolve its own model aided by indigenous resources.

Further, what should be the ultimate destination of man in the process of cultural development through modernization? This debate still remains unanswered by the American and European social scientists. The western exponents of modernization and industrial development have presented the economic parameters such as Gross Domestic Product (GDP) and Per Capita Income (PCI). They are basically the economic parameters and not social or cultural. Development and modernization do not mean merely increasing productivity. It involves qualitative changes such as improvement in lifestyle, easy accessibility to health, hygiene, education, recreation and rehabilitation.

In my perception, the parameters of cultural development in terms of modernization are yet to be developed. Most of the social scientists in India have accepted the paramount role of education and media of mass communication in the process of modernization in developing societies. The informatics and cybernetics have played a very significant role in defusing the value of modernity. The unprecedented changes being brought about in agricultural economy and political and cultural developments are very optimistic signs which show that India is emerging as one of the most powerful nations of the world, but at the same time, the regional voices emerging as ethnic movements in India are obsessive. The claims for retaining specific identities are yet another obsession.

In such a situation, the rational application of science and technology with indigenous resources is essential and while projecting development, the regional, territorial, cultural, ethnic and geopolitical priorities should be put in limelight for an enduring modernised society. The indigenous models and patterns of development should be taken into account in the process of modernization. As a matter of fact, India has to emerge as a fully modernised society which should be socially egalitarian, culturally sensitive and environmentally sustainable.

The post-modernism in the west associated with so-called modern developments in economy and polity has accelerated the need for global developments.

Globalization is a multidimensional open concept that refers to the transformation of trade, technology, industry and economy in a universalising direction. It is a cultural process as well but more specially, it is focused by the Western industrially developed countries *i.e.*, the U.S.A., France, Germany, Italy and the U.K. as a worldwide trade mechanism. In cultural terms it refers to both as compression of the world and intensification of the consciousness of the world as a whole (Robettson, 1992). It is a process that transforms institutions of modernity in universalising directions (Giddens, 1991). Capitalism, industrialism, surveillance and monopolisation of means of violence are its major institutions. Some of the constraints and features of Globalization are mentioned below.

Globalization as a worldwide trade mechanism is a new approach but its roots lie in last six decades of Post-World War II period. The decades of 1960, 1970, 1980 and 1990 started with the agenda of growth, modernization, social transformation, development, and sustainable development and finally at the turn of the twentieth century led to Globalization with emphasis on liberalisation and privatisation (Pandey, 1997). The chief motivators for Globalization are (*i*) Search for market place, (*ii*) Multinational investments, and (*iii*) New tools of technology and electronics with computer network. Next, the most paradoxical aspects of Globalization are disparity, inequality, injustice, insecurity prevailing in the economy, polity and social structure of different societies of the world. The industrially developed countries of the world represent 20 per cent of the world population and hold control over 80 per cent of world resources while the developing world represents 80 per cent of the world population with 20 per cent of the resources of the world. The U.S., the U.K., France, Germany and Italy are moving towards post-industrial economy from manufacturing to service economy. They are in urgent need of market place for their products. It is developing countries of Latin America, Africa, and Asia which appear as alternative grounds for market. These countries are apprehensive of identity loss. They do not want techno-electronic imperialism.

Sad Impressions of Modernization, Development and Sustainable Development

The so-called sad impressions of modernization, development and sustainable development have created more disparities, discrepancies and discriminations, though the slogans of Globalization are more attractive.

The outcome of the western developmental programmes have disheartened the developing nations. The ever increasing social and economic disparities, discrepancy, differentiations and the gap between the rich and the poor indicate that the very ideology of development based on egalitarianism and equity has proved elusive and dilemmatic to the societies of Asia and Africa (Michael Hudson: 1971, P.T. Bauer: 1972, Tiber Mende: 1973, Teresa Hayter: 1972, Andre Beteille: 1993, Immanuel Wallestein: 2000).

Western developed countries have created adverse consequences in these countries. Tiber Mende (1973: 36) has traced out that a tendency of strong resentment and protest has been evoked among the developing nations against the developed western countries. The developing nations are realising that foreign aids are instrumental in perpetuating long term dependency in the developing nations and as such a strategy to place the developing societies in the grip of their trade and technology. The profiteering motives and interference in the economy and polity of the developing countries by the western nations will always put them in the subservient condition. Hence, they are threatened about their identity loss. In this state of affairs, the developing countries must evolve their own indigenous models and parameters to their social and economic development. This will help them restore their identity. Theresa Hayter (1971: 151-52) goes a step forward and emphatically argues that the policies and programmes initiated by development agencies such as International Monetary Fund, World Bank, United States Agency for International Development, Inter American Development Bank accord and approve the international and national character of western capitalist countries and aim at maintaining their supremacy over these countries. These agencies motivate for creating free market, trade and technology and to rely on them with a sense of attachment and commitment. Bauer (1972: 4968) is another social scientist who has given a critical assessment of the nature and form of western aid and has concluded in his investigations that the western developed countries have attempted more to create a vicious poverty circle in the Third World countries rather than improving their economy and social standards of life. Immanuel Wallerstein in one of his latest works entitled 'After Liberalism' (2000) has expressed apprehension about the immanent crisis sprouting out of the late capitalism. A contemporary economist of the U.S. George Shoraz in one of his latest works entitled *The Crisis of Global Capitalism: Open Society Endangered* (2000) is very vocal and clearly highlights that Globalization is an inevitable outcome of the crisis of post-industrialisation in the western world. A well-famed Canadian economist Sislia Ostry (1999) observes that the western industrially developed capitalist countries are facing crucial problems in the sale and consumption of their products and are setting their eyes towards the countries of Asia and Africa. The excessive technologised production in the west requires a large and wide market place for effective sale and consumption. The increasing demand of consumption is a decisive factor for the success of technologised production and this is feasible only when there is extensive market place for consumption. In this context, the Third World countries appear as the only alternative market place for the west.

The principles of justice associated with socialist welfarist states are ridiculed in the agenda of Globalization. The nature and quantum of availability of electronic appliances, computer, e-mail, Internet etc., are not equally available to all the countries of the world. Research and Development (R.D.) is lifeblood in any economy. The initiatives are taken by multinationals more frequently. Hence, infringement of powers and capacity in policy marking. It means multinational corporations will have upper hand in the developing nations. Globalization proceeds with consumerism while 80 per cent of the world is in need of productive economy. Globalization is elusive to the need and expectation of the poor, and the weaker sections. It widens the gap between the rich and the poor. Accepting Globalization means accepting the primacy and rule of integrated minority over a huge majority of the world. At the structural transformation level, the programme of Globalization is against participatory democracy as 80 per cent of world population has little representation and interference in its policies and decision-making. Apparently, the developing nations at Seattle in the U.S. and also at Geneva at the WTO Summits denoted that they are not ready to accept the terms and conditions of WTO as binding on their social and economic liberty. The theft of intellectual property by multinationals and putting on their patent is nothing less than imperial exploitation. It has shattered the nerves of the egalitarian ideology and obsesses the poor countries with ruthless domination and super bossism of the west. The Western industrially developed countries show a deceptive crocodile sympathy to developing countries which have different culture, history, tradition, national ethos and ideology.

This programme of Globalization is the outcome of western crisis of post-industrialisation and is devoid of human concern and issue of uniformity. The Third World countries must come out in a consensual way to make a forte of their own to face the challenges in the new millennium.

The Process of Cultural Change

The most recent theoretical debates about culture centres on the issue whether culture has taken a new turn, entered a new phase, at the end of the twentieth century. The cultural registers analysed by the neo-Marxist and neo-Weberian scholars are essentially modern in character. If society prefers to be dominated by a single set of ideas then Gramsci of Frankfurt school can investigate how these ideas are manufactured; if society is divided by men into a small and fixed number of classes, then Bourdieu, Abercrombie, Hill and Turner can investigate whether culture exhibits similar internal differentiations.

The hardest Marxist version comes from Jameson (1984). He accepts that cultural change is in train but interprets it as the 'cultural logic of late capitalism'. He proposes a threefold perception of capitalism, which comes originally from Mandel:

1. Market capitalism, which involves markets within nation-states.
2. Imperial or monopoly capitalism, in which the capitalism states establish colonies: so that they could catch both suppliers of raw materials and international markets.
3. Multinational consumerist capitalism which establishes a new integrated global place for capitalist expansion and within that expands markets by expanding individual acquisitiveness.

This expansion of capitalism into global arena is percolated by a global expansion of culture which liberates it from particular social context. There is a prodigious expansion of culture throughout the social realm. This is so-called post-modern culture. The post-modern culture which focuses the mind on the centrality of the global space and dislocates individuals from the realities of their own situation has four characteristics:

1. It is depthless (*i.e.*, what you see is what you get) which has risen on the collapse of grand narratives and meta theories.
2. It is historical and immediate. It provides no reference back to human suffering and struggle. Traditions can be mixed and matched in pastiche rather than drown upon or resisted.
3. It is timeless. It focuses on organisation of fragments of culture meanings in space. The time relations of these fragmentations are not signified.
4. It conceives of the world as a technological entity rather than as a natural one. It also conceives social network as a computer network, rather than an ecological balance.

If we count Jameson (1984) and Harvey (1989) along with Bell (1993) and Habermas (1981) as critic of post-modernism then among its best friends must be Lyotard (1984) and Baudrilland (1988). The move from modern to post-modern knowledge parallels social development. The status of knowledge is altered as societies enter what is called as the post-industrial age and culture enters what is known as post-modern age. The post-industrial developments are the computerisation and commodification of knowledge. Increasingly, performatively, the capacity to deliver outputs at the lowest cost, replaces truth as a yardstick of knowledge. Modern culture is highly differentiated but post-culture moves towards hyper differentiation. Post-modern culture can bee seen as a dazzling variety styles which can be mixed and matched with various packages. Modern culture is highly rationalised pattern of technical cultural expertise located either in tradition or its transcendence. Post-culture is so hyper intensified that there can no longer be any claim to expertise or any development of tradition. Modern culture is highly commodified, post-culture is so hyper-commodified that material commodities are subsumed by signs which represent them.

Information Technology and Global Change

The media of mass communication revolutionises culture and the knowledge of science, technology and electronics enhances it to give wider coverage to the global space. The society is transferred into a 'technetronic' culture with computer networking. The 'Culture specifics' are attempted to be subsumed into multi-ethnicity and multi-culturalism as smaller clenches with secondary importance. In addition, printing press, radio, film, television, the computer networking, the cybernetics and informatics are controlling the global network. The information technology and telecommunication systems with digital codifications are reducing the vast pool of human knowledge to a codified structure embedded into the computer websites.

In the words of Habermas, this process of Globalization is going to decouple the integration of life world and the system and is tended to proceed towards internal colonizations. In the modern techno-electronic set-up, individuals are forced to go through purposive rationalisation (in Weber's term Zweck rationalitat). The purposive rationality is marked with contractual morality *i.e.*, non-critical, object oriented and not by communicative rationalisation, *i.e.*, critical reasoning (in Weber's term Wert rationalitat). The character of this so-called post-modern culture which is emerging can be termed as disethesized and shameless. The individual is emerging as a client leaving aside his real identity and the whole world system is being regulated by purposive rationality and is going to emerge as a computerised networking rather than a natural entity, a technological entity rather than an ecological balance.

The developing countries in general, and India in particular, have a long historicity of grand narratives, meta theories, legends and myths. Globalization cannot assimilate all of them. In my assessment, India and other developing countries of Asia and Africa will ever manifest peculiar blend of their historical identity even in the global modernising attempts.

This chapter is a revised and enlarged version of a research paper entitled, "Science, Technology and Changing Power Structure in Industrial Society", presented in the XVIII All India Sociological Conference held on March 3-5, 1989 at Haryana Agricultural University, Hissar (Haryana) and published in *Journal of Social and Economic Studies*, New Series, 3rd Issue, Har Anand Publication, New Delhi, 1991.

1. The terms post-modernism and post-industrial societies have special reference to the societies of Northern and Western Europe and the U.S.A.

2. As the knowledge of science and technology has got central importance in the contemporary world societies, the emphasis is on the centrality of theoretical knowledge in the discussion of post-industrial society.
3. Post-modernism and post-industrialism both are discussed as emerging tendencies leading to the transformation of existing industrial societies with new social structure comprising new serial classes.

References

Ahlestrom, Sydny, E. (1970): The Radical Turn in Theology and Ethics", *The Annals* (January, 1970).

Almond, G.A. and Coleman, J.S. (1960): *The Politics of Developing Area,* Princeton University, Princeton, New Jersey.

Bauer, P.T. (1972): *Dissent on Development,* Cambridge, pp. 49-67.

Beteille Andre (1993): *Equality and Inequality,* Oxford University Press, New Delhi.

Buckhardt, Jacob (1872): *Letters to Von Preen,* April 96, (ed.), Alexander Dru (1995), pp. 151-152.

Bear, Sam (1969): *British Politics in Collectivist Age,* (Vintage) edition, Epilogue.

Bell, Daniel (1967): "Notes on Post Industrial Society", *The Public Interest,* 6 and 7 Winter and Spring, pp. 24-34 and 102-148.

______ (1974): *The Coming of Post Industrial Society,* Arnold Heinemann Publishers (India), Pvt. Ltd., pp. 3-29, 49-54 and 113-119.

Brzezinski, Zbegniew (1967): "The American Transition", *New Republic,* 157, 23. December, pp. 18-21 also reprinted in *Information Technology in a Democracy* (ed.) Alain Western Cambridge, Mass 1971, pp. 161-167.

Birbaum Norman (1971): *Toward a Critical Sociology,* New York.

Boulding, Kennity (1964): *The Meaning of Twentieth Century,* New York.

Bauman Zigmunt (1989): *Modernity and the Holocast,* Ithaca N.Y. Cornell University.

______ (1991): *Modernity and Ambivalence,* Ithaca N.Y. Cornell University.

Bauman Zigmunt (1991): *Post Modern Ethics,* Oxford, Blackwell.

______ (2005): *Liquid Life,* Cambridge, Polity Press.

______ (2007): *Consuming Society,* Cambridge, Polity Press.

Beck Ulrich (1990): *Risk Society: Towards A New Modernity,* London, Sage.

Baudrillard Jean (1975) *The Mirror of Production,* St. Louis Telos Press.

______ (1993): *Symbolic Exchange and Death,* London, Sage.

______ (1990): *Seduction,* New York, St. Martins'.

______ (1983): *Simulation*, New York, St. Martins'.

Bauer P.T. (1972): *Dissent on Development*, Cambridge, pp. 49-67.

Beteille Andre (1993): *Equality and Inequality*, Oxford University Press, New Delhi.

Crook, Stephen, Pakulski, Jan and Waters Malooni (1992): *Post Modernization: The Change in Advanced Societies*, Sage Publications, New Delhi.

Dahrendorf, Ralf (1958): *Class and Class Conflict in an Industrial Society*, Stanford. See chaps. VII and VIII, "Classes in Post Capitalist Society" (*i*) Industrial Conflict and (*ii*) Political Conflict, pp. 272-276, 301-302.

Dube, S.C. (1965): "Human Problems of Economic Development" in *Economic Development and Cultural Change*, Raj Kamal Prakashan, New Delhi.

______ (1976): "Modernization and its Adoptive Demand on Indian Society" in the *Sociology of Education in India*, (ed.) M.S. Gore, L.P. Desai, Seema Chitnis, NCERT, New Delhi.

______ (1994). *Tradition and Development*. Vikash Publishing House, New Delhi, pp. 1-16, 17-44.

Eisenstadt, S.N. (1969): *Modernization: Protest and Change*, Prentice Hall of India. Pvt. Ltd. New Delhi, pp. 1-2.

Elzioni Amitai: (1974): *The Active Society*, New York, p. 7.

Geertz, Clifford (1974): Cited in the Coming of Post Industrial Society by Daniel Bell.

Giddens Anthony (1990): *Consequences of Modernity*, Combridge Polity.

______ (1991): Modernity and Self-Identity, Cambridge Polity.

Holiger, Robert (1994): *Post Modernism and the Social Sciences*—A thematic Approach. Sage Publication, New Delhi.

Hobsbaun, Eric (1971): *Social History and the History of Society*, in Daedualus, issue entitled, Historical Studies Today, winter, p. 36.

Harvey David (1989): *The Condition of Post Modernity: An Enquiry into the Origins of Cultural Change*, Oxford, Blackwell.

Hayter Teresa (1971): *Aid as Imperialism*, Harmondsworth, pp. 151-152.

Kellener, Douglas (1989b): *"Introduction: Jameson, Marxism and Post Modernism"* in D. Kellener (ed.) Post Modernism, Jameson critique, Washington D.C., Maisonneuve Press, 1-2.

Lamert, Charles (1994): "Social Theory at the early end of a short century" in *Sociological Theory* by George Ritzer, 1996.

Lerner, Daniel (1962): *The Passing of Traditional Society*, The Free Press.

Glencoe (1963): 'Toward a communication Theory of Modernization', p. 11 in *Communication and Political Development* (ed) Lucian W. Pye, Princeton University Press, Princeton.

Leonard, John (1970): "Post Literature Culture", *The New York Times*, Nov. 26.

Lichthim, George (1963): *The New Europe: Today and Tomorrow*, New York, p. 194.

McClelland D.C. (1961): *The Achieving Society*, Van Nostrand & Co.; Princeton University, New Jersey.

Mende, Tiber (1973): *From Aid to Recolonization: Lessons of A Failure*, New York, p. 36.

Ostry, Sislia (1999): *The Crisis of Global Trade*, New York.

Pandey, P.N. (1997): *Dilemmas of Development: A Case of the Third World*, Samajiki, *Journal of U.P. Sociological Society*, Vol. 10, Joint issue 1-2, 1997, Varanasi. A previous version of the paper was presented in the XVIII All India Sociological Conference, Deptt. of Sociology, Haryana Agricultural University, Hissar, March 3-5, 1989.

______ (1991): "Science Technology and Changing Power Structure in Industrial Society", in *Journal of Social and Economic Studies*, New Series, 3rd Issue, Harsad Publication, New Delhi, pp. 21-27.

Pool, Ithiel de Sola (1963): *The Role of Communication in the Process of Modernization and Technological Change in Industrialisation and Change* (ed.) Bert F. Hoselitz and Wilbert Moore, UNESCO, Mouton.

Robertson, R. (1992): *Globalization*, London, SAGE.

Simon, Henri de Saint (1816): *L industrie*, Cited in the *Coming of Post Industrial Society* by Deniel Bell, p. 49.

Simmel George (1907/1978) *The Philosophy of Money*, Tom, Bottomore and David Frisby (ed.), London, Routledge and Kegan Paul.

Shoraz, George (2000): *The Crisis of Global Capitalism: Open Society Endangered*, New York.

Tocqueville, Alexis de (1966): "Democratic Nations Have to Fear", pp. 666-667. quoted in the *Coming of Post Industrial Society* by Daniel Bell, New York.

Touraine, Alain (1971): *The Post Industrial Society*, New York, p. 3.

Veblen, Thorstein (1963): *The Engineers and the Prince System*, Haringer Edition, New York, p. 4.

Wellmer, Albrecht (1971): *Critical Theory of Society*, New York, See also Max Horkheimer's *Critiche Theorie, i.e., Critical Theory* (2 vols.), Frankfurt, 1968.

Wallerstein, F. (2000): *After Liberalism*, New York.

Waters Malcolm (1992): *Contemporary Sociological Theory*, NewYork, Columbia, University Press.

Weinsteen Deena and Weensteen Michael, A. (1993): *Post Modern(ized)* Simmel, London, Routledge.

23

Asian Modernity in the Era of Globalization

Some Reflections

ANAND KUMAR

Hegel was the first philosopher to develop a clear concept of modernity—The discovery of the 'new world', the Renaissance, and the Reformation—these three monumental events around the year 1500 constituted the epochal threshold between modern times and the middle ages.

—JURGEN HABERMAS
The Philosophical Discourse of Modernity (1987), p. 5

The spread of modernity beyond Europe, however, was much in the nature of encroachment of eternal forces on traditional societies and civilisations and hence it was indeed the premises of Western European Societies that constituted the major challenge to which different responses developed.

—S.N. EISENSTADT
Patterns of Modernity (1987), p. 9

By the nineteenth century, Europe, with its social, economic and political structure reorganised by the tremendous industrial and political upheavals of the end of the eighteenth century, represented indeed a civilisation on the march. It challenged the basis of the Asian societies; it

> imposed its will on them and brought about social and political changes in Asia which are of fundamental importance.
>
> —K.M. PANIKKAR
> *Asia and Western Dominance* (1959), p. 17

> Modernization in the Third World nations is not only a means of economic and social development but also a process for the projection of their cultural self consciousness and national identity.—The urge for modernity is co-mingled with the urge for identity.
>
> —YOGENDRA SINGH
> *Essays on Modernization in India* (1978), p. 11

> Globalization today is not working for many of the world's poor. It is not working for much of the environment. It is not working for the stability of the global economy—To some, there is an easy answer: Abandon Globalization. That is neither feasible nor desirable.
>
> —JOSEPH STIGLITZ
> *Globalization and its Discontents* (2002), p. 214

The challenge of understanding Asian modernity—in the context of the processes of Globalization and their cultural and political implications at the level of the local and with reference to localisation—requires an overview of the concept of modernity itself. After making sense of the historical context of modernity and sociological understanding of modernization, it may be relevant to explore the factors and processes associated with the idea of Globalization. Then we can look at the idea of Asia and Asian modernity and its engagement with the processes of Globalization and localisation.

Modernization and European Modernity

According to S.N. Eisenstadt (Eisenstadt, 1987): "The contemporary world is a world in which modernity and modernization, modern technology, different patterns of economic development and institutions, modern political ideologies, and modes of political protest and participation constitute central characteristics." He further informs us that Western Europe was the site of emergence of the distinctive characteristics of the modern society. Karl Marx and Max Weber considered the modern European societies as the apogee of the evolutionary potentials of humanity, not achieved or actualised elsewhere. For Marx, European society is the only society in which capitalism developed. Max Weber has argued that the uniqueness of the West was reflected in the tendency toward the overall rationalisation of social life. He underlined (*a*) the emergence of capitalist civilisation, (*b*) the bureaucratisation of different forms of social life, (*c*) the secularisation of the worldview, and (*d*) the development of modern science and scientific outlook as the outstanding features of modern civilisation which was spreading through modernization beyond Europe. But Eisenstadt also alerts us that such an approach to modernity and modernization contains a contradiction as it tended to minimise the internal dynamics of other civilizations and especially the tendency of rationalisation inherent in them. This became much more visible in the later days after World War II with the spread of capitalism and modernization beyond Europe.

What are the specificities of the European modernity? The concept of modernization as reflected in the historicity of European modernity includes a complex of processes that are cumulative and mutually reinforcing. They are the following:

1. the formation of capital and the mobilisation of resources,
2. the development of the forces of production and the increase in the productivity of labour,
3. the establishment of centralised political power and the formation of national identity,
4. the proliferation of the rights of political participation,
5. the enlargement of urban forms of life,
6. the establishment of formal public schooling system, and
7. the secularisation of values.

These features have remained integral to any pattern of modernity since the introduction of modernization as a technical term in the 1950s; at the same time the theory of modernization has performed two abstractions on Weber's concept of modernity. According to Jurgen Habermas, "It dissociates modernity from its modern European origins and stylises it into a spatio-temporally natural model for processes of social development in general. Furthermore, it breaks the internal connections between modernity and the historical context of Western rationalism, so that processes of modernization can no longer be conceived of rationalisation, as historical objectification, of rational structures." (Habermas 1987, 2).

Now it may be asked: What are the determinants of modernity in a non-European, non-Western setting? A close look at European modernity has suggested that it aims at the formation of a rational culture and efficient economy, a civil society, and nation-states along with a social and political order based on citizenship and freedom. In the non-European settings, the processes of modernization have been contingent upon the cultural orientation, social structure, and economic system of a given society. It has been influenced by the point of entry of the given society in the international system which affected specific aspects of its institutional structure as well as created new options for the future. The modes of technology and the nature of economic systems have been a major factor in the internationalisation of innovations and reforms. It is also important to recognise that each society has a tradition of responses to historical changes in their civilizational systems. This tradition is also a major basis for variation in responses to modernization in a given society.

Modernity and Globalization

Globalization has been defined as a process of social change which refers both to the compression of the world and the intensification of consciousness of the world as a whole. The processes and characteristics to which the concept of Globalization now refers have been proceeding with some interruptions in many centres. But Globalization is not equated with or seen as a direct consequence of an amorphously conceived modernity. Globalization is also associated with the discourse of globality and global sociology. Nineteenth century social theorists and sociologists had made modernity and Globalization two central features of their work. But in the late period of classical sociology, the situation became more complex because of expansion of the apparatus of nation-states and the strengthening of nationalism. Currently, the social scientists have been challenged to deal with four features of the contemporary world simultaneously—(1) individuality, (2) community, (3) nationality, and (4) globality. In an increasingly globalised world, there is a hyphening of civilizational, societal, regional, national, and individual self consciousness. There are tensions between the local and global. There is relativisation of local, national, regional, and global. There is simultaneousness of homogenisation, heterogenisation and hybridisation. The increasing intensity of Globalization—which is compression of time and space beyond and nation-states—has several political and cultural implications for the latecomers like the Asians in the discourse about modernization. The local-global interplay is not as smooth and functional in this regard as it has been in Western Europe and North America. There are three prominent antinomies of modernity in full play in the post-colonial parts of Asia concerning orientalism, racism, and nationalism. This tension has been addressed in the discourse on Asian modernity by separating culture, economy, industrialisation, and westernisation. There is also a revival of cultural xenophobia and religious intolerance in the name of resisting the cultural invasion by the West through Globalization.

There is need to look at the dimensions of Globalization and mediators of globality in India for taking a holistic view of the crisis of Asian modernity in facing the challenges of Globalization which necessarily demand a continuous lowering of national barriers and dissolution of nationalism. There are five aspects of Globalization—(1) capital, (2) labour, (3) technology, (4) commodity, and (5) information. There is rapid growth of the Globalization of majority nation-states of Asia. China and Japan had a predominance of familism, low status for the mercantile classes, a tradition of xenophobia, and a centralised political structure. Both engaged in modernization after the breakdown of the traditional political structure. But in China, the political structure was fully dependent upon the cultural structure, and the system of social stratification was in congruence with the political system. This structural congruence between culture, polity, and a system of stratification was not conducive to the growth of modernization which promotes differentiating structures and structural autonomy. In the case of Japan, the cultural and political structures were highly symbiotic and not so congruent. There were many autonomous substructures which gave sustenance to the processes of modernization. In the Chinese case, modernization was achieved in the second stage through communist revolution where China had to fabricate an alternate system of stratification and polity.

The arrival of modernization in India was through the colonial passage. The colonial encounter was basically different from the engagement of China and Japan with modernity. At the same time, the basic structural forms in traditional Indian society were quite conducive to modernization. This speciality of traditional India has led a number of scholars to argue in favour of rejecting the European experience about the radical contradiction between modernity and tradition. According to Rudolph & Rudolph, there is a need to accord tradition a higher priority in exploring the nature and processes of modernity and modernization. They have underlined Gandhi's leadership, the transformation of the caste system, and the continuity and the changes in the Indian legal system as three instances of modernity of tradition as well as modernity incorporating traditional aspects (Rudolph & Rudolph, 1967, 3-15).

There is also a need to recognise the presence of another Asia around the dominance of believers of Islam. Islam is a religion which has experienced tension between reason and tradition in the traditional period of the Arab Islamic world. The genesis of conflict between modernism and traditionalism in Islam today can be better understood by Islamic heritage. It is a fact that the rise and decline of rationalism in Arabic civilization and Islamic societies has coincided with their florescence and fall. During its glorious period, free thinking held its way. Philosophy had the upper hand over theology. Even skeptics were not excommunicated, although they were persecuted on political grounds. Therefore, in any discussion about Asian modernity, separate attention has to be given to the Islamic countries of Asia today.

In short, there is as much space for the concept of Asian modernity as there has been for European modernity. But the desire for modernity in Asia is comingled with the desire for an identity which was not so pronounced in the context of modernization in Europe. Europe engaged in modernity with reference to itself. But Asian modernity has been forced to deal with the hegemonic presence of European modernity. For example, there is an evolution of an eclectic ideology of modernization in India and other post colonial countries to accommodate the contradictions in the system from a short-term perspective. In the long run, however, the systematic restructure of this ideology cannot be postponed. It was argued in the 1970s that there has been a sharpening of choices between Marxism and Gandhism as the modernising ideology in India. At the same time, there was also a push for a pragmatic synthesis which may not promote a doctrinaire discourse (Singh: 1978, 17). But today it is being argued that India is experiencing cultural narcissism, assertion by the *dalit* (depressed) castes, and there is mobilisation for gender justice. It is making a common path toward modernity very difficult. There is also disenchantment with modernity in certain sections. It has promoted social conflicts and lack of mutuality along the lines of caste, gender, and religion. What is the answer? It is suggested that "spiritualising of modernity" is very important for the progress of modernization (Pathak, 2001). From another perspective, the sociologists have found the middle classes totally uncommitted to modernity and unfit to lead the process of modernization as they are "Westoxicated" and self-possessed, without any respect for the rule of law, their role as citizens, or the rights of others. So who can be the flag bearer of modernity in India? They suggest the lower-middle classes and the poorer sections of the nation as the genuine carriers of modernity (Gupta, 2003).

Toward a Conclusion

It may be obvious that modernization and Globalization have different consequences in Europe and Asia. Europe is getting together by lowering the national frontiers as well as accelerating regionalisation as a response to the imperatives of Globalization. In the case of Asia, there is growth of xenophobia as well as economic instability. There is simultaneous growth of economic integration and cultural fragmentation. There are limits to linking the local to the global despite the phenomenal growth of the reach of finance capital, commodity, network, media accessibility, and information technology.

Secondly, the process of Globalization has very limited impact in the context of the challenge of good governance and effective citizenship. There is a continuous decline in the capacity of the state and the legitimacy of the governments due to the increasing role of transnational institutions and processes in the political economy of most of the Asian nation-states.

Modernization through Globalization has acquired a reputation of being rich-friendly and indifferent to the poorer sections of the society. It has adversely affected the local artisans and small and medium-scale entrepreneurs. The formalisation of the economy under the new international division of labour has created regression in the context of institution-building in labour markets and in corporate-union relations.

There is also growth of anti-Globalization pressure in polity and culture through the coming together of a wide variety of groups and communities which suffer from the increasing pressures of the global corporate forces upon the local resource bases like forests, land, and water.

Finally, there is also intensification of global integration in promoting politics of identity instead of citizenship-based politics of nation building. The Globalization related information technology revolution is developing a highway of the global economy which connects the rising technologies around the world. But they are bypassing the traditional localities which have been age-old habitats for millions of men and women who can never be the beneficiaries of the present pattern of Globalization. It calls for exploring the meaning of modernization and Globalization in different local settings to make sense of their life world, life chances, survival strategies, and responses to the imperatives of being in the era of modernity with globality.

References

Eisenstadt, S.N. (1987), *Patterns of Modernity*.

Habermas, Jürgen (1987), *The Philosophical Discourse of Modernity*.

Panikkar, K.M. (1959), *Asia and Western Dominance*.

Rudolph, S.H. and L.I. Rudolph (1967), Modernity of Tradition, University of Chicago Press: Chicago, 3-15.

Singh, Yogendra (1978), *Essays on Modernization in India*.

Stiglitz, Joseph (2002), *Globalization and its Discontents*.

24

Globalization and Modernity

Social Concerns

JAI KANT TIWARY

The synchronisation of social science discourse on Globalization is a striking instance of how developments in the world economy keep impinging on societal processes and institutions, induce new pattern of change and necessitate reassessment of the adequacy of concepts and approaches in social sciences for understanding complex social reality. The Globalization debate in general is focused largely on more recent developments, whose impact is not confined either to a single nation-state or to a subcontinent. Consequences of the global economic integration are seen spread over a wide range of non-economic spheres of life all over the world. It is commonly understood as a process that rapidly transforms the world heterogeneously, yet at the same time it intensifies consciousness of the world as a whole (Robertson, 1992: 8).

Conceptualising Globalization

Some sociologists approach the problematic of Globalization *via* considerations of modernity. Giddens (1990, 64), for example, defines Globalization as intensification of worldwide social relations which link distant localities in such a way that local happenings are shaped by events occurring miles away and *vice versa*. Giddens emphasises four dimensions of Globalization—the nation-state system, the world capitalist economy, the world military order, and the international division of labour. Each of these four, according to him, is an extension of societal modernity and an offshoot of its basic institutional features. He, therefore, postulates modernity as inherently globalising and hence today's Globalization is no more than the fundamental consequence of modernity project of the west.

Today, the concept of Globalization revolves mainly around social consequences of integration with the world economy *via* the market and multinationals. Friedman and Kaplan (2002, 64) defines 'Globalization as a process of integration of markets, finance and technology, especially information technology in a way that shrinks the world to a miniature in size and enables people from different parts of the globe to reach around the world faster, deeper and cheaper'. This characterisation of Globalization, however, projects it as if it is confined to the market and economic activities alone. Anitat (2002: 4) has talked of Globalization as 'the process through which an increasingly free flow of ideas, people, goods and capital leads to integration of economics and societies'. Anitat argues that such global integration has boosted growth and incomes and has thereby helped to raise general standard of living in less developed and underprivileged parts of the world. With Globalization not only sophisticated technologies have become available to developing countries, but also marked improvements in average literacy, quality of health and general life expectancy and above all greater integration have taken place and these have promoted human freedom (Anitat, 2002: 4).

Almost similar logics were propounded by enlightenment theorists of modernity, who characterised it in terms of rationality, reason, empirical, scientific, progress, universalism, individualism, tolerance, freedom, secularism, uniformity in human nature. The theories of Issac Newton, John Locke, Rousseau, Montesque, David Hume, Adam Smith, Immanuel Kant, Peter Hamilton, *et al.* established that modernity is based on scientific knowledge, empiricism and rationality. Max Weber, the classical sociologist, argued that modernity emancipated human being from the iron cage of irrationality and created the ethos of rationalisation.

The Unintended Consequences of Modernity

Modernity is interpreted in a different perspective in post-modern sociological theory. Ulrich Beck (1992) calls modern society as 'risk society'. To him the modernity in classical era of nineteenth century was industrial whereas the modernity of second phase is individualistic, which has created manufactured risk, health risk and socio-cultural risk such as inequality, etc. Advanced industrial society, which is primarily a politicisation of nature, has created environment pollution and various other risks. Zygmunt Bauman (1989) considers modernity as a holocaust. He cites the destructions in Second World War. The Nazies in Germany massacred thousands of Jews by throwing them into gas chambers. Bauman argues that this genocide was neither an act of irrationality nor was it barbarism of pre-modern society. Rather it was the well planned act of modern bureaucracy, who wished to get rid of Jews and rebuild Germany. He also argued that such a holocaust is not merely confined to Germany, several illustrations can be cited all-over the world. Modernity all-over the world, which claims to be civilized, in fact, lacks ethics. Modernity is dehumanisation.

The notion of modernity, thus, has different connotations in classical and post-modern sociological theories. Classical theories of tradition-modernity continuum highlight the evolutionary paradigms of society while the unintended consequences of modernity get significance in post-modern theories. Similarly, we find differences in perspectives among champions and critiques of Globalization. We are of the opinion that the notion of Globalization has to be evaluated in terms of social concerns. What impact the market driven global integration is having on the less industrialised developing countries and their vast population, especially those belonging to the disadvantaged, weaker and marginalised sections such as the small and marginal farmers, i.e., primary producers, agricultural labourers and more so the women.

Globalization and Social Concerns

Social concerns may be defined as those concerns which may not be effectively addressed through individual efforts alone and call for collective responses; or those concerns which emerge because certain costs and benefits get delinked and aside at different points, calling for intervention to rectify the costs inflicted as externalities; or those concerns which pertain to issues that come to be identified with social or collective existence itself and which are supposed to further this collective cause of social beings. Institutional reorganisation through Globalization indeed is meant to deny the relevance of social concerns in defining economic activities. There is an accent on recovery of costs and abandoning the soft corner for those who cannot pay for using public utilities. Marketisation of social issues is the new concern characteristics of Globalization era.

What is accomplished, thus, is not really the separation of social and economic issues but a reversal of their relationship. Social concerns are not expected to interfere with economic processes of state or market, but market principles are supposed to become the defining rule of social issues. Thus, health, education, housing, employment of common man, job security, etc. should be privatised and made to run with profit motive as the guiding norm. This is meant to increase efficiency. The question of access to this efficiency is not considered important. Access comes to be defined as an individual problem and not a social concern. The social content of economic issues is, thus, easily dismissed. Many social problems are simply dismissed as individual problems, calling for individual solutions. Unemployment becomes a problem of acquiring skills, insecurity in job a matter of upgradation of skills, health and education more a subject of consciousness raising. Structural content of problem facing the society is thereby delinked from everything except market opportunities. Markets themselves become an important social concern when redefinition of issues creates legitimacy for them.

The Digital Divide

The most important manifestation of Globalization process is reinforcing existing social division besides creating new one called digital divide. The term digital divide denotes the ever growing gap between those people and communities who have access to information and communication technology, especially Internet technology and those who do not. The Internet has the potential to empower its users with new skills, new perspectives and new opportunities in life. Those groups which remain isolated from this technology, are further segregated into the periphery of public life.

The facts reveal that the diffusion of Internet technology is highly uneven and the Internet users' skill forms a global enclave.

Internet users are predominantly urban and located in certain regions. For instance, Human Development Report (2001:19) reveals that in India, more than 1.3 million of the total 1.4 million Internet connections are in the States of Delhi, Karnataka, Maharashtra and Tamil Nadu. It also reports that most of the Internet users are better educated and wealthier. The problem of digital divide is acute at global level with the West European and North American countries doing fairly well in terms of access to the technology while the rest of the countries around the world struggle with their infrastructural problems to register their presence on the Internet map. The World Development Report, 2001 reveals the intercontinental divide among Internet users. In the year 2000, the percentage of internet users in total population in the United States was 45.3, while in sub-Saharan Africa and South Asia the percentage was 0.4 only. The network society is creating parallel communication systems—one for those with income, education, literally connections, giving plentiful information at low cost and high speed; the other for those without connections, blocked by high barriers of time, cost and uncertainty and dependent upon outdated information.

Deepening of Disparity

Despite the promise that well managed Globalization would make everyone better off, the unheralded side of Globalization is that it does not alleviate poverty and social exclusion but aggravates them. It deepened the economic disparities among the countries as well as the people through opening of global markets and capital flows. In developing countries, unbalanced free trade agreements have also made things worse for many. During the first 10 years of the NAFTA agreement, for example, the income disparity between Americans and Mexicans actually grew by more than 10 per cent. Poor Mexican farmers now have to compete in their own country with highly subsidised American corn, often driving them off the land, into cities or up to the U.S., even if it is true that corn has become cheaper for urban residents. Overall, developed countries impose tariffs on developing countries that are on an average four times higher than the other developed ones. Rich countries have cost poor countries three times more in trade restrictions than they give in total development aid.

Human Development Report 2001 reveals the growing disparities between the rich and the poor over the years after introduction of Globalization. In the decade of 1960-70, the ratio of difference between the 20 per cent richest and the 20 per cent poorest in the world was 30 : 1, which increased up to 74 : 1 by the year 1999-2000. According to an estimate, 143 richest persons of the world have acquired wealth equalling the aggregate wealth of 50 least developed countries of the world. The savage inequality of the world is exhibited by the fact in 1999-2000, the poorest 10 per cent of the world's people had only 1.6 per cent of the income of the richest 10 per cent, while the richest 1 per cent of the world people received as much income as the poorest 57 per cent. The richest 10 per cent of the US population (around 25 million people) had a combined income more than that of poorest 43 per cent of the world's people (around 2 billion people). The evidences suggest that Globalization is deepening disparity.

Growing Ethos of Consumerism

The globalising process accelerated the interaction of native people with global forces of consumption. The process of consumerism defined by Philip Salzman (1993:7) as the 'Cathecing of consumption as an appropriate orientation', has now permeated much of rural India. Consumer goods such as television, electric fans, motorcycles, telephones, mobile phones, VCD and VHS players, satellite dishes, etc., are becoming very common in village homes. The role of advertisement is critical in promoting this new ethos of consumerism. The study of Johnson (2005: 4) reveals how the advertisement has reversed the notion of happiness in rural family. Happiness, which has always been linked to one's relationship to one's family, to one's faith and to one's work now appears to be based on consumption of goods. Each advertisement on TV tells us 'Drink a coke and you will be happy. Wash your clothes with a particular detergent and your husband will love you'. From soap to toothpaste, from hair removal cream to exercise equipment, the message is always the same—happiness is gained through the purchase and consumption of objects. In other words, happiness comes from the market.

According to Samir Amin (1997:128), Globalization is the ideology of capitalist superpowers that labour a utopian vision of running the world like a market. The market forces led by Globalization destroy the indigenous culture and generate consumerism. The cultural invasion through films, music, games, toys, T-shirt fantasies, etc., disseminate global dream which undermines the indigenous value, culture, interpersonal and intercommunity relations and cultural heritage, Commodification of cultures according to alien tastes generate an ornamental hoax. Dhanagare (2003: 15) remarks that the final aim of Globalization is to render nation-states economically parasites, politically powerless and socio-culturally faceless before bulldosing power to the market with MNCs driving from the back seat.

The growing trend of ethnic conflicts and religious fundamentalism has to be understood primarily as a repulsive response to the pernicious impact of the global consumer culture on diverse, even unique, local cultures. Local communities feel both unstable and unsafe in the face of global market forces bolstered up by media that too are controlled by MNCs. The media impact on local communities and cultures is so shattering that the consumer culture has pushed them to the threshold of extinction. Local economies are being swallowed gradually by the global capitalism and traditional cultures are being displaced by the ever expanding global market and consumer culture. Local communities in the developing world are silently, and somewhat, helplessly, watching their plentiful raw material and natural resources are getting depleted and these are replaced by scarce imported materials produced by TNCs. At the same time, local communities are experiencing a study and systematic undermining of their self-esteem.

This kind of erosion of local culture by the process of homogenisation, and particularly by the promotion of global monoculture, has disastrous consequences. To achieve development, at any cost, many developing economies are pressurised to make structural ajdustment, introduce neo-liberal measures, reduce social sector spending and undertake massive programmes of infrastructure development that is unsustainable in the long run. Much of the development initiatives in developing countries are geared to serve the needs of global capitalism to exploit their cheap labour, material resources and vast markets (Dhanagare, 2003: 24).

Pathetic Condition of Farmers

Indian farmers' experience with the Globalization reveals that the farmers are not able to cope with the new competitive environment after economic reforms. Over the last decade we have been hearing from different parts of the country that farmers have been committing suicides or eating rat meat. Why do farmers take these extreme steps? Is income from cultivation not enough to meet consumption and other expenditures? Are farmers heavily indebted due to lower income from cultivation and increased cost of cultivation? Answer to these questions have finally come from the survey initiated by Union Ministry of Agriculture, which is known as Situation Assessment Survey (SAS).

The National Sample Survey Organisation (NSSO) carried out the SAS of farmers during 2003 (July 2002—June 2003) covering 51,770 households spread over 6,638 villages across the country. The NSSO (2005) report reveals dreadful conditions of farmer households, be it income, expenditure or indebtedness of farming households (see Table 24.1).

According to the Survey, at the all-India level, the average annual income of farmer household was Rs. 25,380 which includes cultivation, wages, farming of animals and non-farm business income. What is interesting is that income from cultivation accounts for only 45 per cent of the total income and the remaining receipts are from other sources including wage income, which alone accounts for almost 39 per cent. Clearly, the annual income from cultivation comes to only about Rs. 11,628 per farmer household, after excluding the other sources. The condition of individual state is not very much different from the national level average. Obviously, with such low income of the farmers, the basic issues arise—Can the farmer survive with this low income? Do farmers have any incentive to remain in farming? Is it possible for farmers to meet the consumption expenditure with this income?

The Survey also provides that average annual expenditure on cultivation comes to Rs. 8,791 per household at the all-India level. We notice a wide variation in the expenditure on cultivation across States, the highest in agriculturally developed States like Punjab followed by Haryana and Andhra and the lowest expenditure in Orissa. The situation is bleaker while comparing the annual income with the average annual consumption expenditure of the farmer

Table 24.1: Income, Expenditure and Indebtedness of Farmer Households (July 2002—June 2003) in Rs.

State	*Annual Cultivation Income*	*Annual Total Income*	*Annual Cultivation Expenditure*	*Annual Consumption Income*	*2-4*	*3-5*	*Incidence of Indebtedness (Per cent)*	*Extent of Indebtedness*
1	2	3	4	5	6	7	8	9
Andhra Pradesh	8916.00	19608.00	12085.00	283632.00	–3169.00	–9024.00	82.00	23965.00
Assam	21504.00	37932.00	3370.00	32568.00	18134.00	5364.00	18.10	813.00
Bihar	10152.00	21720.00	6809.00	29508.00	3343.00	–7788.00	33.00	4476.00
Gujarat	13968.00	32208.00	11456.00	37524.00	2512.00	–5316.00	51.90	15526.00
Haryana	17928.00	34584.00	18270.00	52968.00	–342.00	–18384.00	53.10	26007.00
J & K	29112.00	65856.00	6342.00	49308.00	22770.00	16548.00	31.80	1903.00
Karnataka	15192.00	31392.00	10344.00	31296.00	4848.00	96.00	61.60	18135.00
Kerala	13440.00	48048.00	7793.00	51000.00	5647.00	–2952.00	64.40	33907.00
M.P.	11952.00	17160.00	8886.00	28068.00	3066.00	–10908.00	50.80	14218.00
Maharashtra	15156.00	29556.00	10793.00	32268.00	4363.00	–2712.00	54.80	16973.00
Orissa	4032.00	12744.00	3143.00	20364.00	889.00	–7620.00	47.80	5871.00
Punjab	33864.00	59520.00	25945.00	58080.00	7919.00	1440.00	65.40	41576.00
Rajasthan	4308.00	17976.00	7668.00	39456.00	–3360.00	–21480.00	52.40	18372.00
Tamil Nadu	7908.00	24864.00	8597.00	30072.00	–689.00	–5208.00	74.50	23963.00
U.P.	10032.00	19596.00	9151.00	34788.00	881.00	–15192.00	40.30	7425.00
West Bengal	8844.00	24948.00	8429.00	32016.00	415.00	–7068.00	50.10	5237.00
All India	11628.00	25380.00	8791.00	33240.00	2837.00	–7860.00	48.60	12585.00

households (ACEFH). The average ACEFH for the country as a whole was Rs. 33,240. The highest annual ACEFH was reported in Punjab followed by Haryana and Kerala, while the lowest annual consumption was in Orissa. This clearly suggests that farmers are in severe distress and the income that they get from all sources is not even enough to meet the consumption expenditure of the households. The situation leads them to take loans from various sources so as to meet the consumption as well as the productive expenditure of the households.

The incidence of indebtedness as well as the extent of indebtedness is found to be higher in all the States where consumption expenditure exceeds the income of farmer households. The data concerning indebtedness status of the households reveal that the debt per farmer houshold is very high in all the States except Assam and Jammu & Kashmir. Farmers from Andhra Pradesh, Haryana, Karnataka, Kerala, Madhya Pradesh, Maharashtra, Punjab, Tamil Nadu and Uttar Pradesh are heavily indebted possibly because the income of the household is not enough to meet the consumption expenditure. In fact, the average debt per household varies from Rs. 24,000 to Rs. 42,000 in the relatively developed States like Andhra Pradesh, Haryana, Kerala, Punjab and Tamil Nadu.

The results of SAS sufficiently prove that the farmers are not getting enough remuneration from their produce. This could possibly be because of a sharp deceleration in the growth of prices of many agricultural commodities and increase in the cost of cultivation after the introduction of reforms. It is reported from various parts of the country that the use of spurious inputs (seeds, fertilizers and pesticides) in cultivation is one of the major reasons for crop failure and low ouput. Another reason for the low income of farmer households could be the dominant role played by the middlemen in the market. Studies reveal that farmers were not able to get even 40 per cent of the money that the consumer pays for various agriculture commodities in the market. Despite the significant increase in the flow of institutional credit, the SAS data shows that still over 42 per cent of rural credit supply comes from the non-institutional sources like moneylenders, where the rate of interest is not only exorbitant but the terms and conditions of the loans are often exploitative.

All these facts clearly suggest that the farmers are in great distress. SAS report (NSSO, 2005: 11) also indicates that given a choice 40 per cent of the farmers would quit agriculture and take up some other career. The situation can aggravate further, if adequate measures are not taken immediately to improve the income level of the farmer households. Potentially, this can harm the growth of agriculture and food security of the country (Narayanamoorthy, 2006: 472).

Plight of Working Class

Conditions of working class, in both organised and unorganised sectors, in developing countries seem to be not better under a globalising economy. Throughout the history, working class movements and trade unions have always sought to influence and humanise capitalist system within the nation-states framework. In the Globalization phase of capitalism, however, MNCs and TNCs have undercut the capacities of national governments to regulate them, particularly in developing countries (Ross, 2000:1-2). Consequently, the labour is facing new problem under Globalization, as markets keep expanding in their reach and power beyond labour organisations' will and capacity to affect MNCs.

The most important challenge Indian labour facing as a result of Globalization is that traditional industrial working class is practically pushed into the background and is likely to become invisible soon because of four processes, namely, tertiarisation, feminisation, casualisation and precariarisation (Dhanagare, 2003: 18). These processes unleashed by Globalization are adversely affecting labours and their unions that hitherto depended on the traditional support base of organised blue-collar workers.

The Future of Nation-States

The triumph of TNCs and their finance capitalism over microcosms of nation-states raises the question whether Globalization will strengthen or weaken nation-states. A more optimistic view is that Globalization actually strengthens the State by redefining its role in changed economic conditions resulting from global interaction *via* market and finance capitalism. The other more pessimistic view is that Globalization process will not only weaken but will also hasten the demise of the nation-state.

The dominant market oriented and state limiting ideas have come from the proponent of public choice theory, most prominently by Milton Freidman, James Buchanan, Gordon Tullock, William Niskanen, *et al.* Freidman argues that market is more effective than government in achieving social goals. Once a technology driven Globalization sets in, it starts shrinking the world. As the need for morality of order gets reinforced, naturally then everyone is willing to give up a share of one's independence for the sake of 'world government'.

In the context of growing anxiety over the future of nation-states, Martinelli (2002:9-11) views Globalization process as eroding the very foundation of sovereignty and autonomy of nation-states. This is largely because global finance capitalism compels nation-states to adopt neo-liberal economic policies to stay in the competitive world market. Sovereign states have, therefore, no option but to come to terms with gradual loss of sovereignty and erosion of their power. The consequence is that the vulnerable strata of society will be deprived of the benefit of nation-state. Bhambhari (1996:263) rightly opines that without state intervention, social equalisation cannot take place and if the state does not control national economic and productive resources, it cannot implement welfare programmes, like food security and job guarantees, etc. The evidences of economic history of the world reveal that market has never been a pro-poor institution.

Summing Up

The universe of social concern is indeed vast. We have covered a host of issues pertaining to Globalization and modernity. A very significant feature of the global economy is the integration of the emerging economies in world markets. The pace of change is unprecedented, far exceeding what was witnessed during the industrial revolution in Europe. Nevertheless, the achievements of the era of Globalization should not blind us to the new anxieties that Globalization has brought in its wake. The reach of Globalization is yet to touch many parts of the world. The evidence suggests that the process has not removed personal and regional income disparities. The gap between the rich and the poor is widening. This coupled with the inability of public sector to provide adequate and quality service in health and education and cater to the needs of the poor, is causing resentment and alienation. This is nurturing divisive forces and putting pressure on the practice of democracy.

The issue is how to make Globalization an inclusive process which addresses the vital social concerns. This calls for a new global vision which ensures that gains from Globalization are more widely shared. Economist and Nobel laureate Joseph Stiglitz (2006:11) visualises that Globalization will work only if the winners share with the losers.

It is also important to examine the fact of cultural contradictions of modernity. Reactionary modernists display a great enthusiasm for technological modernization, overlaid with a deep aversion to rationalism, secularism and individualism that comes with modernization. They want the fruits of modernization without the pain and joys of cultural dislocations that modernity brings. Economic and technological modernization is no guarantee for secular culture. The creation of a secular culture requires active engagement with scientific and rational spirit of the people. The process of Globalization, which claims to brighten the face of modernity, needs to be examined in the context of vital social concerns causing universal anxiety and discontentment. Devoid of welfare insurance, Globalization can compound the miseries of the poor and the marginalised people, more particularly in a developing society.

References

Amin, Samir (1997), *Capitalism in the Age of Globalization*, Delhi: Madhyam Books.

Anitat, E. (2000), 'Surmounting the Challenge of Globalization', *Finance and Development*, March: 4-7.

Bauman, Zygmunt (1989), 'Modernity and the Holocaust', *Ithaca*, New York: Cornell University Press.

Bhambhri, C.P. (1996), 'Globalization, Liberalisation and the Welfare State', *The Indian Journal of Public Administration*, Vol. XLII, No. 3, July-September.

Beck, Ulrich (1992), *Risk Society: Towards a New Modernity*, London: Sage Publications.

Dhanagare, D.N. (2003), 'Globalization: Towards an Alternative View', *Sociological Bulletin*, 52 (1), March.

Friedman, T. and Kaplan, R. (2002), 'States of Discord' (A Debate), *Foreign Policy*, March-April.

Giddens, A. (1990), *The Consequences of Modernity*, Stanford, CA: Standford University Press.

Human Development Report (2001), *Making New Technologies Work for Human Development*, UNDP, Oxford University Press, Oxford.

Johnson, Kirk (2006), 'Globalization at the Crossroads of Traditions and Modernity in Rural India', *Sociological Bulletin*, 54 (1), January-April.

Martinelli, A. (2002), 'Market, Government, Communities and Global Government', Presidential Address delivered at the XV World Congress of Sociology, Brisbane, 7-13 July.

Narayanamoorthy, A. (2006), 'State of India's Farmers', *Economic and Political Weekly*, February 11-17, Vol. XLI, No. 6.

NSSO (2005), *Situation Assessment Survey of Farmers: Indebtedness of Farmer Households*, Report No. 497 and 498, 59th Round, Ministry of Statistics and Programme Implemantation, Govt. of India, New Delhi.

Robertson, R. (1992), 'Globalization: Social Theory and Global Culture', London: Sage Publications.

Ross, G. (2000), 'Labour *versus* Globalization', Annals of the American Academy of Political and Social Sciences, Vol. 570 (July).

Salzman, Philip (1993), 'The Electronic Trojan Horse: Television in the Globalization of Para-modern Cultures', Presented at the Thirteenth International Congress of Anthropological and Ethnological Sciences, Mexico City.

Stiglitz, Joseph (2006), Dialogue with Nathan Gardels, *The Hindu*, 29 September.

World Development Report (2001), United Nations Development Programme, Oxford University Press, Oxford.

25

Globalization and Local Culture

The Case of Varanasi (Banaras) in India

MANJULA RATHAUR

What is Globalization and what are its consequences for local cultures and traditions?

There are several definitions of Globalization. Similarly, there is no consensus about its impact on cultures. On the one hand, it is conceptualised as a process of social change which involves compression of time and space beyond the 'nation-state'. On the other hand, it is suggested that Globalization is severing cultures from their roots in distinct 'space-time' niche. The arrow of 'cultural time' has been broken: technological advances in mass media and transport now make it possible for the past of one culture to become the future of another. To paraphrase Arjun Appadorai, easy and frequent interactions allow cultures to free themselves from territorial moorings and float freely in an ever-changing global context of multi-culturality (1997). 'Multicultural' points out to the visible and universally accessible products of cultural diversity—food, clothes, music, theatre and films, and sometimes specialist occupations— and on the whole it has a positive resonance. Because, essentially, it adds to the variety and colour of lifestyles available to us, increasing the breadth of our choices as consumers (Watson, 2002). It is also getting promoted by inter-state cooperation in the domain of economy, communication and governance. It is a process that is increasing the opportunities for interaction between people all around the globe. The interaction can be economic as well as cultural, social, political, scientific or otherwise.

Here culture is used as an assemblage of definitive characteristics. It is essentially a way of life and closely identified with a language, a shared history, a set of religious beliefs and moral values (ethos), and a shared geographical origin. The notion of distinctiveness of cultures is not appreciated by anthropologists as they see culture as a dynamic process of the constant evolution of forms—institutional, textual and ethical. In this context, the increasing significance of 'the global' along with 'the local' and 'the national' has direct consequences for four sets of individual and collective experiences–(*i*) identity, (*ii*) belongingness, (*iii*) territorial locality, and (*iv*) sense of history.

The critiques of Globalization present a contradictory perspective about its cultural consequences—not multi-culturality but cultural conflicts and ethnocide. Such observers suggest that "First Globalization empties cultures of their economic and material base by transferring control over production and markets to transnational corporations. Materially emptied cultures are then pitted against one another, because their common economic base has disappeared. Cultural diversity is then pushed into conflict and ethnocide as in the cases of Rwanda, Somalia, Sri Lanka, and ex-Yugoslavia" (Shiva, Vandana). Such a view further argues that there is need to be aware of several superstitions about Globalization which promote the impression about its inevitability and universality, because it is neither a natural phenomenon nor a new process. There are many alternatives to Globalization which is primarily a political process which has been forced on the weak by the powerful through political institutions such as the structural adjustment projects of the World Bank and IMF and the free-trade arrangements of the World Trade Organization. It leads to growth of non-sustainable production and consumption patterns—more cars and more fossil fuel consumption, more industrial agriculture and more consumption of pesticides and fertilizers, more use of toxics and more trade in toxics. Globalization is basically a takeover of the rights of citizens by corporations through a dismantling of the structure of the state that protect people and it is being resisted by the movements of women, peasants, small fishworkers, indigenous people and tribals.

There is a third view of the process of Globalization. Such analyses demand a better understanding of the underlying issues in the context of the debates about Globalization and its consequences. According to this perspective, it is neither new nor it is just Westernisation. It has progressed over a long period through travel, trade, migration, spread of cultural influences and dissemination of knowledge and understanding (including science and technology). It is not a folly in itself but the central issue is related with inequality between and within the nations. The central question cannot be whether or not to make use of the market economy. The market economy can generate many different results depending on the distribution of physical resources, development on the human resources and nature of prevalent rules. Furthermore, the state and society have roles in all these contexts within a country and in the modern world system. It is also pointed out that the current economic, political and financial architecture of the world was created in the 1940s, following the Bretton Woods Conference in 1944. It was a period when the bulk of Asia and Africa was still under imperialist dominance. The tolerance of insecurity, poverty and dominance was much greater. The issues of human rights and environment were not prominent and democracy was not seen as global entitlement. Therefore, global reconstruction is the needed response to the global doubts (Sen, Amartya, 2001; Stiglitz, 2003).

The Indian engagement with Globalization is preceded by modernization which has its roots in Westernisation inaugurated during the colonial era (1860:194). If modernization is a special kind of social change which is anchored in the centrality of rationality and scientific knowledge, then Globalization is that social change which supplants modernity with globality. The Indians are simultaneously experiencing homogeneity of information and heterogeneity of cultures through opening of markets to global brands, consumerism as a way of life, migration, STD booths, cyber cafes, cable TV, Internet interactions, and other forms of information and communication technologies. These factors are accelerating 'Globalization' in the spheres of community identity, group dynamics, and youth culture. At the same time, there are sources of resilience in the context of local cultures which are contributing towards minimisation of disintegrative tendencies despite the macro-imperatives of 'homogenisation' of culture.

This chapter is an endeavour towards uderstanding the response and resilience of 'local' culture of Varanasi, also known as Benares (in Persian, Urdu and English) and Kashi (in Sanskrit and Pali literature) with reference to the impact of Globalization. It aims at exploring the role of pluralism and diversity which is so well engrained in the cultural climate of an old city like Varanasi, which has been also described as 'City of Light' by cultural historian from Europe and America. Here metaphor of light is used to describe the function and significance of the Varanasi in the context of culture and knowledge.

According to Yogendra Singh (2000), there is a paradoxical relationship between Globalization and 'local culture' in India leading to contradictory impulses of acceptance and rejection. As a nation of peasants and workers totalling about 70 per cent of rural population with illiteracy among about 35 per cent of the total people, it has the tendency of limiting the influence of Globalization. But the presence of a growing middle class, ranging between 150 to 200 million, offers opportunity to the forces of Globalization. On the one hand, the technologies revolution in the systems of communication and institutions of finance, banking, trade, and fiscal relationship have created social, cultural and institutional forces that surpass the boundaries of the nation-state. Their impact upon local culture and social forms such as family, neighbourhood and the community is quite destabilising which generate many forms of anomie. At the same time, the universal reach of the communication media have made it possible to produce of locality. It goes hand in hand with the erosion of real time and real space bonds of communitarianism and local cultures. There is disintegration of the folk culture and the folk societies due to marketisation of economy and commodification and production processes under the umbrella of consumerism and expansion of the logic of market and capitalism.

Due to the colonial past, the Indians are very self-conscious about their cultural identity. Significance of 'locality' and its role as the building-block of Indian culture and civilization has been increasingly accepted. The cultural and social boundedness of Indian culture by locality and region has been recognised in the studies of caste, family and rural communities—the three basic institutions of India. The changes in the economy, media and information system, the leisure and style of life with direct impact upon the symbolic contents and the foundations of the tradition have created anxieties. Varanasi is the epicentre of great traditions of India as it has maintained a continuity of cultural centrality for nearly 2,500 years since the Buddhist era, if not even earlier. Therefore, the impact and anxieties in the context of Globalization is much pronounced in the life and culture of it.

What are the socio-cultural realities of India? The social and cultural realities of India have a plural character in terms of (*a*) language, (*b*) geography, (*c*) ethnicity, (*d*) religions, and (*e*) culture. The national survey of the communities by the Anthropological Survey of India has provided an insight into the plurality of caste-community structures and their socio-economic diversities. According to the People of India Survey (1992), there are 4,635 communities in India. Is this plurality divisive or integrative in terms of the macro-system of the nation-state and its political sub-units, i.e., the States of the Union of India? More than 71 per cent of the communities are located within the boundaries of the State/Union Territories. Furthermore, this diversity is also characterised by linkages and shared commonalities of culture traits, rituals, beliefs, and customs as the processes of universalisation (integration) and parochialisation (locality) have been simultaneously going on in India in respect of sacred rituals, myths, legends and their symbolic representations over the centuries. The language-based diversity is also a significant aspect of local cultures and plurality of cultural regions. According to the national survey, there are 325 languages spoken by communities in India. But there is increasing 'bilinguality' as it was found to increase from 13.4 per cent in 1971 to 64.2 per cent in 1991. Thus, the linguistic particularism is also getting interactive through linkages with wider communities in the domain of culture and communication leading to 'cerography' of linguistic usages. India is also a land of the migrants. There are memories of migration among nearly all major communities. It is engrained in their folklores and community/caste history. The whole of India is considered a civilizational habitat and an Indian has much wider territorial attachment due to it than her immediate locality of residence and work.

What are the characteristics of the socio-cultural architecture of Varanasi? It has an intimate relationship with religion, education, and trade for last five millenniums. Therefore, history of Varanasi has evolved into history of a cultural complex which provides an inner view of a whole civilization. It has been known in the classical and traditional literature by several other names also including 'Kashi', 'Anandvan', 'Avimukta', and 'Mahashamshan'. Its making has been a cumulative contribution of several ages and phases of Indian history. Its significance as a city of faiths is related with the rise and spread of several sects, movements, and belief systems from the city in the long history of Varanasi. It is amazing that the basic role of Varanasi as a perennial source of Indian civilization has remained intact despite the ups and downs in the political fortunes of the city over such a long period of time and so many waves of social and cultural changes (Motichandra, 1962).

Varanasi, 'the eternal city', is situated on the banks of the Ganga river in Uttar Pradesh, one of the largest States of India in the Indo-Gangetic river plain. It is spread over an area of 1550 sq. km. The first comprehensive population survey of Varanasi was conducted by James Princep (1799-1839). According to the survey of Princep conducted in 1821-27, the city of Varanasi had a population of 1,80,000 with another 20,000 people settled in nearby township. It was more than the population of Edinborough and Bristol and double of the population of Rotterdam and Brussels. The city used to attract around 1,00,000 persons regularly for special 'baths' on major religious occasions without any disorder. It was more urbanised and well organised than Calcutta, according to the Princep report which was published in 1833 as Benares Illustrated (Kejariwal, 2005). The total population of Varanasi was found to be 25,08,000 in the national census of 1991 and was divided between rural and urban segments (60: 40 ratio) with population of 1618 per sq. km. It had a large number of the Scheduled Caste population (7,56,590) which was mostly rural. But there were only negligible number of persons from the Scheduled Tribes (only 155 persons).

Religionwise, the Hindus and Muslims are the two largest faith communities. But there is also visibility of Christians, Sikhs, Buddhists, and Jains in terms of places of worship, learning, and festivities. It has an active presence of all major sects of the Hindus, Muslims, Buddhists, Jains, and Sikhs through their institutions like monasteries, pilgrim centres, publications, and seats of sect leaders, etc. Languagewise, it is a centre of Hindi and Urdu language. But the rural and urban masses of Varanasi speak a dialect called 'Bhojpuri'. There is a vibrant multilingual atmosphere in the city as it includes clusters of Bengali, Punjabi,

Sindhi, Marathi, Tamil, Gujarati, Nepali, English, Arabic, Persian, Tibetan and Sinhala speaking people.

According to culture observers, the essentiality of Varanasi has been in the context of its continuous significance in the fields of spirituality, philosophy, literature, performing arts and education. The unbroken tradition of spiritual engagement from the Upanishadic and Buddhist discourses to the contributions of Tulsi and Kabir attracted people from all-over the world since the era of the Chinese traveller Fa Huan and Arabic scholar Al Beruni to the 'counter-culture' American poet Allen Ginsberg to Varanasi for having a glimpse of the Indian culture through a glance at this centre of learning, faith, arts and crafts, and way of life. There are a large number of traditional seats of classical Sanskrit scholarship spread from one end of the city to the other end at the bank of the Ganga river. In modern times, Annie Besant, Malviya, Gandhi, Krishnamurthi, the Dalai Lama and Jayaprakash Narayan – all found it important to establish institutions of higher studies at Varanasi during the twentieth century. The tradition of folk theatre was cultivated by saint-poet Tulsidas in the form of Ramlila in the 1580s which has continued to grow its roots deeper in the region for the last 5 centuries in the face of Mughal rule, British Raj and the post-colonial modernization.

Varanasi is simultaneously a cultural-religious complex in the traditional sense as well as a growth point for the modern economic life of the region. It has a dynamic economic base in the fields of agriculture, financial services and transport and communication sector related activities enveloping a large urban population as well as 1262 settled villages organised in 8 blocks. It is one of the most sacred pilgrimage centres for the Hindus, Buddhists and Jains which ensures a steady flow of religious pilgrims round the year from India and abroad. There are 5 universities specialising in the knowledge traditions of classical Hinduism, Tibetan Buddhism, Islam, liberal arts and social sciences, and modern science, technology and humanities. These centre of higher studies provide space for continuous presence of communities of students and scholars from different parts of India and the world. Economically, it is a hub of a variety of rural and urban economic enterprises ranging from traditional crafts like silk sarees and carpets to software export. According to official sources, there were 1,19,386 non-agricultural and 1,871 agricultural enterprises in Varanasi district on the eve of inauguration of the liberalisation-privatisation-Globalization paradigm (Uttar Pradesh, 1999).

It is pointed out that Globalization is causing discontent in several sections of societies as it is resulting in pressure on local culture through market economy powers of media and information technology, and consumerism. It is also promoting acceleration of homogenisation and hybridisation of cultural forms and practices causing anxiety about the future of cultural plurality and autonomy. It may be progressive or disintegrative depending upon a variety of factors. There are at least five aspects of Globalization which have been seen as associated with changes in the 'local culture' in India:

1. Trade and market,
2. Communication and media,
3. Migration,
4. Tourism, and
5. Cultural identity.

There are four general observations about the impact of trade and market related liberalisation-Globalization. First of all, there is a distinct impact of these changes in the lifestyles and orientation of the adolescents and the youth. Secondly, there is a prominent gender dimension to the trade and marketing of cosmetics, soaps, detergents, health and hygiene and related items. There is increasing presence of beauty parlours, health centres and boutiques in smaller towns also. A remarkable change in the style and pattern of women's wear has taken place. These changes are not unrelated with the wave of fashion parades and beauty competitions which are sponsored by a variety of commercial enterprises and where Indian women have found frequent recognition as 'Miss World' and 'Miss Universe'. Thirdly, the middle classes are engaging in new found consumer freeedom which has created global choices for their requirements. From shirts, shoes and shampoos to watches, cars and vacations there is visible preference for global brands companies and destinations. Finally, there are periodic resistance activities by peasant bodies, Swadeshi proponents, and coalitions of anti-capitalist Globalization individuals and groups against promotion of multinational companies and their products which are considered as culturally subversive and economically 'neo-colonizers'.

Duality of Resistance and Acceptance

In this context, Varanasi has emerged as one of the sites of resistance against a Coca-Cola plant at the periphery of the city. A number of awareness campaigns, human chains, and *Satyagrahas* have been organised in the last few years. The participants include political workers, college students, peasant leaders, Gandhian activists, environmentalists and the mobilisation aims at removing the bottling plant of the famous American soft drinks company as it is causing water crisis for farmers, ignoring the environmental considerations, and promoting health problems by sale of sub-standard Coca-Cola. But there was no significant response to the campaign against the sale and consumption of Coca-Cola in the city. On the other hand, there has been uninterrupted growth of consumption of these global brand soft drinks and similar items at homes and hotels of Varanasi. The local and national media continues to accept the advertisements from Coca-Cola company. Some of the adverstisements included popular film heroes and heroines and there has been aggressive advertising with the emergence of resistance from different corners. The menu of most of the restaurants have been enlarged to include the list of 'western items' like pizza, pastry, burger, noodles, and other dishes which have made there entry into the homes also.

There were also protests against hosting of 'fashion show' and 'beauty competition for women' as efforts of violating the cultural code of the city. But there has been existence of 'beauty parlours' in the city for several decades and they have increased in their numbers in the recent years. In fact, the profession of 'beautification' is becoming a new opening for young women in terms of the occupational openings. The demand and availability of global brands of cosmetics is also an indicator of this change. Similarly, the opening of 'Western style gyms' for men has not been opposed as it is associated with the tradition of *akharas* and *vyayamashalas* which have been part of the youth culture for a long time. This duality has to be further analysed to understand about the complexity of the culture code of Varanasi and the differential orientation of the men and women of this cultural centre towards different elements of trade, commerce, commodity and consumption related changes due to promotion of Globalization.

Globalization at the Level of Media and Communication

The most remarkable and resistance free change in Varanasi related with Globalization has taken place in the field of media and communication. Being a university town, there was always reception to Hollywood films and western literature among the students and English educated elite of Varanasi. But there has been explosion of such material in the last decade through the expansion of (*i*) cable TV network, and (*ii*) Internet based access to English language websites. The cable TV network has captured the imagination of nearly every section of the people of Varanasi. It is reasonably priced. There can be a cable connection to the homes through a local cable vendor by paying a modest sum of around rupees 100 to 150 per month charge. In return, the homes are receiving a large number of programmes through 40-50 channels. Several programmes from the western sources are also available in Hindi language on the cable channels. It is quite a revolution for Varanasi homes as there used to be a TV system with only two national channels till the early 1980s. Now, there are so many channels from so many Indian and foreign companies with such a wide range of shows and offerings. These programmes have caused some concern among the parents due to the presence of adult themes, violence, nudity, late hours, and potential problem for 'too much' of TV watching. But these are more often mentioned in the discourses of the religious 'Gurus', media pages, neighbourhood chats, and teacher-parent meets than in the households. At the same time, these concerns have been noticed by the managements of the channels also.

The Hollywood films have arrived in every neighbourhood through the overnight emergence of video libraries, a new phenomenon around 'video technology'. They have all the popular old and new Western English films available in video, DVD, and CD formats. These films are arriving without any hindrance in the market as there are multiple channels opened up through trade liberalisation—the dealers are located in several countries including India, Nepal, Singapore, etc. They are placed on the shelves side by side with the Bollywood films and music cassettes.

This component of media and Globalization ('Westernisation'!) is popular among students-youth, educated housewives, and middle classes and professional classes. It has affected the 'film going' practice of the people of Varanasi as the new technology and supply system provides global level of entertainment within the private surroundings of a home or a room.

The other significant change around the processes of Globalization-liberalisation-privatisation policies has taken place in the realm of communication technologies. There are three new developments in Varanasi around the telephone system due to it. First, there is growth of PCO/STD/FAX booths with facility of long distance calls within and outside India through direct trunk dialling and at an affordable rate. These booths got introduced in the early 1990s and have been growing in the urban and rural settlement in and around Varanasi in an impressive manner as they are so functional. A telephone used to be a status symbol in the homes of the middle classes of Varanasi. But now it is being used as an essential instrument of communication also by the working classes and their members of the family.

Secondly, there is the arrival of mobile telephone in the life of the urban people of Varanasi. It began as an elite item in the 1990s. Within a decade it has become a necessity for a large number of occupational groups. Most of the better 'mobile phones' are from global companies like Nokia, Siemens, Motorola, Erikson, and Sony. There is no problem of availability of this machine and its components. There is a large variety of low cost schemes to encourage people to use it. But there has been no insistence on using the indigenous brands in this field. The competition among mobile phone companies is continuously intensifying to the advantage of the average customers. It is suggested that the mobile phones have been the most favourite technological component of Globalization for 'the talkative Indians'. It appears very true for the people of the eternal city of Varanasi where it is seen in use in temples of worship to temples of learning (colleges and universities); by the customer as well as the shopkeeper, by the priests and the patrons.

Thirdly, the creation of cyber cafes and its affordable rates have created a new site of get together for the computer literate youth of Varanasi. A number of cyber cafes have come up in different parts of the city and are being frequented by the youth for a variety of activities ranging from learning and information to entertainment and communication.

Migration

Globalization has created more and more opportunities for circulation of capital, commodities and people in the context of demand and supply. There has been existence of diaspora communities in India since the colonial times. Varanasi has been a traditional seat of indentured labour supply for the commercial agricultural enterprises since the British Raj. People used to go from here to the far-off island colonies of the West Indies, Fiji, Mauritius, Surinam, etc. It has also been a zone for labour migration to industrial centres of India like Kanpur, Calcutta, Mumbai, and Delhi.

Globalization has intensified the links with the labour markets of the Arab world, Confederation of Independent States (CIS), Western Europe and North America. It is another welcome feature of Globalization as Varanasi has not been an area of advancement in the context of new investment and job opportunities in India. Therefore, the semi-skilled and skilled workforce of this region has been found to be attracted to migration to various job zones. There is growth of job agencies with linkages in the city and its hinterland. It has also promoted enlargement of the travel service centres to meet the needs of job-seeking migrants which includes doctors, software engineers, scientists, nurses, teachers, masons, drivers, and several other categories of skilled and semi-skilled people.

Varanasi is a centre of crafts and commerce. It has attracted a number of business houses of Asia and Europe to establish link points and production units in the fields of silk, carpets, food processing, traditional medicine, small-scale industries, printing industry, etc. It is significant that there is also a little stream of in-migration of 'culture-seekers' and spiritually inclined people from different parts of the world including Asia and Europe. The presence of international migrants from neighbouring countries like Nepal and Bangladesh is also well recognised as most of them provide labour input into the economy of the city life as domestic helpers, rickshaw drivers, guards, vendors, casual labourers, etc.

The city of Varanasi seems to welcome the migration related aspects of Globalization. It is becoming an acceptable dream of a talented young person to prepare for going abroad for education and jobs. The presence of workers from the neighbouring countries has kept the cost of labour stabilised. Similarly, there is a tradition of treating 'the foreigners' with due courtesy as their presence is perceived as an essential indicator of worldwide fame of their unique city. Conversion of the domestic airport of Varanasi into an international airport in recent years is only one of the several indicators of this trend.

Cultural Tourism

Tourism is not a new phenomenon for Varanasi as it has taken pride in its traditional status as a 'place of pilgrimage for the Indians' and 'a centre of cultural interest for foreigners'. Yet tourism has the potential of creating 'cultural pollution'. It can cause cultural intrusion and invasion if it gets intensified beyond a certain level. In fact, the presence of foreign tourists in a large number has been affecting the quality of services and facilities for the traditional visitors who come from relatively modest background, mostly rural and small town men and women. It is argued that foreign tourists are a source of cultural problems like drugs, HIV-AIDS, prostitution, etc., which may promote disintegrative processes. Whereas, the traditional religious pilgrims promote cultural reinforcement and integration. They also patronise the sacred places without promoting consumerism around culture. Similarly, there is increasing visits by the diasporic communities from far-off places in search of roots and memories. They are strengthening the value of cultural traditions of Varanasi through their contribution as believers and worshippers of the city in its totality.

Varanasi was always a point of interest on the cultural map of Asia as it is one of the ancient centres of Indian civilization where the plurality of faith systems and ways of life is fully manifested. Multiculturality in terms of language, faith, customs, rituals, festivals, food, dress pattern, music, art, and learning has been a source of identity for the city for several millenniums. It has been a place of bliss deeply permeated by spiritual consciousness and light of knowledge. But arrival of ill-informed and curiosity seeking travellers may not allow it to remain like it has been for so long.

The growing engagement with highly diverse variety of global tourists is causing concern among the observers. First of all, the global tourist is pushing out the traditional religious pilgrims in terms of availability of space, facilities and services. Secondly, there is increasing prominence of commercial considerations in responding to the growing global interest in Varanasi due to its inclusion in the global websites and travel guides in the recent decades. The introduction of 'five-star facilities' is just one of the several causes of concern as it may destroy the simple ways of living and interacting with each other at Varanasi. Thirdly, easy connectivity and Internet based accessibility may introduce a new kind of global tourism which has limited interest in the traditional sites and spaces of Varanasi. The city may get transformed into a tourist centre with attractive restaurants, shopping malls, mobile carrying touts instead of a pilgrim city. On the other hand, it is also remembered that the city is not facing such a situation for the first time in the modern phase. In fact, it was a globally-known shelter for the war deserters and 'hippy' generation youth in the Sixties. There was arrival of pot-smoking, promiscuous, culturally uprooted youth from the European and American cities. They stayed here for the whole period of the Vietnam War. They used to shuttle between Kashi and Kathmandu. But there was no major cultural crisis for the pilgrims or regular inhabitants of the *ghats* and the lanes of the city. In the end, the city and its culture got into their lifestyle and many of them returned to their countries better educated in the philosophy, religion, customs, and arts and music of India.

Cultural Identity

The question of cultural identity is recognised as a serious concern in the context of the wave of Globalization as this process of compression of time and space beyond the nation-state is influencing the life and setting of Varanasi at many levels. The household is in the grip of consumerism. Every member of each family is getting engaged in the process of media and information revolution. The labour process is getting influenced by liberalisation, contractualisation and computerisation. The labour market has become influenced by the imperatives of global labour market and international migration. Internet has brought us information power and mobile phone and cyber cafes are getting us connected with persons without territorial hindrance. Computers have given a place of honour in the educational process of the new generation of Indians and they are becoming an object of desire for educated households. There is cultural intrusion from global tourist community which has limited commitment for the sanctity of the places of worship and articles of faith. If all of these trends are put together then there are many reasons of concern about the cultural identity of Varanasi. Sociologists have already alerted that Globalization, market economy and powers of the media or information technologies are bound to put pressures on the local cultures. Some degree of homogenisation may also be envisaged (Singh, 2000).

In fact, there are two examples of increasing concern about the identity aspect among the people of Varanasi. It is significant that this city has emerged a major source of support for the nation-wide campaign for protection of the Hindu heritage particularly the temples associated with Rama, Krishna and Shiva. There was continuous victory of the candidates of the Hindutva platform from 1992 to 2004 for representing the city in the Lok Sabha (national parliament). The other example is associated with the resistance to a film project where the condition of Hindu widows was proposed to be depicted in a negative light by an America-based Indian film-maker. It was charged that there is conspiracy to malign Indian culture through such films where the film-makers have no sense or understanding of the elements of Indian culture and customs. A 'culture protection association' was launched to make it sure that there was a total withdrawal of the film team from Varanasi. This was an internationally noted event which marked the making of a new attitude about the self-perception among a section of well educated and well integrated citizens of Varanasi and their aggressiveness about any negative depiction by the 'others' belonging to the forces of Globalization.

Is there a threat to the cultural identity of Varanasi due to Globalization related influences? The empirical setting of Varanasi points out three factors which may help in finding an answer to this critical question. First and foremost, the communities and groups of Varanasi have a segmentary character with high degree of autonomy and plurality in terms of cultural aspects, like the rest of India. This autonomy has been the source of cultural resilience for centuries. They also create 'refractory' adaptations as in the case of the previous waves of westernisation and modernization. This may hold true for the interface with the forces of Globalization also. Second, Globalization has been strengthening the self-consciousness among the cultures around the world. It has led to 'ethnicisation' and awareness of identity. Finally, there is a good opportunity of enlargement of the elements of Varanasi culture beyond the territorial space towards universalisation of its arts, crafts, music, knowledge, medicine and food. Globalization has caused increasing frequency of contacts and communications, use of new information technology for spreading the knowledge about the city and its culture through multimedia, and increasing availability of global resources for protecting the heritage of Varanasi (as in the case of campaign for checking pollution of Ganga river, resource mobilisation for the maintenance of the spiritual centres like Kashi Vishwanath Temple, the Buddhist sites, Kabir Math, or protection and promotion of the musical traditions of Varanasi). Thus, there is possibility of a new vigour through the renewed sense of self-awareness about Varanasi. This identity consciousness may promote the possibility of adaptive reconciliation with the forces of Globalization as there is a growing reality of increasing local-global interaction through consumption, migration, and communication which will never allow *status quo* in the affairs of the peoples of Varanasi and their cultural life.

Conclusion

Globalization is a market, machine and money mediated process of integrating men, women, places, and cultures in a common web of information, ideas, institutions, and processes and governance through inter-State treatise and transnational actors. The great traditional sites of indigenous cultural traditions are getting increasingly exposed to the forces of Globalization. These forces are creating waves of change in the economic, social and cultural set-up of such significant places of culture causing anxieties about identity.

City of Varanasi is no exception to this global process. Despite its historical identity, the city has been an example of continuity and change for a long time. At the present juncture, there are five dimensions of Globalization which have contributed towards new changes in the setting of Varanasi—(*i*) Trade and commerce, (*ii*) Media and communication, (*iii*) Migration, (*iv*) Tourism, and (*v*) Cultural identity.

There is a new wave of identity consciousness around the world including India and Varanasi. The city has received many of the opportunities around trade, commerce, media and communication inherent in the process of Globalization with great enthusiasm. But there is equal amount of apprehension about the increasing intensity of culture contact through global tourism and identity incursions. It is expected that the pre-existing traits of cultural resilience will get envigorated with increasing sense of self-awareness and Varanasi will be able to evolve a refractory response to the cultural implications of Globalization.

References

Appadorai, Arjun (1997), *Modernity at Large: Cultural Dimensions of Globalization*. Oxford University Press, Delhi.

Kejariwal, Omprakash (2005), "James Prince aur Benares", Kalpana, Kashi Ank, Hyderabad.

Motichandra (1962), *Kashi Ka Itihas,* Mumbai, Hindi Granth Ratnakar Private Limited.

Sen, Amartya K. (2001), "If it's fair, it's good: 10 truths about Globalization", *International Herald Tribune,* July 14-15, 2001.

Shiva, Vandana (No date), "Globalization, Gandhi and Swadeshi". New Delhi, *Research Foundation for Science, Technology and Ecology*. p. 3.

Singh, Yogendra (2000), *Culture Change in India*. New Delhi. Har-Anand.

Stiglitz, J. (2003), *Globalization and its Discontents*. London, Penguine.

Uttar Pradesh (1999), *Statistical Diary,* Uttar Pradesh, 1998. Lucknow, State Planning Institute.

Watson, C.W. (2002), *Multiculturalism,* New Delhi, Viva Books.

26

The Actor and Institution

A Structuration (The Role of BHU in Anti-Colonial Struggle)

VISHWANATH PANDEY

[I]

The advent of the new century has come with the bankruptcy of ideology promoting market rationale in a world which has become mosaic of multicultural society. The conventional ideologies have lost ground; the cultural resurgence has brought up the debate of actors and structure on forefront replacing the thrust of agencies and agents in the era of colonial building and modernization. It was presumed that the new world order after the demise of the Cold War will set the terrain of democracy flourishing across the globe. It did not happen, instead created a world more fragmented and filled with uncertainties. The market rationale might be a signalling force, but it is not a controlling mechanism to articulate the expressions of new social formations. It is why the persons and places along with the lines of communicative rationality are becoming not only significant, but also socially relevant categories to understand the process of structuration in historicity. It is in this chapter that the case study of Banaras Hindu University has been analyzed in the context of multiple convertibility of capital, from economic to cultural and finally social. The founder of the institution, Pt. Madan Mohan Malviya is the 'Actor' and the university is the structure, the relationship of the two has made a structuration possible for the social transformation of the entire society, as well as instrument of creating a new social and political consciousness of identity with institutional ideology. The analysis of this case study reveals a holistic relationship of text, contest of history and structure in understanding the person and the institution in the process of structuration.

[II]

The very foundational edifice of Banaras Hindu University rests on the late nineteenth and early twentieth century social reform movements as well as the new renaissance dawning upon the continent. Banaras Hindu University's profile cannot be separated from this historic process of transformation. The genesis of the synthetic view of the founder Pt. Madan Mohan Malviya lied in the labyrinth of Reformative movements of the day. The Government's initiatives in this regard were expressed through Indian Education Commission of 1882 which suggested the establishment of a university in the then United Province. The demand of the university was fulfilled by an Act of 1887 which brought the Allahabad University into being. Along with this progress on the education side, there was developing a new social, political and economical consciousness in the country. The Brahmo Samaj under the leadership of Shri Keshav Chandra Sen was spreading its tenets far and wide. Swami Dayanand Saraswati founded the Arya Samaj in the year 1872 and kindled national spirit in the country. In Bombay, the Prarthana Samaj, Social Reform movement and the industrial movements under the leadership of Mahadeva Govind Ranade were awakening the people to bring about the social and religious regeneration. The Theosophical movement also set foot in India by this time. It was established in South India in 1881. This movement was endeavouring to bring about recognition of universal brotherhcod by reviving spirituality in major part of the world. It treated every religion holy, as a path towards the supreme to enrich the eternal aspect of the spiritual life on which rests the destiny of man. The message of Shri Ram Krishna Paramhansa also helped in bringing about the synthesis of the Eastern and Western civilisation. His teaching brought new hope.

These movements were tending to bring about the national

renaissance, the Indian National Congress also came into existence which marked the beginning of a new era in the history of the country. In its very second session held at Calcutta in December 1886, the country saw an emerging personality on horizon; it was Pt. Madan Mohan Malviya.

During his tour of the country while attending the Congress session, Pt. Malviya had an opportunity of observing the conditions in different spheres of national life existing. He felt that universalistic spiritual message of religion was pushed out of agenda everywhere; he felt that patriotism was impossible without proper grasp of message of religion. The essence of religion is also the basis of morality and of all true patriotism. A fairly large number of patriots in the history religion were men of spirituality. Religion does develop spirit of unselfishness. A selfish person can be a patriot. Pt. Madan Mohan Malviya, therefore came to the conclusion that in order to revitalise India as a Nation, it was necessary to feed her youth with its old spirit and moral reservoir. While Pandit Malviya was trying to revitalise the nation in this way, as the Theosophical movement was spreading fast throughout the country. The movement had gained new impetus with the arrival of Mrs Annie Besant in India in 1893. Annie Besant felt that the needs of India were among others, the development of national spirit through an education founded on the ideal and enriched—not dominated, by the thought and culture of the West. She, therefore, felt that in order to develop the Indian nationality and spirituality, religious ethics must be made part of the training of every child. This would generate patriotism, inspired by ideals of self-realisation, self-sacrifice and spirituality. With this idea, she set about to establish the Central Hindu College in Banaras in 1898. The college was established to give to its students the best learning of the East, while training these in religion and morality on the lines of the Hindu Shastras, by encouraging Sanskrit learning and reasearch to acquire a model institutional status all-over the country. There was a time when India could claim to be the largest contributor at least in the Indo-European language family of the human race, not only to study of religion and philosophy, but to science, arts, crafts and all else that makes up a civilization. European scholars and investigators acknowledge that India is the birthplace of arithmetic, algebra, geometry, astronomy and medicine and owe their indebtedness to our ancestors for their discovery of another most important material factor of our civilization, *viz.*, the use of metals. But the process of retrogression took toll of all that was important.

India cannot, it was visualised, regain its prosperity until the study and application of modern science becomes, so to speak, naturalised in the country. A wide diffusion of science in India is a means for rescuing the people from the abject poverty into which they have fallen. Freedom from poverty is not possible until science, both theoretically and practically, can be absorbed by Indians in their own country and in their own vernacular.

The twenty-first session of Indian National Congress was held in the city of Banaras in 1905 under the chairmanship of Gopal Krishna Gokhale. On the occasion Pt. Malviya convened a select meeting of distinguished educationists and representatives of the Hindu community. On 31st December, 1905, the prospectus of the Hindu University was discussed. During Kumbh at Allahabad in 1906, Pt. Malviya took a resolve to dedicate his life for the establishment of the proposed Hindu University. On 12 March, 1906, first prospectus of the university was issued to the public by Pt. Malviya. The scheme met with much approval and support both from the press and public. *The Pioneer*, a newspaper, noted in its editorial... a University which 'would combine the best in the east and west', which could be not sectarian and conducted on national lines by national agency, is assured of ample recognition and ought to meet a crying want.

Mrs. Annie Besant came to India in 1893 and soon accepted India as her home. In the year 1898, Mrs. Besant established the Central Hindu College at Banaras. She felt that religion is the foundation of all true education as it is the foundation of family and state. Religion and moral institutions were, therefore, introduced by her as a part of school and college teaching. Very soon Mrs. Besant began to hope that Central Hindu College would be the centre of a great circle of related institutions all giving education on the same lines until it becomes the Hindu University of India.

During this period several developments took place in the country. The Aligarh College trustees began to think of turning their college into a residential university. The idea of community educational instruction was being welcomed not only by the leaders of the Muslim community in India but got inspiring blessings of the British officials in high quarters. The colonial rules had their agenda, Lord Curzon himself, when he paid a visit to the College expressed the hope that the Muslims of this country, Shias and Sunnis alike, would exert themselves not to be left behind while their rivals were pressing forward in the race. Record subscription was raised in 1904 for the Aligarh College in the conference held at Lucknow. In the beginning of 1911, the Muslims under the leadership of H.H. the Agha Khan, submitted their demand for a University charter for establishment of Muslim University at Aligarh and because of the solidarity of the Muslim community, the scheme succeeded to the extent of higher expectations. The Government of India had practically promised them their University if they could collect a sum of twenty-five lakhs of rupees as collateral. Consequently, a number of Muslim gentlemen, who had given their names to Mrs. Besant's scheme, withdrew from it.

The Hindu community was also roused at this juncture by the sight of the success of their Muslim brothers. The workers of the Central Hindu College received invitations from several districts and held very enthusiastic and successful meetings at Hardoi, Rai Bareli and Barabanki, collecting large sums for the Central Hindu College. Aroused by strong feelings of emulation, the Hindu population wished to have a University of their own. It was just at this time that Pt. Malviya also revised his old scheme. It was during the 25th session of the Congress at Allahabad in 1910 that Malviya decided to resume the work of the University, which had been put off year after year, till now.

Mrs. Besant and Pt. Malviya met in Calcutta in March 1911, talked over the situation and decided to join hands. A further meeting was held between them and few other leading Hindus at Allahabad on 8th April, 1911 and it was agreed to send the petition for a Royal approval with certain modifications. These proposed changes were printed in a circular letter dated the 11th April, 1911 issued by Mrs. Besant which was also published in various dailies and weeklies. This is how the work of the institution of Banaras Hindu University started. The proposal to establish a Hindu University at Banaras was first put forward at a meeting held in 1904 at the 'Mint House' at Banaras, which was presided over by H.H. the Maharaja of Banaras. A prospectus of the proposed University was published and circulated in October 1905, and it was discussed at a select meeting held at the Town Hall at Banaras on 31st December, 1905, at which a number of distinguished educationists and representatives of the Hindu community of almost every province of India were present. It was also considered and approved by the Congress of Hindu religion which met at Allahabad in January, 1906. The scheme met with much approval and support and both from the press and the public. 'To the scheme for establishing a Hindu University', said the daily *Pioneer* in a leading article, 'the most cordial encouragement may be offered. A crore of rupees does not seem to be an excessive sum for a purpose so clearly excellent, and which no doubt appeals to a very numerous class.... Even if Mahomedans and Christians do not hasten to embrace the opportunities offered under the most liberal constitution of this new centre of learning, there are two hundred million Hindus to whom it should appeal as a true Alma Mater, and surely no greater constituency could be desired'. The Hon. Sir James la Touche, the then Lieutenant-Governor of the United Provinces, was pleased to bless it in the following words:

> "If the cultured classes throughout India are willing to establish a Hindu University with its colleges clustered round it, they have my best wishes for its success. But if the institution is to be first-rate, the cost will be very great and the bulk of the money must be found elsewhere than in this province. At this era of the world's progress no one will desire or approve a second-rate institution."

The scheme had ever since 1906 been kept alive by discussions and consultations with a view to begin work, but owing to circumstances which need not be mentioned here, an organised endeavour to carry out the proposal had to be put off year after year. As the result of the discussion which had been on, the scheme has underwent some important changes as further discussion took place. It agreed that the proposed University should be a residential and teaching University of the modern type. All the five Universities which existed at the time were mainly examining Universities. They had done and were doing most useful work. But the need for a University which will teach as well as examine, and which by reason of being a residential University, will realise the ideal of university life as it was known in the past in India as well as in the western countries in modern times.

The Objects

The objects of the University have been thus formulated:

(*i*) To promote the study of the Hindu *shastras* and of Sanskrit literature generally as a means of preserving and popularising for the benefit of the Hindus in particular and of the world at large in general, the best thought and culture of the Hindus, and all that was good and great in the ancient civilisation of India.

(*ii*) To promote learning and research generally in arts and science in all branches.

(*iii*) To advance and diffuse such scientific, technical and professional knowledge, combined with the necessary practical training, as is best calculated to help in promoting indigenous industries and in developing the material resources of the country.

(*iv*) To promote the building up of character in youth by making religion and ethics an integral part of education.

Following is the excerpt of speech made by Sir Rameshwar Singh Bahadur of Darbhanga and President of the Hindu University Society explaining the objectives:

> "There was another equally powerful reason for inaugurating the movement. While we highly appreciate the value and need of education in European arts and science, we cannot divest ourselves of the consciousness that we have inherited a culture and civilization of our own which reaches further back in time than that of any other people, and which possesses as we believe in a special degree the elements of social stability as well as the fundamental principles of physical, intellectual and spiritual progress and welfare. Amidst all the vicissitudes through which Hindu society has passed, it has in all essential, clung to that civilization and has ever been governed by it. There was naturally a widespread desire

> in our community our distinctive civilization and culture, and to instruct our youth in the sacred precepts of our religion. The promoters of the University believe that if our students are brought up in our tradition and culture instructed in the precepts of our religion, they will grow up into men of vigorous intellects and high character, who love their motherland, are loyal to the king and are in every way fit to be useful members of the community and worthy citizen of a great Empire."

In his address to the first convocation at the Banaras Hindu University, the Vice Chancellor, Sir P.S. Siraswamy Aiyar exhorted the students and distinguished gathering: "You will have to play an important part in the regeneration of India and making of her future, so as to enable her to take an honoured place in the League of Nations."

Pt. Malviya had from the earliest years of his public life passionately pleaded for the revival of indigenous industries to relieve the peasantry of grinding poverty, as a recurrent theme in his speeches before the congress. He made a memorable speech on *swadeshi* in 1893 and moved a resolution at the 1898 session urging government to foster native industries and native arts. Pt. Malviya also moved a resolution in the Viceroy's Legislative Council for the appointment on the industrial commission consisting of a representative of people. This was accepted and seven or eight names were suggested to Government out of whom Pt. Malviya was chosen.

The Industrial Commission gave a masterly survey of the urban and rural industries of the country, a description in some details of the conditions obtaining in the leading industrial centres, Calcutta, Bombay, Ahmedabad, Kanpur and in the leading industries cotton, jute, tea, coal, indigo and account of the country's transport system and of its resources in raw materials and manpower. It described the very scanty provision for technical and commercial education and research. The conclusion arrived at by the Commission was that Indian industries were unevenly and inadequately developed, that valuable raw material was either left unutilised or the manufacturer of it and the profit arising from such manufacturer were left largely to foreign countries. The Commission also took note of the rising demand all-over India for economic progress. It emphasized the need for well directed technical, financial and administrative assistance being provided by Government so that India could become 'strong by its own strength and a worthy partner in the empire' of Pt. Malviya subscribed to the recommendations, nevertheless he was also determined that the responsibility of government for the ruin of the once prosperous Indian industries should be clearly brought out in the report, that the myth of the Asiatic apathy to industrial pursuit must be exploded and efficient conducting of vital economic activities like banking should be further explored. He was equally insistent that the deplorable effects of the neglect of technical and commercial education should be brought to notice as should also the government's habit of making a pretext for recruiting Europeans to man the services and excluding Indians from them.

He had a good deal to say about the education, the neglect of which in his opinion largely accounted for the backwardness of India. Before 1870, neither India nor Britain had a national system of education. But since then Britain had, he opined, risen to the pinnacle of power and prosperity by virtue of measures which had transformed its educational system and India would not have lagged behind but the Commission on the part of Government to do the same in India where it had not agreed even to the modest Primary Education Bill sponsored by Gokhale and supported by Malviya himself.

While welcoming the Commission's recommendations for the establishment of an Industrial Development Department at the centre and also in each of the provinces, he strongly opposed the creating of an Imperial Industrial Services and of a cadre of scientists styled 'Imperial Chemical Service' for carrying on scientific research in aid of industries. Such steps, he apprehended, would place the future of Indian industries in the hands of bureaucrats recruited in England like the existing Imperial Services, who would be both costly to this country and indifferent to its interest.

Malviya's basic aim was to ensure that the state should promote Indian industries and that they should utilise Indian raw materials, and be run with Indian capital by Indian personnel and under Indian control. Malviya was the author of the prospectus of the proposed Hindu University issued in 1911, containing a remarkably comprehensive educational programme. Later, he took a leading part in framing the recommendations of the Indian Industrial Commission in regard to technical educations. He was, moreover, at pains to consult leading scholars and educationists at home and abroad. His speeches and writings among which are the addresses, he delivered at the convocations of the BHU (in 1920 and 1929) and at other universities and the speeches with which he inaugurated the annual meetings of the University Court during the twenty years of his tenure of the Vice Chancellorship, bear testimony to his deep understanding of the subject. This very exposure to the need of modern nation building exercise induced Pt. Malviya to move further towards formation of Banaras Hindu University which was supposed to provide an answer to the needs of a nationalist regeneration in economy, industry and nation building enterprise.

Pt. Malviya's consistent work in the Central Legislative Council helped expanding his vision of the Banaras Hindu University.

The Miracle of the Twenties

Malviya's achievement in building the Banaras Hindu University from the small beginning from the premises of the Central Hindu College in October 1917 and turning it into the leading university of the country, with an imposing campus and offering the largest number of courses including courses of highest standard in Engineering and Technology, not available anywhere else in the country, was indeed phenomenal. It surprised Malviya himself as much as it impressed others.

Colonel J.C. Wedgewood, British M.P., a well known friend of India, described the BHU as the greatest thing in Asia and Malviya as the greatest constructive statesman in India.

The eminent American journalist Edgar Snow who visited the University in 1931 and had a long interview with Malviya, gave a glowing account of the University in a dispatch dated June 28, 1931 to his paper, *The New York Sun*. He wrote of it as the full fruited realisation of a man of practical genius which belies the remarks of skeptical Europeans that Indian though admirable agitators and excellent destructionist are incapable of improving upon what they seek to destroy. Here was 'the finest university in modern India conceived, constructed and administered solely by

Indians'. Of Malviya, he said, 'his future prestige would rest on the University and it would secure for him a peculiar niche in the Indian Hall of Fame'.

Pt. Malviya had devoted much thought to the problem of prevalent poverty which was one of the most glaring features of India's life in his days and unfortunately continues to be so even today. He spoke feelingly about the grinding poverty of the masses and powerfully advocated revival of industries as one effective remedy for it. He pressed for it in his speeches in the Legislative Councils of India as well as United Provinces, at sessions of the Congress, in industrial conferences held under Government auspices and under the auspices of the Congress. He pleaded forcefully in the note he appended to the report of the Indian Industrial Commission for removal of poverty. He realised also that industries carried on with antiquated technology could not withstand the competition offered by industries run by modern machines and processes evolved by modern science. Training of personnel to organise and run industries on up-to-date lines was one of his most cherished aims in starting the Hindu University. He has given *Sthapatya Veda* or 'Constructive Arts' an important place in the comprehensive scheme of the University drawn up in 1911.

Four years after the foundation of University, Pt. Malviya had to face the storm raised by the Congress programme of boycott of educational institutions, to which he was strongly opposed. His own son (Govind) led the revolt against him. Worse followed when the Prince of Wales came to the University by invitation to receive an honorary degree at a special convocation and the benches meant for students, which were left almost entirely unoccupied were filled by inferior servants of the University and sundry other simulating as students. The Prince wrote about this to the Viceroy bitterly complaining 'what a bloody fool' they had made of him hoping that he would not come to know of it. In the decade that followed, the youth of the country were organised, as never before, in the cause of various political parties, communal organisations and secret societies. At one end were the Boy Scouts and the Khudai Khidmatgars and at the other the Rastriya Swayam Sewak Sangh, the Khaksars and Razakars. Malviya himself presided over an all-India rally of the Youth League in 1928.

The Civil Disobedience call of the early thirties affected some teachers and many students. The University was forced to close down for a while despite the best efforts of Pt. Malviya to keep it open. Later, he himself assumed leadership of the civil disobedience movement as a protest against the repressive measures of the government and went to jail. Government wanted him to give up the Vice Chancellorship and contemplated stopping its grant. The Executive Council made a spirited reply contending that the University has to take note of wave of national sentiment which has been passing over the country. In reply to the threat of stoppage of grant-in-aid, the teachers and officers of the University offered, in writing, their services to Malaviya on whatever terms he chose to lay down.

In those years revolutionaries found refuge in the University and Government had a well founded suspicion that they received encouragement from the entire University Community.

More prominent was the participation of this University's teachers and students in the Quit India Movement of 1942. The widespread damage to railway, telegraph and telephone lines in the eastern districts of the UP was ascribed by Government to members of the University since the methods employed required a high degree of technological skill which the common man did not have. The University remained closed for three months; the campus was occupied by the military who coveted its magnificent building as suitable for the purpose of a Base Hospital.

From the rapid review of the impact of politics, the University drew conclusions on discipline:

1. Defiance of authority in a righteous cause such as freedom of the country, which recognised as not only laudable; (The possibility of this technique being applied for the achievement of less noble and even positively ignoble aims was ignored.
2. The University was divided internally for some time over the issue of suspending studies and later over other issues.

This, in short, defines the very essence of University which was ever ready to protest against unjust colonial authoritarianism but emphasised very heavily on maintaining its academic discipline.

In retrospect, we find that the predicament of the Banaras

Hindu University was anti-colonial. The very concept of a multi-faculty University at this juncture of history, was nothing less than revolutionary. Under the impact of Indian renaissance, Malviya conceived a mega institution for awakening of the younger generation. Strategically, he proposed to work for a synthesis of tradition and modernization. Malviya had no other viable medium, at that juncture, except liberalism in politics and regenerating universal values of Hindu way of life. The *Gita* and the *Upanishads* had a patriotic mission and those patronising classes (the native rulers, etc.) came forward to support his project. Besides it must be taken note of that all major political ideologies and movement steeped in anti-colonialism found a welcoming shelter in the precincts of this great university. The ideas of secular nationalism, ideas emanating from our glorious past all submerged in this novel institution, which very deeply generated an anti-colonial fervour. The anti-colonialism growing in BHU was an amalgam of all the major political ideological stream of anti-colonialism struggle in field of art, education, science and technology and above all in disciplines like ancient Indian history and modern history. The anti-colonial mission of this great national institution cannot be bypassed. Banaras Hindu University was at the very 'CORE' of the anti-colonial mainstream as an institution, as an educational ideology, as reflected in its resurgent rebellious faculty and students seen particularly in the 1942 Quit India struggle.

The University latently had a patriotic mission. Its functions were patriotic in design and intent. Of course, they were not so confrontist in nature, being educative and consciousness raising. The University was at the same time, a nodal point of creating and building a nation. For these reasons, the University had to encounter wrath of the British rulers. The galaxy of the eminent scholars as Vice Chancellors had often persuaded the colonial masters to spare the institution.

The active core of anti-colonialism were the organisations of the students and certain groups of teachers. They took active part in the national movement of 1942.

[III]

The analysis of Banaras Hindu University is an exercise to understand the convertibility of capital in one form or another through the process of structuration (actor and structure). It is also a focus on social transformation of a society, at time when histories are competing. Since the University itself was a product of enlightenment without taking break from the past, it has a potential to overcome the impediments of the periodation. Its first role as a transforming agency for promoting political and technical elites all-over the world is an agenda that it has fulfilled substantially. With the change of epoch, the new agenda is to identify the strength of tradition without undermining the scientific temper. The cultural resurgence was already an inbuilt agenda of the institution. Now it is with measured modernization. The trend is to reinterpret the colonized countries, as viewed as cultural products in terms of Eurocentric past. The other emphasis is to disassociate from the colonial past as a referent of western centring. It is a move to bring culture as an indigenous movement back to development paradigm. But this cannot be without reformation. Therefore, the new agenda is radicalisation with reformation of the human project.

27

Globalization and National Identity

D.K. SINGH *AND* S.B. SINGH

Here are the two terms 'globalization' and 'national identity'. One must clearly understand what both stand for. Two concepts are involved in defining national identity—nation and its identity—and there are a number of definitions of both. "A nation is a soul, a spiritual principle. Only two things constitute this soul. One is the past and the other is present. One is the possession in common of a rich legacy of remembrances, the other is the actual consent, the will to continue to value the heritage which all hold in common. To have common glories in the past, a common will in the present: to have great things together, to wish to do so again, that is essential condition of being a nation"[1] (Anthony D., Smith: 1994: 17). To Max Weber, "A nation is a community of sentiment which would manifest itself in a state of its own; hence a nation is a community normally tends to produce a state of its own[2] (Weber, Max: 1967: 176). Much more comprehensive both historically and descriptively, however, is Joseph Stalin's definition, "A nation is a historically constituted and stable community of people formed on the basis of a common language, territory, economic life and psychological make-up manifested in a common culture"[3] (Stalin Joseph: 1992: 5).

A nation's identity is the sum of its perceived qualities that defines it in terms of both what it is and what it is not, for instance, a Hindi speaking nation and not an English speaking nation. It also distinguishes a nation from other collectivities such as class and caste. Objective inputs into the process of identity perception include the character of the state, methods of economic organisation, level of technological progress, military and economic strength, language, ethnicity, etc. Subjectively, perception is a function of consciousness and is influenced by thought process, emotions and one's sense of values, which are culturally determined. This will become clear, if we recall that "cultures involve the process and organisation of experience" common to a community and embody its "standards of perceiving, predicting, judging and acting"[4] (Ward Hunt, 1963: 259). The fate of a nation's identity will depend on the fate of its culture, which undoubtedly stands for much more than the functions just described.

Culture has been differently defined. According to Edward B. Taylor (1871), culture is "that complex whole which includes knowledge, belief, art, morals, laws, customs and any other capabilities and habits acquired by man as a member of society"[5] (Taylor, Edward B., 187: 1). Kroeber holds that one can roughly "approximate what culture is by saying that it is that which the human species has and other social species lack. This would include speech, knowledge, beliefs, customs, art and technologies"[6] (Bose, Nirmal Kumar, 1977: 15).

Nirmal Kumar Bose's definition of culture refers to economic aspects much more clearly. "Culture", he says, "is a term in anthropology which covers everything from the traditional manner in which people produce, cook, or eat their food; the way they plan their houses, the manner in which men are organised into communities to the moral and religious values which are found acceptable, or the habitual methods by which satisfaction is gained in respect of the higher qualities of mind"[7] (Valentine Charles A., 1968: 3). Hence, from the dynamic point of view, culture can be analysed into a number of aspects such as education, social control, economic, systems of knowledge, belief and morality and also modes of creative and artistic expression.

Under each of these definitions, culture covers important aspects of life and the circumstances determining people's lives. As Valentine puts it, "Culture in the anthropological sense, has come to mean most simply, the entire way of life followed by the people"[8] (World Development Report 1999/2000: 173).

Is Globalization a threat to national cultures? The search for an answer, we must begin with a look at what Globalization stands for. The World Bank defines Globalization as "the continued integration of the world's economics, through expanding flow of goods, services, capital, labour and ideas and through collective action by countries to address global evironmental problems"[9] (Marx, Karl and Friedrich Engels, 1975: 42). Gathering momentum since 1985, the process has three operational dimensions. At the economic level, it means a process leading to the completely free movement of capital, currency, raw material finished products and people across national frontiers. It involves increasing economic openness and interdependence among countries and Oganisation of economic activities overarching a multiplicity of countries. At the political level, it means a corresponding diminution of the sovereign authority of states and domination of bodies like the World Trade Organisation (WTO) and multinational corporations. At the cultural level, it means the increasingly unhindered movement of cultural products and ideas across national boundaries. All the three levels are closely interlinked.

Globalization has its roots in the rise of international trade. There has been trade between continents and countries from almost the beginning of recorded history. It was, however, only with the coming of the age of geographical discoveries and the rise of capitalism that the beginnings of global trade in modern sense began. Marx writes in the Communist Manifesto, "The discovery of America, the rounding of the cape, opened up fresh ground for the rising bourgeoisie. The East Indian and the Chinese markets, the colonization of America, trade with the colonies, the increase in the means of exchange and in the commodities generally gave to commerce, to navigation to industry, an impulse never before known"[10] (Nayyar, Deepak, 22).

Deepak Nayar points out, "Globalization is nothing new. There was a similar phase of Globalization that began a century earlier, *circa* 1870, and gathered momentum until 1914, when it came to an abrupt end"[11] (Nayyar, Deepak: 22).

"These four decades", he adds, "were the age of *laissez faire*. There was almost no restriction on the movement of goods, capital and labour across national boundaries. Government intervention in economic activity was minimal"[12] (Nayyar, Deepak, 23). There was, in this period, a massive increase in international trade and direct foreign investment including in the developing countries of the third world. "There was also a significant integration of international financial markets in the late nineteenth century and earlier twentieth century. The only dimension missing was international transactions in foreign exchange which were determined by trade flows and capital flows given the regime of fixed exchange rate under the gold standard"[13] (Hermain, Edward S. and McChesney Robern W., 1998: 2).

It may be pointed out here, there are significant differences between the two periods of Globalization. In the earlier one, the maximum proportion of international trade was intersectional trade in which primary commodoties were exchanged for manufactured goods. There has now been a sharp decline in the importance of primary goods and sharp increase in that of manufactured goods. There has also been a sharp decline in foreign investments in developing countries which in 1914 accounted for 45 per cent of the stock of long-term foreign investment in the world economy, with the industrial world accounting for the remaining 55 per cent. In the 1980s, industrial countries absorbed 80 per cent. In 1992, the corresponding figures were 78 per cent and 22 per cent of the flow of foreign investment, whereas developing countries received only 70 per cent respectively. Also, whereas there were few restrictions on the flow of labour across national boundaries in the earlier round, there are numerous ones in the current one. Finally, unlike in the earlier period when Globalization was dominated by imperial powers, both in the realm of politics and economies, the key players are now multinational corporations. They are now dominating trade, investment and production in the world economy and international banks or financial institutions which control the world finance.

There is a very important reason behind studying. The difference between two periods of Globalization is crystal clear. The first did not raise the question of process impact on national identities anywhere near the way the second has. Why? This is partly because the first was a period of imperialism in which national identities were strongly etched in the colonising nation-states as well as colourized countries were waking up to an awareness of their national identities as a part of their incipient struggle for freedom. Today, the multinational corporations and global financial institutions consciously blur whatever national identity they have, to increase their global acceptability. Nor does their presence trigger the kind of intense nationalist backlash that the imperial powers did because such dominance is the result not of wielding governmental power but subtly generated influence. Also, there was then no single accepted ideology of Globalization which is now market-oriented capitalism. This new capitalism now integrates diverse economic functions globally, is fuelled by internationally highly mobile short and long term capital, and is supported by an increasingly global market propagating the same consumption pattern. Nor did it have then a unipolar world where a single dominant power, like the U.S.A., is able to project its own way of organising its social and economic life, and its cultural values as a means of a global transcendence to prosperity and freedom.

Such a development would not have been possible without a radical transformation of the global political environment in the last decades of the twentieth century. As long as the Soviet Union remained there, the East European countries remained satellites in its orbit, and China shunned the capitalist path, more than half of the globe's landmass remained outside the reach of the market economy. This, as well as support from the Soviet bloc and China, enabled third world countries to resist more effectively than now, pressures to open up their economies to import from the US and other western countries. Therefore, there could be no Globalization in the present sense until the collapse of Soviet Union. The emergence of the East European countries into independence and China's march towards a market economy has helped in strengthening the processes of Globalization all-over the world.

The change in the political environment alone, however, would not by itself have made the current round of Globalization possible without the change in the nature of capitalism. The communication revolution in the second half of the twentieth century has enabled, in combination with tremendous advances in information technology and macroeconomic management on the global scale. It has now become possible to receive and interpret information and communicate decisions within seconds. The result has been the rise of integrated production and of a rapidly expanding global market, E-commerce has arrived. Marketing has emerged as one of the most important departments of the capitalist system, and advertising as a separate industry with a staggering turnover. The same has happened with the media and the entertainment industry. The striking new arena for global commercial development is television[14] (Hermain, Edward S. and McChesney Robern W., 10). The significance of this development can hardly be overemphasised because television is the defining medium of the age and it provides the basis for an integrated global commercial media market as in the case of Globalization, the global media has roots that stretch long back in history. The establishment of an integrated global media market began in earnest only in the 1980s and achieved its full potential only in the 1990s[15] (Hermain, Edward S. and McChesney Robern W., 38).

The results have been dramatic. Advertising, media and the industry are part of the capitalist substructure and not the superstructure, as they were considered to be by Marx. They no longer merely reflect and articulate the capitalist ideology in various ways but have become proponents of that ideology. As a result, the ideology and culture of the market where consumption takes place have become the ideology and culture of capitalism itself. This lends to Globalization a cultural dimension which international trade lacked in the period before it began.

The ideology of Globalization has been described as neoliberalism, which stands for minimising the role of state and giving virtual sovereign status to the market whose price dynamics should determine resource allocation. According to it, policies of state should facilitate and not hinder the working of market forces, which now emphasise consumption much more than saving and accumulation as it did earlier. Nor should domestic economic compulsion hinder the free flow of trade and capital.

It is now easy to see why Globalization is perceived as a threat to nationalism and national identities. Nation-states of our time are, however, very different from the earlier nation-states committed to mercantilism. Many of them manage to retain their distinctiveness in identities while participating in the global economies. The experience of Western Europe, perhaps the most globalising region of the world, clearly shows that neither the ideology nor the economic dynamics of Globalization are destructive of national identities.

National identities are still strong in most developing countries of the Third World, which have achieved freedom after long struggles against colonial powers. These are unlikely to wither soon. Besides, Globalization is a two-way process. Diasporas, which keep on growing despite the best efforts of the industrialised-developed countries to restrict the entry of people from developing countries, become centres to Third World's culture. These can also influence, as the Non Resident Indians in the USA have shown respect for the policies of the last countries.

A country's culture, however, evolves with social and economic changes. Of crucial importance is the impact of the globalised media and entertainment industries on national culture, which plays a critical role in defining national identity. There is a growing feeling that their domination by the US tends to turn them into instruments for globalising American culture at the cost of individual national identities. Many of the latter are losing their distinctiveness and the young people of the countries concerned are increasingly emulating the lifestyle and cultural preferences of their American counterparts.

Besides, a nation's identity also changes, for example, with its transcendence into an industrialised one from a purely agricultural one. Yet it remains a nation, and perhaps stronger and better administered than in its previous incarnation. The basic problem with the culture dished out by the globalised media is not that it is threatening national identities but it is spreading mindless consumerism and trivialising discourse. This, in turn, results from the fact that such media units are privately owned and seek to maximise profits by maximising revenue by dishing out programmes which draw the largest number of viewers by catering to the lowest common cultural denominator in the market. Unfortunately, the problem is compounded by the fact that Indian media are doing precisely the same thing for the Indian people.

The question here is how to have private media companies without their adversely affecting a nation's culture. It can arise even in a country, which remains outside the reach of Globalization. The answer would lie in a host of correctives from public vigilances, regulatory mechanism, to measures to civilize capitalism. Meanwhile, it would be useful to remember that the champions of neo-liberal economies have not been the only one to talk of Globalization. Karl Marx had also visualised, although in a different way, the worldwide spread of capitalism before it exhausted all its inherent potential and collapsed under the weight of its own contradictions and assaults by the organised revolutionary proletariat.

Notes

1. Anthony D., Smith, *Nationalism*, Oxford University Press, Oxford, 1994, p. 17.
2. Weber, Max, *From Max Weber: Essays in Sociology*, London, 1967, p. 176.
3. Stalin Joseph, quoted in Hobsbawm H.J. *Matron and Nationalism since 1780: Programme, Myth and Reality*, Cambridge University Press, Cambridge, 1992, p. 5.
4. Ward Hunt, *Cooperation in Change: An Anthropological Approach to Community Development*, New York, 1963, p. 259.
5. Taylor, Edward B., *Primitive Culture: Researchers into the Development of Mythology, Philosophy, Religion, Language, Art and Custom*, London, p. 1.
6. Bose, Nirmal Kumar, *Culture and Society in India*, Asia Publishing House, Bombay, 1997, p. 15.
7. Valentine Charles A., *Culture and Poverty: Critique and Counter Proposals*, University of Chicago Press, London, 1968, p. 3.
8. Entering the 21st Century, World Development Report 1999/2000, Published by Oxford University Press for the World Bank, 1999, p. 173.
9. Marx, Karl and Friedrich Engels: *The Communist Manifesto*, Moscow, 1975 (reprint), p. 42.
10. Nayyar, Deepak, 'Globalization: What does it mean for Development', In *Challenges for Globalization* by Bibek Debroy (ed.) Konark Publisher, p. 22.
11. *Ibid.*, p. 22.
12. *Ibid.*, p. 23.
13. Hermain, Edward S. and McChesney Robern W., *The Global Media, The New Missionaries of Corporate Capitalism*, Madhyam Books, 1998, p. 2.
14. *Ibid.*, p. 10.
15. *Ibid.*, p. 38.

28

Emerging Power Structure in Modern Societies

The Role of Science and Technology

ANUPAMA PANDEY

The role of science and technology is instrumental in changing and transforming the developed as well as the developing societies on the goal level. The scientific inventions, discoveries and the technological expertize all-over the world have established an unprecedented records of achievements. The industrial revolution emerging from the western world is a noted outcome of the scientific and technological developments which has led to the growth of the techno-economic development in the West and later in other parts of the world.

It is through the growth of science and technology that the world has progressed up to definite steps from early primitive culture chiefly dominated by superstition, folkways, mores, magic and animism to modern so-called industrial and super industrial techno-electronic orders of society which is being dominated by technocratic, electronic and scientific expertise and innovations. It is really a shift from primitive to modern, manual to technical, mechanical to organic, theocratic to secular and egalitarian, particularistic to universalistic, specific to diffused, pre-industrial to industrial and on towards super industrial, economic order of society and, therefore, it can be regarded, perhaps, as the science and technology. The technological and scientific changes have divided the world into two major categories of social systems. One is maintained by the big powers which the social scientists denote as industrially developed nations while the others are known as the developing nations or the Third World Countries.

Growth of Capitalism and Euphoria of Post-Modernism

The most recent theoretical debates about culture centres on the issue whether culture has taken a new turn, entered a new phase, at the end of the twentieth Century.

Jameson (1984) proposes a three-fold perception of capitalism, which comes originally from Mandel:

1. Market capitalism, which involves markets within nation-states.
2. Imperial or monopoly capitalism, in which the capitalist states establish colonies so that they could catch both suppliers of raw materials and international markets.
3. Multinational consumerist capitalism which establishes a new integrated global place for capitalist expansion and within that expands markets by expanding individual acquisitiveness.

This expansion of capitalism into global arena is percolated by a global expansion of culture which liberates it from particular social context. There is a prodigious expansion of culture throughout the social realism. This is so-called post-modern culture. The post-modern culture which focuses the mind on the centrality of the global space and dislocates individuals from the realities of their own situation has four characteristics:

1. It is depthless (i.e., what you see is what you get) which has risen on the collapse of grand narratives and meta theories.
2. It is ahistorical and immediate: it provides no reference back to human suffering and struggle. Traditions can be mixed and matched in pastiche rather than drown upon or resisted.
3. It is timeless. It focuses on organization of fragments of culture meanings in space. The time relations of these fragmentations are not signified.

4. It conceives of the world as a technological entity rather than as a natural one, as computer network, rather than an ecological balance.

- Modern culture is highly differentiated but post-culture moves towards hyper differentiation. Post-modern culture can be seen as a dazzling variety of styles which can be mixed and matched with various packages.
- Modern culture is highly rationalized pattern of technical cultural expertise located either in tradition or its transcendence. Post-culture is so hyper intensified that their can no longer be any claim to expertise or any development of tradition.
- Modern culture is highly commodified, post-culture is so hypercommodifed that material commodities are subsumed by signs which represent them.

Emerging Features of Social Structure

In the words of Habermas, this process of Globalization is going to decouple the integration of life world and the system and is tended to proceed towards internal colonization. In the modern techno-electronic set-up individuals are forced to go through purposive rationalization (in Weber's term Zweck rationalitat), the purposive rationality is marked with contractual morality, i.e., non-critical, object oriented and not by communicative rationalization, i.e., critical reasoning (in Weber's term Wert rationalitat). Excessive bureaucratization and commodification of knowledge are the outcomes of post-industrial development. The character of this so-called post-modern culture which is emerging can be termed as disethisized, shameless. The individual is emerging as a client leaving aside his real identity and the whole world system is being regulated by purposive rationality. The whole world is going to emerge as a computerized networking rather than a natural entity, a technological entity rather than an ecological balance. The developing countries in general and India in particular have a long historicity of grand narratives meta theories, legends and myths. Globalization cannot assimilate all of them. In my assessment, India and other developing countries of Asia and Africa will ever manifest a peculiar blend of their historical identity even in the global modernizing attempts.

The panorama of scientific development and technological growth in the industrially developed societies in the West, specially the U.S.A., the U.K., France and Germany, indicates that these societies have reached the zenith of their techno-industrial and economic development. Japan in the eastern world also presents a similar picture. A new social transformation is taking place in these countries which can be observed as post-Industrialism, the term by which their structural configurations can be differentiated from the industrial society. They may also be called technocratic societies because of the power that dominates them. Alain Touraine (1971), a French Sociologist of the present time talks of such societies as 'programmed societies' to define them according to the nature of their production methods and economic, organization. Such societies can be described as technocratic societies, or techno-electronic societies, which conduct their activities by technological, electronic and nuclear sources and resources. They are also regulated by technological and electronic machines and equipments. In these societies, we find that their economic, political and social systems operate through electronic machines and technological devices. In other way such societies are called as computerized social systems. Brzezinski (1967), one of the contemporary social scientists has made his observation of American society in regard to post-industrial development and has pointed out that America is in the midst of transition, that is both unique and baffling. It is ceasing to be an industrial society and is being shaped to an ever increasing extent by technology and electronics and thus is going to be the first 'techno-electronic society.' Such societies, undoubtedly, have paramount importance of knowledge of science technology, electronics and nuclear resources as they are being generated, regulated and controlled by the techno electronic resources. Therefore, sociologically it appears that the empirical knowledge of modern technology, electronics nuclear resources and computer science formulate the very edifice of the post-industrial social structure of societies in the western world. Daniel Bell (1967) in his study of the post-industrial society stresses upon the functional significance of the knowledge derived from techno-electronic resources in the system of economic production and the shift from a manufacturing economy to a service economy.

The perspective of this chapter is to analyse social, economic and political systems of industrially developed capitalist societies of the West which are passing through a stage of super industrialism. The Science, Technology and Changing power Structure aim of this chapter is to focus on emerging class structure and class character as well as the nature of dominance over social movements and political actions by new social groups in these societies. It has also been attempted to emphasize the functional significance of an intermediate stratum emerging as a new social group, composed of technocrats, electronic experts, computer scientists, administrators and other educated personnel who have come amidst the working class.

Post-Industrialism and Emerging Power Structure

The industrially developed capitalist societies in the West which are reaching the stage of super industrialism or post-industrial systems have annihilated the Marxist concept of class structure (bourgeoisie and proletariat) because the perspective of Marxist sociology was the industrial society in which there was conflicting relation between the capitalists and the proletariats and overall dominance was vested that the hand of the capitalists. In another words, one can observe that Marxism arose as a response to industrial era. Now that power of dominance is shifting from the hands of the industrialists and the capitalists to the technocrat's electronic experts and nuclear technologists who are becoming more and more involved in public and private sector undertakings, special Government enterprises and become in effect the 'house ideologues' for those in power in the contemporary states of affair. If we analyse the social structure of western developed societies, it appears that the importance of social conflict between the capitalists and labourers which was predominantly imbued with economic interest is losing its central importance in the capitalist societies which are treading on towards the closure of twentieth century but new forms of dominance and new social conflicts are evolving in these countries which can be observed even in socialist countries which are developing. These new conflicts arise between those who control the institutions of economic and political decision making and those who have reduced to a condition of dependent participation. The new dominant class can no longer be defined by property ownership, and ownership of means of production but by new techno electronic efficiency skill and knowledge. The revolt against it takes the will of the dependent class to break away from its dependence and embark upon an autonomous development. This can be observed in relation to new social movements. In this way, if we analyse the social structure of these developed nations, it seems that most of the radical and active social movements are not conducted or evoked by the working class in different undertaking and enterprises such as railroad negative because in modern post-industrial societies class conflict emerges as political conflict. This conflict is opposed to integration and transformation of the contemporary system. In such movements political and cultural activities are more influential than the economic actions and this is the fact which differentiates it from the labour movements of liberal capitalism. Such movements are scarcely yet beginning which are imbued in essence more with power and authority than with the questions of salary, employments, increments and property ownerships.

Norman Birnbaum (1969) has also made his observations in regard to developed societies of the West. He has observed that the class structure in these societies itself has been transformed: A new intermediate stratum of administrative technical and service personnel often possessing a considerable degree of education has emerged who serve as experts to the new rulers of the society. In Indian context too, a similar account of the intermediate class is given by D.P. Mukherjee (1958) and B.B. Mishra (1960). This has shown the emerging potential of the middle class which replaces the significance of working class at least in the initiation of social movement in the industrially developed capitalist societies. This is also perceptible in the developing socialist societies.

This, according to Wellmer, provides the starting point for an erroneously technocratic interpretation of history. One may critically examine and hold that Marx's concept of class has largely last its utility as an instrument of analysis. This is also because science has become the 'form of life' of industrial societies and intellectual development and dominance of technical expertise over society. The decision making of political actions economic institutions is possible only when the experts directly or indirectly participate in progress development and impacts of science. Hence, the interpretation of contradiction between critical and conservative ideas can no longer be interpreted in purely political terms as the expression of class conflict but must be settled on the ground of science itself. The increasing use of resources of science and technology has brought about significant changes in class situation of social systems in the post-industrial society. The conflicts which are emerging are not between the capitalist and the working class. It is emerging as political conflict between new classes. This can be derived from the present analysis that the potentiality of post-industrial society from sociolinguistic perspective presents a picture of the possibilities of such changes in which new social groups of the educated personnel, technocrats, nuclear scientists, administrators and other experts may develop a critical outlook and radical political action.

Workers, dockers, miners and the factory workers, rather such movements in these societies are generated and initiated by the economically advanced groups and the research agencies, the technologists and electronic experts with skill but not authority. The aims and the objectives of their movements are related with demand for sharing in the status, prestige and authority systems in the power structure.

Instances may be cited of the historic movements and struggles launched by Negro professionals in the late sixties in the United States; the emergence of radicals in the seventies; the resurgence of expertized intelligentsia and youth activities and Germany in seventies.

The Third World countries too, though yet completing the full industrial development, have overtaken some of the features and attributes of post-industrial societies by way of their 'demonstration effect'. The movements and struggles in the countries of Latin America, Africa and Asia are not based on economic interests but for sharing in the status, prestige and authority systems in the power structure. The struggles in South Africa and Sri Lanka, Sikh militancy in Punjab, ULFA extremists in Assam, GNLF in Darjeeling, Terrorists in Kashmir in India are the glaring instances.

The entire nineteenth century renaissance movement and struggle against the British imperialism in India were led by an intermediate stratum composed of enlightened thinkers, ideologists and revolutionaries for sharing in the authority system in the power structure. The contemporary movements in the garb of Naxalism and Terrorism are also launched by a group of misguided middle class composed of technical experts, educated personnel and service professionals and not by working class. The present agrarian movements are being organized on ideological basis in several parts of India.

It is true that any social or political movement of any potentiality develops only in a situation in which there is dominance of the working class because it is the working class which includes a sizable population of the dependent workers but the question in the present chapter in the present context is a different one. This formulation in regard to post-industrial societies is marshalled with a questioning argument whether or not the working class or the prolatariat according to Marxist conception play an important active role in initiating social conflict and historical changes that are taking place in the societies which are passing through the post-industrial stage. Our observation and analysis of the content of contemporary texts on post-industrial societies enable us to reply in negative.

To conclude, it can be pointed out that the present analysis does not mean the denouncement of Marxism. It has been and will continue to be relevant for the analysis of class structure in specific industrial situation. What appears from the intensive observation of the post-industrial march of the industrially developed societies in the Western world, is a completely new demand of interpretation of power structure beyond Marxism. Changes in the character of the working class and the problems that arise within Marxism in attempting to analyse these changes hammer the brain of sociologists, and social critics to a revision of Marxism or its new interpretation or to the elaboration of a new theory which builds upon or above Marxism. It is mainly because of the situational emergence of the potentials of expertise intelligentsia of the technocrats, nuclear scientists, computer experts and administrators who serve as "experts" or "house ideologues" to the ruling class and capitalists. Hence, their role is more pivotal, more surmounting and more strategically influential than that of the working class because of the super advancement of technology. Though the new class can no longer be defined by property ownership but by techno-electronic efficiency, skill and knowledge as integral attribute of their personality potentials of which the working class is deprived. Therefore, this new social group of 'knowledge elites' evokes and embosses an ideology which diminishes the hypnotic shadow and magic-effect of Marxist reality prevailed over for about a century on the industrial societies of the world and admirers of Marxism. Although some inadequacies and inconsistencies lie in full interpretation of the post-industrial societies of the West since they do not show complete break of their ties from the industrial societies. It is because of the relative nexus between industrialism and super-industrialism. Further, the course of the super-industrialism is yet to be defined and delimited.

The studies and investigations made by Western social scientists during the recent years about the socio-economic development of the Third World countries themselves show a major contradiction. Michael Hudson (1971) concludes in his survey that the foreign aid to these countries have created adverse consequences in these countries. Tiber Mende (1973) has traced out that a tendency of strong resentment and protest has been evoked among the developing nations against the developed Western countries. The developing nations are realizing that foreign aids are instrumental in perpetuating long term dependency in the developing nations and as such is a strategy to place the developing societies in the grip of their trade and technology. The profiteering motives and interference in the economy and polity of the developing countries by the Western nations will always put them in the subservient condition. Hence, they are threatened about their identity loss. In this state of affairs, the developing countries must evolve their own indigenous models and parameters to their social and economic development. This will help them restore their identity. Teresa Hayter (1971) goes a step forward and emphatically argues that the policies and programmes initiated by development agencies such as International monitory fund, World Bank, United States Agency for International Development, Inter American Development Bank motivate for creating free market, trade and technology and to rely on them with a sense of attachment and commitment. Bauer (1972) has given a critical assessment of the Western aid and has concluded in his studies that the Western developed countries have attempted to create a vicious poverty circle in the developing countries rather than improving their economy and social standards of life. Wallerstein (2000) in his latest works entitled *After Literalism,* has expressed his apprehensions about the immanent crisis emerging out of the late capitalism. George Shoraz

(2000) an economist of the U.S. in one of his latest works entitled *The Crisis of Global Capitalism: Open Society Endangered* clearly highlights that Globalization is an inevitable outcome of the crisis of post-industrial development in the West. A Canadian economist Sislia Ostry (1999) observes that the Western industrially developed capitalist countries are facing crucial problems in the sale and consumption of their products and are looking forward towards the countries of Asia and Africa. Thus, the proper coordination between man, machine and social values in the Western world is disturbed and is coming to an end. The Western social theory is silent on the issue of cultural destination of man through the process of globalization. The excessive technologized production in the West requires a large and wide market place for effective sale and consumption. The increasing demand of consumption is a decisive factor for the success of technologized production and this is feasible only when there is extensive market place for consumption. In this context, the Third World countries appear as the only alternative market place for the west.

REFERENCES

Alain Touraine: *The Post-Industrial Society*, New York, 1971, p. 3.

B.B. Mishra: *The Indian Middle Class*, Oxford University Press, 1960, pp. 380-389.

Daniel Bell: "Notes on the Post Industrial Society", *The Public Interest* 6 and 7 winter 1967 and spring 1967, pp. 24-34 and 102-118.

D.P. Mukherjee: *Diversities*, People Pub. House, New Delhi, 1958, p. 73.

Norman Birnbaum: *Towards A Critical Sociology*, New York, 1971.

Ostry, Sislia (1999): *The Crisis of Global Trade*, New York.

Shoraz, George (2000): *The Crisis of Global Capitalism: Open Society Endangered*; New York.

Wallerstein Immanuel (2000): *After Liberalism*, New York.

Zbigniew Brzezinski: The American Transition", *New Republic* 157(23) Dec, 1967, pp. 18-21, also reprinted in *Information Technology in a Democracy*, ed. By Alain Western Cambridge, Mass, 1971, pp. 161-67.

29

Modernity and Empowerment through Global Development

MUKESH KUMAR SRIVASTAVA *AND* ANUPAMA PANDEY

Globalization is a carrier of culture and modernity. Sociologically, Globalization carries out modernity and empowerment both. Without modernity empowerment cannot flourish and without empowerment modernity is a dream project. Therefore, there is close sociological nexus between modernity and empowerment.

Modernity is a term used to describe the condition of being modern. In other words, it denotes the acceptance of common behaviour patterns associated with technological innovations, new value orientations and motivations. It provides a wider scope for increasing skill efficiency and potentialities in structure and agency both. That is to say the social set-up or the system and the individual. The term modern is derived from the late fifth century Latin term *modernus* which was used to distinguish an officially Christian present from a Roman pagan past (*c.f.* Calinescu, 1977; Habermas, 1981). Thereafter, the term was employed to situate the present in relation to the past of antiquity, appearing and reappearing exactly during those periods in Europe when the consciousness of a new epoch found itself through a renewed relationship to the ancients (Habermas, 1981: 3-4). However, with the *Querelle des Anciens et des Modernes* and the emergence of the French enlightenment, a different conception developed of modernity as distinctive and superior period in the history of humanity. In relation to reason, religion and aesthetic appreciation, it was argued that moderns were more advanced, more refined and in the possession of more profound truths than the ancients (Block, 1979).

In the discussion of the emergence of modernity, consideration is frequently given to the respective philosophical analysis of Kant and Hegel. But if Kant is acknowledged to have inaugurated the modern age and Hegel is considered to have provided the first clear philosophical conception of modernity and to have identified its problem as self-assurance or the necessity of constituting its own grounds, it is the work of Baudelaire which is frequently considered to provide the turning point in the development of and understanding of modernity (Smart, 1996). Baudelaire has been credited with identifying the price for which the sensation of the modern age may be had (Benjamin, 1973: 196); recognising the distinctively transient..., fleeting...contingent character of modernity (Habermas, 1987: 8); illuminating modern life's complexities and conditions (Berman, 1983: 8) and for contrasting aesthetic modernity...to the practical modernity of bourgeois civilization (Calinescu, 1977). Modernity and modernization are the notions of two different processes. Historically, modernization is a process of change, which emerged during the seventeenth and eighteenth century in Western Europe and America and expanded up to Eastern Europe. Later on during nineteenth and twentieth century, it has expanded to Africa, Asia and South American nations. It is a concept in the sphere of social sciences that refers to a process in which society goes through industrialisation, urbanisation and social changes that completely transform economy, polity and social structure. As a result in the modern and post-modern era, economy is being controlled by market, polity by the state and social structure by the civil society, *i.e.*, people's combined effort, collective ventures, NGOs and self-help groups (Smart, 1996). It is a process to renovate social and political system. Modernity has been described in various forms by different social scientists. Marx, Weber, Durkheim and Simmel were working at the point of the emergence and ascendancy of modernity. All four were aware of the advantages of modernity. For Marx, of course, modernity was defined by the capitalist economy (Marx, 1867/1967). To Weber (1904/1905), the most defining problem of the modern world was the expansion of formal nationality at the expense of the other types of rationality and the resulting emergence of the iron cage of rationality. In Durkheim's view, modernity was defined by its organic solidarity and the weakening of the collective conscience. Simmel has recently been described as both a modernist (Frisby, 1992) and as a post-modernist (Weinstein and Weinstein, 1993). Frisby accepts that Simmel is the first sociologist of modernity (1992: 59). Simmel is seen as investigating modernity primarily in two major interrelated sites—the city and the money economy (Frisby, 1992: 69).

Poggi (1993) picks up the theme of modernity as it relates to money, especially in Simmel's 'Philosophy of Money'. Poggi finds three views of modernity in that work. The first is that modernity brings with it a series of advantages to human beings, especially the fact that they are able to express various potentialities that are unexpressed, concealed and repressed in premodern society. In this sense Simmel sees modernity "As an Epiphany", that is as the express manifestation of powers intrinsic to the human species but previously unrevealed (Poggi, 1933: 165). He deals with the powerful effect of money of modern society. Simmel is also interested to explain the adverse effects of money for modernity, especially alienation and talks about tragedy of culture in regard to the issue of alienation. That means a growing gap between objective and subjective culture or as he put it "the atrophy of individual culture and the hypertrophy of objective culture" (cited in Frisby, 1992: 69).

Anthony Giddens (1990) has described the modern world with its origin in the seventeenth century in Europe as a juggeranut. More specifically, he is using the term to describe an advanced stage of modernity—radical, high or late modernity. Modernity in the form of a juggernaut is extremely dynamic, it is a runaway word with great increase in the pace, scope and profoundness of change over prior systems (Giddens, 1991: 16). He explained modernity as a *risk culture* (1991: 3-4).

Beck (1992: 10) argued that modernization dissolved the structure of feudal society in the nineteenth century and produced the industrial society; modernization today is dissolving industrial society and another modernity is coming into being.

Ritzer (1996) has addressed the issue of modernity in three interrelated ways—through the concepts of hyper-rationality, McDonaldisation and Americanisation. The concept of hyper rationality is employed to describe today's highly rational world, especially Japanese industry (Ritzer and LeMoyne, 1991). The issue of modernity also arises in the McDonaldisation of society (Ritzer, 1993).

Zygmunt Bauman has adopted formal rationality in the form of a holocaust (1989: 149). According to Bauman, the holocaust was the product of modernity and not, as most people view it, a result of breakdown of modernity. Habermas (1987b) sees modernity as an unfinished project implying that there is far more to be done in the modern world before we can begin thinking about the possibility of a post-modern world. Habermas observes that the hallmark of modernity has been the colonization of life world by system. Smelsor (1968) equates modernization with economic development, which he defines in terms of four shifts—from traditional to scientifically based technology; from subsistence to commercialised agriculture; from animal power to power-driven machines, and from farm and village to urban centres.

Giddens (1987) while explaining the interrelationship between sociology and modernity, documents the major parameters of modernity, namely, economic, administrative, military and cultural parameters. Global development as a vehicle of modernity has launched a process that moves forward in a straight way to attain some particular goal. Modernity leads to the emergence of new social order, bringing new tools and techniques for individual to become skilled. Becoming skilled of a person or community can be explained in terms of empowerment which includes the active participation in technical works, adoption of new technology, mixing in technetronic society along with the adoption of new social order. Modernity as a means of Western cultural contact, in the wave of global development, has brought technological and scientific innovations, electronic boom and economic blast in society. All these are means of empowerment of a community or individual. In the process of modernity, the traditional or conservative boundaries of social structure have been replaced by development; international cultural exchange has been accelerated much. This exchange is a source of modernity and it spreads the multiculturalism and better individual access to cultural diversity. A process of global development contains a multiplicity of cultures which is taken together or viewed by individual participations as constituting 'the world' in a phenomenological sense (Wallerstein, 1974: 347-8).

Adopting the parameters given by Giddens, as mentioned above, it can be explained that all the four factors are integral for empowerment of the people. For empowerment, economic sufficiency as well as administrative power is considered as among the most important factors. The cultural factor is also of immense significance. In the wave of global development, the greater international cultural exchanges make people to think in a broad range. It also accelerates much international travel and tourism. This cultural exchange is also responsible for the spread of local foods to other countries and worldwide fads and pop culture such as Pokemon, Sudoku, Numa-Numa, Origami, Idol Series, Youtube, Myspace, animated series and many others. All these are creating a form of awareness among the masses that ultimately leads to empowerment. Modernity, in the wave of global development, has brought various economic and commercial promotions such as promotion of free trade of goods capital and reduction of tariffs, construction of free trade zones with small or no tariffs and reduced transportation costs. These promotions are, somehow, responsible for strengthening of human beings by enforcing them to be engaged in various types of trade and commercial activities. All these are fitted well with the explanation given by Giddens in terms of modernity and these factors lead to the empowerment of people as well. When people are getting economic sufficiency and better climate for their livelihood, they try to bring 'something nascent, unique and something unoccurred in the past' in their lives. Thus, it can be said that both modernity and empowerment are running as the two wheels of a coach run on the parallel track of railways.

While talking about empowerment and modernity, it may be injustice if we are ignoring debate about post-modernity. The modern society has now been replaced by a post-modern society particularly in the Western world (Smart, 1993). The post-modern encompasses a new historical epoch, new cultural products, and a new type of theorising about the social world. Something new and different has happened in recent years that can no longer been described by the term 'modern'. In a simpler sense, this can be credited with the global development that has increased the interdependence in the economic, social, technological, cultural, political and ecological sphere.

Sociologically, the modern period has moved towards post-modern period that brings various new structural and cultural transformations. What post-modern society brings with it is a question to be explained. The superficial character of society and lack of depth are profound. This implies the breaking of primary relations and predominance of contractual relations. Peoples' affection to one another is more sophisticated with superficiality and formality than a natural reality of relationship. In the post-modern world, alienation has been replaced by fragmentation (Jameson, 1984: 64). In a post-modern society, there is a loss of historicity. This loss of historicity was led to the "random cannibalisation of all styles of the past" (Jameson, 1984: 65-66).

In the post-modern age, capital access is open for all. Capital access in any society is a basic prerequisite for the empowerment. This age involves easy circulation of taking and returning, giving and receiving cycle of gifts and counter-gifts (Baudrillard, 1973/1975: 83). This cycle is also in the form of sharing values and ideas. This sharing of values and ideas is also a milestone to achieve the goals of empowerment. The young generation in the society is adopting new values and ideas by the cultural and philosophical contacts with Western society in the global world. In the process of global development, whole universe is being transformed into a global circle of interactions having common economy, culture and lifestyle, for example, European Union.

In the post-modern age, basically cultural attributes are involved in the alteration of society. In this age, there is a predominance of scientific knowledge, informatics, cybernetics, computer languages and modern mathematical concepts. Due to the development in telecommunications and informatics, the thousands of miles has been replaced by even a millimetre distance, i.e., the places where people reach in 24 hours or more can be accessed within half an hour. It is the outcome of post-modernity that people, while sleeping on their bed, can have access to all the information of every nook and corner of the world. The transformation in technology has a considerable impact on knowledge. Knowledge has become the principle force of production over the last few decades. This has an enormous effect on the composition of the workforce of the developed as well as developing countries. The knowledge filled with technology will minimise the ever gap between developed and developing nations. When this gap minimises, people will realise themselves to think rationally and they will be free to go ahead based on their own decision. When people feel themselves to be free from any bindings, this is the condition of empowerment. This minimising gap between nations due to the expansion of technology and knowledge can be termed as global development. Knowledge as a commodity of information and source for production is a major stake in the wordwide competition for power. It can be conceived that one day nation-states will fight for control of information (Lyotard, 1984). Now, a new field is opened for industrial and commercial strategies on the one hand, and political and military strategies on the other.

As stated above that modernity and empowerment are closely related and empowerment leads to modernity whereas modernity in turn leads to greater empowerment. Modernity can also be ensured by the boost-up of economy. In the process of global development, the economy is strengthening and this economy in turn prepares a strong and solid background for empowerment. The process promotes direct foreign investment and thus, it enables the masses of developing countries to raise capital without any international financial assistance. It also enables people from developing nations to maximise the use of technology developed by advanced countries without any type of investment in research and development.

To conclude, it can be held that the very process of global development is to be considered in terms of supplementation and substitution by the process of modernization. The empowerment of economy, political structure and sound democratic development along with improvement in health, hygiene, recreation and optimum level of calorie intake are possible by modernising the economy and society. The education particularly in the developing society as a multiplier of opportunities and awareness among the people is indispensable. This is also indispensable so far as reducing the gap between the rich and poor is concerned and this ultimately is the *summum bonum* of globally accepted development Empowerment presupposes strategic procedures of action and modernity aims at making the traditional constraints by promulgating rationalisation and scientific outlook. Therefore, the two processes—modernization and globally-oriented development—are essential for empowering the nation-states. The plans and projects of modernization and development must proceed in accordance with the ecology, environment and requirements of the different nation-states. Mere carbon copy of Western development programmes is not enough but while projecting and implementing the project for empowering of society, the planners and administrators must chalk out the specific areas of consideration such as ethnic, cultural, religious, regional, sub-cultural and so on.

References

Baudrillard, Jean (1973/1975), *The Mirror of Production,* St. Louis: Telos Press.

Beck, Ulrich (1992), *Risk Society: Towards a New Modernity,* London: Sage.

Benjamin, W. (1973), *Illuminations,* London: Fontana.

Berman, M. (1983), *All that is Solid Melts into Air,* London: Verso.

Bock, K. (1979), 'Theories of Progress, Development Evolution' in T. Bottomore and R. Nisbet (eds.), *A History of Sociological Analysis.* London: Heinemann.

Calinescu, M. (1977), *Faces of Modernity,* London: Indiana University Press.

Derrida, J. (1978), *Writing and Difference,* Chicago: University of Chicago Press.

Frisby, David (1992), *Simmel and Since,* Essays on George Simmel's Social Theory, London: Routledge.

Giddens, Anthony (1990), *The Consequences of Modernity,* Standford, California: SUP.

______(1991), *Modernity and Self Identity: Self and Society in the Late Modern Age,* Standford, California: SUP.

Habermas, Jurgen (1981), *Modernity* versus *Postmodernity,* New German Critic, 22.

______(1987), *The Philosophical Discourse of Modernity,* Cambridge: Polity.

______(1987b), *The Philosophical Discourse of Modernity*: Twelve Lectures, Cambridge, Mass: MIT Press.

Jemeson, F. (1984), "Postmodernism, or the Cultural Logic of Late Capitalism", *New Left Review,* 146: 53-92.

Lyotard, J.F. (1984), *The Postmodern Condition,* Manchester: ManchesterUniversity Press.

Marx, Karl (1867/1967), *Capital: A Critique of Political Economy,* Vol. I, New York, International Publishers.

Poggi, G. (1993), *Money and the Modern Mind: George Simmel's Philosophy of Money,* Berkeley: California University Press.

Ritzer, George and LeMoyne, Teri (1991), "Hyperrationality: An Extension of Weberian and Neoweberian Theory" in G. Ritzer, *Metatheorizing in Sociology,* Lexington, Mass: Lexington Books: 93-115.

Ritzer, George (1993), *The McDonaldization of Tata Society,* Thousand Oaks. California, Pine Forge Press.

Ritzer, George (1996), *Sociological Theory*, Tata McGraw Hill.
Smart, Barry (1993), *Postmodernity*, London: Routledge.
_______ (1996), 'Modernity, Postmodernity and the Present' in B.S. Turner (eds.) *Theories of Modernity and Postmodernity*, London: Routledge.
Smelsor, N. (1968), *Essays in Sociological Explanation*, Englewood Cliffs: Prentice Hall.
Wallerstein, I. (1974), *The Modern World System*, New York: Academic.
Weber, Max (1904/1905), *The Protestant Ethic and the Spirit of Capitalism*, NY: Scribner's.
Weinstein, Deena and Weinstein, M.A. (1993), *Postmodern (ized) Simmel*, London: Routledge.

30

Globalization and the Indian Society

A Dilemma of Civilization

S.K. SRIVASTAVA

When we look at the scientific, structural and functional meaning of globalization, we may appreciate different interpretations and perceptions. Globe means *prithvi* but it also stands for *vasudha* which goes beyond the physical, temporal and spatial concept and stands for more inclusive and cosmic viewpoint.

Globalization in the Western epistemology is the product of modernization and westernization. It stands for the following characteristics:

1. Globalization establishes market centres promoted by nexus of multinational corporations and transnational financial bodies.
2. It centres around Capital formation. The consequences of globalization in spite of increasing contact and communication and interaction between different continues and their major capital and market centres, have resulted into the following influences, and consequences:
   (*i*) It increases disparities between different countries as reported by the various reports of U.N.O, UNDP and ILO.
   (*ii*) It also commercialises the basic services, such as, health, education, transport and housing and creates poor bargaining power of the low income groups.

(*iii*) Globalization has increasingly helped economic powers of USA and Europe.

(*iv*) South Asia, India, Africa and South America are the worst sufferers.

(*v*) Globalization has latently established neo-colonization and Imperialism under the hegemony of I.M.F. and W.T.O.

(*vi*) It has resulted into increasing inequalities between and within the countries of the world.

(*vii*) Globalization has increased instability in the developing nations and has perpetuated dominance of U.S.A. and Europe.

(*viii*) Globalization manipulates but the question is for what, for whom and mobilization by whom.

Globalization has mainly the motives: Market, money and manipulation of whom, for whom and for what.

It is Nexus of multinational corporations and transnational financial bodies that managed and controlled by richest persons, power groups in Europe and USA.

Capitalists and industrialists for whom they plan to maximize profits and capital gains aim for maximization of profits and to achieve the wealthiest status in the world. Therefore, globalization is antithesis of civil society.

It is perpetuating all the sensate values and sensate culture and sensual personalities all-over the globe since it has all the characteristics which stand for antithesis of civil society.

(*a*) The Lust for power to rule and reign through manipulation and control over market, is now a days a worldwide phenomenon.

(*b*) The Lust for wealth—To earn money at any cost by multinational network is resulting into scams and scandals and conspicuous consumption leading to increasing poverty to the developing nations.

(*c*) The Lust for pleasure is Obscene literature, blue films, Discos, and such International events such as world Football Match in Germany, Imported prostitutes from all-over the world. International nexus and networking for promotion of sexual pleasures.

(*d*) The Lust for conspicuous consumption is seen with jewellery, a separate mansion for pets and exhibitionism of wealth to show of their sensualision and sensual satisfaction.

(*e*) Lust for military and economic exploitation resulting into a nexus between the Military supremacy and economic dominance over the poor nations.

On the other hand we have another concept of *vasudha* 'The globe' denoting 'The Indian' contest globalization is also based on human relationship of the man and woman of the world tied by the bonds of kinship of an extended family and community relationship based on love, self respect, equality and above all bond of everlasting brotherhood the *Vasudhaiva Kutumbakam*.

(*a*) Unlike globalization based on market relationship *vasudha* on the other hand stands for humane relationship, the most important tenets of civil society.

(*b*) Money is power and power is money in the case of western globalization while the Indian concept of *vasudha* represents love, compassion and human sympathy as the treasures of love of human kindness.

(*c*) It does not believe nor practice through any institution the disparities between individuals and groups, castes and classes, religions, societies and nations on the other hand, it treats equality as its core values is basic foundation of civil society.

(*d*) Basic services like education, health, shelter, etc., are the responsibility of a Welfare State not based on commercialization and privatization.

(*e*) Consumerism and conspicuous consumption and the order of the day in globalization because marketing the consumable goods and services were of gaining profits to the owners and contributions through money and market manipulations.

In *vasudha* the goal is to meet the basic needs of food, shelter and clothes, housing, health and education of the people irrespective of their economic and social status.

What a Civil Society Stands for?

(*a*) In *vasudha* there is no problem of bargaining power of the poor and the labour. The distinction between the Haves and have-nots is maintained at the minimum.

(*b*) In *vasudha* there is no concentration and accumulation of wealth as it is enshrined even in our Constitution and also in Gandhi's Trusteeship principle.

Globalization is the consequential resultant of a services of stages of social transformation which also speaks of crisis in Western civilization today.

Right from the seventeenth century at the time of Scientific Revolution and nineteenth century Industrial Revolution along with two World Wars and emergence of powerful nation-states born out of various revolutions in France, Germany, Russia, and USA to Globalization in terms of market and money power, have been making deeper inroads into the non-European world. Colonialism and Imperialism were imposed on Asia, Africa and other parts of the world to capture and control market, rule over the people by impoverising them and of their basic rights of dignity and respectable human existence. The bondage of political slavery was superimposed by economic exploitation of the people in slave countries. The world has witnessed that countries which had won their freedom and wanted to stand on their self reliant independence with economic policies of national reconstruction came under the ghost of globalization in the world *via* very subtle and far reaching mechanisms through very powerful lobbies of the multinationals which they could control and regulate all the profits in goods and services in the field of food, health, education, etc.

Therefore, these developed nations through industrial, scientific and technological might have impressed upon the developing nations, the notion and the principle of the development on western lines like capitalist or industrialist models of USA, France, Germany, Italy and the U.K. Then they provided extensive loan grants and funds for development of the poor nations. They influenced and even manipulated the political leaders, business and industrial houses with a positive intent that if you want to develop then follow our model and keep our market and money in great circulation. Thus, modernization and liberalization became great *mantras* on the cardinal principles of at the end of twentieth century. It worked for some time with great fun and fury. Then came the wave of globalization, a more neutral term specifying and emphasizing that it is the market which holds the key for the development of poor nations. Compete and earn money through global competition. Today globalization is a watchword for development in twenfy-first century. Here I may emphasize that the West and particularly the US and Europe are facing a crisis of civilization. Therefore, the West has very clearly managed to transfer their crisis of civilization to great civilizations of Asia and South Africa. India is no exception to this onslaught. Consumerism and conspicuous consumption have taken toll in the developing countries. Who has gained most in the wake of globalization? It is the West and US. Marketing and money making have not only confined in consumer and capital goods but has influenced the entire range of defence, space, communication and health and even in supply of atomic equipment and knowledge. This is an example of neocolonialism and post-modern capitalist, economic and social order. The Western civilization is in crisis and, therefore, why not globalize it and earn money in all sector of human endeavour. Coming to Indian scenario we have seen how Indian society right from pre-Vedic period to this day has established an unbroken course of continuity for six thousand years because Indian civilization has withstood the rise and the fall, stresses and strains during last six thousand years of its existence. While several civilizations of the world have perished, since they could not face the onslaughts, Indian society on the other hand, has maintained its unique character in assimilating, adopting and adjusting with different influences brought by Islam and Christianity.

The entire history of knowledge is enshrined in the literary, scientific technological and medical, writing of the *Vedas*, *Upanishads* and *Puranas*. They had transverse and crossed all the frontiers of knowledge in all its manifestations and coverage—be it science, metaphysics, philosophy, medicine, art and music, literature, etc. They could achieve all this because they were not running after market and money.

On the one hand India's contribution to the world's civilization other than their own particularly, Middle East, Europe and South

Asia are historical landmarks that led to the diffusion of knowledge in different fields in the past.

It also had the rare distinction of seventy years world peace during Asoka's times. During 4-5 centuries India had developed navigational skills and had launched their ships to Africa, Europe and South Asia for trade and commerce. Indians searched for markets not for expanding colonies. Our goal was trade without exploitation also without imperialistic and colonial designs. We believed in the dictum of *Vasudhaiva Kutumbkam* because we did not have any army of traders nor any army of soldiers to conquer other countries. Their markets were not only selling and purchasing merchandise but were establishing cultural ties and people to people contact with a real humanistic vision, peace and goodwill, equality and social justice—a key for civil society.

Whenever and wherever the Indians in the past indulged in conspicuous consumption and sensual pleasures, Indian society declined. If we have to learn any lesson from our past history, we should never deviate from the path of Buddha and Gandhi. Otherwise, the present wave of globalization will sweep us away from the righteous path of *Vasudhaiva Kutumbakam* —the world of human sympathy and love. Today the danger before us is that the crisis of Western civilization is spreading its tentacles over our holy land. Let us, therefore, resolve to be firm and determined not to import the western crisis on our soil. Our shoulders should be strong enough to combat and face this onslaught. After all what has been the sustaining power and inner strength of our ancient civilization? Which has maintained its unbroken continuity and unique identity? That is, we have not marketed our society and culture for global goals and are determined to establish and perpetuate non-sensate social order and culture and demonstrate to the world at large that market, money and manipulation cannot last long. To treat society as a mere market place will not be able to conquer the spirit and soul of India.

What was India, and What India is today.

To us globe does not mean earth only. It means *Vasudha* the Globe which is one family, one fraternity, where equality not only stands for men and women but also transcends the animals, plants, hills and mountains—all creatures of nature and God—a symbiotic relationship of Man, Nature and Universe with fusion of cosmic vision.

Indian civilization has faced rise and fall, stress and strains during last six thousand years of different attacks during its various periods of history, while several civilizations have perished. Perhaps the last one was Soviet Union. India has maintained its unique character in assimilating, adopting and adjusting while interacting with Islamic and Western civilization. What was the power, the spirit, the essence and central core value which sustained us and maintained us, through our thousands of years of existence.

It was the will to conquer the sensate values and sensuality and sexual pleasures and take the society to achieve the universal values of *Sarva Dharma Sambhava* and *Vasudhaiva Kutumbakam*.

The core values which sustained our society against onslaught of Western civilization, the cardinal universal and secular values were enshrined in the *Dharma*. The *Dharma* may be defined as *YAMA, NIYAMA, DHARMA* which are based upon the following principles:

1. Abstinence.
2. Control and conquest of senses—such as lust for power, money, sex, etc.
3. Minimization of Wants (*Apargarh*).
4. Conquest of ego-1 personalization of ego.
5. Peace and peaceful existence with man and society with all the animate and inanimate objects of the entire universe.
6. To follow *Dharma*—Moral path for a civil society and polity.
7. Conquest of Good over Evil—*Ramayana* and *Mahabharata* as reflected in freedom struggle led by Gandhi on the principles of Non-Violence and Truth.

All these ancient values of Indian civilization have found a respectable place in our Constitution of India.

The guiding principles enshrined in our Constitution have to be implemented through the Directive Principles of State Policy and fundamental rights to equality and justice against all exploitation of men, women, children and the bonded labourers.

Liberalization through globalization was thrust upon us and our leaders who swear by our Constitution and take a solemn oath by following the Constitution have fallen prey most tempting adventures and are not able to resist the temptation and onslaught and have, therefore, fallen into the trap of the crisis of the Western civilization. The West, therefore, in a very subtle and shrewd way has invaded our civilization, our State and the nation. The lust for power, money, sex, conspicuous consumption has increased beyond all boundaries of civilized society. Money and market are manipulated by three thousand houses and corporations to earn huge profits at the cost of the poor and the needy. They have, therefore, ushered in a new era of cultural invasion upon our society and culture. Therefore, the crisis of Western civilization is purposefully transferred to Indian society through these agents of liberalization and globalization. The agents of globalization both inside and outside the country have planned that *Vasudha* and our *Kutumbakam* should never reach the boundaries of *Vasudha* and our emblem of *Satyameva Jayate.* (Truth alone shall triumph) Thus, they (Western Powers) have designed and planned to plunder and loot our *Vasundhara* of its riches, i.e., the heritage of our ancient civilization.

Index